# Social Regeneration and Local Development

Social regeneration is about the transformative processes that, through institutional choices that embody cooperation and inclusion, develop opportunities and capabilities for weak categories and, transversally, for society. The challenge of social regeneration can be addressed, in part, through organisational solutions increasingly identified with social economy organisations, since they are characterised by a social objective, cooperation, and inclusive democratic governance.

Besides the organisational element, Social Regeneration and Local Development provide a new perspective on interacting socio-economic factors, which can work in synergy with the social economy organisations model to promote and sustain social regeneration and well-being. Such elements include civic engagement and social capital, the nature of the welfare system, and the use of physical assets in urban and rural areas, leadership, technology, and finance.

By analysing organisational and contextual elements, this book offers an institutional perspective on how socio-economic systems can reply to challenges such as social and environmental degradation, financial crises, immigration, inequality, and marginalisation.

**Silvia Sacchetti** is an Associate Professor of Economic Policy at the University of Trento, Department of Sociology and Social Research, Italy.

**Asimina Christoforou** is an Adjunct Professor at the Department of International and European Economic Studies, Athens University of Economics and Business, Greece.

**Michele Mosca** is an Associate Professor of Economic Policy at the Department of Political Science, University of Naples, Federico II, Italy.

# Routledge Studies in Social Enterprise & Social Innovation

Series Editors:
Rocio Nogales, Lars Hulgård, and Jacques Defourny

A Social Enterprise seeks to achieve social, cultural, community economic, or environmental outcomes whilst remaining a revenue-generating business. A Social Innovation is said to be a new idea or initiative to a social problem that is more effective, efficient, sustainable, or just than the current process and which sees the Society it is operating in receive the primary value crated rather than a private organization or firm.

Routledge Studies in Social Enterprise & Social Innovation looks to examine these increasingly important academic research themes as a central concept for social theories and policies. It looks to examine and explore the activities of social participation among civil society organisations, SMEs, governments, and research institutions by publishing the breakthrough books of the new frontiers of the field as well as the state-of-the-nation-defining books that help advance the field.

# Social Regeneration and Local Development

## Cooperation, Social Economy, and Public Participation

**Edited by Silvia Sacchetti, Asimina Christoforou, and Michele Mosca**

Routledge
Taylor & Francis Group

LONDON AND NEW YORK

First published 2018 by Routledge

2 Park Square, Milton Park, Abingdon, Oxfordshire OX14 4RN
52 Vanderbilt Avenue, New York, NY 10017

*Routledge is an imprint of the Taylor & Francis Group, an informa business*

First issued in paperback 2019

*Library of Congress Cataloging-in-Publication Data*
Names: Sacchetti, Silvia, editor. | Christoforou, Asimina,
    editor. | Mosca, Michele, editor.
Title: Social regeneration and local development : cooperation,
    social economy and public participation / edited by Silvia
    Sacchetti, Asimina Christoforou, and Michele Mosca.
Description: New York, NY : Routledge, 2017. | Includes index.
Identifiers: LCCN 2017035791 | ISBN 9781138236394
    (hardback) | ISBN 9781315302478 (ebook)
Subjects: LCSH: Social planning. | Social policy. | Public-private
    sector cooperation. | Political participation.
Classification: LCC HN18.3 .S5965 2017 | DDC 306.3—dc23
LC record available at https://lccn.loc.gov/2017035791

ISBN: 978-1-138-23639-4 (hbk)
ISBN: 978-0-367-88512-0 (pbk)

Typeset in Sabon
by Apex CoVantage, LLC

The Editors would like to dedicate this book to Giulio Regeni, who was brutally tortured and killed in Cairo while undertaking academic research.

# Contents

# Illustrations

## Figures

## Tables

## Box

# About the Contributors

**Francesca Battistoni** is the co-founder of Social Seed (www.socialseed.eu), a company that helps and supports social enterprises to innovate. She worked for several years in the field of social innovation as a consultant for public administration as well as in the evaluation of social impact. She has a PhD in Public Policy and Planning from IUAV (University of Venice).

**Carlo Borzaga** is a Professor of Economic Policy in the Department of Sociology and Social Research at the University of Trento (Italy). His research interests include cooperatives, social enterprise, the economic and social roles of non-profit organisations, and their interactions with welfare policies. From 1997 to 2008, he was chairman of the Institute for the Development of Nonprofit Organisations (ISSAN), based at Trento University. From 2003 to 2006, he was Dean of the Faculty of Economics. Currently, he is President of the European Research Institute on Cooperative and Social Enterprises (EURICSE). He sits on the editorial board of several Italian and European journals. He has written and co-edited numerous books and papers on labour economics, labour and welfare policies, and social and cooperative enterprises. He has participated in and coordinated numerous research projects funded by the EU, the Italian government, and local authorities.

**Leslie Budd** is a Reader in Social Enterprise at the Open University Business School. He is an economist who has written extensively on urban and regional economies in relation to the European Union, digital social inclusion, and global financial markets. His current work focuses on linking city leadership to economic citizenship and governance. Leslie was Special Economic Advisor to the Committee for Enterprise Trade and Investment (CETI) at the Northern Ireland Assembly, providing briefings, in particular on the impact of Brexit. He is currently Chair of the Urban and Regional Economics Seminar Group (URESG).

**Sara Calvo,** PhD, is a Senior Lecturer in Organisational Behaviour and the Social Enterprise Coordinator at the Enterprise Development Hub at Middlesex University Business School. Her research interests include social enterprise, social innovation and the social and solidarity economy, the informal sector, ethnic minority enterprise, social enterprise support policy, and visual research. She has carried out research in South America, Africa, Asia, and Europe. She is also the co-founder and director of a social enterprise organisation, Living in Minca and Minca Ventures, and a documentary filmmaker, having participated in a number of international film festivals. She has published several book chapters, reports on online websites, and academic papers in established international journals.

**Colin Campbell** is the founder and Executive Director of Assist Social Capital CIC (ASC). He has been working in the third sector in Scotland since 1995 and around sustainable socio-economic development in Biospheres since 2011. He has conducted many workshops and keynote presentations at international events. He is the co-founder and co-leader of the Social Enterprise in Biosphere Reserves Global Working Group, whose efforts have influenced the Lima Action Plan (2016–25), which includes actions on promoting and supporting social enterprise and social entrepreneurship. He is also the co-founder of the Social Capital World Forum (SCWF).

**Massimo Caroli** was born in Faenza in 1959 and holds a laurea in philosophy. He has always dedicated his time to the work integration of fragile or vulnerable people and people with disabilities. For some years now, he has been working to promote active citizenship and the reorganisation of social services, with a participatory and communitarian approach. He undertakes these activities as director of research and development at Fare Comunità (www.farecomunita.com), a consortium of social cooperatives based in Ravenna, as well as in his role as president of the Azienda dei Servizi alla Persona della Romagna Faentina (www.aspromagnafaentina.it).

**Asimina Christoforou** is an Adjunct Professor at the Athens University of Economics and Business. She has a PhD in economics and does research on topics such as social capital, regional development, European integration, ethics in economics, and the social economy. She is on the editorial boards of the *Journal of Economic Issues* and the *Forum for Social Economics* and is a member of the Board of Directors of the *Association for Evolutionary Economics* and the *Association for Social Economics*. She is also coordinator of the Social Capital Working Group for the *International Initiative for Promoting Political Economy*. She has participated in a number of Greek and EU research projects, as well as national and international conferences. Some of her publications include: 'Social capital and human development: An empirical investigation across European countries', *Journal of Institutional Economics*, 2010; 'On the identity of social capital and the social capital of identity', *Cambridge Journal of Economics*, 2013; A. Christoforou and J.B. Davis (eds.) *Social Capital* *and Economics: Social Values, Power, and Social Identity*, Routledge, 2014; A. Christoforou and M. Lainé (eds.) *Re-Thinking Economics: Exploring the Work of Pierre Bourdieu*, Routledge, 2014.

**Paolo Cottino** is an urban planner and policy designer, committed at two complementary levels of academic activity and professional practice. He received his PhD in 2005 in Town Planning and Public Policies at IUAV (University Institute of Architecture of Venice) and is the winner of the IVth edition of the "Giovanni Ferraro" National Awards for doctoral dissertations in Town Planning. In 2014, he obtained the National Scientific Qualification—Associate Professor in Sector 08/F1 Urban and Territorial Planning and Design. In 2009, he was a founding member of KCity Ltd (www.kcity.it), one of the first multidisciplinary firms in Italy specialising in strategic design for urban regeneration, and he works with public and private organisations, as well as with NGOs, to develop innovative territorial transformations and projects of urban reuse.

**Safa Husni Dhaher** is a university Assistant Professor and a freelance consultant. Born in Jerusalem, she holds a PhD in Local Development and Global Dynamics from the University of Trento, Italy, and a Master's degree in Social Sciences and Humanitarian Affairs from La Sapienza University of Rome, Italy. Currently teaching in Birzeit University/ Palestine, she was the Vice Head of Human Resources Department and the Library at al-Quds University/Palestine.

**Luca Fazzi** is a Full Professor of Sociology at the University of Trento, Italy. His research interests include social policy, voluntary action, and non-profit organisations. He is the director of a Master's programme in "Management of Social Enterprises" and coordinates the Graduate Course of Social Work at the University of Trento.

**Luigi Ferrara** is currently an Assistant Professor/Research Fellow in Administrative Law at the University of Naples Federico II. In 2014, he obtained the National Academic Qualification as Associate Professor in Administrative Law. At the University of Naples Federico II, he teaches Comparative Administrative Law and Environmental Law in the Department of Law and the Department of Pharmacy. He is responsible for international agreements with the Universities of Kobe (Japan) and Goerlitz (Germany). He delivered several papers in conferences in Italy and abroad. He published books, papers, and articles on the topics of EU administrative law, immigration law, and cultural heritage law. A complete CV with a list of publications and papers delivered can be found at www.docenti. unina.it/luigi.ferrara

**Rudolf Lewanski** (1950) is Associate Professor at the School of Political and Social Sciences, University of Bologna, where he presently teaches courses in deliberative participation and policy analysis. From October 2008 to

March 2013 as independent 'Participation Authority' he has been responsible for implementing law no. 69/07 of the Tuscany Region promoting citizen engagement. He is co-founder and past president of the Associazione Italiana per la Partecipazione Pubblica, affiliated to Iap2. His his most recent publications in the field of deliberative democracy is La prossima democrazia, 2016 available at www.laprossimademocrazia.com

**Mike Lucas** is a Senior Lecturer in Management at the Open University Business School. Over a lengthy career at the Open University, Mike has written and developed online learning courses in management, leadership, and organisation, most recently co-producing a MOOC on public leadership (with Prof. Jean Hartley) and developing an Open Educational Resources on collaborative problem solving in communities. His ongoing research on community festivals draws on his interests in organising practice, ethnography, and visual methods and has led to publications in *Culture & Organisation* and the *Journal of Organisational Ethnography*.

**Andres Morales** is a PhD researcher at the Open University in the UK. He also works as a Project Manager and is the co-founder of Living in Minca and Minca Ventures. He is also a documentary filmmaker and has participated in a number of international film festivals; all the documentaries made are based on bottom-up experiences from social entrepreneurs and social economy initiatives around the world. He has a wide range of experience working as a social enterprise consultant as well as an educator in several European, African, Asian, and Latin American countries. More recently, he has deepened his knowledge and experience researching and publishing academic articles, book chapters, and blogs about social enterprises and solidarity economy in the Global South.

**Michele Mosca** is an Associate Professor of Economic Policy at the University of Naples 'Federico II'. He holds a PhD in Development Economics and Policy at the University of Naples "Federico II" and a Master's in Economics (MA Economics) at the School of Economics and Social Sciences of the University of Manchester, UK. His research interests include social enterprise, non-profit organisations, criminal organisations, and the attempt to contrast them through the role of social economy and the reuse of assets seized from organised crime for social aims. He is the coordinator of a Master's programme in "Common Goods and Environmental Cultures" and co-coordinates a Master's programme in "Analysis of Organised Crime Phenomena and Strategies of Social Re-use of Assets Seized from Mafias" at the University of Naples 'Federico II'. He has published several articles and books on different topics, among which are the economics of organised crime and optimal law enforcement.

**Darcy Overland** is the Research Manager at the Centre for the Study of Cooperatives at the University of Saskatchewan. She oversees the undertaking of research initiatives at the Centre. She has been with the Centre for two years and previously spent 15 years working for the Government of Canada and Province of Saskatchewan in labour market adjustment programming, focused on youth, rural, and Indigenous populations. She holds a Master's of Public Administration from the University of Saskatchewan and Bachelors' of Education and Arts from the University of Regina.

**Silvia Sacchetti** is an Associate Professor of Economic Policy at the University of Trento (Italy) and collaborates with Euricse (European Research Center on Cooperative and Social Enterprise). She holds a PhD from the University of Birmingham (UK). She is interested in the inclusive development of economies and localities. Her research addresses in particular the study of participatory governance structures and resource coordination mechanisms. She focuses on cooperative firms and social enterprises, recently studied in the context of welfare services. Her research has addressed also the role of creativity, social capital, and individual motivations in local development. Her most recent publications have appeared in *Journal of Business Ethics*, *Annals of Public and Cooperative Economics*, and the *Journal of Entrepreneurial and Organisational Diversity*. She is the Co-Chief Editor of the *Journal of Entrepreneurial and Organisational Diversity* and an Associate Editor of the *European Management Journal*. She is a member of the European Research Board of the International Cooperative Alliance.

**Alessandro Sancino** is a Lecturer in Management at the Open University Business School. His research focuses at a macro-level on the changing relationship between state and society and its impacts on the co-creation of public value; at a meso-level on the role of leadership in and of places; and at a micro-level on processes of citizens' engagement across the public policy cycle (e.g., co-production of public services). He is a member of the Executive Board of PUPOL (International Academic Network on Public and Political Leadership). He has published in *Public Administration Review*, *Public Management Review*, *International Review of Administrative Sciences*, *Voluntas*, *Local Government Studies*, and *Public Money & Management*.

**Ermanno Tortia** is an Associate Professor of Economic Policy at the University of Trento. His research focuses on the theory of the firm, business economics, labour economics, human resources, and organisational behaviour as applied to third sector research and the organisational forms in the social economy (cooperative and social enterprises, nonprofit organisations). He has authored several empirical studies dealing with happiness economics, on-the-job satisfaction, organisational justice, and worker motivations. He has also authored several studies in the institutionalist theory of social economy organisations. He has been research fellow at the University of Stirling (UK), School of Applied Social Science. He collaborates closely with EuRICSE (European Research Institute on Cooperative and Social Enterprises, Trento, Italy). He is also a member of the scientific committee of JEOD (*Journal of Entrepreneurial and Organisational Diversity*, www.jeodonline.com) and a member of the teaching committee of the PhD Programme in Development Economics and Local Systems (DELoS) at the School of Social Science, Trento University.

**Salvatore Villani** is currently an Assistant Professor in Public Economics at the University of Naples Federico II, Department of Political Science. He also taught Finance of Public Administration at the School of Administrative Law and Administration Sciences of the University of Teramo, Italy. He was also a tax specialist lawyer and a member of the Lawyers' Committee for the Environment at the Bar Association of Naples, Italy. He was a member of the HDCA (Human Development and Capability Association) and the SVIMEZ (Association for the Industrial Development in Southern Italy) Working Group on the Implementation of Fiscal Federalism in Italy. He published several articles and books on the topics of migration policies, income inequality, fiscal federalism and decentralisation, local business taxation, non-profit taxation, and the economics of organised crime. A complete list of his publications and papers is available at www.docenti.unina.it/salvatore.villani.

**Flaviano Zandonai** is a senior researcher at Euricse (www.euricse.eu). He graduated with a degree in sociology and has been working for more than ten years in the consortia of Italian social cooperation. Also, he is the coordinator of the Iris Network, the Italian network of research institutes on social enterprises. His research interests focus on the specificity of the social enterprise and the whole third sector phenomenon in Italy and on studies regarding the regeneration of community assets and the potential forms of social enterprise financing. Apart from his research activities, he has well-established experience as a consultant and educator.

# Introduction

*Silvia Sacchetti, Asimina Christoforou,
and Michele Mosca*

"Regeneration" has been a topic of study and policy since the advent of industrialisation across the globe. The word has been associated mostly with urban and rural areas, as the capitalist organisation of production and the rise in growth were often accompanied by the intensification of disparities between urban and rural regions, the increase in inequality and poverty in the city slums and agricultural areas, the over-exploitation of the natural environment, the marginalisation of disadvantaged groups, and the degradation of the quality of life. These inequalities, resulting from material and non-material forms of deprivation, have been addressed in the literature and have often been related to conceptions and policy measures for so-called renewal and reconstruction with a focus on urban development and spatial planning and reconstruction.

However, limited attention has been given to the social and political dimensions of the physical space within which these localities face problems and pursue policies for regeneration. As a result, contextual historical and cultural factors, like power relations and social inequalities, which affect how problems are perceived, what institutional and organisational solutions are sought, and how policies are implemented, were overlooked and this hampered attempts to renewal and development. Social and political participation and cooperation play a crucial role in regeneration by enabling local actors and communities of interest to voice diverse needs and interests, including those of the marginalised and disadvantaged groups, to organise concerted efforts to discuss problems and promote solutions, and to create a public space of deliberative, democratic participation to re-assess values and priorities regarding the means and ends of development and welfare. There are theoretical and empirical studies from different parts of the world, which touch upon these aspects of urban planning and cover various approaches and dimensions of community- and culture-led regeneration that address the impact of the social economy on urban regeneration (see, for instance, Leary and McCarthy, 2013).

We feel that our volume takes the argument further by focusing on social regeneration, that is, on the processes of transformation based on inclusion and cooperation that are informed by the goal of improving peoples' lives through participation and deliberation, or by the active involvement of beneficiaries and other communities of interest. This volume addresses specific modalities to achieve social regeneration by emphasising forms centred on inclusion and cooperation within and across territories, which require appropriate public spaces—organisational, relational, political, and physical spaces. These solutions, as social economy scholars have remarked, go beyond the use of material resources and the production of monetary outcomes and involve the use and production of relational goods, behavioural norms of reciprocity and cooperation, values of inter-generational solidarity and respect for the environment, as well as new models of people participating in the planning and delivery of general interest services.

We feel this approach is consistent with two of the most prominent challenges that societies face today, namely social exclusion and inequality. Territories reveal increasing difficulties in addressing the complexity of the answers required, and what can be a good solution for one locality may not be for another. The diversity of needs and aspirations across communities requires an effort to understand whether there are modalities which are conducive to the identification of needs and solutions which respect such diversity. The challenge is to identify decision-making methods that allow the recognition of needs which are not necessarily satisfied by traditional organisations, as well as the formulation of appropriate answers, building on the peculiarities of each territory and on the interests of multiple publics (Dewey, 1927; Sacchetti and Sugden, 2009; Sugden and Wilson, 2002). Global disparities have been repeatedly addressed in UN reports, which denounced the widening gaps between skilled and unskilled workers, educated and illiterate people, the weak and healthy, and citizens with access to the political debate and those to whom such access is denied (UN, 2015). A greater level of societal inclusion, therefore, remains the central aim also of developmental actions against poverty.

This volume focuses on specific forms of poverty, which are crucial to local development but have received limited attention. This is the poverty of social relations, inclusion, and empowerment, which require actions aimed at social regeneration (Becchetti et al., 2008; Sacchetti and Sugden, 2009). Social regeneration, in this sense, identifies with processes of transformation based on inclusion and cooperation that are informed by the goal of improving peoples' lives through the active involvement of beneficiaries and other communities of interest (a perspective that was forcefully brought in the academic and policy debate by the work of Amartya Sen and his approach to human capabilities and democracy; Sen, 2002). Social regeneration poses a huge challenge across diverse contexts, needs, and aspirations, and, so far, the question remains on how these goals can be achieved. The challenge was also recently indicated by Europe's Net4Society, an International network set up to consult and support socio-economic research, which advocates the need for research to address "the development of new forms of organisations and interactions to respond to societal challenges" in order to determine and satisfy community needs (NET4SOCIETY, 2014, 21).

To deal with these open questions, this volume studies social regeneration and addresses specific modalities of achieving it by emphasising forms centred on inclusion and cooperation within and across territories. We adopt an interdisciplinary outlook and investigate how values and institutions of cooperation and deliberation can be embedded in the physical space of the community to enable social stakeholders to determine the means and ends to local development. In this context, we embrace the unity between the choice of processes (cooperative and inclusive) and the choice of aims (social inclusion, empowerment, and well-being). Thus, we embrace an alternative approach whereby social values and institutions of cooperation and deliberation are not only conducive to growth, which is the dominant view in the literature, but are also constitutive of a sense of development that incorporates material and non-material means and objectives of well-being.

The aim of this volume is to shed light on the emergence and evolution of social economy organisations in different contexts of social, political, technological, and financial structures and thus evaluate their impact on regeneration and development. For instance, we consult the work of Elinor Ostrom and John Dewey to benefit from their insights on coordination mechanisms, polycentric and cooperative forms of governance, and public spaces for democratic solutions and critical thinking. Social capital, that is, norms and networks of reciprocity and cooperation, is an essential building block by supporting the network and governance structures among social stakeholders to act, cooperate, and deliberate for their own development and wellbeing. Our theoretical reflection is combined with empirical analyses and case studies from around the world that focus on the obstacles posed on social regeneration, especially in underdeveloped regions of Southern Europe and the Third World, or even areas in the developed world that face the challenges of the post-industrial era, where deprivation and social exclusion for some segments of the population are often no different, if not worse, to those encountered in less developed countries.

This book focuses on socio-economic dynamics, combines the insights and recommendations of various social sciences, brings together theory and practice, and compares different social and political contexts and dimensions. In this way, it aspires to take account of context and the additional constraints imposed by the global crisis in order to delineate specific steps to be taken for regenerating social values and institutions of cooperation and participation via the social economy and public participation.

The chapters featured in this book emphasise how solutions pertain a variety of public spaces, namely organisational, relational, political, and physical spaces. In so doing, the volume addresses governance solutions that can provide decision-making principles for social regeneration and improved well-being. It contributes to an interpretation of the organisations and interactions that promote the common good by providing answers to needs that are not normally addressed through conventional market organ-isations (see also Laville et al., 2015). These solutions have been theorised in the work of institutionalist scholars, such as Elinor Ostrom, who analysed polycentric and cooperative forms of governance aimed at the sustainable use of specific common goods, or in the earlier studies of John Dewey, who theorised democratic solutions aimed at creating deliberative and creative spaces to inform public interest (Ostrom, 2010; Dewey, 1927; Sacchetti and Sugden, 2009; Sacchetti, 2015). The chapters highlight the ways in which participatory and cooperative forms of interaction and decision-making can activate transformative answers to valued problems, which may not find desirable modalities in traditional market or public administration solu-tions. Cooperative solutions, as social economy scholars have remarked, go beyond the use of material resources and the production of monetary out-comes, and involve the use and production of relational goods (intangible elements characterised by communicative and affective nature, produced through encounters and interactions (e.g., Gui, 2000), behavioural norms of reciprocity and cooperation (e.g., Borzaga and Tortia, 2017), and values of inter-generational solidarity and respect for the environment (e.g., Coraggio et al., 2015).

Thus, the authors contributing to this volume reflect on the ways that specific solutions, such as social economy organisations, and other inter-acting contextual factors (such as relations and civic engagement, the use of physical space, urban regeneration, leadership, technology, and socially oriented finance) can achieve social regeneration and promote the develop-ment and welfare of a good life within and across territories. Their study of social regeneration includes cooperative and collaborative solutions at several levels (that of individuals, organisations, and institutional networks) and can be applied to different areas of local development (such as the use of cooperative, collaborative, and participative processes to address issues of urban and rural regeneration, as well as diverse forms of poverty and social exclusion resulting from immigration, unemployment, illness, digital illiteracy, and diverse forms of addiction). On the one hand, the contribu-tors emphasise the forms of life experience that individuals can enjoy collec-tively, and, on the other hand, they investigate the resources that can make this possible, such as: norms and rules reflected in legal frameworks and entrepreneurial organisations; forms of leadership and political practices that favour democratic deliberation and civic engagement; a supporting system of social relations; and the availability of aggregative and pleasant physical spaces where people can deploy and develop relatedness, ideas, and opportunities. Specifically, these factors are considered to the extent that they are capable of contributing to societal regeneration by favouring greater social inclusion and environmental sustainability.

The implication for social regeneration is clear. In order to put forth sus-tainable solutions to the problem of social poverty, values such as inclusion, deliberation, cooperation, solidarity, reciprocity, participation, and respect for the environment need to be embedded in the nature of institutions, social relations, organisations, as well as in the nature of the physical space. This unity between the choice of processes (cooperative and inclusive) and the choice of aims (social regeneration) is what Sen calls a "comprehensive outcome", or the idea that specific processes are selected in view of their foreseen ability to achieve certain results or avoid undesired ones (Sen, 2002, 159; Sacchetti, 2015).

In terms of organisational solutions, the volume focuses on organisations whose main objective is the creation of societal value through inclusion and cooperation. These are increasingly identified with social economy organisations, like social enterprises. Social enterprises are business organisations that have the explicit aim of seeing people and their needs, thus playing a key role in improving social integration, equality, and well-being. However, the need for social regeneration, which until now has been confined to the needs of particular groups of individuals, touches upon territories and their communities in a widespread manner. Studies on social capital have shown that where the fabric of social relationships has eroded and isolation prevails, communities lack also the ability to share ideas and responsibility on issues of common interest. Virtuous behaviours, such as cooperation and social responsibility go astray, thus compromising the capacity of a community to enhance the value of private as well as common (or public) assets. Consequently, the community as a space for relations, cooperation, communication, deliberation and democracy, development, and self-determination is being threatened by collapse and disappearance (Putnam, 2000; Christoforou and Davis, 2014).

Against this risk, engagement and cooperation have been promoted not only by social enterprises, but also by developmental policies with a focus on deliberative democracy, participation, and social capital. This requires specific policy and finance solutions as well as elements of public leadership that recognise the desirability of fostering processes based on deliberative democracy that can create capabilities for civic engagement and leadership.

Where appropriate tools of engagement and deliberation are recognised at the system level, social organisations become an integral part of a broader socio-economic environment where issues surrounding social regeneration are decided inclusively and cooperatively, with an emphasis on enhancing the quality of the life experience. The challenge for engaging cooperative processes is to include multiple needs and interests, prototyping and applying the deliberative method so as to give voice to multiple communities of interest, whilst accounting for the wider impacts of regeneration in the longer run (Sacchetti, 2015). The approach fosters the development of democratic and deliberative skills within and amongst community constituencies (for example, through community development forums, festivals, or other engagement initiatives), bringing together actors from different sectors (private non-profit, private for-profit, public sector, families, etc.) and expertise (such as in business, local development, health, social services, arts, education, housing, urban and rural regeneration, and the environment). Likewise, the financial dimension can deploy its function consistently with long-term social objectives. In this respect, social regeneration is also achieved by means of financial processes which emphasise participatory and monitoring procedures that allow us to identify the community's socio-economic needs and solutions. Finance can promote social regeneration beyond traditional corporate social responsibility, by being shaped around the territory's strengths and playing an intermediary's role in promoting social transformation and development. As cooperative experiences emphasise, financial institutions that support social regeneration reflect the existence of a community of actors who share pro-social values, detect skills and resources, whilst providing a locus for engagement in order to develop the appropriate solutions for social regeneration.

The interconnections amongst factors of regeneration requires creating a system for territorial governance, or a dynamic socio-economic network of like-minded actors sharing fundamental values on methods of engagement (inclusion, cooperation) and purpose (social regeneration). Yet, we have very limited knowledge of what solutions are being introduced to foster cooperation and inclusion in processes of social regeneration, in a context defined by the multiple and at times conflicting interests of a variety of stakeholders and communities. In passing, this is one instance of a wider gap—the need to shift the organisational, and particularly the social enterprise, debate from the level of the firm to the level of the system and system governance.

The volume addresses those issues following an inter-disciplinary and innovative line of reasoning:

- Social regeneration requires the creation of an institutional context where opportunities and capabilities for weak categories, and transversally, for society, can be developed.
- This unity can be achieved, in part, through organisational solutions increasingly defined as social enterprises because they are characterised by a social objective, cooperation, and inclusive democratic governance.
- Additionally, besides organisational solutions, values of cooperation and inclusion must be reflected in other socio-economic elements, which can work in synergy with the social enterprise model to promote and sustain social regeneration and well-being. Such elements include civic engagement and deliberation, social capital, urban and rural spaces, leadership, technology, and finance.

## Structure of the Book

Following the introduction, the volume is separated in three parts. The first part of the volume (Chapters 1 and 2) introduces the main framework of analysis along the lines outlined above. The second part of the volume

(Chapters 3 to 7) focuses on organisational solutions based on inclusion and cooperation that can support social regeneration at different levels. These organisational solutions mainly draw from theories, practices, and policies related to the social economy. Finally, the third part (Chapters 8 to 14) positions contextual elements which are complementary to organisational solutions and which, consistently with the approach of third sector organisations, potentially foster cooperative and inclusive values that are conducive to social regeneration.

In the first part of the volume, in **Chapter 1**, Silvia Sacchetti and Carlo Borzaga argue for the need of social regeneration "wherever a specific form of poverty becomes endemic". The authors take a behavioural perspective and define social regeneration as "the transformative processes which, through institutional choices that embody cooperation and inclusion, develop opportunities and capabilities for multiple categories of actors, and especially weak categories, leading to societal benefits and community resilience". It is argued that this behavioural transformation is able to address the poverty of social relations, which is at the heart of the failure of societies to address major challenges, such as inequality or urban and environmental degradation across world regions. The authors combine conceptual elements of cooperation and deliberation from institutional theory (recalling authors such as E. Ostrom and J. Dewey) to identify key institutional solutions that are able to generate surplus for communities and reduce social poverty. In particular, they identify three institutional features at the heart of social regeneration processes. The first refers to participatory procedural features and the formation of deliberative forms of problem-framing and decision-making. The second refers to structural features and requires the inclusion of multiple stakeholders in organisational governance. The third extends these features at the system level, arguing that inclusive institutional solutions are required at multiple levels of nested private, public, or community action.

The idea of social poverty and the social regeneration imperative come alive in **Chapter 2**, where Luca Fazzi illustrates the waning of solidarity and social cohesion in the traditional welfare model and proposes new institutional solutions aimed at social regeneration, public participation, and reorganisation of the production of services. The author's analysis starts from the idea that the scope of the welfare model is to build solidarity among individuals, generations, and social classes. This aim, however, contrasts with the tendency of society to become increasingly individualistic. For a whole range of reasons, most people today no longer have experience of shared collective political and social action, and their lives are increasingly separate from those of others. The author then observes that under these circumstances, it is becoming harder to sell traditional themes of solidarity and social inclusion as foundations of welfare and much easier to promote divisions between social classes, generations, and people. He builds his argument by tracing the political and historical development of welfare as a moral institution. He then focuses on specific areas that are central to restructuring welfare states, and discusses the tensions and risks related to the weakening of the solidaristic function of welfare. Conclusions stress the importance of supporting new processes and institutions aimed at social regeneration, public participation, and reorganisation of service production.

The second part of the volume begins with **Chapter 3**, where Asimina Christoforou discusses the participatory dimensions of social enterprises and their potential contribution to social regeneration. The author builds on the European Commission perspective, according to which the social enterprise is "an operator in the social economy whose main objective is to have a social impact rather than make a profit for their owners or shareholders. It operates by providing goods and services for the market in an entrepreneurial and innovative fashion and uses its profits primarily to achieve social objectives. It is managed in an open and responsible manner and, in particular, involves employees, consumers and stakeholders affected by its commercial activities" (*Social Business Initiative*, October 2011). Therefore, there is an entrepreneurial, social, and governance dimension that distinguishes social enterprises from for-profit and non-profit organisations. The aim of this chapter is to theoretically and practically determine the ways in which social enterprises can build social capital and sustain the capacity of the organisation and locality to promote social regeneration and pave the way toward a more participatory economic system. To examine the actual potential of a social enterprise to contribute to social regeneration and a participatory economic system via social capital, the chapter provides preliminary results of a case study conducted in Greece, where concepts of social economy and social entrepreneurship are rather novel and are promoted by EU-supported policies and funds to deal with the crisis in the country.

In **Chapter 4**, Flaviano Zandonai, Paolo Cottino, and Francesca Battistoni explore experiences of social and urban regeneration. In doing this, the authors exceed traditional organisational solutions centred on corporate social responsibility and highlight the role of (social) impact investing by focusing on models of territorial governance based on coordination between private enterprises and local authorities. The chapter takes a very practical angle and contributes to the debate on social regeneration by defining new guidelines for the development of financially sustainable processes, which combine social and urban regeneration objectives. The re-combination of social, urban, and specific financial elements gives rise to different models of interaction between enterprise and local authorities, which the authors illustrate with case studies. Specifically, the authors consider the case of the recovery of unused railway stations as *community assets* promoted by the Ferrovie dello Stato Italiane. They highlight both the limitations of a compensation logic and the added value from recovering property for social use within the new chains of value production.

In **Chapter 5**, Darcy Overland reports results from the Cooperative Innovation Project (CIP), which looked at cooperative development in western Canada. The CIP project was aimed at exploring whether cooperative development can be considered as a tool for social and spatial regeneration in rural and Indigenous communities that have unique local challenges. These communities are facing diminished possibilities as a result of changing economies and populations. The cooperative model, which balances both business and associative capacity, can succeed where other business models or government provision aren't practicable and can form an important part of regeneration in these communities. However, cooperatives are a unique model of organising, so it takes leaders with a unique set of attributes to start and sustain cooperatives. The study conducted interviews with experienced coop development practitioners to investigate the leadership qualities that are considered conducive to community cooperative development. Commitment to the community and shared leadership, possession of business acumen and controlled energy, knowledge of the community and group dynamics, and an ability to put a project over politics were identified as attributes that successful cooperative leaders possess.

Chapter 6 analyses policies for social regeneration taking place in difficult territories. Michele Mosca takes the example of the land of Gomorra in Italy, where, in compliance with the Italian law, third sector organisations are involved in the regeneration of social capital through the social re-use of assets confiscated to the mafia. The author investigates how these policies have outlined a new role for the organisations of the social economy and how this has contributed to creating an alternative development model which is beneficial not only for marginalised or disadvantaged people, but for the community as a whole. He argues that in territories which have suffered the domination of the mafia and the deterioration of their endowment of social capital, social regeneration has occurred by means of policy actions that were able to remove social capital from the mafia's control. In this context, the author suggests that social capital regeneration may consist in re-orienting social capital to support and promote the substantial freedoms of people and the general interests of a democratic community. The chapter stresses the importance of social cohesion policies in preventing the expansion of the mafia, alongside more traditional crime-repression strategies. In addition, it discusses the role of third sector organisations and social cooperatives which have been recognised by the law as privileged concessionaries in the assignment of confiscated assets for their social re-use. The chapter indicates that the seizure and confiscation of illegally acquired assets, paired with suitable policies aimed at promoting and supporting the development of social cooperatives and non-profit organisations, can have a direct impact on work opportunities and on individuals' life choices, reducing the incentive for illegal activity and improving emancipation and development within communities.

In Chapter 7, Massimo Caroli and Ermanno Tortia adopt a territorial governance approach to deal with a major European and global issue, namely the marginalisation and social exclusion of migrants and asylum seekers. They use the concept "systemic governance", discussed in Chapter 1, to analyse systems of migrant reception and integration implemented across Italy. They focus on the role of multiple territorial actors in generating innovation and social inclusion in pair with the regeneration of abandoned spaces and localities. The authors suggest legislative, policy, and administrative initiatives in order to build integration and avoid exclusion and conflict, contributing to the social regeneration of regions. First, they introduce the general trends of immigration and the legislative and policy measures adopted in Italy. Then, they contextualise the patterns of migrants' inclusion, the allocation of national resources, and the implementation of administrative and reception measures at the local level. Finally, they turn to the case of the Union of Municipalities of Romagna Faentina in Central Italy. The Union has recently started several dedicated integration programmes in a country that has recently been the destination of migration flows in Europe. The case study demonstrates how reception and integration are managed through a web of public, civil society, and third sector organisations. With the support of the National Agency for Personal Services (NASP), specific organisations have been created and run by both Italian and immigrant citizens in order to teach the Italian language to migrants, offer administrative services, and enable cultural integration.

In the third part of the volume, in **Chapter 8**, Rudolf Lewanski supports the view that social regeneration requires a process of political regeneration. He argues that the alienation of citizens in contemporary democracies from the polity in general and from specific decisions takes away the locus of power from elected institutions and Nation States. He observes that over the last decade, an innovative form of citizen engagement has been developed and put into effect in many parts of the world: *deliberative* participation. In this chapter, the author illustrates the specific features of deliberative participation, differentiating it from other forms of engagement, and discusses the added value it may contribute to social regeneration. He suggests we go back to the original meaning of democracy, which requires citizen participation in a credible and meaningful way. He then proposes a specific application of deliberative democracy for regenerating civic engagement and social capital in a 'time-poor' society, as well as mobilising collective intelligence in a highly sophisticated technological society.

In **Chapter 9**, Leslie Budd and Alessandro Sancino look at place leadership as a way for enhancing the social regeneration of communities. The authors draw from their previous research that identifies and classifies various types of city leadership: *managerial leadership*, which deals with public services (e.g., housing, health care, education, regeneration, leisure, etc.) delivered within a city; *political leadership*, which deals with the democratic processes and decisions affecting a city and its citizens; *civic leadership*, which deals with all the community processes provided by the community and its actors operating outside the traditional realm of the public and private sectors; and *business leadership*, which deals with the processes of (co-)creation of value provided by the private sector. Then the authors discuss for each type of place leadership (managerial, political, civic, and business) which actors, structures, processes, and followership patterns can boost social regeneration. Some main themes emerging are: the new roles and skills required by public managers; the need of integrating representative and deliberative democracy in designing processes of political leadership; and the potential of empowering citizens' capabilities for sparking civic leadership. The authors finally suggest that place leadership for social regeneration requires a paradigmatic change in the way we traditionally frame the identity of local governments and the role of public managers and politicians.

In **Chapter 10**, Sara Calvo and Andres Morales examine the role played by digital technology, using the example of Web 2.0 as a tool for social regeneration. They introduce basic theoretical discussions and debates about Web 2.0 and digital divide studies. Notably, the authors do not overlook the rising concern about the emergence of new inequalities and therefore a need for a more critical approach in relation to digital technology as an instrument for socio-economic, political, and cultural transformation. This is especially important due to the fragility of economic recovery and uneven progress in major economies, in which social conditions are not only expected to recover slowly, but also to encounter societal distresses beyond the economic dimension such as political, social, environmental and trust crises. Furthermore, the authors attempt to explain the role of Web 2.0 technology amongst different groups and how far-reaching digital technology serves the purpose of participation, access for all, and its use and knowledge-implementation amongst the global communities. Good practices are included. A Social Enterprise MOOC programme and two social and solidarity initiatives (Citizens Foundation and Million Kitchen) illustrate the importance of digital technology when aiming at generating social and environmental change and therefore social regeneration through participatory, collaborative, and inclusive processes.

In **Chapter 11**, Luigi Ferrara and Salvatore Villani address the role of the legislative framework in promoting urban regeneration and, through it, opportunities for local development. On the one hand, they describe the successful case study of the "Barriera" district of Turin, which shows how a wise management of integration policies and a greater involvement of all actors (public institutions and private stakeholders) in the planned urban regeneration can favour the economic and social exploitation of the territory, as well as the human development of residents. On the other hand, they discuss the fallacy of public decision-making and why opportunities have been missed in Southern Italy by illustrating the case of Bagnoli and the bankruptcy of the urban regeneration programme in this important site of national interest. In particular, the authors stress that attempts to exploit and convert early industrialisation areas have failed in Southern Italy because of the lack of a national strategy for strengthening and developing interconnections between urban areas and effective multi-level governance structures. They go on to argue that this failure has had serious effects on the territory, especially in the metropolitan areas of Southern Italy, where local public agencies governing Provinces and Metropolitan Cities fail to deliver public goods and services, leading to the exclusion and marginalisation of a growing number of citizens. The authors juxtapose the missing opportunities in Bagnoli with opportunities created by migratory flows in Turin, where local governments have been able to maximise cultural diversity and foster local economic and social development by encouraging greater participation of immigrants in economic and decision-making processes.

In **Chapter 12**, Safa Dhaher illustrates research results on the Wall between East Jerusalem and the West Bank and its implications for social capital among Palestinian people. The author observes that social capital provides a safety net for improving the Palestinian people's chances in their daily survival efforts in the Occupied Palestinian Territories (OPT). She discusses the effects of the Wall, which was constructed not only to separate Israel and East Jerusalem from the West Bank but also to separate Palestinian communities in the West Bank from each other. In this complex geopolitical context caused by the different sources of political hegemony over its components and the unjust distribution of land and resources, this chapter examines the role of social capital and what it implies for social regeneration. The author explains how the Wall in East Jerusalem separates Palestinians from Palestinians, highlighting the different comprehensive explicit policies that Israel has used in order to change the demographic balance in favour of the Israeli population in the city of Jerusalem. The author shows how the confinement of the population caused by the Wall has enforced social capital in all its manifestations at the individual, community, and the governmental levels in order to overcome problems related to education and health care services and security. The chapter concludes that social capital has and still has the capacity to soothe the problems in these specific areas, but has no power in solving them without a concrete political solution.

In **Chapter 13**, Silvia Sacchetti and Colin Campbell combine the idea of social regeneration with that of natural justice by considering community development within biosphere reserves (BRs). BRs have been identified by UNESCO since the 1970s and are located across the globe. The challenge of environmental sustainability within BRs meets a variety of cultures, histories, natural settings, and forms of economic organisations. In the chapter, the authors acknowledge that although the need for compatibility between human activities and BRs has been invoked at several policy levels, solutions on how to achieve this outcome have not been considered in the same detail. The authors think that part of the issue may be methodological, since BRs may have common aims, but greatly differ in terms of their contextual elements. To explore contextual diversity, the chapter offers illustrations from BRs in Vietnam, Italy, Australia, and Zimbabwe. The chapter then identifies a number of 'spaces' or contextual dimensions that differentiate BRs, focusing on dimensions of policy, relations, and organisations that can be consistent with social regeneration and natural 'justice'. The authors argue that the presence and features of these dimensions can determine the ability of community members to cooperate with a long time horizon. The existence of policy and relational spaces, in particular, suggest the presence of place-awareness (e.g., being aware of living within a BR and a specific community), leading to the formation of organisational solutions that are consistent with social regeneration and natural justice.

In **Chapter 14**, Mike Lucas addresses community engagement in the production of festivals. A community festival is a particular form of event which offers intensive relational engagement. This chapter focuses on how, as part of their collaborative practices of organising an annual festival event, a local community group co-produce the space used to celebrate the festival as a form of relational good produced—in this case—by a group of volunteer organisers of an occasional festival. Recent studies of what are termed relational goods suggest a blurred relationship between their production and their consumption. Involvement in the organisation and delivery of such events as the community festival discussed here contribute to the production of a relational good, but also provide a time-space of engagement which may be viewed as a form of relational consumption. Using ethnographic data from the author's own research, the chapter explores the nature of the relational practices and goods which are produced and consumed in the organisation and delivery of a community festival. The particular focus on the space or site which is utilised as part of the community's work is supported in part by Lefebvre's (1991) theorisation of the social production of space and in part by Ricoeur's (1971) use of the text paradigm to understand broader social practices of meaning-making. The author examines how a community festival space becomes a relational text, a form of relational good linked to the development of shared meanings amongst the members of the volunteer organising group.

## Research Implications and Future Research

The main objective of the chapters featured in this volume is to discover ways to promote local development by means of social regeneration which relies on cooperation and public participation among local actors. The chapters focused on the potential of social economy organisations to provide the principles and institutions that underpin cooperation and public participation for social regeneration because they are built on values of social inclusion and democratic deliberation for social welfare and empowerment. The studies presented in this book adopt a multi-disciplinary approach and apply both theoretical and empirical analyses to delineate the capacities and limitations of social economy organisations, particularly social enterprises, in supporting social regeneration and local development. Generally, we could say that these studies observe the following:

- Social regeneration is not exclusively determined by calculative and instrumental considerations that underlie the maximisation of personal utility or profit in accordance to mainstream economic approaches.

It also relies on underlying motivations and visions for pursuing cooperation and solidarity among various groups and serving generalised
interests in the community. Thus, social economy organisations may be
able to support social regeneration because they combine economic and
social objectives.

- Social regeneration is essentially driven by a process of political regeneration. Nowadays, even in the modern democracies of the developed
world, people show distrust towards public institutions and question
their ability and willingness to preserve public values such as redistribution and justice, reducing their effectiveness and legitimacy. This calls
for new forms of democratic participation and governance on the basis
of deliberation and inclusiveness of all interested classes and parties.
More often, it is stressed that legal frameworks and public policies must
recognise and protect the autonomy of bottom-up initiatives that aim at
mobilising groups and satisfying specific social needs and values. Social
economy organisations may function as a forum, which applies, culti-
vates, and disseminates autonomy and participation in decision-making
processes not only within but also outside these organisations by building networks among various local actors that operate in the economy
across firms and sectors.

- The processes of social regeneration specifically require patterns of
citizen participation in the decision-making processes for goods and
services of general interest to be produced. As stressed above, these
patterns of participation are crucial in light of the multiplicity and
diversity of needs and aspirations across communities, which are not
necessarily satisfied by traditional organisations. The challenge is to
identify decision-making methods that allow us to recognise multiple
and diverse needs and find appropriate solutions by building on the
peculiarities of each territory and the interests of multiple publics.

- In this way, social regeneration is a highly complex phenomenon. On
the one hand, it is determined by both context-specific characteristics of
the locality, as well as systemic factors at broader levels of social organisation and governance. On the other hand, it is shaped by the interaction among various kinds of public spaces—organisational, relational,
political, and physical spaces. Therefore, business strategies and public
policies should be planned in ways that take into account the multiple
dimensions that characterise social regeneration processes. To take a
simple example, it is not possible to set out strategies and measures for
economic growth without considering the impact on the physical space,
particularly the natural environment. It is also not possible to engage in
social and political deliberations without considering the impact of the
physical space that will bring people together, 'shelter' ideas and practices of dialogue and participation, and educate people in developing
shared values and identities. Social economy organisations may have
the potential to address these dimensions and combine spaces thanks

to their democratic principles of participation in conjunction with their commercial objectives for growth, employment, and competitiveness. The difference is that economic means and objectives are not the outcome of a handful of corporate executives, shareholders, bureaucrats, and politicians, but of all those affected in the community and the economy as a whole.

- Finally, social regeneration is concomitant with a vision of social change. The point of introducing values and institutions of public participation, deliberative democracy, inclusiveness, and solidarity is to enable processes of reflection that will lead to the redefinition of the means and ends needed to respond to ever-changing social needs and achieve social welfare. These processes are important especially in times of crisis, when everything is being questioned and undergoing transformation, like the times we are living today. Social economy organisations are usually considered to be held back by their non-economic considerations and values. However, they have shown that under certain circumstances they may be the drivers of social change. It is precisely because of their dual role that social economy organisations are capable of understanding innovation in its holistic sense, that is, not only as technical advancement and digitisation of the economy, but also as the emergence of new forms of cooperation and governance that places technology in the service of social welfare.

Indeed, the present volume documents a number of cases in which social economy organisations have been able to reduce the gap in inequality, even during the crisis, by providing opportunities, goods, and services to disadvantaged and marginalised people. These organisations have been able to incorporate the perverse effects generated by neoliberal policies that exacerbated this gap. However, the volume also discusses the obstacles and lost opportunities faced by these organisations due to both internal and external factors in different spatial and historical contexts. Therefore, it is imperative to continually explore the basis on which a new idea of enterprise, development, and welfare can be built. Social economy organisations are new forms of enterprise which pursue economic objectives in order to serve social objectives by producing goods and services of general interest. Further insight is needed to understand how these organisations can be entrepreneurial subjects that are capable of 'contradicting market laws', while being efficient in the markets they operate in (labour market, credit market, market of goods and services). Some questions for future research may include:

- What social economy organisations provide? What are the potentialities, and what are the limits? In which way they can compensate the causes of the global crisis? How can they absorb the social consequences of the neoliberal policies of the last 30 years?

- When values of individualism, competition, and profit prevail in the national and global economies, what are the conditions that will enable local agents, and particularly social economy organisations, to foster and disseminate values and institutions of cooperation and public participation?
- When conditions of social segregation, human rights violations, and environmental destruction prevent certain segments of the population from participating in decision-making processes, how can social economy organisations build advocacy and voice without compromising the daily provision of services and goods that target these vulnerable groups and contribute to their empowerment?
- What strategies and policies have to be implemented in order to enable social economy organisations to access the economic and social resources they need to flourish? What are the contextual and systemic factors that determine which strategies and policies are appropriate?
- What institutions need to be put in place to foster participatory networks and structures not only within social economy organisations, but also within the broader national and global economic system? What institutions need to be established to build processes of reflection and redefinition at the individual and collective levels and educate people in the principles of these processes?
- How can social economy organisations redefine work in order to combine employment and income with respect to human needs, like environmental protection, creativity, sociality, and family obligations? How can they perceive, produce, and redistribute surplus among agents? How can they contribute to building a new and broader understanding of growth, one that goes beyond its monetary elements (as income and wealth) and incorporates people's capabilities and emancipation (Sen's approach to human development)? What are the motivations and rules that would underpin these principles and processes?

As summarised by Gibson-Graham (2003, 157), there are two lines for research that will further enhance development of "alternative communities and economies". The first is a more sophisticated analysis of the economics of surplus distribution. Though principles and structures of surplus distribution are at the core of the philosophy and operations of social economy organisations and participatory economic systems, they have received relatively little attention in theory and practice. The second line for research is developing a better understanding of the processes by which "communal subjectivities" are created and fostered. Solidarity is a relational aspect of human nature and is cultivated within the diverse and complex interactions people engage in. Yet few studies give merit to the evolution of these processes and their combined impact on people's values, behaviours, and identities. To deal with these open issues, the authors suggest that we play an active and constructive role in community conversations about "ethical economic decisions and personal political becomings".

In other words, we could say that principles and institutions of democratic deliberation and public participation among researchers, policymakers, and local actors, which are at the heart of this volume, can offer technically and socially sound solutions to these questions and open ways to regeneration and development.

## References

Becchetti, L., Pelloni, A., and F. Rossetti. 2008. "Relational Goods, Sociability, and Happiness." *Kyklos*, 61(3): 343–363.
Borzaga, C., and E. C. Tortia. 2017. "Cooperation as Coordination Mechanism: A New Approach to the Economics of Cooperative Enterprises." In *The Handbook of Mutual, Cooperative, and Coowned Business*, edited by J. Michie, J. Blassi and C. Borzaga, 55–75. Oxford: Oxford University Press.
Christoforou, A., and J. B. Davis. 2014. *Social Capital and Economics: Social Values, Power, and Social Identity*. London and New York: Routledge.
Coraggio, J., Eynaud, P., Ferranini, A., de França Filho, G. C., Gaiger, L. I., Hillenkamp, I., Kitajima, K., Laville, J.-L., Lemaitre, A., Sadik, Y., Veronese, M., and F. Wanderley. 2015. "The Theory of Social Enterprise and Pluralism: Solidarity-type Social Enterprise." In *Civil Society, the Third Sector and Social Enterprise: Governance and Democracy*, edited by J.-L. Laville, D. Young and P. Eynaud, 234–249. London and New York: Routledge.
Dewey, J. 1927. *The Public and Its Problems*. Denver, CO: Holt.
Gibson-Graham, J. K. 2003. "Enabling Ethical Economies: Cooperativism and Class." *Critical Sociology*, 29(2): 123–161.
Gui, B. 2000. "Beyond Transactions: On the Interpersonal Dimension of Economic Reality." *Annals of Public and Cooperative Economics*, 71(2): 139–169.
Laville, J.-L., Young, D. R., and P. Eynaud. 2015. *Civil Society, the Third Sector and Social Enterprise*. London: Routledge.
Leary, M. E., and J. McCarthy, eds. 2013. *The Routledge Companion to Urban Regeneration*. London and New York: Routledge.
Lefebvre, H. 1974/1991. *The Production of Space*. Oxford: Basil Blackwell.
Net4Society. 2014. *Opportunities for Researchers From the Socio-economic Sciences and Humanities (SSH)*, October. Accessed from www.net4society.eu.
Ostrom, E. 2010. "Revising Theory in Light of Experimental Findings." *Journal of Economic Behaviour and Organisation*, 73(1): 68–72.
Putnam, R. D. 2000. *Bowling Alone: The Collapse and Revival of American Community*. New York: Simon and Schuster.
Ricoeur, P. 1971. "The Model of the Text: Meaningful Action Considered as Text." *Social Research*, 38: 529–562.
Sacchetti, S. 2015. "Inclusive and Exclusive Social Preferences: A Deweyan Framework to Explain Governance Heterogeneity." *Journal of Business Ethics*, 126: 473–485. First published November 2013. doi:10.1007/s10551-013-1971-0
Sacchetti, S., and R. Sugden. 2009. "The Organisation of Production and Its Publics: Mental Proximity, Market and Hierarchies." *Review of Social Economy*, 67(3): 289–311.
Sen, A. 2002. *Rationality and Freedom*. Cambridge, MA: Harvard University Press.
Sugden, R., and J. Wilson. 2002. "Economic Development in the Shadow of the Consensus: A Strategic Decision-Making Approach." *Contributions to Political Economy*, 21(1): 111–134.
United Nations. 2015. *The Millennium Development Goals 2015*. New York: United Nations.

# Part I
# Social Regeneration

# 1 Social Regeneration and Cooperative Institutions

*Silvia Sacchetti and Carlo Borzaga*[1]

## Social Regeneration and Social Poverty

In a recent conversation with a Scottish general practitioner, she noted that the major sources of illness in her patients were loneliness and isolation. Albeit anecdotal, this conversation pointed at one of the paradoxes of the socio-economic development model that has dominated economic policy after the Second World War. The paradox can be phrased as follows: how come, in an era of material and technological progress, people are overly falling into problems caused by isolation and emotional dissatisfaction? Why have intended solutions, such as, for example, redistributive welfare policies or some spatial regeneration experiences, increased isolation, not only of single persons but also of entire communities, instead of promoting socio-economic integration (see Barber and Hall, 2008)?

In *The Spirit Level*, Richard Wilkinson and Kate Pickett take on this challenge. Their results point to the fact that some of the major societal problems we face today originate from uneven wealth distribution (Wilkinson and Pickett, 2010). It is almost needless to remind that this follows an era dominated by globalisation. Its implications for deindustrialisation, the worsening of the living conditions of entire urban and rural areas, indicate that traditional welfare policies are not effective anymore in contrasting these trends (see Fazzi in this volume). The economic crisis, moreover, seems to have hit social groups asymmetrically, improving the purchasing power of some categories (e.g., in some countries, typically, public servants)[2] and reduced that of others. Re-distributive policies, in the current situation, run the risk of pushing regions into excessive protectionism, strengthening global inequality rather than reducing it. For this reason, economic policies cannot be conceived, as in the past, as an exclusive prerogative of the central authority and cannot be based only on monetary transfers and standardised social services.

Given this problem, the objective of this chapter is to identify some alternative institutional solutions to the interrelated issues of social degradation and inequality. We build on the idea that the richness and poverty of social relations, and the outcomes that originate from this, are in part caused by the unequal distribution of income and wealth, but also by the type of socio-economic institutions that a society gives itself and the behavioural attitudes associated with them. We discuss how, by reinstating cooperation and inclusion strategies within economic institutions, it becomes possible to deal with and balance at the same time individual behaviours and distributional issues.

Over time, deindustrialisation and economic crises made more evident what effects institutions based on self-interested behaviour could have (one amongst others, the decline of Detroit, Michigan, in the US). The decline and ruin of cities in so-called developed or rich countries were not only visible in the buildings and material assets of cities. The degradation of income and physical assets was a reflection of uneven policy interventions (see Barber and Hall, 2008), but also of the paucity of social relations, of how people and organisations had neglected acting together for their common and mutual benefit. The chapter starts, therefore, by outlining the need to recover this ability, or the need for social regeneration.

The idea of social regeneration has a clear policy appeal and can be traced in policy agendas,[3] often in relation with social deprivation, urban regeneration, social housing, and social policy more broadly, overall meaning actions aimed at improving people's quality of life (Ginsburg, 1999; Blanc, 2002; Osman et al., 2015). Our take on social regeneration is not confined to specific areas of deprivation and social exclusion. More broadly, it takes a behavioural stand and addresses the problem of reinstating cooperation between and among actors in pursuit of collective benefit and asks what institutional solutions can favour this process. In this work, social regeneration is about the transformative processes which, through institutional choices that embody cooperation and inclusion, develop opportunities and capabilities for multiple categories of actors, and especially weak categories, leading to societal benefits and community resilience.

Although it is not the aim of this chapter to discuss social regeneration policy and the underpinning ethical arguments in favour or against the idea of social regeneration, we nonetheless reason why social regeneration is needed, and where. Our answer is that social regeneration requires to be addressed wherever a specific form of poverty becomes endemic. We are thinking of "social poverty", or a paucity of those relations that are not necessarily mediated by power asymmetries, authority, contracts, and prices. It occurs when relations are dominated by consumerism, opportunism, and when conflict is high, leading to an erosion of other relational types based on cooperation and, ultimately, to isolation and a feeling of not counting (Sacchetti et al., 2009; Hirschman, 1979). The damaging consequence of social poverty is the widespread idea of being constrained by a horizon of set, inadequate, and damaging alternatives in the face of major personal and societal challenges, leading to public and community failure, or the failure of socio-economic relations and decision processes to identify and address multiple needs and interests across society and communities (Ostrom, 1990; Sacchetti and Sugden, 2010; Sacchetti and Campbell, 2014). Social poverty, in this sense, is the outcome of a deterioration process of a key resource in society, which is the human motivation to cooperate, formally or informally, in collective processes of decision-making. The phenomenon is not a prerogative of economically poor regions and can occur transversally in so-called "advanced" and "impoverished" regions. So, how can this failure be explained and are there solutions?

An understanding of social poverty and social regeneration opportunities is supported by social capital theory. Social capital scholars associate individual, organisational, and regional prosperity with the presence of rules, behaviours and networks that allow cooperation or collective action for the common good (cf. Coalter, 2007; Cento Bull and Jones, 2006; Cornelius and Wallace, 2010 for applications). For social capital theory, cooperative outcomes require trust between and among social actors, which may reach actors' close bonds, bridge between different groups, or link actors across decision-making layers within and between diverse levels of enterprising (Woolcock, 2001; Putnam, 2000). Social capital has informed developmental models around the world (see Campbell and Sacchetti in this volume). But its formula does not address the problem of continuity and persistence, and it is at risk of failing to deliver expected outcomes, in the long term, if social capital was thought to work in isolation, without consistent institutions in place.

In conjunction with social theory, institutional theory has contributed to explain cooperation and the conditions under which this can happen and persist, using both experimental evidence and case studies (Grimalda and Sacconi, 2005; Sacconi and Faillo, 2010). By developing a wide array of case materials, Elinor Ostrom and institutional scholars have repeatedly emphasised that, in the long run, cooperation benefits all, and that it leads to the creation of the most adequate solutions and greater compliance (Ostrom, 1990). Documented experiences of enduring communities and of their self-designed answers to common resources show that, if the appropriate institutions are in place, cooperation is possible.

This is not to deny, however, that individual preferences can shape institutions in the first place. Rational choice theory has emphasised this point, highlighting that individuals hold preferences on what institutions they want and that such preferences regard the distributional consequences of institutions, that is, what benefits are distributed and to whom (Knight, 1992). However, the limitation to rational choice theory has been presented by Ostrom, who shows that individual preferences require, in turn, that consistent institutions are in place in order to be maintained (cf. Sacchetti, 2015). This perspective will drive our analysis.

Altogether, institutional approaches have shed light on the fact that institutional solutions must be assessed in terms of their distributional consequences and according to the type of preferences that they contribute to reproducing. This requires a new way of thinking about economic solutions to societal problems. The aim of this chapter is to contribute to this reflection by framing the problem of social poverty and by outlining new forms of publicly accessible goods, by which we refer to economic institutions which nurture cooperation and contribute to overall social regeneration.[4] In synthesis, a social poverty perspective acknowledges that lack of cooperation is at the heart of key societal failures and people's discomfort and that, on the contrary, the quality of social relations underpins the well-being of people and the overall prosperity of communities. It then emphasises the role of institutional solutions to the problem.

The chapter proceeds as follows. Starting from Ostrom's idea of commons, Section Two discusses the role that community self-management can play in solving collective problems. In Section Three, we use some of the analytical categories developed in the theory of commons to outline the relation between institutional resources and cooperation. Section Four addresses the societal surplus produced by cooperation, leading to a reduction of social poverty. Finally, Section Five discusses some institutional solutions in support of cooperation: multi-stakeholder participatory structures and deliberative nexus. Section Six discusses the outcomes of institutional solutions and addresses surplus socialisation. Section Seven concludes.

## Theory of Commons: The "Cooperative Way"

The theory of commons developed by Ostrom has been introduced in the policy and economics curricula of most of the major universities. Her theory does have a policy urgency and an immediacy generated by humans' need to act collectively and preserve the environment in which they live and, therefore, their own livelihood. Ostrom reveals the behavioural foundations of collective action in a practical, applied context, that of common-pool resources (CPR). In "Governing the commons", Ostrom says that:

> the term 'common-pool resource' refers to a natural or man-made resource system that is sufficiently large as to make it costly (but not impossible) to exclude potential beneficiaries from obtaining benefits from its use.
>
> (1990, 30)

The idea of CPR as resource system is crucial, as this is the "stock" that should not be compromised by usage. Resource systems are, for example: fishing grounds, irrigation canals, lakes, alpine meadows. Ostrom is clear on the need to distinguish between the stock variables and the flow of resource units which can be produced by the resource system under particular conditions, for example, fish, water for the fields, food for the cattle. These units represent what individuals can appropriate when using the resource system. The condition for system resilience is that the maximum quantity of flow variables appropriated does not harm the stock of the resource system (Ostrom, 1990, 31). However, while the system can be used collectively, the units produced cannot. This means that, for example, "the fish harvested by one boat are not there for someone else" (ibid.). Resource units are said by Ostrom to be "subtractable".

If costly improvements to the resource system are made, everyone (that is, appropriators who contributed and appropriators who did not) will be able to benefit. The collective action problem derives from joint access to the system *and* subtractability of the resource units. Traditional approaches say that appropriators will refuse to contribute to the maintenance of the system, which will collapse as a consequence. This analysis reflects the neo-classical behavioural assumption about individuals' self-interest. To use an analogy, consider a situation in which your sustainable fishing practices are being disregarded by uncaring boats. As their activity is quickly using up all the resource units (fish) in the sea, you realise you do not want to be a fool and start fishing irresponsibly too, as the resource is going to be exhausted by others anyway. Collective action theory would predict this—that a person's principles would be subdued by short-term economic self-interest.

What is remarkable in Ostrom's theory is that her application of behavioural, group theories to CPR comes from ideas around institutions that, when she wrote, were not conventional at all. From her work, we learn that there is not one best way that fits all situational contexts and that neither the 'Leviathan' (or state centralised authority) nor private use via property rights and the market can resolve the problem of the impossibility of individuals to achieve their common, group interest. Ostrom suggests a third way, which involves cooperation among actors and community self-management. This complements the other two, and it is related to her findings from game theoretical analysis, building on Axelrod (1984) and others. Her findings support the view that even though self-interest may push people to behave uncooperatively and confrontationally, they have nevertheless an inclination and an interest in cooperating, since cooperation enables to preserve the resource system which, in turn, sustains users.

Cooperation, specifically, is the coordinating mechanism used to define rules and their application. In addition, cooperation must be widespread, between and among interdependent institutional layers and sectors of activities. Her theory predicts that in the absence of rules that regulate who can access the system and how resource units can be appropriated after access has been granted, the system will collapse. If rules are not designed/ implemented/ enforced, the resource system is compromised and—without a resource system—no appropriation of resource units can occur. The important conclusion of Ostrom's work is that cooperation can play an important role in many situations, but it operates only under specific conditions, that is, if the institutions that enable it are in place. These institutions correspond in many instances with self-management.

## Institutions as a Resource System

The idea of social regeneration through the creation of specific institutions that reinforce and enable cooperation is supported by the theory of commons, which proves that cooperation can engender benefits for individuals and for the collectivity more broadly. A way to approach social poverty, therefore, is to foster institutional solutions that enable cooperation. Though we are not trying to build an analogy with CPRs, which would be inappropriate given the different nature of the resources discussed, it is nonetheless useful to apply some of the analytical categories of that theory.

Specifically, it is fruitful to distinguish between the resource system and the resource units produced by a particular good. Let's think of institutions that favour cooperation as a non-excludable resource system that can produce resource units, represented by individual's preferences towards cooperation and the surplus deriving from it (Figure 1.1). Experimental results support the view that such system, over time, engenders preferences towards cooperation even among those individuals that entered the system because of a binding requirement (Grimalda and Sacconi, 2005). Preferences towards cooperation, hence, can be considered as the resource units produced by the institutional solution. Now, albeit we could not say that such preferences are subtractable, experimental results make it plausible to argue that if a cooperator is repeatedly cheated upon by a non-cooperator, she will change her preferences towards selfishness, reproducing results predicted by collective action theory. We could therefore say that cooperative preferences are "erodible" resource units.

The fact that nobody wants to be fooled is what Ostrom has described in her studies. The cheaters are users of the institutional system who abuse

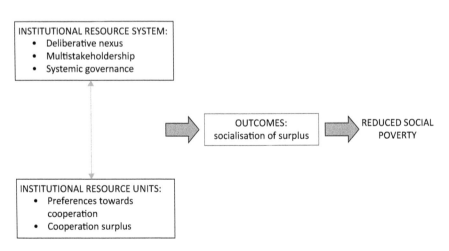

*Figure 1.1* Social Regeneration Approach: The Resource System Supporting Cooperation and Reduction of Social Poverty

diffused cooperative preferences. In so doing, they can weaken cooperators' preferences, or else cooperators may move out to seek a more cooperative endeavour (cf. Ben-Ner and Ellman, 2012). The system of institutions that supports cooperation will collapse as a consequence.

An example of this is the demutualisation that occurred in the UK. This ceased the existence of cooperative firms, which were explicitly structured around mutualistic principles and governed democratically by members. Authors have explained demutualisation with undercapitalisation (Tortia, 2007, 2017; Pérotin, 2013). Furthermore, if we take a social poverty perspective, it may be argued that such conditions are a result of the individualist values dominant in the broader social context that crowded out cooperative activities. This can happen alongside the erosion of cooperative preferences inside the organisation, which may then be contagious for other organisations, where more members may nurture preferences to behave selfishly and sell their assets (Sacchetti, 2015). Birchall (2010), in particular, sheds light on the role of managers, who had lost touch with the meaning and consequences of directing self-managed organisations as if the cooperative element was absent, in order to earn higher salaries and bonuses. For example, managers expanded the business in new risky markets with strategies that were not included in the mutual's original mission. This, in turn, favoured the conversion of the mutual into investor-owned businesses.

## The 'Cooperation' Surplus

Cooperation produces a variety of effects that work towards social regeneration. These effects can be identified with the surplus produced. It follows that every institution should be assessed in terms of its ability to generate cooperation and surplus, or resource units, without jeopardising the institutional resource system. The problem with interpreting surplus as resource units is that normally surplus is confused with economic profit, and, consequently, the evaluation of effects is done on a partial basis. In this work, surplus is defined as the value added produced by socio-economic activities and is only in some measure reflected in the difference between revenues and costs. Besides, the idea of surplus as profit is associated with the interests of one main stakeholder, i.e. the investor, which is what cooperative institutions aim at avoiding.

Counterfactually, we can say that the surplus produced through cooperation mirrors the costs that would be born in its absence, by actors and, more broadly, by society (Borzaga and Sacchetti, 2015). So, here surplus is used broadly, meaning the positive outcomes generated by cooperation, including material and immaterial elements.

Material surplus is reflected in economic output. Economic output is qualified by the fact that it can be appropriated. However, when the rules that define its appropriation are guided by cooperative preferences, it enables a distribution that can differ for the one typically provided following the market rules, and the accumulation of common capital resources. As Tortia (2017) suggests, common capital resources which cannot be appropriated, such as in cooperative firms, can be interpreted as a form of organisational common.

In addition, immaterial elements that are especially relevant for social regeneration are psychological benefits to individuals, improved social capital, and overall democracy. Psychological surplus is generated because cooperation includes actors, and in so doing, it improves their sense of belonging, accomplishment, and overall health and well-being (Deci and Ryan, 2008). Moreover, the fact that actors can bring into the debate their interests, ideas, knowledge, and experience creates surplus in terms of the quality of services or products. This happens because cooperation furthers the advantages of diversity rather than its limitations,[5] generating benefits in terms of problem framing,[6] use of creativity amongst participants, and a better match between the innovations introduced and societal needs.[7]

Diversity represents a starting point for recognising and addressing the interconnectedness of interests and generate new solutions. On this, political scientists have also argued about the advantages of plural decision-making whereby shared processes of deliberation are functional not only in identifying where conflict resides, but also in appreciating how points of intersection and mutual understanding can be fostered (Dewey, 1927; Ostrom, 2010; Sacchetti and Sugden, 2009, Young, 2000; Lewanski in this volume). This strengthens the legitimacy of solutions and generates democratic surplus.

Finally, cooperation reinforces social capital. Empirical findings in the work of Sabatini et al. (2014) show that across types of organisations, those that activate overall social trust of workers are firms that place cooperation at the centre of their governance structures.

Having discussed the benefits of cooperation, the question to be addressed is what type of institutions can support cooperation.

## Institutional Solutions

"Certainly not all the social institutions that underlie the web of interests . . . are favourable to the poor or marginalised; many are themselves a source of repression" (Meinzen-Dick and Mwangi, 2009, 41). Partaking concerns for social poverty and the need for social regeneration require developing institutional solutions and practices that embed and promote cooperative preferences, as well as the identification of specific modalities to include multiple actors, and especially the marginalised. Besides the classic (but uncomprehensive and possibly ineffective) alternative between public and private for-profit solutions, and avoiding overreliance on the effects of social capital alone, this section presents some institutional arrangements which have become observable in organisations, specifically, in those that are explicitly pursuing cooperation and, more recently, in social enterprises.

We are not addressing here other forms of institutional solutions; namely, we will not touch on collective political processes or social movements (on which cf. Hargrave and Van de Ven, 2006). We hope, however, that the focus on economic organisations provides a useful starting point to discuss institutions that back cooperation more broadly.

Because of the social role of enterprising, here we focus on production organisations and on the solutions developed to embed cooperative preferences and re-produce them. New ways of conceiving economic organising have occupied legislators and policy makers for some years now, at least in Europe (as demonstrated by the recent approval of the Social Business Act) but also elsewhere. Though private, these solutions embed cooperation between and among a variety of actors using specific forms of governance, and are able to contribute to the production of goods and services of public interest, thus reinforcing the value of cooperation. And, as Ostrom (1990) has repeatedly observed, this may occur even in the absence of regulation or state intervention. We build on lessons learned from this literature to develop a discussion on the institutional arrangements that can favour cooperative preferences in general within and among organisations.

### The Deliberative Nexus

A precondition for cooperation has been identified in communication (Ostrom, 1990). Again, experimental results and case studies show that when individuals can communicate between and among each other, agreements are respected (Sacconi and Faillo, 2010). More forcefully, experimental results show that cooperative agreements are respected also by those who are not cooperative in the first place. In their work, Grimalda and Sacconi (2005) show that this happens because, as individuals interact within a cooperative institutional setting, they develop preferences that enable them to respect the agreement. In other words, preferences towards cooperation (our resource units) are shaped by the interaction of actors within an appropriate agreement, formal or informal (our resource system). In this analysis, communication emerges as a key determinant of cooperation.

Communicative processes can take various forms. Here we consider institutional solutions that support open and non-opportunistic communication between and among stakeholders. This form of communication has been discussed as deliberation, especially in the context of democratic and participatory institutions (cf. Lewanski in this volume).

The deliberative element becomes a fundamental component of the resource system, which is suited to account for the diversity of participants. Cooperation amongst a variety of partakers is achieved by emphasising a 'nexus of deliberation'.[8] This view embraces the inter-subjective nature of participants' interests (as in Dewey, 1927) and a relational conception of resource systems (as in Granovetter, 1991; Yeung, 2005) and suggests that institutions that support cooperation must pair binding agreements with deliberative processes. This logic applies, for example, to the shaping of organisations and their networks when these institutional systems are based on principles of symmetry and even distribution of decision-making power on the one hand, and practices of deliberation on the other (Allen, 1997; Bridge, 1997; Sacchetti and Sugden, 2009, 2010).

For example, the nexus of deliberation can pre-exist formal institutions when it occurs among individuals who share common aims and values, without necessarily formalising their cooperative activities via an organisation. Casari (2007) illustrates this point by analysing the process that led to the definition of community governance in the Italian Alps. The work sheds light on the role of informal interactions among villagers to sustain the management of common pastures and forests, but also on the limitations of this modality, especially where the complexity of the system grew, which led to the institutions of formal agreements ("charters").

Instead, in the case of more complex aims, production processes, and complementarity of investments (as in the case of social service production whereby service continuity is essential), cooperation is supported by specific organisational solutions. These are costlier, but serve the function of supporting cooperation with binding agreements. In this context, deliberation would work as a form of substantive involvement which goes beyond the formal engagement entailed in the right to vote in organisational assemblies or the contractual obligation to deliver a service. Rather, it is based on communication amongst actors, on a genuine intention to assess ideas and generate solutions based on argument rather than on power unbalances among actors. An example is cooperation between public administrations and social economy organisations in the co-production of specific community services (Pestoff, 2012; Ostrom, 1996; Sacchetti, 2016).

The deliberative nexus, therefore, can be interpreted as a space populated by one or more actors, with different interests, who not only occupy equal positions or power structurally, but who practice deliberation as a way to exercise their cooperative preferences. The structural and procedural elements go together, with a specific function: to achieve cooperative solutions to shared problems. This function is intrinsic in the meaning of "interest", which is made of two distinct words: *inter* and *est*. It means that what concerns individual actors or groups of patrons is 'what exists in between' or what places us in relation with others. Given the inter-subjective nature of interests, the function of the deliberative nexus is to emphasise the relational nature of each actor's interests, make it explicit and yet transformed by the cooperative interaction. The existence and reproduction of the nexus depends on the disposition of actors to ground their decisions on impartial arguments rather than power asymmetries, thus supporting the production of preferences towards cooperation (Dewey, 1927; Sacconi, 2015). The type of cooperation generated within the deliberative nexus is what Ertell (1957) calls 'deep cooperation' as an integrated level of cooperation that happens at the grassroots of an organisation (Blackwood, 1977). It implies a shared understanding around the value of deliberative practice and mutual expectations of trust. Through the deliberative nexus, cooperation can go beyond contractual obligations or initial agreements. Because decisions are based on impartial arguments, the deliberative nexus is transformative of institutional individualities, identities, or programmes (Ertell, 1957; cited in Blackwood, 1977).

In addition, deliberation is a way to increase learning and knowledge creation in production organisation (Sacchetti and Sugden, 2010), as well as the legitimacy of decisions (Benhabib, 1996; Cohen, 1989; Dryzek, 2001), to create trust and prevent opportunism, thus complementing formal monitoring solutions (Borzaga and Sacchetti, 2015; Tortia, 2017).[9] The dialogic and participatory nature of this process acknowledges the existence not only of multiple interests, but also of multiple knowledge bases and experiences (Sacchetti et al., 2009). By bringing these together and effectively socialising knowledge (M. Polanyi, 1966; Nonaka and Takeuchi, 1995), the deliberative nexus promotes creativity, learning, and enquiry (Dewey, 1927). In doing so, it can be argued to motivate stakeholders and renew their cooperative attitude (McGregor, 1960; Hirschman, 1979).

## *Multi-Stakeholder Organising*

The deliberative nexus underpins institutional solutions in which strategic direction is exerted collectively. In particular, multi-stakeholder organising is a way of governing the production of goods or services where multiple actors (such as managers, workers, volunteers, users, donors, funders) share strategic control for their common good. It is meant to give voice and to empower all the relevant stakeholders in an organisational context, normally designed to produce meritorious goods, such as welfare and community services, including public utilities, but not exclusively. Strategic control functions can be held through ownership or by other coordination mechanisms (Borzaga and Sacchetti, 2015). The role of multi-stakeholder structures has been discussed by scholars who have emphasised its role in the provision of social and welfare services (Pestoff, 1994, 1996; Borzaga and Mittone, 1997; Laville and Nyssens, 2001; Sacconi, 2006; Sacchetti and Tortia, 2008; Cafaggi and Iamiceli, 2009). In parallel, the spread of multi-stakeholder governance in some countries, such as France, Italy, and Spain, was explicitly enabled by the evolving public regulation on specific types of organisations, namely social enterprises (SEs).[10]

The distinguishing feature of multi-stakeholder organisations is that diverse actors with an interest in the activities of the organisation can contribute to decide what and how to produce, or how economic surplus is distributed. Case studies show that multi-stakeholder forms capitalise on the resources of multiple actors at different levels by involving them as member owners or by including them in the board of directors or through consultative or controlling committees (Sacchetti and Tortia, 2014; Sacchetti,

2016). By sharing decision-making power, this socially participated form of governance leads to a unique feature, which is that the activities of the organisation are run cooperatively. In this way, the outcomes can benefit multiple categories, including members but also non-members (Borzaga and Mittone, 1997).

This last point sheds light on the challenges of multi-stakeholder structures, which require, amongst other things, valuing and implementing participatory decision-making processes. As the above-mentioned studies document, multi-stakeholdership historically emerges from an evolving 'percorso' during which the organisation interprets community unmet needs, contextual changes (e.g., in service demand, in the legal framework), or stakeholders' changing preferences towards engagement and cooperation. The open organisation transforms production activities and creates the structural conditions for the inclusion of each emerging stakeholder (for example, the inclusion of workers with disabilities as members may require the introduction of a psychologist within the organisation and the reformulation of human resource strategies). A gradually growing network of stakeholders gains voice in the definition of socio-economic activities and creates space to stakeholders and community interests. As a result, multi-stakeholder solutions can be expected to be open projects, or institutional solutions that are 'means to multiple aims' (cf. Sacconi, 2015, 282 and his analysis of commons).

In summary, organisations with an open approach to beneficiaries will require that the actors involved engage in collective action, meaning that they will cooperate and develop preferences towards cooperating. Exclusion will be limited to the presence of conflicts of interest and the possibility of opportunistic behavior. These organisations are run in a genuine democratic way, which is not limited to formal voting rules (e.g. one-head-one-vote), but by the establishment of practices that ensure continued participation and deliberation on relevant decisions, especially those related to economic surplus distribution.

## Nested Systemic Governance

In a section entitled "*Similarities among enduring, self-governing CPR institutions*", Ostrom (1990, 90) illustrates the patterns of binding agreements observed in a number of situations worldwide.[11] All these institutional solutions specify who can access the common and under what conditions, as well as monitoring, sanctions, and enforcement of sanctions. The last point in the list, specifically, tells us that all these agreed functions must be organised 'in multiple layers of nested enterprises'. The theory of commons identifies the principles that would make self-management work, but adds that these principles must be pervasive across the institutional system that supports the common.

This implies that institutional solutions are looked at multiple, nested complementary levels. What we obtain is a nested system of institutions where many centres of decision-making that are formally independent come to constitute, to different extents, an interdependent system of relations, building on common cooperative values and aims. Actors (not only organisations but also individuals and other community constituencies) who recognise reciprocal interdependencies enter in various formal and informal cooperative undertakings (cf. Ostrom, 2010 on polycentric governance). Nested networks of institutions form what can be called systemic governance and are evidenced by the densely knitted relationships in the co-production of community services. They enable long-term interactions with public administrations, private organisations, and their federations. The presence of thematic networks, regional networks, and federations can support the development of institutional communities, building deliberative processes on the common cultural roots within a region or a sector (Campbell and Sacchetti, 2014). In this sense, systemic integration can be based on self-regulation of economic actors which, as explained by Ostrom (1990), becomes self-constraining, leading to cooperative behaviours also where there are no property rights defined (Heath, 2006). Self-regulation includes multiple stakeholders and—because of their active participation—supports long-term investments and planning. It builds on complementarities and it can aim at increasing coordination along the social value chain of service provision. At this level, cooperative preferences define how organisations link and work together to coordinate on production. Each organisation promotes cooperative behaviours also outside the organisational borders, without the constraints imposed by profit maximisation, but with the aim of accruing collectively beneficial outcomes (cf. Sacchetti, 2016 for an illustration).

## Outcomes: Socialisation of Surplus

Let us go back to Figure 1.1, which sketches the relation between the institutional resource system and cooperative preferences. It is because of the institutional system interacting with cooperative preferences that output works as a generator of surplus, or social value, in terms of workers' material welfare, psychological satisfaction, social capital, user surplus, accessibility, and service quality. The theory of commons is again useful to shed light on the appropriation of surplus and its different components. The idea suggested in the chapter is that surplus is produced by the interaction between institutional resources and cooperative preferences. Surplus, therefore, is part of the resource units produced by the system and represents what actors 'appropriate or use' from the resource system (Ostrom, 1990, 90). In order to ensure the sustainability of the resource system, the appropriation of this 'flow' of units should not jeopardise the institutional system or erode cooperative preferences.

Let us now consider the economic element of surplus, which derives from the institutional system. In non-monopolistic markets, economic surplus is the return to innovation, which is conventionally seen as the outcome of entrepreneurial activity. The entrepreneur is therefore seen as the appropriator. Differently, in institutional solutions that promote cooperation, entrepreneurial activity occurs within a multi-stakeholder structure and using deliberative praxis. The stakeholders who took part in surplus production and towards whom surplus is directed vary depending on the type of service provided and, within each enterprise, according to the actors involved in the deliberative nexus.

The deliberative nexus specifically allows to balance the allocation of surplus amongst these possible different destinations. Since multiple actors are part of the organisation's decision-making bodies, they can engage with deliberative processes for the allocation of economic surplus, which does not coincide with allocation to the entrepreneur.

Participants' cooperative preferences are expressed by the willingness of stakeholders to pursue collective benefit, whilst improving the welfare of the weakest actors (Sacconi, 1991; Rawls, 1971). In this sense, for example, in SEs (which are, as a norm, not-for-profit or are subject to limited profit distribution) decision-makers can opt for distribution by transferring rent to the weakest users, for instance, by setting service price lower than the cost of production (Bacchiega and Borzaga, 2001; Borzaga and Tortia, 2010) or by promoting aspects of community development through public benefit policies. One interesting aspect of empirical evidence is that multi-stakeholder enterprises exhibit a greater tendency to redistribute economic surplus towards users than single-stakeholder enterprises (Borzaga et al., 2011). Otherwise, surplus can be redistributed to workers by increasing salaries, or be re-invested, or placed into common assets.

Common assets serve the purpose of increasing the financial stability of the organisation but, mostly, to allow for re-investment in the community, provided that sufficient levels of resources are placed in the common asset. These resources, moreover, can be leveraged by matching other financial resources from external partners. The use of common assets is determined by the presence of cooperative preferences, which are influenced, in turn, by multi-stakeholder institutional arrangements and by the deliberative nexus. They depend on the presence of common norms and solidarity values. In this way, it can compel joint planning among stakeholders on a long-term basis. Common assets, therefore, are not static. Rather, through surplus reinvestment, they are the dynamic element of the system, which allow it to address emerging needs over time. For example, in SEs that offer work integration services to disadvantaged categories, asset lock and surplus reinvestment not only operate towards the rehabilitation of individuals in need. Through reinvestment, they create activities where disadvantaged individuals can work, and, in doing this, they create jobs for ordinary workers in the community.

The example sheds light also on the fact that besides sharing work and salary, cooperation between disadvantaged and ordinary workers extends to include the sharing of relations, which are built within the work environment and can extend beyond it. Together with the enhancement of deliberative processes, the possibility to build relations facilitates the emergence of multiple perspectives and experiences across stakeholders, which represents a first step towards challenging non-cooperative attitudes at a broader societal level. Interestingly, this example sheds light on the fact that economic surplus is not the only aspect to be re-socialised or re-distributed or re-invested. By integrating multiple actors, in fact, the institutional system enables sharing surplus at the collective level, including the relational, psychological, and democratic surplus that originates from partaking in the making of choices that impact on people's lives.

## Discussion: Implications for Social Regeneration

When asking the question of what can be changed in the way socio-economic systems work, we are inevitably framing a complex problem. Too many policy makers are looking for a formula, but even good formulas need to interact with a variety of other ideas about how communities and society more broadly understand economic organising and social interactions.

Specific forms of organisations or enterprises, such as commons or SEs, to which this chapter has referred for illustrations, cover now an important role across continents. Compared to other sectors and ways of organising, they are still growing out of the initial stage of their life cycle. Like social capital, specific organisations or enterprises cannot be considered a solution to social poverty if left on their own. The most complete formula, then, would be one that encompasses areas of organising, transacting, and relating, which empower individuals, communities, and society overall to contribute to the identification of assets, opportunities, and ways to eradicate social poverty.

Regeneration, in this sense, requires enabling and supporting institutions that use participatory and deliberative modalities, leading to cooperative preferences, surplus generation and its re-investment. Perhaps, if asked about what difference a system of participatory and deliberative socio-economic institutions would make, the answer would be to judge from its non-existence. What if these institutions were lacking? If these ways of organising were absent, many more communities would be crippled by social poverty and marginalisation. We have presented specific forms of organising that are extremely effective and will grow in importance. However, their cooperative principles should be more pervasive, albeit not unique, across all socio-economic systems. If they become the prevalent way of socio-economic organising (besides standard hierarchies and contracting), their effects will be less likely to be countervailed and, on the whole, nullified by conflicting ways of doing things.

## Notes

1. Correspondence: silvia.sacchetti@unitn.it; carlo.borzaga@unitn.it.
    The authors wish to thank Asimina Christoforou and Michele Mosca for comments and suggestions on how to improve earlier drafts. Silvia Sacchetti wishes to thank colleagues from the Citizenship and Governance strategic research area at the Open University for fruitful debates on these issues.
2. This may not be true for countries that initiate fiscal consolidation or new public management practices, resulting in the reduction of public sector services and employment.
3. Definitions tend to be rather vague in policy making. For instance, Scotland's Big Nose initiative for promoting health through music provides the following: 'Social regeneration' refers to social interventions and approaches which are typically embedded alongside physical and economic dimensions of a 'holistic' regeneration strategy, where an overarching vision for the community or area coordinates all three aspects of regeneration (social, physical, and economic) (Glasgow Centre for Population Health, 2016, 5).
4. Our perspective on social poverty carries an explicit Polanyian flavour by placing emphasis on the negative consequences of contemporary modalities of social interaction and organisation (Polanyi, 1977).
5. Economic literature has traditionally focused on the limitations of diversity and especially on the reasons why diversity inflates the costs of decision-making (Williamson, 1985; Hansmann, 1996).
6. The problem of coordinating dispersed knowledge and using it effectively has been addressed in a variety of ways, not necessarily through cooperation. A crucial benefit of cooperation, however, is the creation of a shared understanding about the surrounding context, or the mental model that defines it (Dosi and Marengo, 1994; Cefis et al., 2008). In this sense, cooperation can help "problem framing" or "all those activities leading from the identification of the problem to the selection of possible actions" (Dosi and Egidi, 1991, 150).
7. This interpretation is consistent also with rational choice theory, which has emphasised substantive uncertainty, or the knowledge gaps between decision-makers and the world around them. Likewise, it has shed light on procedural uncertainty, or the gap between problem complexity and the capability to solve it (Dosi and Egidi, 1991; Cefis et al., 2008).
8. The nexus of deliberation can be seen as a specific type of "nexus of treaties", introduced by Aoki and colleagues, which described contractual and non-contractual institutional solutions within and among organisations (Aoki et al., 1990).
9. The problem of deliberation among different interests and discourses in the public sphere has been widely debated, starting from the seminal work of Habermas (1996), and with Bourdieu (1993) speaking of 'discursive field' between opposed actors, where deliberation between different stakeholders has been deemed as possible with the 'de-traditionalisation' of society (Beck et al., 1994). Though it is not the aim of this chapter to enter the deliberation debate, we note that this is understood differently by Habermas and Bourdieu. The former argues in the context of an idealised public sphere, on the basis of a universal reason à la Kant, whereas the latter stresses the power asymmetries and struggles within the public sphere and the conditions for the emergence of 'universality'. See, for instance, Poupeau (2001).
10. SEs are enterprises with a social aim. They are characterised by a non-profit distribution constraint and include stakeholders as organisation members or as part of a governing body of the organisation (e.g., the board of directors).

11. These are (Ostrom, 1990, 90): clearly defined boundaries:

   a. clear appropriation rules, related to local conditions and provision rules

   b. participation in the definition of operational rules by those affected

   c. monitoring, where monitors "audit CPR conditions and appropriator behaviours. They are in turn accountable to the appropriators or are the appropriators" (ibid. p. 94)

   d. graduated sanctions (as for monitoring, sanctions are undertaken by participants themselves)

   e. conflict-resolution mechanisms ("access to low cost local arenas to resolve conflicts" formal or informal)

   f. external government institutions give at least minimal recognition of the right to self-organise

   g. nested enterprises—all the above functions (appropriation, provision of resources, monitoring, enforcement, conflict resolution, governance activities) "are organised in multiple layers of nested enterprises".

# References

Allen, J. 1997. "Economies of Power and Space." In *Geographies of Economies*, edited by Roger Lee and Jane Wills, 59–70. London: Arnold.

Aoki, M., Gustafsson, B., and O. Williamson, eds. 1990. *The Firm as a Nexus of Treaties*. London: Sage.

Axelrod, R. 1984. *The Evolution of Cooperation*. London: Penguin.

Bacchiega, A., and C. Borzaga. 2001. "Social Enterprise as an Incentive Structure." In *The Emergence of Social Enterprise*, edited by Carlo Borzaga and Jacques Defourny, 273–295. London and New York: Routledge.

Barber, A., and S. Hall. 2008. "Birmingham: Whose Urban Renaissance? Regeneration as a Response to Economic Restructuring." *Policy Studies*, 29(3): 281–292.

Beck, U., Giddens, A., and S. Lash. 1994. *Reflexive Modernization: Politics, Tradition and Aesthetics in the Modern Social Order*. Cambridge: Polity.

Benhabib, S. 1996. "Toward a Deliberative Model of Democratic Legitimacy." In *Democracy and Difference: Contesting the Boundaries of the Political*, edited by Seyla Benhabib, 67–94. Princeton, NJ: Princeton University Press.

Ben-Ner, A., and M. Ellman. 2012. "The Effects of Organization Design on Employee Preferences." In *Towards a New Theory of the Firm: Humanizing the Firm and the Management Profession*, edited by J. E. R. Costa and J. M. R. Marti. Bilbao: Fundacion BBVA.

Birchall, J. 2010. *People-Centred Businesses: Cooperatives, Mutuals, and the Idea of Membership*. London: Palgrave.

Blackwood, W. O. 1977. *A Comparative Study of Cooperation in Voluntary and Statutory Consortia*. Doctoral Dissertation, University of Florida.

Blanc, M. 2002. "Strategies for the Social Regeneration of Disadvantaged Neighbourhoods in France (1977–2002)." In *Soziale Stadt—Zwischenbilanzen*, edited by U. J. Walther, 211–228. Wiesbaden: VS Verlag für Sozialwissenschaften.

Borzaga, C., Depedri, S., and E. C. Tortia. 2011. "Testing the Distributive Effects of Social Enterprises: The Case of Italy." In *Social Capital, Corporate Social Responsibility, Economic Behaviour and Performance*, edited by Lorenzo Sacconi and Giacomo Degli Antoni, 282–303. New York: Palgrave Macmillan.

Borzaga, C., and L. Mittone. 1997. "The Multi-Stakeholders Versus the Non-Profit Organisation." *Discussion Paper* 7/1997. University of Trento, Department of Economics.

Borzaga, C., and S. Sacchetti. 2015. "Why Social Enterprises Are Asking to Be Multi-Stakeholder and Deliberative: An Explanation Around the Costs of Exclusion." *Euricse Working Paper*, 75–2015, Trento, Italy.

Borzaga, C., and E. C. Tortia. 2010. "The Economics of Social Enterprises." In *The Economics of Social Responsibility: The World of Social Enterprises*, edited by Leonardo Becchetti and Carlo Borzaga, 15–33. London and New York: Routledge.

Bourdieu, P. 1993. *The Field of Cultural Production*. Cambridge: Columbia University Press.

Bridge, G. 1997. "Mapping the Terrain of Time—Space Compression: Power Networks in Everyday Life." *Environment and Planning D: Society and Space*, 15: 611–626.

Cafaggi, F., and P. Iamiceli. 2009. "New Frontiers in the Legal Structure and Legislation of Social Enterprises in Europe: A Comparative Analysis." In *The Changing Boundaries of Social Enterprises*, edited by Antonella Noya, 25–87. Paris: OECD.

Campbell, C., and S. Sacchetti. 2014. "Social Enterprise Networks and Social Capital: A Case Study in Scotland/UK." In *Social Capital and Economics: Social Values, Power, and Social Identity*, edited by Asimina Christoforou and John B. Davis, 215–235. London and New York: Routledge.

Casari, M. 2007. "Emergence of Endogenous Legal Institutions: Property Rights and Community Governance in the Italian Alps." *Journal of Economic History*, 67(1): 191–226.

Cefis, E., Berlendis, F., and R. Leoni. 2008. "L'impresa Nella Teoria Evolutiva." In *Economia Dell'innovazione*, edited by Riccardo Leoni, 39–63. Milano: Franco Angeli.

Cento Bull, A., and B. Jones. 2006. "Governance and Social Capital in Urban Regeneration: A Comparison Between Bristol and Naples." *Urban Studies*, 43(4): 767–786.

Coalter, F. 2007. "Sports Clubs, Social Capital and Social Regeneration: 'Ill-Defined Interventions With Hard to Follow Outcomes'?" *Sport in Society*, 10(4): 537–559.

Cohen, J. 1989. "Deliberation and Democratic Legitimacy." In *The Good Polity: Normative Analysis of the State*, edited by Alan Hamlin and Philip Pettit, 17–34. Oxford: Basil Blackwell.

Cornelius, N., and J. Wallace. 2010. "Cross-Sector Partnerships: City Regeneration and Social Justice." *Journal of Business Ethics*, 94: 71–84.

Deci, E. L., and M. R. Ryan. 2008. "Self-determination Theory: A Macrotheory of Human Motivation, Development, and Health." *Canadian Psychology/Psychologie canadienne*, 49(3): 182–185.

Dewey, J. 1927. *The Public and Its Problems*. Denver, CO: Holt.

Dosi, G., and M. Egidi. 1991. "Substantive and Procedural Uncertainty." *Journal of Evolutionary Economics*, 1: 145–168.

Dosi, G., and L. Marengo. 2000. "Some Elements of an Evolutionary Theory of Organizational Competences." In *The Theory of the Firm: Critical Perspectives on Business and Management*, edited by N. J. Foss, 49–80. London and New York: Routledge.

Dryzek, J. S. 2001. "Legitimacy and Economy in Deliberative Democracy." *Political Theory*, 29(5): 651–669.

Ertell, M. W. 1957. *Inter Institutional Cooperation in Higher Education*. Albany, NY: State Education Department.

Ginsburg, N. 1999. "Putting the Social Into Urban Regeneration Policy." *Local Economy*, 14(1): 55–71.

Glasgow Centre for Population Health. 2016. "Principles for Effective Social Regeneration and Interventions: Learning From Sistema Scotland." *Briefing Paper*, No. 50, December. Accessed on 30 April 2017 from http://socialwelfare.bl.uk/

subject-areas/services-activity/community-development/glasgowcentreforpopulat
ionhealth/179959BP50_social_regeneration_WEB.pdf
Granovetter, M. 1991. "The Social Construction of Economic Institutions." In
*Socio-economics: Toward a New Synthesis*, edited by Amitai Etzioni and Paul R.
Lawrence, 75–81. Armonk, NY: M.E. Sharpe.
Grimalda, G., and L. Sacconi. 2005. "The Constitution of the Not-For-Profit Organ-
isation: Reciprocal Conformity to Morality." *Constitutional Political Economy*,
16(3): 249–276.
Habermas, J. 1996. *Between Facts and Norms: Contributions to a Discourse Theory
of Law and Democracy*. Cambridge, MA: MIT Press.
Hansmann, H. 1996. *The Ownership of the Enterprise*. Harvard, MA: Harvard
University Press.
Hargrave, T. J., and A. H. Van de Ven. 2006. "A Collective Action Model of Institu-
tional Innovation." *Academy of Management Review*, 31(4): 864–888.
Heath, J. 2006. "The Benefits of Cooperation." *Philosophy and Public Affairs*,
34(4): 313–351.
Hirschman, A. O. 1979. *Shifting Involvements: Private Interest and Public Action*.
Princeton, NJ: Princeton University Press.
Knight, J. 1992. *Institutions and Social Conflict*. New York, NY: Cambridge Uni-
versity Press.
Laville, J.-L., and M. Nyssens. 2001. "The Social Enterprise: Towards a Theoreti-
cal Socio-Economic Approach." In *The Emergence of Social Enterprise*, edited
by Carlo Borzaga and Jacques Defourny, 312–332. London and New York:
Routledge.
McGregor, D. 1960. "Theory X and Theory Y." In *Organization Theory: Selected
Readings*, edited by D. S. Pugh, 358–374. London: Pinguin Business.
Meinzen-Dick, R., and E. Mwangi. 2009. "Cutting the Web of Interests: Pitfalls of
Formalizing Property Rights." *Land Use Policy*, 26(1): 36–43.
Nonaka, I., and H. Takeuchi. 1995. *The Knowledge Creating Company: How Japa-
nese Companies Create the Dynamics of Innovation*. New York: Oxford Univer-
sity Press.
Osman, M. M., Bachok, S., and N. I. M. Bakri. 2015. "Social Regeneration Through
Physical Facilities Provided to the Vulnerable and Disadvantaged Groups."
*Procedia-Social and Behavioral Sciences*, 170: 308–319.
Ostrom, E. 1990. *Governing the Commons: The Evolution of the Institutions for
Collective Action*. New York: Cambridge University Press.
Ostrom, E. 1996. "Crossing the Great Divide: Coproduction, Synergy and Develop-
ment." *World Development*, 24(6): 1073–1087.
Ostrom, E. 2010. "Beyond Markets and States: Polycentric Governance of Complex
Economic Systems." *Transnational Corporations Review*, 22: 1–12.
Pérotin, V. 2013. "Worker Cooperatives: Good, Sustainable Jobs in the Commu-
nity." *Journal of Entrepreneurial and Organizational Diversity*, 2 (2): 34-47.
Pestoff, V. A. 1994. "Beyond Exit and Voice in Social Services. Citizens as Co-
Producers." In *Delivering Welfare*, edited by Isabel Vidal. Barcelona: Centre
D'Iniciatives De L'Economia Social.
Pestoff, V. A. 1996. "Renewing Public Services and Developing the Welfare Society
Through Multi-Stakeholder Cooperatives." *Journal of Rural Cooperation*, 23(2):
151–167.
Pestoff, V. A. 2012. "Co-Production and Third Sector Social Services in Europe:
Some Concepts and Evidence." *Voluntas*, 23(4): 1102–1118.
Polanyi, K. 1977. *The Livelihood of Man*. New York: Pearson Academic Press.
Polanyi, M. 1966. *The Tacit Dimension*. Chicago: University of Chicago Press.
Poupeau, F. 2001. "Reasons for Domination, Bourdieu Versus Habermas." *The Soci-
ological Review*, 49(S1): 69–87.

Putnam, R. D. 2000. *Bowling Alone: The Collapse and Revival of American Community*. New York: Simon and Schuster.

Rawls, J. 1971/2009. *A Theory of Justice*. Cambridge, MA: Harvard University Press.

Sabatini, F., Modena, F., and E. Tortia. 2014. "Do Cooperative Enterprises Create Social Trust?" *Small Business Economics*, 42(3): 621–641.

Sacchetti, F., Sacchetti, S., and R. Sugden. 2009. "Creativity in Socio-Economic Development: Space for the Interests of Publics." *International Review of Applied Economics*, 23(6): 653–672.

Sacchetti, S. 2015. "Inclusive and Exclusive Social Preferences: A Deweyan Framework to Explain Governance Heterogeneity." *Journal of Business Ethics*, 126: 473–485.

Sacchetti, S. 2016. "Governance for a 'Socialised Economy'. A Case Study in Preventive Health and Work integration." *Euricse Working Papers*, 89|16.

Sacchetti, S., and C. Campbell. 2014. "Creating Space for Communities: Social Enterprise and the Bright Side of Social Capital." *Journal of Entrepreneurial and Organizational Diversity*, 3(2): 32–48.

Sacchetti, S. and R. Sugden. 2003. "The Governance of Networks and Economic Power: The Nature and Impact of Subcontracting Relationships." *Journal of Economic Surveys*, 17(5): 669-691.

Sacchetti, S., and R. Sugden. 2009. "The Organization of Production and Its Publics: Mental Proximity, Market and Hierarchies." *Review of Social Economy*, 67: 289–311.

Sacchetti, S., and R. Sugden. 2010. "The Public Interest in Economic Development and Creativity: A Knowledge Governance Perspective." In *Local Economies and Global Competitiveness*, edited by Bruno Dallago and Chiara Guglielmetti, 232–241. New York: Palgrave Macmillan.

Sacchetti, S., and E. C. Tortia. 2008. "Dall'Organizzazione Multi-Stakeholder all'Impresa Reticolare." *Impresa Sociale*, 77(4): 104–124.

Sacchetti, S., and E. C. Tortia. 2014. "Multi-Stakeholder Cooperatives and Social Value: The Case of the CEFF System in Italy." In *Sustainable Cooperative Enterprise: Case Studies of Organisational Resilience in the Cooperative Business Model*, edited by Tim Mazzarol, Sophie Reboud and Elena Mamouni Liminios, 285–300. Cheltenham: Edward Elgar.

Sacconi, L. 1991. *Etica degli affari. Individui, imprese e mercati nella prospettiva dell'etica razionale*. Milano: Il Saggiatore.

Sacconi, L., 2006. "A Social Contract Account for CSR as an Extended Model of Corporate Governance (I): Rational Bargaining and Justification." *Journal of Business Ethics*, 68(3): 259–281.

Sacconi, L. 2013. "The Economics of Corporate Social Responsibility." In *Handbook on the Economics of Philanthropy, Reciprocity and Social Enterprise*, edited by Stefano Zamagni and Luigino Bruni, 372–399. Cheltenham: Elgar.

Sacconi, L. 2015. "Beni Comuni, Contratto Sociale e Governance Cooperativa dei Servizi Pubblici Locali." In *Beni Comuni e Cooperazione*, edited by Lorenzo Sacconi and Stefania Ottone, 175–214. Bologna, Italy: Il Mulino.

Sacconi, L., and M. Faillo. 2010. "Conformity, Reciprocity and the Sense of Justice. How Social Contract-Based Preferences and Beliefs Explain Norm Compliance: The Experimental Evidence." *Constitutional Political Economy*, 21: 171–201.

Tortia, E.C. 2007. "Self-financing in LMFs: Individual Capital Accounts and Bonds." *Advances in the Economic Analysis of Participatory and Labour-Managed Firms*, 10(2): 243–272.

Tortia, E. 2017. "The Firm as a Common. The Case of the Accumulation and Use of Capital Resources in Cooperative Enterprises." *Euricse Working Papers*, 90|17.

Wilkinson, R., and K. Pickett. 2010. *The Spirit Level*. London: Penguin.
Williamson, O. 1985. *The Economic Institutions of Capitalism*. New York: Free Press.
Woolcock, M. 2001. "The Place of Social Capital in Understanding Social and Economic Outcomes." *Canadian Journal of Policy Research*, 2(1): 11–17.
Yeung, H. W. C. 2005. "The Firm as Social Networks: An Organisational Perspective." Growth and Change, 36(3): 307–328.
Young, I. M. 2000. *Inclusion and Democracy*. Oxford, UK: Oxford University Press.

# 2 The Transformations of Welfare

## From Solidarity to Individualism and Back

*Luca Fazzi*

## Introduction

The aim of the present chapter is to examine the impact of the transformation of the welfare state on the processes of social regeneration and public participation. The traditional welfare state that emerged in the first post-war period in Western societies rested on values of solidarity and collective responsibility (Rothstein, 1998). However, from the 1970s onward, market liberalisation and austerity led to the retrenchment of the traditional welfare state and the dominance of individualist values and policies. The failure of these polices to bring growth and equality and the conditions of impoverishment and political instability prevailing in the post-crisis era urgently call for a kind of social regeneration that relies on a new conception and system of welfare supported by social economy organisations and deliberative public participation.

The chapter analyses initially welfare as a moral institution whose purpose is to build solidarity among individuals, generations, and social classes. It then describes the changes that have taken place in welfare systems in the past 30 years, showing how reforms have contributed to the emergence of individualisation and to the weakening of the institutional and social mechanisms that used to ensure social cohesion. The chapter concludes by describing the tensions and risks related to the weakening of the solidarist function of welfare, and it stresses the importance of supporting new processes and institutions aimed at social regeneration, public participation, and reorganisation of the production of services.

## The Welfare State as a Moral Institution

As recently stressed by Andre Gamble (2016), the future of the welfare state is not a mere matter of economic policy. Rather, it has to do with moral questions related to how the economy and society must interact with each other and the purposes for which this relationship should be developed. The modern welfare state is an institution that took a more complete form after the end of World War II as an instrument to promote post-war reconstruction and a social mechanism to compensate for the distorting effects of capital-ist economic growth (Glatzer and Rueschemeyer, 2005). Its founding prin-ciples include: i) the active role of the state in ensuring people's well-being and satisfying their social needs; ii) citizenship as a sufficient condition for entitlement to social benefits; and iii) social rights.

Due to the time and place in which the welfare state was born, its char-acteristics are deeply imbued with values emphasising solidarity among the members of a community (Rodger, 2003). It was the explicit intent of the founders of the social protection system that it should not only deliver ser-vices and benefits but also strengthen the national spirit as the driver of post-war reconstruction (Glennerster, 2006).

In the modern conception of the welfare state, social rights in particular have obtained a status of normative prescriptions. They are considered to be principles inherent in the idea of citizenship itself. For Beveridge and Marshall, being a citizen meant sharing rights and duties and conceiving the social protection system as an institution for which all are responsible both individually and as members of a community (Mau and Veghte, 2007).

In the Beveridgean model of the welfare state, every citizen is required to contribute fiscally to the financing of a system of services and protection addressed to the most vulnerable individuals. The payment of taxes is not only a legal requirement; it is also an act of collective responsibility. Citizens who pay taxes do not purchase services; rather, they provide the community with resources that are spent not only on themselves but also on others in a state of need. Every citizen is thus inserted into a mechanism that theoreti-cally rewards persons who are in need.

On this view, welfare systems are not just the result of negotiations between political and economic interests, according to the traditional notion of the relationship between state and market; they are also systems of ideas and moral values. Kohli (1987) coined the term 'moral economy' to denote this feature of the welfare system. The concept of moral economy refers to the fact that the forms of moral rationality which legitimise the principle of redistribution must assume some form of reciprocity or obligation of reciprocity as their constitutive value. In this sense, the welfare state can be considered a moral and cultural institution, as well as an economic and political one.

Hall (1993) considers the principles and values constituting the criteria with which to assess the extent of welfare changes. He is critical of the approach which measures changes only in quantitative terms, and thus dis-tinguishes three levels of assessment. The first is the level of social welfare benefits. The second concerns the instruments used to deliver services and allowances. The third, which is less visible but equally if not more impor-tant, relates to objectives and values that legitimise welfare systems.

According to Hall and the proponents of the paradigm theory, the rela-tionships among institutions, moral values, and society are not given once and for all but are characterised by dynamics and processes that give them a fluid and evolving nature. In his most recent book dealing with the relationship among welfare, rights, and justice, Dean (2015) notes that contemporary citizens live in a post-Marshallian era. It is increasingly evident that social rights must deal with fluid systems of moral values and norms. Therefore, the very cultural and ethical principles which contributed to building the traditional systems of social protection are subject to change. Rights emerge in this period, not as established facts, but as constructs constantly correlated with policies and social conditions. In particular, rights are increasingly constructed and deconstructed by specific legislative choices and are integrated into national policies through complex processes of political and institutional negotiation involving the state, on the one hand, and civil society and the market, on the other.

From this perspective, the dynamic of the modern welfare systems becomes the framework within which social rights change as political and economic obligations, while their moral and cultural nature is transformed as well. How have the constitutive values of the welfare state changed over time? Through what processes? What are the consequences in terms of economic growth, cultural conceptions, and the resilience of the social bond?

## From the Golden Age to the Era of 'Tough Austerity'

After the 'golden age' of the welfare state, there began a period of profound changes in the political and cultural structure of modern welfare systems. By the end of the 1970s, Margaret Thatcher in Europe and Ronald Reagan in the United States had declared war on the welfare state. In the name of the neoliberal ideology, policies were implemented to weaken the trade union confederations, reduce the protection of labour, and roll back the social protection programmes consolidated in previous decades.

The destructive intentions of neoliberal governments, however, encountered what Pierson (1994) termed the phenomenon of 'path dependency'. Path dependency can be understood as a force acting against substantial policy changes because of the resistance raised by those individuals who are simultaneously the beneficiaries of welfare measures and voters in the political system that has implemented them (David, 1985). According to this theory, the endeavour to dismantle the welfare state by the neoliberal governments of the 1980s was thwarted by the fact that the middle classes—the core beneficiaries of social policy programmes—allowed the erosion of marginal welfare measures but, by exercising their electoral weight, managed to obstruct a more radical retrenchment of interventions. The role of resistance by the median voter and organisations representing the interests of the middle class has induced many scholars to describe welfare reforms as 'recasting' policies which, despite making benefits more selective and reducing target beneficiaries, have remained firmly anchored to a universalist model of social protection (Ferrera and Rhodes, 2000).

Also, the so-called 'marketisation programmes' launched in many countries since the 1990s have only partly fulfilled their potential to replace the founding principles of the welfare state. The main forms of marketisation in the sectors of pensions, welfare, and health care have come about within so-called 'quasi-markets'. These are forms of market in which the behaviour of private providers is regulated by public standards and in which funding is still largely furnished by the state (Le Grand and Bartlett, 1993).

The main result of these programmes has been the creation of a terrain that is more favourable to the 'disorganisation' of the traditional models of welfare system governance. The term 'disorganisation' refers to a situation in which public authorities weakly coordinate the relationships among users, purchasers, and producers (Bode, 2007). In this scenario, welfare services are provided by various institutions, for-profit enterprises, public agencies, and third-sector organisations in the framework of rules defined by the state and local public authorities.

In the new welfare systems based on public/private partnerships, negotiation processes, and mutual adjustment between supply and demand tend to become more fluid and result in the greater flexibility of supply. However, until the late 1990s, despite the emergence of quasi-markets, several studies show that the mentality of the producers of private services was only in part characterised by commercial interests and that universal welfare continued to be the main purpose of goods and services production (Forder et al., 2004).

Until the early 2000s, the changes in welfare were partially mitigated by the legacy of the political and cultural past. However, at the turn of the century, Western countries entered an era of 'tough austerity' (Farnsworth and Irving, 2013), albeit following different trajectories. Even before the crisis of 2008, several countries had accumulated debts in public spending which had grown to dramatically threatening proportions. The resulting increases in the tax burden combined with reductions in average wage levels due to globalisation strongly impacted the living standards of the middle class (Mishel and Shierholz, 2013). Increased life expectancy and declining birth rates at the same time raised severe concerns about the economic sustainability of the welfare system in the medium term, and various countries took action to reform their pension systems, mainly through change from earnings-related to contributions-based schemes (Hemerijck, 2012). The global economic crisis has aggravated the effect of these contradictions (Lavoie and Stockhammer, 2013). It has increased unemployment and poverty and reduced tax revenues, thereby creating the conditions for what various scholars interpret as a radical welfare state retrenchment (Dukelow and Considine, 2014). In an effort to prevent default by banks afflicted by the crisis, governments have launched recapitalisation policies through progressive public spending cuts. They insist that welfare is the first cost to cut and reorganise in terms of social investment (Hay and Wincott, 2013).

Cuts in social spending have been most drastic in the countries with the greatest indebtedness, i.e. Spain, Portugal, Ireland, Italy, and Greece, or those with a more deeply rooted neoliberal ideology, like Britain (Taylor-Gooby, 2013).

In parallel, to stimulate the growth and competitiveness of economic systems, reforms have been enacted to make labour markets more flexible by reducing protection and allocating the task of generating and distributing wealth to the market through economic growth (Allard and Everaert, 2010). Protective measures have been widely sacrificed to the 'moloch of competitiveness' to be achieved in a scenario of increasingly deregulated globalisation.

The new policies, however, have produced controversial results. Slow rates of economic growth and recovery have been counterweighed by extremely high social costs. In almost all European countries, deregulation has exacerbated the negative trend growth rate that began in the 2000s. The reorganisation of labour protection systems centred on contract flexibilisation has increased the risk of unemployment especially for young people (Gebel and Giesecke, 2016), who have also suffered a drastic fall in wages, an increase in job insecurity, and a reduction in youth welfare programmes (McKay and Rowlingson, 2016). Hills and Stewart (2016) calculate that in 2012, the average wealth of British 60-year-olds was fully seven times higher than that of 30-year-olds. The new inequalities affect both citizens and immigrants in various Nation States. As a result of the crisis and social unrest, the criteria for access to benefits tend to become particularly discriminatory against immigrants, who are seen as second-class citizens with respect to natives (Shutes, 2016).

In this crisis situation, the social cleavages are so severe that they are creating a type of welfare that Taylor-Gooby (2016) has recently termed 'divisive'. Divisive welfare can be considered an intermediate stage in a long-time decomposition process whereby society is divided into two blocks. On the one hand, there are social groups politically more resistant to reforms, which seek to mitigate the effects of the cuts. On the other, there are groups with a lower capacity to organise and apply political pressure, and which are also those hit hardest by the reforms. The effect of the segmentation of welfare is a marked increase in inequalities, which have grown substantially in two-thirds of European and OECD countries (OECD, 2015). According to the ratio of top-to-bottom income decile inequality had reached in 2010 its highest level in 30 years. In the UK, inequality in the second decade of the twenty-first century is even ten percentage points higher than a generation ago (Atkinson, 2015).

In the post-crisis era, an instrument important for dismantling the welfare system has been the so-called 'privatisation of social risks' (Hacker, 2004). The privatisation of risks is a process which modifies the expectations of citizens so that, in response to public spending cuts, they are induced to turn to the private market to obtain specific welfare or health services. Even in the presence of formally universalist social protection programmes, the high selectivity of access criteria or long waiting lists incentivise individuals to resort to private providers pursuing typical self-interested goals.

The new millennium has therefore been marked by changes very different from those of the past. They profoundly modify both the architecture and the founding principles of modern social protection systems, and, at the same time, they raise new issues and challenges for the future.

## From Collective Responsibilities to the Individualisation of Welfare

The changes that have taken place in welfare systems over recent decades concern not only the coverage of services, entitlements, and the amount of expenditure, but also the conception of rights and solidarity. Already in the 1980s, and therefore long before the explosion of the global crisis, many areas of everyday life were affected by the rise of individualism. The term 'individualism' refers to a series of processes related to the sphere of rights, individual autonomy, and social ties whereby greater importance is given to individuals than to the idea of community. The development of individualistic attitudes was first analysed as an empirical phenomenon by Inglehart (1990) in studies on cross-country changes in values based on data from the *World Values Surveys* and findings of the "Eurobarometer". According to Inglehart and his research group, the achievement of widespread affluence in contemporary Western societies has generated so-called 'postmaterialist' values which have replaced the old solidarities of social class, language, and nationality with the idealisation of individual freedom, individual initiative, and an aversion to bureaucracy and statism.

Individualism considers welfare as result of individual autonomy and market relations and no longer a social pact that gives priority, also normatively, to collective well-being over that of the individual. Ferge (1997) speaks in this regard of individualism as a pillar of a post-modern welfare paradigm whose predominant features are the following:

i) collective responsibility as the driver of social development is replaced by emphasis on the value of individual responsibility and free enterprise;
ii) the principle of combating inequalities is superseded by acceptance of inequality as a cost necessary to stimulate free enterprise and personal commitment;
iii) economic growth takes place of an economic balance between state and market; and
iv) competition is given priority over social cohesion.

Individualism has become a constitutive dimension of modern welfare systems mainly with the demise of the redistributive principle and the advent of the culture of individual responsibilisation. Welfare as individual responsibility is an ideology that has consolidated through a series of measures and rhetoric with corrosive effects on the principle of solidarity on which the Marshallian and Beveridgean conception of social protection systems rested (Roulstone and Morgan, 2009). Since the 1990s, the legislatures of several countries have enacted financial reforms that give a more active and direct role to citizens through the establishment of supplementary pension and health care schemes. Every citizen is thus required to directly finance a portion of the welfare benefits that s/he may need in the future and no longer pays for services used by the entire community. This system increases individual responsibilisation for social protection, but it inevitably fosters a more privatist conception of the welfare system that puts the welfare of the individual before that of the community.

In parallel, so-called 'activation' has become increasingly important. 'Activation' is an umbrella term denoting programmes designed to: i) improve the employability and productivity of individuals through measures to enhance individual skills and human capital; and ii) offer job incentives to welfare beneficiaries. Whilst these programmes were initially aimed at improving human capital, since the second half of the 1990s, activation policies have been characterised by a 'creeping conditionality' (Dwyer, 2004). The payment of social benefits to the needy and the unemployed has become conditional on their willingness to seek work and to attend vocational training courses. This has led to a substantial change in the role of social policies, which have been theorised, not as means to redistribute resources to provide for the needs of citizens, but as a means designed to enable individuals to manage risks in a responsible manner (Gilbert, 2004). The implicit message often transmitted through the rhetoric of activation is that inactive individuals are to blame for their situation because they are unwilling to improve their social and economic circumstances (Eichhorst et al., 2008).

As emphasised by Scharpf (2010), the new rhetoric of individual responsibility has spread the belief in public discourse and opinion that social exclusion, unemployment, and poverty are not caused by social and political factors, but by the individual's behaviour. Some scholars maintain that there is a political endeavour to portray welfare recipients as scroungers who take undue advantage of the excessive generosity of welfare programmes (Garthwaite, 2014). The problem of welfare dependency has accordingly acquired the nature of a totalising public discourse which often indiscriminately lumps together welfare freeloaders and persons unable, for physical, cognitive, or social reasons, to improve their situation. Recent surveys show that, in this new scenario, a very large number of welfare recipients perceive themselves as subject to growing social reprobation and stigmatisation, and not as persons with recognised needs (Baumberg, 2016).

The problem of post-Marshallian welfare is that the demise of the moral and collective dimension of welfare and the sense of obligation towards persons in need has made the divisions among social classes, ethnic groups, and generations increasingly deep and irremediable. In the individualised and fragmented welfare system emerging from the global economic crisis, elderly and young people constitute groups with conflicting and unrelated interests; foreigners are considered to misappropriate resources that belong to the natives; the poor demand improvements in their living standards in opposition to the middle class that has withstood the crisis and to the wealthy.

In this scenario, contemporary society, devoid of referents and institutions that value solidarity, appears increasingly at the mercy of disruptive forces that open the way to xenophobia, populism, and conflict. According to many observers, the austerity policies which shift the responsibility for social protection to citizens through cuts and liberalisation measures are the main cause of the populist protests against the European institutions and the elites of the nation state manifest in most of the Western democracies. In countries like Greece, where the dismantling of the welfare state has been most radical, the onset of social conflict and organised groups of a more populist and xenophobic stamp is a clear and certified outcome of the decline of the institutions created to ensure social cohesion.

The weakening of the Marshallian social pact which united social classes and generations with a bond of mutual solidarity therefore not only causes severe difficulties in mitigating the effects of the crisis; it is also likely to engender an even greater crisis of the democratic principles on which contemporary societies rest.

## The Prospects of Exiting the Crisis: Between Structural Constraints and New Institutional Models

The debate on the prospects of exit from the crisis is taking place amid economic, political, and social changes of enormous proportions (Crouch, 2009; Béland et al., 2014). The persistence of the economic crisis, globalisation, migration, and international political instability define a frame within which welfare reforms are just one component and no longer the focus of discussion. Inevitably, therefore, the ambiguity and confusion which characterise the current situation have important repercussions on both how the crisis is understood and what strategies can be devised to overcome it.

What one can say concerning the future is that there are three great problems to be addressed in order to move beyond the crisis affecting contemporary welfare systems. For each of them, coherent solutions are necessary.

The first concerns the future sustainability of social protection models. The rhetoric which claims that excessively costly welfare systems have fuelled the economic crisis and caused the collapse of growth is now contradicted by a great deal of empirical evidence (Crouch, 2015). The principal cause of the economic crisis has been the irresponsible behaviour of the great international financial institutions and the domino effects that have ensued. It has only marginally to do with welfare systems as such. This does not mean, however, that the economic sustainability problems of welfare systems are fortuitous. Independently of the political and economic situations of welfare regimes, they share the problems of an ageing population and radical socio-demographic changes. The traditional family model of the husband at work and the wife at home is by now definitively superseded. Simultaneously, the average number of children per household has diminished, and average life expectancy has dramatically increased. In the medium term, these changes entail an explosion of needs that will place severe strain on pension, health care, and welfare systems even if a slow but steady recovery of the economy and consumption occurs. From this, it follows that the welfare of the last century must be integrated permanently with programmes to increase the autonomy, skills, and resources of individuals (Marin, 2015). However, it is important that activation policies remain anchored to a human capital approach and do not, as has happened in the recent past, become subject to a brutal conditionality. In an analysis of 23 European countries, Kuitto (2016) has recently highlighted the need to strike a balance between social investment strategies and protection against old risks. Kutto shows that this is easier for the welfare systems that have financed social investment programmes for a longer time and are in better economic circumstances. Carlin (2012) spoke in this regard of the importance of so-called 'predistributive human capital' to improve the capacities of individuals in a perspective of equal opportunity. In other words, the design of social investment programmes will have to take account of the principles of justice and fairness in order to prevent the use of resources from increasing social and economic cleavages.

The second problem that governments must address in order to overcome the economic and social effects of the crisis is the scant room for manoeuvre available to most of them. For Eurozone countries, in particular, there are stringent spending constraints imposed by monetary union which require the adoption of specific tax measures to remain within the parameters established (Fourcade, 2013). The era of the Nation State that autonomously decided its fiscal and monetary policy choices is over, and the decision-making logic of individual countries is increasingly connected with that of globalisation. Taxation has therefore lost its incisiveness as an instrument to extend the social protection system. In this scenario, a more pluralist welfare system able to mobilise resources even outside the classic taxation scheme becomes the path to be pursued to make future welfare systems sustainable. It is therefore likely that traditional public intervention will be flanked by the greater presence of private providers such as voluntary associations, the third sector, and new social enterprises (both non-profit and for-profit) furnishing services which supplement public ones and are innovative with respect to the traditional ones.

Finally, the third great problem to be addressed is the implementation of reforms able to conjugate economic sustainability, responses to needs, and the values of solidarity and social cohesion. To date, the competition and consumerism paradigm has proved unable to reconcile growth and social cohesion. Indeed, it has severely damaged the bonds that held the welfare pact together. In order to counter the negative consequences generated by neoliberalism and austerity, it is necessary to combine a social investment and productivity strategy with the development of models for the co-production of services based on cooperation and trust among the various actors involved (Brandsen et al., 2012). A welfare system that should conjugate protection against the old social risks and investments to address the new ones must inevitably deal with contradictions and tensions among interests and priorities. In a regime of scarce resources, what may be in the interest of one social group may be against the interest of another group, and vice versa. This makes all the more necessary forms of joint participation and active involvement in the solution of problems that concern multiple actors simultaneously. In this regard, development at the local level is a crucial arena for testing new initiatives and action programmes. Many phenomena, such as poverty and unemployment, recorded with data aggregated at national and international level in fact exhibit very wide variations at the local level. All welfare reforms have an impact at the local level, and it is to the latter that greater attention should paid, with the design of initiatives that involve multiple actors in the solution of shared problems. It is essential to stimulate collaboration in order to move beyond the merely contractualist logic that has been dominant in the neoliberal rhetoric but has played an important role in the division of society and the weakening of solidarity between generations, groups, and social classes. It is clear that the societies of the new century are no longer characterised by the forms of traditional solidarity of the post-World War II period. Consequently, what was profoundly weakened was the basic social fabric on which the welfare states were constructed. Nevertheless, the relationship between values and institutions continues to play a central role in building the culture and social perception of reality. Having or not having institutions and processes that focus on collaborative mechanisms inevitably makes a difference in promoting and cementing the minimal sense of social solidarity and shared values without which the gloom of social fragmentation becomes more likely.

From this point of view, the relationship among local development, collaboration, participation, and welfare constitutes a new frontier for reform programmes which makes it possible to conceive changes to welfare not only in economic terms but also in those of recovering and consolidating values crucial or the resilience of democracies. The challenges raised by the new 'welfare' are broad and important.

The problem of territorial imbalances and inequalities impacts primarily on the possibility of local resources and actors to construct collaborative responses to social risks. Areas richer in social capital and economic resources are likely to be more advantaged than poorer and more marginal ones. For this reason, programmes to incentivise local development measures require a very well-calibrated allocation of resources and laws.

Secondly, welfare based on local development requires the implementation of a multidisciplinary approach to social problems. Issues such as social exclusion, the regeneration of physical spaces, protection and recovery of the environment, and the creation of employment and income closely interweave. Considering welfare from the perspective of local development therefore means adopting an integrated and comprehensive approach that encompasses within one frame of reference the so-often separated issues of social protection, economic and human development, social investment, environmental protection, and regeneration of social ties.

From this point of view, public participation and the involvement of various local actors from the bottom up is of key importance in redefining priorities and interventions based on the real needs of communities. Consequently, greater importance is acquired by the processes and institutions that foster and promote participation in both the governance of intervention programmes and their implementation (Bridge et al., 2013).

Finally, the welfare and local development perspective requires the widespread presence of actors that not only produce material goods and create economic wealth but are also able to produce relations of reciprocity and cooperation and to promote the values of solidarity. The social economy is the 'humus' for the birth and evolution of these actors (Doherty et al., 2014).

It is within this economic and social ecosystem that there arise and operate organisations and enterprises which are more open to participation and which have competitive advantages in addressing issues concerning social problems with respect to other forms of business due to their degree of embeddedness in the community (Allen, 2005). One of the key characteristics of social enterprises and social economy organisations is the participation of diverse actors in their governance and their bottom-up development on the initiative of community actors (Borzaga et al., 2016). These features enhance the capacity to interpret needs in their entirety, and they make it possible to mobilise community resources to solve various social problems, while at the same responding to collective needs and empowering individuals and disadvantaged groups.

The social economy's contribution to and participation in social regeneration can vary, and it depends on the type of organisation involved and the legal and political context of reference. The main factors in the spread of social enterprises are access to secure and sustainable sources of funding and the need to maintain a balance between economic and social results (Peattie and Morley, 2008). The challenge of promoting these forms of enterprise is therefore relative to the construction of rules and policies which enhance their competitive advantages and reward the economic and social value produced.

## Conclusions

As stressed by Streeck and Thelen (2005), the dimension of welfare in which the most important changes occurred over the last 40 years has been the institutional one. There has been greater liberalisation of welfare and an explicit 'decline in resistance to change' from the founding pillars of social protection systems. The global economic crisis has enormously accelerated the 'elephant movement' and helped to create profound social and economic cleavages (Hinrichs and Kagas, 2003). Many observers believe that the proposals to cure the disease of welfare by implementing austerity policies have dramatically aggravated these problems. On the one hand, budget and wage cuts and neoliberal reforms have increased inequalities without being able to solve the problem of economic growth. On the other hand, slowly but inexorably, they have radically weakened the values of solidarity among classes, social groups, and generations that the traditional model of the welfare state assumed as implicit. This is fostering the emergence of irreparable social and economic divisions that constitute the breeding ground for the rise of populisms and social conflicts. In very few words: these changes are undermining the democratic principles on which advanced societies and economies were founded. Consequently, to formulate a new welfare project, it is necessary to consider not only the economic and sustainability aspects of social spending, but also the type of processes and institutions that are required to innovate social protection systems. It is important to ensure that the process of institutional change is based on policies favouring the emergence of new economic actors able to conjugate a focus on local development problems, the mobilisation of local resources, and a capacity to generate trust and cooperation among producers, consumers, and citizens. After the intoxication of individualistic values and social inequality, it seems that the bell of history is tolling to declare that it is time to restore value to solidarity and social relations and to invest once again in equality of opportunity as the prerequisite for any possible economic growth.

## References

Allard, C., and L. Everaert. 2010. "Lifting Euro Area Growth: Priorities for Structural Reforms and Governance." *IMF Staff Position Note* SPN/10/19, 22 November.

Allen, B. 2005. "Social Enterprise: Through the Eyes of the Consumer." *Social Enterprise Journal*, 1: 57–77.

Atkinson, A. B. 2015. *Inequality: What Can Be Done?* Cambridge, MA: Harvard University Press.

Baumberg, B. 2016. "The Stigma of Claiming Benefits: A Quantitative Study." *Journal of Social Policy*, 45(2): 181–199.

Béland, D., Blomqvist, P., Andersen, J. G., Palme, J., and A. Waddan. 2014. "The Universal Decline of Universality? Social Policy Change in Canada, Denmark, Sweden and the UK." *Social Policy and Administration*, 48(7): 739–756.

Bode, I. 2007. "New Moral Economies of Welfare: The Case of Domiciliary Elder Care in Germany, France and Britain." *European Societies*, 9(2): 201–227.

Borzaga, C., Fazzi, L., and G. Galera. 2016. "Social Enterprise as a Bottom-Up Dynamic: Part 1. The Reaction of Civil Society to Unmet Social Needs in Italy, Sweden and Japan." *International Review of Sociology*, 26(1): 1–18.

Brandsen, T., Pestoff, V., and B. Verschuere. 2012. "Co-production as a Maturing Concept." In *New Public Management, the Third Sector and Co-Production*, edited by V. Pestoff, T. Brandsen and B. Verschuere. London: Routledge.

Bridge, S., Murtagh, B., and K. O'Neil. 2013. *Understanding the Social Economy and the Third Sector*. Basingstoke: Palgrave.

Carlin, W. 2012. "A Progressive Economic Strategy." *Policy Network Paper*, October.

Crouch, C. 2009. "Privatised Keynesianism: An Unacknowledged Policy regime." *Journal of British Politics and International Relations*, 11: 382–399.

Crouch, C. 2015. *Governing Social Risks in Post-Crisis Europe*. Cheltenham, UK: Edward Elgar.

David, P. 1985. "Clio and the Economics of QWERTY." *The American Economic Review*, 75(2): 332–337.

Dean, H. 2015. *Social Rights and Human Welfare*. London: Routledge.

Doherty, B., Haugh, H., and F. Lyon. 2014. "Social Enterprises as Hybrid Organizations: A Review and Research Agenda." *International Journal of Management Reviews*, 16(4): 417–436.

Dukelow, F., and M. Considine. 2014. "Outlier or Model of Austerity in Europe? The Case of Irish Social Protection Reform." *Social Policy and Administration*, 48(4): 413–429.

Dwyer, P. 2004. "Creeping Conditionality on the UK." *Canadian Journal of Sociology*, 25: 261–283.

Eichhorst, W., Kaufmann, O., Konle Seidl, R., and H.-J. Reinhard. 2008. "Bringing the Jobless Into Work? An Introduction to Activation Policies." In *Bringing the Jobless Into Work? Experiences in Activation Schemes in Europe and the US*, edited by W. Eichhorst, O. Kaufmann, R. Konle Seidl and H.-J. Reinhard, 1–16. Berlin: Springer.

Farnsworth, K., and Z. Irving. 2013. "Varieties of Crisis, Varieties of Austerity: Social Policy in Challenging Times." *Journal of Poverty and Social Justice*, 20(2): 133–147.

Ferge, Z. 1997. "The Changed Welfare Paradigm: The Individualization of the Social." *Social Policy and Administration*, 31: 20–44.

Ferrera, M., and M. Rhodes. 2000. "Recasting European Welfare States: An Introduction." *West European Politics*, 23(2): 1–10.

Forder, J., Knapp, M., Hardy, B., Kendall, J., Matosevic, T., and P. Ware. 2004. "Prices, Contracts and Motivations: Institutional Arrangements in Domiciliary Care." *Policy & Politics*, 32(2): 207–222.

Fourcade, M. 2013. "The Economy as a Morality Play, and Implications for the Eurozone Crisis." *Socioeconomic Review*, 11: 620–626.

Gamble, A. 2016. *Can the Welfare State Survive?* Cambridge: Polity Press.

Garthwaite, K. 2014. "Fear of the Brown Envelope: Exploring Welfare Reform With Long-Term Sickness Benefits Recipients." *Social Policy & Administration*, 48(7): 782–798.

Gebel, M., and J. Giesecke. 2016. "Does Deregulation Help? The Impact of Employment Protection Reforms on Youths' Unemployment and Temporary Employment Risks in Europe." *European Sociological Review*, 32(4): 486–500.

Gilbert, N. 2004. "Welfare, Poverty and Social Services: International experiences." In *Social Welfare: Innovations From Abroad*, edited by Midgley and Hokenstad. Washington, DC: NASW Press.

Glatzer, M., and D. Rueschemeyer, eds. 2005. *Globalization and the Future of the Welfare State*. Pittsburgh, PA: University of Pittsburgh Press.

Glennerster, H. 2006. *British Social Policy: 1945 to the Present*. Oxford: Blackwell.

Hacker, J. 2004. "Privatizing Risk Without Privatizing the Welfare State: The Hidden Politics of Welfare State Retrenchment in the United States." *American Political Science Review*, 98(2): 243–260.

Hall, P. A. 1993. "Policy Paradigms, Social Learning, and the State: The Case of Economic. Policymaking in Britain." *Comparative Politics*, 25: 275–296.

Hay, C., and D. Wincott. 2013. *The Political Economy of European Welfare Capitalism*. London: Palgrave Macmillan.

Hemerijck, A. 2012. *Changing Welfare States*. Oxford: Oxford University Press.

Hills, J., and K. Stewart. 2016. "Socioeconomic Inequalities." In *Social Policy in a Cold Climate*, edited by R. Lupton, T. Burchardt, J. Hills, K. Stewart and P. Vizard, 245–266. Bristol: Policy Press.

Hinrichs, K., and O. Kangas. 2003. "When Is a Change Big Enough to Be a System Shift? Small System-shifting Changes in German and Finnish Pension Policies." *Social Policy & Administration*, 37(6): 573–591.

Inglehart, R. 1990. *Culture Shift in Advanced Industrial Society*. Princeton: Princeton University Press.

Kohli, M. 1987. "Retirement and the Moral Economy: A Historical Interpretation of the German Case." *Journal of Aging Studies*, 1(1): 125–144.

Kuitto, K. 2016. "From Social Security to Social Investment? Compensating and Social Investment Welfare Policies in a Life-Course Perspective." *Journal of European Social Policy*, 25(5): 442–459.

Lavoie, M., and E. Stockhammer. 2013. "Wage-led Growth. Concept, Theories and Policies." In *The Palgrave Macmillan Wage-led Growth*, edited by M. Lavoie and E. Stockhammer. New York: Palgrave McMillan.

Le Grand, J., and W. Bartlett. 1993. *Quasi-markets and Social Policy*. Basingstoke: Macmillan Press.

Marin, B. 2015. "Introduction: The Future of Welfare in a Global Europe." In *The Future of Welfare in a Global Europe*, edited by B. Marin. London: Routledge.

Mau, S., and B. Veghte. 2007. "Introduction: Social Justice, Legitimacy and the Welfare State." In *Social Justice, Legitimacy and the Welfare State*, edited by S. Mau and B. Veghte, 1–19. Aldershot: Asghate.

McKay, S., and K. Rowlingson. 2016. "Social security under the coalition and Conservatives: shredding the system for people of working age; privileging pensioners". In *The Coalition Government and Social Policy: Restructuring the Welfare State*, edited by H. Bochel and M. Powell. Bristol: Policy Press.

Mishel, L., and H. Shierholz. 2013. "A Decade of Flat Wages: The Key Barrier to Shared Prosperity and a Rising Middle Class." *EPI Briefing Paper*, No. 365, Economic Policy Institute, August.

OECD. 2015. "Growth and Income Inequality: Trends and Policy Implications." *OECD Economics Department Policy Notes*, No. 26, April.

Peattie, K., and A. Morley. 2008. "Eight Paradoxes of the Social Enterprise Research Agenda." *Social Enterprise Journal*, 4(2): 91–107.

Pierson, P. 1994. *Dismantling the Welfare State? Reagan, Thatcher and the Politics of Retrenchment*. Cambridge: Cambridge University Press.

Rodger, J. 2003. "Social Solidarity, Welfare and Post-emotionalism." *Journal of Social Policy*, 32(3): 403–421.

Rothstein, B. 1998. *Just Institutions Matter: The Moral and Political Logic of the Universal Welfare State*. Cambridge: Cambridge University Press.

Roulstone, A., and H. Morgan. 2009. "Neo-Liberal Individualism or Self-Directed Support: Are We All Speaking the Same Language on Modernisation?" *Social Policy and Society*, 8(3): 333–345.

Scharpf, F. 2010. "The Asymmetry of European Integration, or Why the EU Cannot Be a Social Market Economy." *Socio-Economic Review*, 8(2): 211–250.

Shutes, I. 2016. "Work-related Conditionality and the Access to Social Benefits of National Citizens, EU and Non-EU Citizens." *Journal of Social Policy*, 45(4): 691–707.

Streeck, W., and K. Thelen. 2005. "Introduction: Institutional Change in Advanced Political Economies." In *Beyond Continuity: Institutional Change in Advanced Political Economies*, edited by W. Streeck and K. Thelen. Oxford: Oxford University Press.

Taylor-Gooby, P. 2013. *The Double Crisis of the Welfare State and What We Can Do About It*. Basingstoke: Palgrave.

Taylor-Gooby, P. 2016. "The Divisive Welfare State." *Social Policy and Administration*, 50(6): 712–733.

# Part II

# Inclusive and Cooperative Organisations

# 3 Social Enterprise and Regeneration

## A Participatory Approach

*Asimina Christoforou*

## Introduction

The current financial crises brought to the fore the "social" deficit created by the sole pursuit of profit. The quest for financial gain had primacy over and above social considerations, such as the preservation of the natural and cultural environment, access to health and education, the protection of human rights, and the inclusion of disadvantaged groups (e.g., women, immigrants, ethnic groups, etc.), compromising community development and social welfare. As discussed in the introduction of this book, nowadays many researchers, policy-makers and practitioners at the EU and national levels claim that the solution to these problems lies in the transmission and adoption of collective and cooperative values and institutions fostered by the social economy and social enterprises. The social economy includes organisations, such as cooperatives, foundations and social enterprises. Social enterprises identify with alternative forms of management and production which combine economic goals of efficiency and competitiveness with social priorities, such as the provision of social goods and services, as well as the establishment of participatory governance and ownership structures.

Social economy organisations and particularly social enterprises are seen as entities that potentially play a critical role in the local economy and society by supporting social regeneration. In the introduction of this book, social regeneration is defined as processes of transformation based on inclusion and cooperation that are informed by the goal of improving peoples' lives through democratic empowerment. Though regeneration research and policies have recently stressed the considerable role of the community and the social enterprise, they have rarely theorised the ways in which these entities impact social dynamics and urban development. More importantly, they have hardly engaged in practically assessing their influence on building a locality's capacity to form partnerships and foster values of cooperation.

The chapter puts forth the argument that social enterprises and social regeneration should be understood as a step toward a participatory economic system; otherwise, their social means and objectives will be compromised. A participatory economic system relies on generalised participation and social ownership. It may be more efficient in the allocation of resources in the economy and society precisely because it invites all those in the community with an interest in the use of these resources to determine the criteria and judgements for their allocation through a discursive process of cooperative interaction. In this chapter, it is argued that social capital could be of paramount importance in building a participatory economic system. It identifies with intangible resources of norms and networks of trust, reciprocity, and cooperation, which could cultivate and sustain participatory principles, values, and institutions. It could also provide the concepts and means to assess the locality's potential to build networks and partnerships for the promotion of broader developmental and welfare goals.

The aim of this chapter is to theoretically and practically determine the ways in which social enterprises can build social capital and sustain the capacity of the organisation and locality for social regeneration as a path toward a participatory economic system. Section II discusses the social enterprise as a vehicle for social regeneration, and Section III places social entrepreneurship within a participatory economic system. These sections focus on the important, yet understudied, role of social capital in these processes. To examine the actual potential of a social enterprise to contribute to social regeneration and a participatory economic system via social capital, Section IV provides preliminary results of a case study conducted in Greece, where concepts of social economy and social entrepreneurship are rather novel and are promoted by EU-supported policies and funds to deal with the crisis in the country. The chapter closes with some concluding remarks.

## The Social Enterprise as a Vehicle for Social Regeneration

Traditionally, the social economy in Europe hosted cooperatives, mutual societies, and associations to address the adverse social consequences of increased poverty, the miserable working and living conditions, and the environmental destruction that accompanied the rapid growth of capitalist production since the Industrial Revolution. However, by the end of the 20th century, these organisations were subject to global transformations due to the liberalisation of domestic and international markets and the reduction of state intervention and public funds. They were under considerable pressure to adapt to this environment by engaging with commercial activities, beyond charitable donations and voluntary work, and by making efforts to increase the efficiency of capital raised. Despite challenges faced within a competitive economic environment, the modern social economy was determined to preserve its social character, acquire institutional recognition, and seek a new compromise between social benefit and profitability, social cohesion, and economic efficiency (Vienney, 1994/2008; European Commission, 2011).

These developments led to another type of social economy organisation, the social enterprise. Though there is no universal definition of the term, in Europe, the social enterprise is: ". . . an operator in the social economy whose main objective is to have a social impact rather than make a profit for their owners or shareholders" (European Commission, 2011, 2). There are entrepreneurial, social, and governance dimensions that distinguish social enterprises from for-profit, welfare state, and non-profit organisations. According to the European Commission (2011, 2–3), a social enterprise: 1) engages in commercial activity to pursue social goals and serve general interest, including the creation of new forms and institutions of cooperation; 2) reinvests profits in the organisation and uses them to support its mission; and 3) adopts organisational structures that are based on principles of democratic participation of a range of stakeholders, including workers, users, or volunteers.

Some authors, such as Ginsberg (1999) and Campbell (2011), see the social enterprise as a vehicle of social regeneration, especially one driven by community involvement. They distinguish various facets of the social regeneration process, such as giving voice to marginalised groups, investing in social capital, enabling the participation and empowerment of local communities, encouraging bottom-up initiatives, forging private-public partnerships, and improving access to social goods, like education, health, and housing. However, they also point to the difficulties that local actors and policy-makers encounter in these processes. Briefly, social regeneration may be hindered by: 1) the absence of government support at various levels of administration with the provision of financial, professional, and technical resources and the creation of a legal and policy framework; 2) the social inequalities and power structures within communities leading to heterogeneity and conflicts among groups and the exclusion and isolation of the more disadvantaged segments of the local population; and 3) the severe resource constraints, in both quantity and quality, of the more deprived urban areas and groups and the restrictions they impose on mobilising local agents to re-build their capacity for participation and development (Ginsberg, 1999, 66–67). Obstacles to community involvement may also include: 1) the transfer of responsibility for regeneration to the more deprived areas and groups; 2) the lack of knowledge and confidence on behalf of local groups to participate in collective processes and decision-making (language and social barriers for illiterate individuals, immigrants, and ethnic minorities); 3) scepticism toward established collective arrangements that weaken motivation; 4) lack of legitimacy, recognition, and acceptance within organisations and communities; and 5) the long time it takes for social learning processes to unfold and contribute to changes in values and institutions that make people more trusting, participatory, and cooperative (Campbell, 2011, 16–20).

According to Ginsberg (1999) and Campbell (2011), social enterprises may be able to overcome these difficulties precisely because they introduce economic and social objectives in the provision of goods and their organisational structures, and they combine objectives of growth and competitiveness with social participation and inclusiveness in ways that market, state, and traditional social economy organisations alone fail to do so. There are some studies that point to the positive impact that social enterprises potentially have on the regeneration of the economic, social, environmental, and physical dimensions of the urban space (cf. Sacchetti and Campbell, 2014).

However, for social enterprises to thrive and produce sustainable outcomes, they need a supportive environment that enhances the flow of financial and social resources among agents in both the public and private spheres and at different levels of governance. The European Commission (2014a) discusses the difficulties that social enterprises encounter in Europe and proposes the social economy eco-system at the national and supranational level. The eco-system comprises a set of factors integrated into a single institutional framework, which supports, evaluates, and monitors the efficiency and sustainability of social enterprises. Key components include: 1) an appropriate legal and policy framework; 2) systems for social accounting and auditing; 3) systems of certification and branding; 4) financial institutions for social (impact) investments; 5) mutual networks with other social enterprises or social economy organisations; and 6) public-private partnerships at the local, regional, national, and supranational levels (European Commission, 2014a, xiv). It becomes evident that the European eco-system places the social enterprise at the centre of a complex set of multiple and diverse network relations, synergies, and partnerships that transcend the private and public realms. Thus, social capital can play a crucial role by providing norms and networks of trust, reciprocity, and cooperation that facilitate the pursuit of a mutual benefit across multiple and diverse groups (Borzaga and Sforzi, 2014; Sacchetti and Campbell, 2014).

In this framework, limited attention is given to the physical and public spaces within which the social enterprise and its networks are embedded. It hardly addresses critical aspects of social relations, such as underlying motivations, the politics of recognition and identity, the dynamics of conflict and struggle, and the pursuit of generalised participation via alternative values and practices of social ownership. Little is said about the ways in which the social enterprise becomes a source for social change, a force for establishing new ways of doing business, which challenge the primacy of competition and profits over cooperation and social welfare. Where competition and profits prevail, social capital can be used only as a means for more financial gain, instead of being valued as an end in itself. Notably, social capital measures suggested by EU agencies (European Commission, 2014c) tend to focus more on the list of major stakeholders and the ways they participate in a social enterprise's operations and decision-making processes, and less on factors, such as power struggles, identity building, and social learning, which influence values and practices of participation and development within organisations and communities.

Put differently, the framework described above does not take heed of the development models that exist within and outside the social enterprise and the ways these interact in determining its efficiency and sustainability. According to Sacchetti and Campbell (2014), a model of community ownership can create conditions that are more favourable to the promotion of participation and development within and outside social enterprises, compared to a model of community failures. Community ownership is grounded on pro-social values of cooperation, trust and networking, inclusive and creative spaces, public-private synergies, and the satisfaction of community needs via innovative activities, leading to community responsibility and generalised participation. To the contrary, community failures identify with the dominance of individualist values, exclusive and constraining spaces, and particularised interests which foster paternalistic links with powerful groups and state bureaucracy and thus fail to meet community needs, leading to inequality, mistrust, and conflict (Sacchetti and Campbell, 2014, 34–35).

In other words, building a socially beneficial development model requires the participation and cooperation of the broader community in the planning and delivery of services. It depends on the synergy among institutions and organisations functioning across the public and private spheres. To assess the kind of development model that prevails in the locality, researchers, practitioners and policy-makers would need to evaluate and re-define ways in which cooperation and synergy could conceptually and practically be identified. To this end, some studies examine whether certain collective processes have been put in place, particularly those that encourage stakeholders to become actively involved, build cooperative values and institutions, take part in decision-making, and provide efficient and sustainable solutions to social problems (Campbell, 2011; Sacchetti and Campbell, 2014). The case study presented in Section IV elaborates further on these practical issues. At this point it is important to stress that, to avoid reducing networking relations and private-public synergies into a mere means for more financial gain, downplaying the value and pursuit of social objectives, any discussion on social regeneration and social entrepreneurship should move toward a participatory approach.

## Toward a Participatory Approach in the Economy and Society

Galera and Borzaga (2009) stress the various meanings of social enterprise and social entrepreneurship, due to the differential historical, political, and ethical contexts within which they are embedded. They describe two distinct approaches, the US and European approach. The US approach qualifies social enterprises as organisations running commercial activities, which are not necessarily linked to the social mission and are instrumentally employed to fund a social activity. In fact, the existence of an institutional arrangement specifically designed to pursue a social goal is not considered as a necessary condition for being qualified as a social enterprise. There is emphasis on the individual dimension of the "social entrepreneur" as an agent capable of implementing innovative solutions apt to tackle social problems that are overlooked by other actors in a wide variety of fields of general interest. On the other hand, the European approach describes social enterprises as alternative forms of business and social provision, different to those performed by conventional for-profit, non-profit, and public organisations, by combining entrepreneurial operations with the cooperative movement. The distinct feature here is a balance between social and economic dimensions, which is supported by a social and legal institutional framework that sees the social enterprise in its new role as service provider and worker-integration organisation and determines key aspects of its function, such as general-interest objectives, the adoption of a non-distribution constraint, and the participation of major stakeholders.

Yet even within Europe, there is no common definition due to the variety of conceptions, institutions, and practices across countries. In their study, Galera and Borzaga (2009) devise a more encompassing definition whereby social enterprises are conceived as private, autonomous institutions, which engage in the supply of services and goods of general interest in a stable and continuous way. Notably, this definition stresses the idea of "collective entrepreneurship", which focuses on the needs of the most fragile segments of the population, applying non-distribution clauses and adopting participatory governance structures. Thus, it goes beyond the individual aspects and instrumental considerations of the social "manager" in the provision of goods and services. In this way, social enterprises are conceived as specific institutions for social entrepreneurship, which is distinct from commercial entrepreneurship. Though the latter is attracted by large or growing market sizes that might offer profitable opportunities, the former is attracted by an unmet need, demand, or market failure that offers the opportunity for social change. In fact, the authors argue that the upsurge of social enterprises paves the way for alternative perceptions and practices of entrepreneurship where the supply of general-interest goods and services is placed over and above profit maximisation.

An important characteristic of social enterprises, enabling them to deliver social goods and services and create impetus for social change, is their participatory nature and their multi-stakeholder governance structure. In their attempt to theoretically account for the emergence of participatory and multi-stakeholder governance structures in social enterprises, Borzaga and Sacchetti (2015) argue that this is a response to a governance failure rather than a market failure. In mainstream economics, the gap between the public and private spheres of interest and the failure of market and state agents to account for the public dimensions of private choices—the knowledge, needs and interests of numerous stakeholders, including workers, users, suppliers, and the broader community—have created exclusionary governance structures within organisations. These structures concentrate control of strategic decisions within a restricted group and generate negative social effects, including uneven distribution of income, rights, knowledge, and opportunities at a broad societal and spatial scale. In this way, solutions often suggested in mainstream economic theory, like taxation and regulation, cannot be completely effective. The solution lies in revising decision-making processes and governance structures to make them more inclusive and participatory. The social enterprise may be able to provide a solution in this regard by introducing alternative forms of governance, which derive from the cooperative movement and determine the rules and institutions for broader participation and ownership.

Laville and Salmon (2015) suggest a move from conceptions of *"good governance"*, with its neoliberal overtones, to perceptions of *"democratic governance"*, with its emphasis on plurality, participation, deliberation and self-organisation. Third-sector organisations are not considered as a mere response to market and government imperfections. They are seen as a result of the "re-embeddedness" of the economy à la Polanyi to counter the power of capital and money. Thus, the authors challenge the economistic and homogenising view of third-sector organisations à la Hayek and opt for an alternative approach, the solidarity economy, which is constructed on the basis of citizens' initiatives determined not only by considerations of efficiency, but also of legitimacy and meaning. The solidarity economy approach reveals the institutional reality and diversity of third-sector organisations and the ways they are constituted as a hybridisation of the different poles of the economy, namely exchange (market), redistribution (state), and reciprocity (civil society). In this manner, third-sector organisations transcend traditional public-private and market-state dichotomies. What is noteworthy in this analysis is that the solidarity economy is determined by a certain model of society that provides an understanding of the common good, as well as processes of pluralist and deliberative democracy. The authors are also concerned about the new private initiatives of the third sector, which may be perceived and practiced in ways that revert to doing "business as usual", undermining the democratic and participatory processes, which the solidarity economy relies on.

Yet, according to Pestoff (2012), social enterprises have the potential to promote greater citizen involvement and co-production between actors in the public and private spheres. They might fare better than private enterprises, which rely on profit maximisation principles, as well as state organisations, which adopt new public management approaches, transferring the kind of calculative and individualist considerations of private corporations to state welfare agencies. Multi-stakeholder participation and democratic decision-making within social enterprises can be sustained by external rules as well as internal motivations for cooperation, such as solidarity, democracy, and normative considerations for social welfare. Moreover, third-sector organisations like social enterprises take part in the co-production of public services not only in the restricted sense of delivering social services to its members, but also in the broader sense of participating actively in the design and implementation of public policy. This broader meaning of co-production constitutes a kind of co-governance between private, third-sector initiatives and public institutions as a way to respond to the complex, diverse needs and interests emerging in modern societies, especially in a neoliberal environment that opts for the rolling back of the state. Thus, as Pestoff stresses, social enterprises seem to enable a shift from "new public *management*" to "new public *governance*", which implies a more pluralist model of governance and provision of welfare services based on public-private networks, in which citizens have both choice and voice.

Adaman and Devine (2002) delineate a possible way of introducing alternative forms of entrepreneurship that are participatory and democratic. They argue that participatory values and institutions within the enterprise require alternative forms of participatory entrepreneurship, which depend on different organisational structures at the level of the firm, but also at the level of the economy. The authors observe that in economics entrepreneurship is usually identified with innovative activity in conditions of uncertainty. However, by critically reviewing the neoclassical, Austrian, and Schumpeterian schools, as well as modern competence theories, they find that these approaches do not discuss how the entrepreneurial function is embedded in different types of organisational structures at both micro and macro levels and how these interact with one another to produce change and development at the level of the firm and the economy. Innovation and entrepreneurship must be understood as social processes of knowledge, learning, and re-constitution, where means-ends structures are not given and have to be set up by agents themselves. In this context, the entrepreneur's job is to nurture the firm's discursive practices; to develop a consensus around the new means-ends structures that emerge; and to promote the specific organisational forms that manage these processes and produce beneficial outcomes at the level of the firm and the economy as a whole.

In their study, Adaman and Devine (2002) argue that a participatory economic system, via principles and institutions of generalised participation and social ownership, may mobilise knowledge more efficiently and thus may consciously shape economic change to serve social welfare. To the contrary, the capitalist system may prevent actors from achieving the efficient mobilisation of knowledge, due to private ownership and the one-dimensional criterion of profitability. In particular, a participatory economic system "is defined as an interlocking network of social relationships, mediated through a set of interlocking institutions, in which the values and interests of people in the different aspects of their lives interact and shape one another in a discursive process of decision-making through negotiation and cooperation". Generalised participation is identified as "the direct or indirect involvement in social practice, on an equal footing, of all those with either a relevant input to contribute or a legitimate interest in the outcome, i.e. all those who are affected by an activity". Social ownership is considered "the institutional form corresponding to generalised participation" and implies "ownership by those with an interest in the use of the assets involved in the activity in question" (Adaman and Devine, 2002, 345). The process of negotiated coordination is envisaged as being mediated through an inter-locking set of institutions which extend beyond the firm and is constituted at different levels—industry or sector, locality, national region, nation, inter-national region, global—with an aim to jointly determine the allocation of resources within and across firms in the economy (Adaman and Devine, 2002, 347).

In this way, participatory entrepreneurship embraces both the firm, as the institution within which entrepreneurial activity results in innovative output, as well as the extra-firm processes and institutions that allocate capital across firms for future entrepreneurial activity. The process of nego-tiated coordination would make it possible for competition to be combined with cooperation. Moreover, it could create "an ethos, a moral community, in which responsibility and accountability to others is part of the gener-ally accepted underlying assumptions for social-including economic-life" (Adaman and Devine, 2002, 351).

This chapter suggests that a vision for a participatory system could truly inspire modern-day social enterprises in pursuing their objectives and bring-ing about social regeneration. Additionally, it argues that social capital can further help build the norms and networks of trust, reciprocity, and coop-eration that support multi-stakeholder governance structures, democratic decision-making processes, and negotiated coordination systems within social enterprises and the economy at large. It potentially provides the moti-vations and channels for knowledge exchange, social learning, inclusive and pluralist networks, and discussion on the means and ends of development and welfare. The case study presented in the following section empirically investigates the relationship between social enterprise and social regenera-tion via the concept of social capital.

## An Example from Greece: The Case of "Eu Zin"[1]

### *Methodology*

The case study focused on the organisation "Eu Zin" ("Ευ Ζην", meaning "Well Being"). "Eu Zin" is a work integration social cooperative enterprise[2] and aims at the rehabilitation and employment of people with mental health problems who have limited access to the labour market. This section exam-ines the sustainability and social impact of "Eu Zin" in relation to the social capital it has access to, within and outside the organisation, in order to determine its participatory nature and its potential for social regeneration. A variant of the community development framework used by Sacchetti and Campbell (2014) is applied to examine the role of social capital in the social enterprise. Thus, social capital is studied with regard to: the social values and needs addressed by the organisation; the collaborations and networks developed and pursued within and outside the organisation; and its social impact on members and the broader society. The case study uses information from printed and electronic material prepared by the organisation and made publicly available via brochures and the social media.[3] Further details were provided by Ms. Nikolaou, the chairwoman of the organisation, via in-depth interviews conducted during the course of several meetings between September 2015 and December 2016.

"Eu Zin" was selected for several reasons. One reason is that "Eu Zin" is among the first social enterprises to be founded in Greece. It has been in business for more than a decade and has successfully been serving its social mission. Thus, it is aware not only of the difficulties but also of the possibilities that social enterprises encounter in their pursuit of economic and social objectives, especially in a country dealing with debt crisis and austerity. Second, it provides an abundance of printed and electronic material, including annual financial and social account statements, organisational charts, SWOT analyses, and business plans used to systematically assess and publicly communicate information regarding the cost effectiveness and social impact of the organisation. Third, Ms. Nikolaou is a founding member and elected chairwoman of the organisation, as well as the Secretary of the Greek confederation of work integration social enterprises in the field of mental health, so she is well aware of the conditions that social enterprises face in Greece. She was particularly keen to participate in the study, believing that scientific research and knowledge generate added value for social enterprises.

Finally, the study presented here is of further interest because concepts of social economy and social entrepreneurship have recently gained increasing attention in Greece in the post-crisis era. They are often seen by researchers and policy-makers at the national and EU levels as a solution to rising unemployment, particularly among young people, social exclusion, and poverty. In fact, they are at the heart of EU Cohesion Policy and the National Partnership Agreement for the programming period 2014–2020, which is one of the few remaining sources of funds for public investments in the country, due to fiscal consolidation. The new law on social and solidarity economy in Greece reflects the legal and policy framework, which has been set by EU bodies and is linked to the socio-economic goals of the Europe 2020 Strategy for sustainable development and social inclusion. At the same time, despite the country's long cooperative tradition,[4] social entrepreneurship is a relatively new phenomenon, which poses further challenges in efforts to cultivate participatory principles and structures and thus enhance the sustainability of social enterprises.

*Description*

Before assessing the sustainability and social impact of "Eu Zin", it would be useful to briefly describe its operations and progress. The organisation was founded in 2005 as a Limited Liability Social Cooperative (KOISPE) under the Law 2716/1999 regarding reforms in the national mental health system. The 1999 Law particularly emphasised the reintegration of individuals with mental health problems in the labour market through economic activity and sustainable development with a view to de-institutionalise and de-stigmatise these groups. Under Law 4013/2011 on the social economy and social entrepreneurship, as well as the more recent Law 4430/2016 on the social and solidarity economy, KOISPE are automatically and legally considered as a Social Cooperative Enterprise (KOINSEP) specialising in work integration. According to these laws, a Work Integration KOINSEP aims at the economic and social rehabilitation and reintegration of vulnerable groups, who have limited access to the labour market, by combining social objectives (solidarity, investment in civil society, Corporate Social Responsibility) and economic objectives (quality services and economic competitiveness).

At the time of writing "Eu Zin" had 83 members, of which over 50% are individuals with mental health problems. It employed in total 20 young people with mental health problems and 16 people from the general population with a focus on vulnerable groups (e.g., a single mother with limited resources). The organisation operates in the following sectors: Food and Catering services (including catering for personal and business events, three Social Kitchens and a School Meal Programme); Cleaning Services; and Travel Consultancy Services for Vulnerable Groups. Its headquarters are located in an urban area near the capital of Athens, but it also maintains stores in other sub-urban areas mainly via its social kitchens.

The organisation's socio-economic performance is assessed on the basis of account statements that show its turnover, employment, and profits. During the period 2010–2015, the annual changes in turnover, employment, and profits were, on average, 11.6%, 30.6%, and 25.8%, respectively. Turnover and employment were steadily rising till 2013. After a fall in employment in 2014, there was a significant increase in the past year, due to the expansion of the organisation's activities by opening a new social kitchen. As a result of its social obligations as a cooperative and the corresponding provisions of the law, profits are reinvested in the organisation. Though profits fell soon after the crisis broke out in Greece in 2010, they increased significantly in 2012. In the past year, the organisation undertook new activities, so profits were negative. However, it is clear that the crisis did not hold the organisation back, but rather mobilised it to look for dynamic solutions in order to maintain its competitiveness in the market and meet its social goals for work integration and social inclusion.

The competitiveness of a social enterprise is of particular importance. As Ms. Nikolaou stressed, competitiveness does not simply translate into a constant flow of profits; it also ensures permanent employment and continuous training for people with mental health problems. "Eu Zin" operates first and foremost as a mental health unit under the 1999 Law for national reforms in the field of mental health. Thus, the cooperative does not merely undertake the provision of specialised services that the market and state fail to offer; it contributes to public policy in mental health.

## Participatory Action and Social Impact

### Social Values and Needs

The cooperative's website reads that its primary objective is not profit, but investing in solidarity, civil society, and Corporate Social Responsibility. It states that concerned citizens and individuals with mental health problems come together and collaborate with one another to create a cooperative that offers work to members of vulnerable groups who have limited access to the labour market. These objectives are summarised in the cooperative's slogan: *We engage in enterprise[5] together for a society with a human face, by investing in the strength of society.*

As described by Ms. Nikolaou, "Eu Zin" was founded on the need to improve our knowledge and skills for supporting people with mental health problems by preparing them to work, placing them in a job and helping them keep the job. Before the Law of 1999 and the establishment of the first KOISPE in 2002, the mental health environment involved sheltered workshops, which offered training and enabled trainees to produce and sell products in a rather informal way without maintaining a shop, or hiring paid work, or registering with tax services. Despite improvements in social reintegration, relapse prevention, and the overall therapeutic target, there was still a huge gap:

> All these efforts did not ensure continuity. It was like placing a person on top of a mountain and leaving him without a parachute at the edge of the cliff. . . . In other words, the resources that were invested, all the work that was done, would actually start to slowly disappear. Therefore, resources were not being capitalised and specialised knowledge and skills were not being developed.

When asked why the founding members of "Eu Zin" chose the legal form of KOISPE rather than that of a for-profit enterprise or a non-profit organisation, Ms. Nikolaou replied that it was the best option given some of the privileges that the law offered at various levels. For example, users of mental health services working at the organisation would equally participate in employment and decision-making mechanisms and not forego social benefits and pensions received by the state. Indeed, she finds that the 1999 Law is quite innovative, even to this day, because it shows "the ideological context within which the field of mental health is placed and which supports values of solidarity and equal participation in society . . ." In fact, in 2007 this law was awarded the title of European "best practice" in public policy for the economic and social inclusion of vulnerable groups.

However, in the beginning, there were difficulties. As Ms. Nikolaou explained, "Eu Zin" was one of the first founded KOISPE in Greece, and the specific institutional framework was being implemented for the first time. Social entrepreneurship was a novel way of understanding and doing business, so prior knowledge and experience were practically absent, especially for the founding members of the organisation. Actually: "It was a step to nowhere . . .".

The organisation managed to confront difficulties and become successful, even in the midst of the crisis. According to Ms. Nikolaou, major success factors include the members' vision, dedication, and determination to create a solidarity society, support vulnerable groups, and fulfil their social mission. This is consistent with the profile of a social entrepreneur who channels personal knowledge and skills to serve the general interest, inspire others to join and pursue social objectives, and create partnerships and networks within and outside the organisation to enhance generalised participation.

*Collaborations and Networks Within and Outside the Organisation*

Within the organisation, the active participation and collaboration of members enables the cooperative to fulfil its work integration objectives. The cooperative adopts and implements a Model of Supported Employment for individuals with mental health problems. As described by Ms. Nikolaou:

> Work integration requires a specialised, scientific methodology that prepares and supports users of mental health services. In this process, it is important to look for the best possible match between the professional profile of the candidate and the job position. Those two parameters considerably contribute to the two basic indicators of the quality of employment: satisfaction and continuity [for users of mental health services] . . . Working has a therapeutic effect on all of us. This is particularly true for those who have mental health problems, because working enhances their image and their self-esteem . . .

Hence, the organisation's sustainability significantly depends on the effectiveness of this model "to support and prepare users to accept the job and participate in a productive and solidaristic manner". The productivity of users could be stabilised, but usually falls short of the productivity of individuals who do not face health problems. So, for example: "Today one [user] can produce 200 dishes in three hours, but tomorrow or for ten days one cannot even produce 20". And this kind of variation and temporary loss in the organisation must be instantly and effectively managed and replaced, so it will not adversely affect the organisation's sustainability in the long-run. For "Eu Zin", a major obstacle in this process was the absence of specific entrepreneurship skills and know-how, because the education system in Greece does not have degree programmes in social management. Most professionals working in the particular organisation specialised in mental health and voluntarily invested considerable time and effort to learn how to manage a business and make their way around the market.

In the organisation's decision-making mechanisms, one member has one vote, regardless of shares. Furthermore, two of the board members are users of mental health services. These outcomes are determined by relevant legislation, but are also in line with the principles of cooperative and democratic participation. Apart from that, there are no formal, institutionalised decision-making processes that include all interested parties other than the members of the organisation. However, in the past, "Eu Zin" has participated, without a vote, in discussions with local community networks and local government bodies in order to exchange views and contribute to the development of broader public-private partnerships.

Beyond the organisation, "Eu Zin" aims at expanding and establishing public-private synergies, collaborative networks, and partnerships with customers, suppliers, other social economy organisations, and public authorities, as well as members of the broader community who believe in the organisation's vision and actively support it.

At its inception, "Eu Zin" was actively supported by the Greek Mental Health and Research Centre (EKEPSYE),[6] a private charitable organisation, which is the largest provider of outpatient mental health services nation-wide and represents the country as a voting member at the World Federation for Mental Health. The organisation's founding members—both mental health professionals and users of mental health services—came from the vocational training workshops of EKEPSYE, which constitutes an umbrella-institution and continues to support "Eu Zin" by supplying facilities and staff.

Among its variant operations, "Eu Zin" maintains three social kitchens that prepare traditional, home-made food and are located in different sub-urban areas of Athens. According to Ms. Nikolaou, the success of this project relies on the supply of quality food at social prices, targeting mainly low-income groups, such as pensioners, students, and families with unemployed individuals, who were severely affected by the Greek crisis. It was also based on a favourable customer response motivated by a sense of social responsibility and solidarity. Apparently, the crisis led to an increase in cooperation and solidarity among members of the local community, which reveals that consumers' motivations are driven by both economic and social considerations.

To cover the initial capital required mainly for physical infrastructure, the organisation relied on private and public grants supporting social responsibility and development initiatives. These grants were offered by the VINCI Foundation, the Central Bank of Greece, the National Bank of Greece, the Development Partnership "Synergy" of the Community Initiative EQUAL, as well as other programmes supported by the European Structural Funds. In 2016, "Eu Zin" opened its third social kitchen in Chalandri in collaboration with the municipality, which is the first to cooperate with a KOISPE in Greece. During the same year, "Eu Zin" started collaborating with the

Ministry of Labour and the National Bank of Greece (via its crowdfunding project "Act for Greece") in setting up a School Meals Programme in order to deal with the deterioration of household incomes and their children's nutrition in the post-crisis period. For this programme, "Eu Zin" prepares and distributes 1,130 portions of food daily to schools in the Attica region.

In Greece, sources of funding for social enterprises are limited, while markets for social impact investments are non-existent. Provisions for the establishment of a Social Economy Fund in Law 4019/2011 and Law 4430/2016 have not yet been realised. Also, there is no specific institutional framework for the establishment and operation of micro-financing networks, despite proclamations in the Strategic Actions for the social economy developed by supranational, national, and local administrative bodies. Finally, traditional banking and financial institutions rarely have corporate social responsibility programmes targeted at social economy organisations and activities.

There are official collective bodies through which KOISPE and KOINSEP social enterprises are represented at the national level, as well as cooperation networks between social enterprises (e.g., KOINSEP Network). Members of these bodies and networks can exchange experiences and good practices, create partnerships for the provision of goods and services, and organise collectively in order to address social problems and voice social demands, including those faced by social enterprises in setting up their operations and delivering goods and services. Ms. Nikolaou, as secretary of the confederation of KOISPE, explained that they are keen on collaborating with universities and educational institutions in producing scientific knowledge in order to provide answers to the practical problems and daily needs faced by these organisations.

Generally, what is needed, according to Ms. Nikolaou, is a support mechanism that would provide social enterprises with advisory and educational services and opportunities for building networks and partnerships with other private and public institutions. In 2014, the Ministry of Labour announced the creation of mechanisms to support the promotion and development of KOINSEP and the social economy at the national and regional level. The announcement stipulated that these support mechanisms should adopt principles of generalised participation, multi-level governance, and bottom-up initiatives. However, the outcome of these mechanisms remains to be seen.

Social economy and social entrepreneurship also rely on state support. The state should not affect the autonomy of these organisations and undermine their efforts to serve economic and social goals. As argued above, this means that the role of the state should also be re-assessed and re-defined on the basis of participatory and redistributive principles, rather than the individualist and calculative principles dictated by prevailing new public management approaches. In Greece, state support seems to be troublous. As Ms. Nikolaou pointed out, after the crisis broke out, the austerity measures of the fiscal consolidation programme have significantly reduced public support to "Eu Zin", both financial and in kind. Furthermore, there were significant delays in public funds in development programmes in which the organisation had participated. Finally, the legal framework raises critical issues for the organisation. "Eu Zin" is both a social cooperative enterprise and a mental health unit, so as a KOISPE, it is accountable to the Ministry of Health, in accordance with the Law of 1999, and as a Work Integration KOINSEP, it is accountable to the Ministry of Labour, in accordance with the laws of 2011 and 2016. As Ms. Nikolaou distinctly stated, "in fact, we have two 'dads' . . ." She continued saying that it is important to maintain the distinct role of KOISPE as mental health units, while at the same time broadening its participatory basis to insure collective and social solidarity. But she believes that most of these problems will be addressed in large part, if the provisions of the new law of 2016 are implemented regarding the specialised funding agencies and financial institutions, the support mechanisms of social entrepreneurship, and public procurement aimed at social economy organisations serving social objectives.

*Social Impact*

According to Ms. Nikolaou, the social effects of "Eu Zin" briefly include increasing the employment of users, promoting de-institutionalisation in the field of mental health and building a solidarity society. In spite of deep recession, capital controls, and fierce competition from large companies operating at the national and global levels, the organisation continued to offer its services, produce liquidity, and expand its activities in different sectors by opening new shops.

Ms. Nikolaou explained that the source of their success could be found in the organisation's competitive advantages, which had a significant social impact both within the organisation and within the broader community. These advantages can be summarised as follows:

- *The organised and specialised efforts to prepare users of mental health services via the Model of Supported Employment, which aims at creating jobs with social and therapeutic benefits.* With this model, users: acquire knowledge and skills; become actively involved in production and in the labour market; acquire income and self-confidence; equally and jointly take part in making decisions regarding the organisation's operations; contribute to the development of social entrepreneurship and the welfare of the local community; provide for other vulnerable, socially excluded groups (via the social kitchens, for example); and help society see them "through different eyes". In this manner, the organisation secures employment and de-institutionalisation.
- *The pursuit of balanced partnerships between the private and public spheres, even in the midst of the crisis.* Collaborative networks and generalised participation might have played a crucial role in ensuring

the sustainability of the organisation where effective mechanisms that foster a solidarity society were absent. They enable social enterprises to realise their added value in the economy and society, to raise community awareness regarding their social objectives, and to gain recognition for their contribution to the general interest. In this way, social enterprises manage to de-stigmatise social entrepreneurship and remove doubts about its ability and commitment to consistently serve both economic and social objectives.

- *The organisation's passion, love, and orientation toward its social objectives that help them cope with adversities and commit to their social mission and ideology.* These factors made up for the lack of expertise in social entrepreneurship, allowing members of the organisation to gradually obtain the specialised knowledge and skills they needed via processes of learning and reflection. In other words, those who had the initiative to create "Eu Zin" collaborated in developing new skills and potential in the market, which enhanced the organisation's sustainability.

Furthermore, it should be noted that commonly accepted methods and tools for the evaluation of cooperatives' social impact are not widely used in Greece. The relevant legislation requires all KOINSEP to write up annual accounting and programming statements, which are submitted to the Ministry of Labour. For the first time, the new Law 4430/2016 defines the concept of "social impact" as the collective and social benefits produced by the organisation, the former referring to benefits that accrue to the collective of the organisation, and the latter concerning benefits to community development, including environmental protection, the provision of social goods and services, and the creation of values and institutions of cooperation and participation. However, it provides no detailed description of the methods that can be used to measure social impacts. The problem was pointed out by Ms. Nikolaou who looked for appropriate tools to measure the quantitative and qualitative dimensions of users' employment and the social impact of the organisation.

Overall, despite difficulties in combining economic and social objectives in a competitive market, this combination may become the driving force of the organisation's sustainability as long as it fosters a social vision, collaborative networks within and outside the organisation, continuous support to users of mental health services, and a steady orientation toward its dual role, as an enterprise and health unit. These are elements which characterise the participatory spirit of the social enterprise and lead to social regeneration.

## Conclusions

This chapter addressed the ways in which social enterprises can build social capital and sustain the capacity of the organisation and locality for social regeneration as a path toward a participatory economic system. It began with a theoretical discussion regarding social enterprises and their role in social regeneration and a participatory economic system by focusing on the important, yet understudied, contribution of social capital in these processes. Then it presented an empirical investigation of the actual potential of a social enterprise to contribute to social regeneration and a participatory economic system via social capital by presenting preliminary results of a case study conducted in Greece. The social economy and social entrepreneurship are considered important in dealing with the crisis in the country.

The main conclusion is that an environment characterised by competitive markets, welfare state retrenchment, and the European and global financial crises may threaten the sustainability and effectiveness of entrepreneurial endeavours and policy initiatives with a "social face". However, social enterprises may have the potential to promote social regeneration and community development precisely because they are founded on the pursuit of economic objectives in conjunction with social priorities that favour the provision of social goods in a participatory and democratic system of governance and ownership. To achieve this outcome, as argued in this chapter, certain conditions must be met: social entrepreneurship should be understood and practiced with a view toward a participatory economic system, which relies on generalised participation, social ownership, and negotiated coordination within and across firms. Various aspects of social capital, such as social values and collaborative networks within and outside organisations, enable social enterprises to build participatory principles and institutions, to serve the general interest, and to produce palpable social outcomes in the form of the provision of social goods and the inclusion of disadvantaged groups. As evidenced in the chapter, these elements were present in "Eu Zin" and considerably contributed to its economic—and social—success.

Evidently, there is still a long way to go in establishing a participatory economic system that will support social entrepreneurial activities and social regeneration. On the one hand, social enterprises in Greece face serious obstacles, due to the crisis and the absence of support mechanisms. According to data from the Social Economy Register, only a small share of social enterprises is a Work Integration KOINSEP, far less than those designated by the national plan for mental health services (one KOISPE for each municipality), and therefore fewer than those required to cope with the magnitude and diversity of social needs across the country (Balourdos and Geormas, 2012; Nasioulas and Mavroeidis, 2013; European Commission, 2014b). On the other hand, social enterprises everywhere may as well be up against the pressures of a national and global economic system where financial gain still prevails over social welfare, and collective mechanisms of collaboration and coordination on the basis of generalised participation and social ownership are still lacking. Further studies in different countries and sectors could shed light on the variant ways that social enterprises can exploit opportunities and overcome threats in pursuing their objectives via the expansion of social capital.[7]

Yet it is worth noting that for Ms. Nikolaou, collective determination and commitment to a social vision were the organisation's driving forces, leading to success against all odds. On many occasions during the interviews, she would correct the researchers and insist they use the term "solidarity *society*" instead of "solidarity *economy*" to represent the organisation's main goals. Perhaps this is not simply a matter of linguistic style or marketing rhetoric; it specifies that the ultimate goal is *social change*, gearing the organisation's collective efforts, entrepreneurial strategies, and daily operations toward that goal.

## Notes

1. I am very grateful to Ms. Paula Nikolaou and everyone at "Eu Zin" for graciously sharing their time and stories and making our meetings a truly enlightening experience. I also extend my thanks to Prof. Yannis Caloghirou and his team at the "Innovation and Entrepreneurship Unit" of the National Technical University of Athens for their kind support, scientific and financial, in carrying out this study.
2. As mentioned later in the chapter, "Eu Zin" was founded under the legal form of what is termed a *limited liability social cooperative*. According to the new law, it is also considered what is termed a *social cooperative enterprise*. In discussions with members, it was stressed that given the cooperative values and structures adopted by the organisation, legally and practically (e.g., general assembly, cooperative shares), they identify more with a *social cooperative*, which they feel belongs to the broader spectrum of social entrepreneurship. Thus, the term *cooperative* will be used hereon in specific references to "Eu Zin".
3. www.koispe-euzin.gr; www.facebook.com/koispe.evzin.
4. The CIRIEC study considers *The Common Company of Ampelakia* as the first modern cooperative in the world founded between 1750 and 1770 in the Greek Tempi area (CIRIEC, 2012, 13, footnote 1).
5. In Greek, "επιχειρούμε" does not only mean "we engage in enterprise", but also "we make a (joint) effort".
6. www.ekepsye.gr.
7. For example, see Sacchetti (2016) for a study in Italy on work integration social enterprises in the field of health.

## References

Adaman, F., and P. Devine. 2002. "A Reconsideration of the Theory of Entrepreneurship: A Participatory Approach." *Review of Political Economy*, 14(3): 329–355.
Balourdos, D., and K. Geormas. 2012. "Social Economy in Greece: From Childhood to Adolescent." Paper prepared for the *Peer Review in Social Protection and Social Inclusion Programme Coordinated by ÖSB Consulting, the Institute for Employment Studies (IES) and Applica*, and funded by the European Commission.
Borzaga, C., and S. Sacchetti. 2015. "Why Social Enterprises Are Asking to Be Multi-stakeholder and Deliberative: An Explanation Around the Costs of Exclusion." *Euricse Working Papers*, 75|15.
Borzaga, C., and J. Sforzi. 2014. "Social Capital, Cooperatives, and Social Enterprises." In *Social Capital and Economics: Social Values, Power and Social*

*Identity*, edited by Asimina Christoforou and John B. Davis, 193–214. London and New York: Routledge.

Campbell, P. 2011. *Community-led Regeneration: A Review of the Literature*. Scotland: Scottish Government Social Research.

European Commission. 2011. *Social Business Initiative, Creating a Favourable Climate for Social Enterprises, Key Stakeholders in the Social Economy and Innovation*. COM(2011) 682 final.

European Commission. 2014a. *A Map of Social Enterprises and their Eco-systems in Europe, Synthesis Report*. ICF Consulting Services.

European Commission. 2014b. *A Map of Social Enterprises and their Eco-systems in Europe, Country Report: Greece*. ICF Consulting Services.

European Commission. 2014c. *Proposed Approaches to Social Impact Measurement*. GECES Expert Sub-group on Social Impact Measurement.

Galera, G., and C. Borzaga. 2009. "Social Enterprise: An International Overview of Its Conceptual Evolution and Legal Implementation." *Social Enterprise Journal*, 5(3): 210–228.

Ginsberg, N. 1999. "Putting the Social Into Urban Regeneration Policy." *Local Economy*, 14(1): 55–71.

International Centre of Research and Information on the Public, Social and Cooperative Economy (CIRIEC). 2012. *The Social Economy in the European Union*. The European Economic and Social Committee.

Laville, J.-L., and A. Salmon. 2015. "Rethinking the Relationship Between Governance and Democracy: The Theoretical Framework of the Solidarity Economy." In *Civil Society, the Third Sector and Social Enterprise: Governance and Democracy*, edited by Jean-Louis Laville, Dennis R. Young and Philippe Eynaud, 145–162. London and New York: Routledge.

Nasioulas, I., and V. Mavroeidis. 2013. "The Social Business Sector in Greece, Systematic Failures and Positive Action Potentials Based on Strengths of the Hellenic Ministry of Development and Competitiveness." *European Commission, Social Business Initiative Group of Experts on Social Entrepreneurship (GECES)*, Report 10#.

Pestoff, V. 2012. "Co-production and Third Sector Social Services in Europe: Some Concepts and Evidence." *Voluntas*, 23: 1102–1118.

Sacchetti, S. 2016. "Governance for a 'Socialised Economy'. A Case Study in Preventative Health and Work Integration." *Euricse Working Papers*, 89|16.

Sacchetti, S., and C. Campbell. 2014. "Creating Space for Communities: Social Enterprise and the Bright Side of Social Capital." *Journal of Entrepreneurial and Organisational Diversity*, 3(2): 32–48.

Vienney, C. 1994/2008. *The Social Economy*. Athens: Polytropon (in Greek).

# 4 Regenerating the Commons

## Policy Design Models Beyond CSR

*Francesca Battistoni, Paolo Cottino, and Flaviano Zandonai*

## Introduction: The Commons as a New Paradigm?

The emphasis on the search for a new paradigm—i.e. a set of meanings from which an overall vision and an organisational model of the society are generated—is indicative of momentous transformations redefining relations between individuals and the basis of institutions. It is in this perspective that we may frame the growing interest in "common goods". Common goods are being employed as an archetype to interpret the changes in political systems and economic models and, therefore, to identify the need of innovation in the governance's and management's tools, in order to promote a new model of development based on a more complex notion of "well-being" and "integral human development" (Bruni and Zamagni, 2013). In particular, the idea that the collective interest may and must be satisfied by searching for direct synergies between resources and different stakeholders' expectations leads to a shift in perspective, which involves not only the domain of public policies in the strict sense, but generally all those tools regulating and organising the relation among different actors, as well as their relationship with their context.

The goal of this paper is to analyse the solicitations to which the social function of enterprises is subjected within this emerging paradigm. With regard to the implementation of new and more effective systems of production of social value in localised socio-economic contexts, it is clear that traditional Corporate Social Responsibility (CSR) policies show the limits of a mostly passive attitude towards the external world (between ethical certification—or lack of ethical nature—of business behaviours and the philanthropic contribution of actions promoted and led by non-profit actors) without direct accountability (Garriga and Melé, 2004). It is also clear that the time is ripe for models and processes of social value production based on a more systematic cooperation between enterprises with different stakeholders, putting into play not only mere externalities, but also their core business, in order to increase efficiency and competitiveness. In this sense, enterprises are fostered to adopt a long-term strategic approach overcoming CSR in order to create a value that can be shared by all stakeholders (Porter and Kramer, 2006).

The field of urban regeneration, considered as a context of re-organisation of relations between space and actors in the city by creating new synergies, defines a promising context to cultivate this perspective. Indeed, given the new focus on the territory promoted by economic institutions, any intervention for the renovation of inherited real estate and abandoned or underused spaces is an interesting opportunity in which companies, though gradually and with outcomes that are not yet consolidated into real business models, could invest to pursue forms of integration and synergy between their own mission and "general interest" goals. Specifically, considering the case of the recovery of unused railway stations as community assets promoted by the Ferrovie dello Stato Italiane, it is possible to highlight both the limitations of an approach inspired by a logic of compensation and the elements of challenge and added value that could result from the recovery of such property for a social use within the new value chains. We speak of a value that is inherently multidimensional and better (or shared) distributed among by a number of different actors. The importance of this challenge also increases because of the need to attract dedicated financial resources, in order to scale up the social impact of initiatives that at present are extremely localised and specific. From this point of view, impact investing represents another variable in understanding the conditions that influences the social goal of entrepreneurial action in the domain of common goods and the synergy with other more localised financing tools like grants and donations (Boiardi and Gianoncelli, 2016). This variable is important for two reasons: 1) the evident availability of resources; 2) the evaluation tools of financial products assign value also to intangible resources and play a key role in regeneration processes, where social entrepreneurship are often invoked but not always put into practice (Warren and Jones, 2015). These topics are undoubtedly ambivalent, but they are also introducing positive discontinuities in a field whose narration is scattered with good practices, which are now becoming a real industry. This brings to the fore not only efficiency issues and scale economies, but also the challenge of a growing offer of spaces, whose state of abandon or lack of use coincides more and more often with a deficit in their collective use.

The first part of the chapter reconstructs the recent debate on the transformations that concern, on the one hand, CSR strategies of for-profit firms and, on the other hand, the entrepreneurial evolution in the field of nonprofit organisations, highlighting ambivalent elements of convergence and divergence of this processes. The second part analyses the relation between enterprise and social and economic local context, considering "the territory" not as an unchanging background and taken for granted, but as a factor still relevant for chains that recombine economic and social value, in particular considering initiatives of regeneration of real estate assets for purposes of collective interest. The third part of this chapter deepens opportunities and risks, with reference to the financial solutions for social regeneration processes, which involve coalitions of different actors: individuals and associates, public and private institutions, and non-profit and for-profit enterprises. From this point of view, we will analyse, in the fourth part, the case of the social regeneration of railway assets in Italy, highlighting the still partial successes of this strategy. Finally, we suggest some conclusive considerations about tools and approaches useful to draw new strategies and policies that strengthen the role of social regeneration, as a "engine" for a new, place-based development model.

## The "Cooperative Race" for Social Value

The structural transformations that characterize this historical period are more and more determined by institutions' and various organisations' capability to acquire new chains of value creation, wherein the elements of social value assume an ever-growing importance (Mulgan, 2010). In particular, the social dimension is less and less an "oligopoly" of public and non-profit institutions and is getting closer to the varied world of enterprises, not only those that are motivated by an explicit social mission, but also those that operate within mainstream economy, are profit-oriented, and are active on a global scale (Porter and Kramer, 2006). This openness of the field of social value creation fosters both juridical forms and underlying regulatory mechanisms: in this perspective, the social dimension can be generated not only through mechanisms of public redistribution and informal reciprocity (Polanyi, 1971), but also through market transaction, particularly in the domain of service economies. This new "great transformation" redefines, with remarkably ambivalent features, the relationship between the market and social dynamics. In fact, it is not clear to what extent the market as an institution will recover those elements of sociality it progressively abandoned or, on the contrary, whether an efficiency-driven process will lead market institutions to progressively integrate a significant element of sociality into their business models (Pais and Provasi, 2015). The origin and probably the outcome of this process are largely linked to changes occurring within consumption models which, in a more systematic and broader way, are questioning quality that is influenced by variables of social and environmental sustainability (Arvidsson, 2008). Those transformations in consumption are, in turn, not exclusively connected to individual choices but rather to the development of new sociality pattern concerning: i) the adoption of lifestyles determined by new forms of vulnerability (Deaton, 2013); ii) the emergence of new forms of collective action aiming at "voice" but also production on a collaborative basis (Manzini, 2015); and iii) the dissemination, as an element of transversal empowerment, of information and knowledge technologies which are now usable as commodities and operate as facilitators of networks within society (Benkler, 2016).

The combined effect of these factors allows, in the first place, to segment the social field into three macro dimensions, which lead to a framework that determines new ways of producing economic value.

The first dimension corresponds to an interpretation of the concept of social value as a production of collective interest goods with accentuated features of meritocracy (Borzaga and Zandonai, 2009). This is the field where non-lucrative organisations operate and over time have acquired an entrepreneurial structure to produce goods and services, whose character of "social utility" is linked to the existence of a relatively widespread consensus on the fact that these goods satisfy requirements of social justice. These goods may be enjoyed especially by people who, for different reasons, do not own sufficient resources (in monetary, informations and competences terms) to acquire them by standard market exchanges. This is the case, for example, of social enterprises particularly in the field of work inclusion (WISE) which, progressively, spread both on an Italian and European level thanks to a *sui generis* entrepreneurial model which is characterised by the following features (European Commission, 2016):

1. Enterprises specify their function, by claiming their social nature through the pursuit of a "general interest" objective.
2. Inclusive models of governance are adopted, thus allowing different stakeholders to participate in management, with the aim not to maximise a specific (economic, professional, political) interest, but rather on the basis of a relevant objective which is the outcome of a sharing process. Inclusion increases the degree of sharing and creates a common ground to realise a real social impact whose benefits may be redistributed on a wide scale (Borzaga and Galera, 2016).
3. The continuity of production, which is linked to the capacity of these organisations to intercept and combine a mix of resources: economic and non-economic, market-based or donations, public and private (Nyssens, 2006).

The second social dimension may concern the contribution of traditional economies and enterprises to the creation and strengthening of social cohesion, especially on a local scale. This field is especially characterised by small and medium enterprises, capable of valorising the material and immaterial assets included in specific geographical, social, and anthropological contexts (Putnam et al., 1993). The more an entrepreneurial action is pursued through an intentional strategy of opening towards the territory—in particular, by redistributing and generating positive externalities—the it contributes to a business dimension. This is evident in recent surveys of Italian enterprises, whose "cohesive" nature contributed to the realisation of better economic and occupational performance (Fondazione Symbola, 2014).

The third social dimension stems from the progressive diffusion of the co-production paradigm, which is based on the systematic participation of all users, consumers, and beneficiaries as co-producers of the goods and services used. We are referring to complex processes concerning different areas of intervention mainly managed by non-profit organizations, but where an important element consist in the participation strategies adopted by enterprises. These enterprises are usually large companies which invest in platform technologies and are able to exploit the prototypes of devices and software, because they have an immediate feedback system and the opportunity to access information and source codes, fostering cooperative and bottom-up production (Arvidsson and Giordano, 2013).

These macro areas are characterised by a number of peculiarities and overlaps, and they all emphasise a model of "social enterprise" or "social business" defined in a rather different way, which may lead to terminological and conceptual misunderstandings (Guida and Maiolini, 2014). In the case of production of collective interest goods, for example, a model of social enterprise is proposed, which has an explicit influence on objectives, governance, and production, thus acquiring features of a *sui generis* institution with specific juridical forms (Borzaga and Galera, 2016). In the case of cohesion generation on a local scale, the enterprise is social because it adopts orientations and behaviours where owners do not pursue interest maximisation through "low profit" models, and, thanks to specific benchmark, it maximises the impact of those positive externalities which were realised by juridical models such as that of a benefit corporation (Honeyman, 2014). Finally, the systematic application of co-production strategies recalls a model of "social enterprise" that further makes reference to the use of technologies capable of developing the relations between various subjects in a dialogical sense, thus impacting, in many cases, on organisational models (Benkler, 2016). Accordingly, at a micro level, co-production itself generates new streams of community entrepreneurship (Mori, 2017), which periodically develop in different territories and socio-economic contexts, such as the case of community assets regeneration, as we discuss in the following paragraphs. Besides relevant differences, all these experiences of social entrepreneurship deviate from traditional policies of CSR.

The first element of deviation consists in the fact that these different ways of organising and managing social value production seek elements of continuity and centrality within business models. If the goal of CSR policies is to play an advocacy role within the enterprise and with main stakeholders by emphasising the positive outcomes of entrepreneurial activity, then in the processes of social value creation, these externalities are less extemporary and more systematically sought in core business activities. This breaks the duality between, on the one hand, traditional management oriented to interest maximisation of both shareholders and managers, and, on the other hand, CSR with redistributive/compensation functions characterised by discontinuity and residuality. Such a break leads to a process of change in organisational and governance structures (Grandori, 2015), potentially leading to new hybrid subjectivities, which combine profit, non-profit, and public elements

(Venturi and Zandonai, 2014). The second element of deviation from a traditional CSR concerns the action of the enterprise within its environment, overcoming, on the one hand, classic engagement and stakeholder procedures characterised by pre-existing identity categories (customers, workers, investors, and local authorities) and, on the other hand, a relation with indefinite "crowds" (customers, users, etc.). The final outcome is represented by complex forms of community building that make boundaries less defined and recombine roles, because these communities are founded on identity substrata and common values, though of a different origin and intensity, which do not enable extemporary cooperation forms that simply aim at sharing the means and ends of economic action (Pais and Provasi, 2015).

The diffusion and relevance of these cooperative processes, which do not only overcome traditional CSR models but also "go beyond" classical forms of cooperative mutualism, are deeply questioning the forms and contents of production (Dardot and Laval, 2014). From this point of view, the growing diffusion (and ambivalence) of the concept of the "common good", such as the one of social enterprise, may be used as a sort of "proxy variable" to capture changes that are taking place and to measure its effective dimension. In other words, will the change we are witnessing be processed by the entirety of classical models of social responsibility through their "upgrade"? Otherwise are we experiencing an overall transformation of the economic paradigm and, with it, of institutional models and forms, particularly those of an entrepreneurial nature, thus causing a new cycle of organisational innovation and institution-building (Billis, 2010)? In order to provide an answer to such a complex question, it is necessary to operationalise the concept of common goods by demystifying the nature of the "buzzword" applied in the most varied contexts and situations, which leaves the most important and problematic issues unresolved, i.e. its implications at a productive, managing, and governance level (Vitale, 2013). In this sense, the analysis suggested by Ottone and Sacconi, based on Elinor Ostrom's thought (Sacconi and Ottone, 2015), allows us to apply large-scale cooperative action to the management of the so-defined "common infrastructures", which are characterised by the following distinguishing features:

- The existence of discursive processes of a pre-deliberative kind and of an informal but not extemporary nature (cheap talk) fostering cooperation among actors.
- Economies based on the intentional research of externalities (spill-over effects) through the creation of infrastructures suggesting different ways of using the good (including non-calculable ones in both space and time).
- Multi-stakeholder governance of an inclusive nature, shaped on the beneficiaries of the good, and balancing openness (open access) and sustainability (in order to avoid exploitation of goods: overconsumption, obstruction, etc.).

This definition succeeds in underlining the importance of producing social value in the field of common goods, or the need to create new kind of cooperative platform (Conaty and Bollier, 2014), particularly at a moment when a correlation between entrepreneurship and social value, community and social transformation is clearly sought (Daskalaki et al., 2015). From this point of view, the regeneration of properties and spaces to pursue social goals represents nowadays one of the most relevant "epicentres" of the observed dynamics because it questions the effective nature of these infrastructures (not only in a material sense) and because it defies the actors—public, private, civic—who apply for the role of developers and managers in economic and governance models which restore the genuine value of common goods (Borzaga and Sacchetti, in this volume). To sum up, we look at the intersection of regeneration initiatives on a social scale with the role of finance in fostering the scalability of these localised innovations in order to grasp the potentialities and deviations of the "cooperative race" for in the production of social value in the field of commons.

## Investing in Territorial Infrastructures as Common Goods

Various examples of abandoned areas and unused buildings are recurrently dominating the debate on innovative urban management approaches. Most cases deal with issues and suggestions that, though in different ways and connotations, recall the perspective of common goods in relation to the "territory". To simplify, it is possible to identify two types of representations. On the one hand, the first one claims that the "territory *is* a common good", which originated from and is mostly used in contrast with the logics and interests of the bottom-up (re)appropriation of these spaces (Salzano, 2009). On the other hand, the second representation looks at the "territory *as* a common good" and suggests the idea of sharing opportunities and ways to recover spaces in order to satisfy multiple needs and interests (Donolo, 2007).

This chapter does not engage in a deeper analysis of these different representations, because then the whole issue would be reduced to the mere juxtaposition between those who deny the ideological nature of the position "everything is in common" and those who are critical of addressing interests other than the public ones in a strict sense, as a way of refusing the project of public city. It might be more interesting to grasp the stimulus provided by this juxtaposition in order to question the notion of "territory" and its use within the debate on public goods (Cottino, 2009). In fact, the second representation (i.e. territory as a common good) recalls an idea of the territory that is substantially different from the one we are currently using in everyday language, where territory is defined as a set of material resources (spaces and products) representing the "objective" invariant on which social relations are built. Rather, in the second case, the idea of the territory depends on a way of using goods as a vehicle to social relations. In the first case, the territory is a datum (the background or the context of social norms); in the other, it is a construct (activated by social norms).

As Crosta (2010) argues, the difference between the two standpoints becomes clear in terms of "policies", i.e. the actions we wish to embark on with the goal to influence the relation between society and territory. Traditionally grounded on a statist culture, urban planning identifies in the (preventive and binding) allocation of certain resources (spaces and/or products) to specific uses the necessary and sufficient condition to ensure the pursuit of public utility objectives. The spectrum of negotiation practices and social interactions activated around those goods may only confirm the accomplishment of those objectives. A different approach to planning policies considers the realisation of public utility objectives through a certain use of available material resources as a possibility which cannot be predetermined and may be influenced by many different actors. From this point of view, the creation of collective benefits represents the combined effect of multi-stakeholder governance action (intentional and, sometimes, not completely intentional), which organises the territory as a system of in-common resources. It may be particularly interesting to establish a link with the definition provided by Sacconi and Ottone (2015), according to which in-common resources are physical-material resources subjected to a model of management that transforms them into "infrastructures", i.e. means used to generate additional activities and social benefits and, at the same time, externalities which cannot always be determined *ex ante*.

From this point of view, the common goods' approach re-orients the action field of urban policies, shifting the focus from planning the best use of spaces to managing the transformation of urban resources into infrastructures that are conducive to the production and the multiplication of collective benefits. Urban regeneration, in particular, may be redefined as a field of intervention specifically aimed at conceiving, negotiating, and testing possible reformulations of the "social contract" that once regulated and organised the use of spaces and structures, which are now in a condition of abandon or under-use, by designing and exploring various opportunities to activate forms of social resilience (Colucci and Cottino, 2015) and win-win mechanisms.

Urban regeneration defines a policy field that has recently experienced (together with the growing interest in common goods) a significant success within government practices at different levels. Looking at the concrete developments of this policy field, we notice that the integration between practices of regeneration of available spaces and the redefinition of relations between actors who in the past were engaged at different (sometimes even contrasting) levels is occurring in a bidirectional way. On the one hand, starting from the need to give new life to spaces, interactive processes take place among cooperating actors (following a trend "from the good to the common"); on the other hand, starting from the need to implement forms of governance that are different from the past, we are exploring the chanches offered by the conversion of unused territorial resources to make partnership opportunities effective (following a trend "from the common to the good").

In any case, regardless of the origin of this combinatory process, a positive and effective outcome is still dependent on the capacity to imagine, plan, and create models and integration strategies between actors, spaces, and opportunities. The complexity of the systems where this activity is performed justifies the implementation of innovative approaches and methods for the management of complex processes and for a multi-actor policy design, together with the competences that traditionally represented the tools for territorial planning. Recent developments of project theories in the field of planning (Cellamare, 2012)—integrated and fostered by studies in other disciplines, e.g., those of political sciences and organisation—go in the same direction.

For example, Mäntysalo et al. (2011) hint at this perspective. They suggest a re-examination of Lindblom's negotiation theories grounded on the concept of mutual partisan adjustment, i.e. on the search for efficient solutions to collective problems by combining various actors' interests, starting from the use of two key concepts: trading zone, which was introduced by Galison (1999), and boundary objects, which Galison himself recalled from Susan Leigh Star and James Griesemer. It is interesting to notice how Galison, in his thoughts on the conditions favouring the development of exchange relations between different actors, underlined the local and "localised" dimension of the trading zone: "it is a specific site in a specific time—partly symbolic, partly special—in which local coordination between theory and action takes place" (Galison, 1999: 138). With the concept of boundary object, however, Mäntysalo et al. (2011: 9) hint at all those "tools allowing the use and the exchange of information between different communities, even though they do not necessarily share the same system of meanings, values and strategies; objects that are flexible enough to conform to local needs and to the users' requirements, but also resistant to the point that they can keep their own identity".

However, accepting the framework of common goods should lead to the pursuit of more ambitious results concerning the synergy between the parts. In fact, the type of sharing that is at the heart of the management model of common goods implies a level of interaction that cannot be reduced to a mere relation of exchange (as in the case of private goods), but it is rather to be understood as a social contract based on an economic relation of a cooperative kind. In the perspective of common goods, the collective value is neither reducible nor comparable to the "exchange value" of material resources or to the activities needed to realise the common good. Conceiving the territory "as" a common good entails the creation of a different and superior type of value because it takes into account not only the production of the infrastructure, but also, and, most importantly, other activities, the benefits/social impacts and the externalities determined in the long run by the implementation of the infrastructure. It can be defined as a "shared value" because all the elements are contributing to its creation and its enjoyment: it is a sort of collective investment aimed at generating returns for all the interested actors.

The change towards a new way of conceiving social investment is not to be taken for granted. This is a change that nowadays represents the main focus of attention by multiple actors and fields of intervention, even those belonging to the private sector in a strict sense. One of these domains is CSR, which in general represents an interesting and current topic and whose particular assessments on how tools can be progressively improved and made more efficient became a topic of interest among both scholars and enterprises. In support of these arguments, recent research (Guida and Maiolini, 2014) emphasises the transformation of CSR from a tool used to improve the reputation of the enterprise and help stakeholders "gain private benefits" (CSR as a necessary cost) towards an investment aimed at improving the performance of the enterprise (CSR as an incentive for value creation) through investments implying a strategic cooperation with other stakeholders on social innovation and urban regeneration.

## Impact Investing: Tools and Approach

In recent years, following the economic downturn and the crisis of trust towards the current development model, there was an increasing need to implement innovative approaches in building new relations between economy, community and the territory developed within the for-profit sector. This restructuring is taking place not only through the relaunch of alternative models different from the dominant capitalist one, but also through efforts to reposition mainstream economy and finance. Whereas non-capitalist enterprises—cooperatives, social enterprises—have to strengthen their economic model by emphasising its more characteristic elements and opening its activities to wider markets, in the case of for-profit enterprises, the main challenge consists in realigning production and strategies towards sustainability and societal goals. The aim is to demonstrate that investing in business models that harmonise the interests of a plurality of actors, especially local communities, requires concrete actions within markets that are characterised by more sustainable demand and consumption models (International Finance Corporation, 2012).

Therefore, the recombination of the economic and social dimensions in the enterprise's value chain is the basis of the so-called "impact investing" approach. The term "impact investing" was coined at the Rockefeller Centre on Lake Como, in Italy, in 2007 (Rodin and Brandenburg, 2014).

The main goal consisted in originating "a sector to invest in projects with social or environmental outcome" (Rockefeller Foundation, 2012) by ensuring promoters a financial return. For this reason, both dimensions (social and financial) are subject to a measurement of results (Social Impact Investment Taskforce, 2014). This approach is based on the idea that the driver of transformation are linked more to investors' behaviours and motivations about to the use of capital to generate social and environmental impact, than to the "social" nature of beneficiary organisations. Therefore, "less emphasis is placed on making capital available to existing social sector organisations on terms suitable to them" (Daggers and Nicholls, 2016, 7). In this sense, impact investing develops a dialectic with the tradition of social investment which refers to the whole set of repayable capital tools created to satisfy the demand for financial resources by organisations that operate in the social field, aggregated in third sector and social economy domains. On the other hand, it is the neutrality of forms characterising impact investment that lend itself to significant applications even within for-profit enterprises wishing to strengthen the social and environmental component of their value chain.

Different contributions, more operational than scientific, analyze impact investing, in the strict sense, as a combination of the capacity to generate social impact and to ensure a financial return on investments (Austin et al., 2006) and, in a wider sense, as an evolution of the dynamics of corporate social responsibility and stakeholder engagement towards the shared value. Considering these two research branches, impact investing consists not only in a set of financial tools, but also in a broader approach to the investment dimension by looking in particular at the socio-economic and territorial system in which the enterprise operates. Therefore, we will try to synthetically define the necessary conditions to invest, according to an impact mindset, by going beyond the traditional logic of CSR.

- Intentionality: It refers to an investment approach that determines a non-extemporary strategy involving the core business of the enterprise and at the same time representing the distinguishing feature of impact investing compared to other traditional approaches to investment. The role of the territory, in this context, represents a critical variable intended to be not only an immutable background, but also a complex variable of available resources which are recombined in actions and policies that redefine the role of the enterprise.
- Additionality: It suggests that the investment has to increase the quality of the social outcome compared to the traditional investments of the enterprise. This means adopting a theory of change which implies the need to ask questions on how and why to invest in the territory, and requires that the enterprise undergo change in organisational and governance terms (Foss, 2000).

- Generating a financial return: This marks the main difference with respect to a redistributive approach of resources, and thus deviates from philanthropic models, which consider, even in their venture approach, a more marked orientation towards non-profit actors (Boiardi and Gianoncelli, 2016).

Therefore, impact investing aims at generating value in a way that is different from the past, because it induces the enterprise to re-discuss its business model and to play a role that is more than a financial tool connected to a *modus operandi*. To this end, in 2012, the United Nations Global Compact published "A Framework for Action: Social Enterprise and Impact Investing". This document defines, for the first time, the term *Corporate Impact Venturing* as an innovative model of corporate philanthropy. Corporate Impact Venturing may develop along three different models corresponding to three ways of action of the enterprise:

- Investment Model: It is based on the cross-functional competence to create investments in a social enterprise within a market that is different from the core business of the enterprise; thereby markets for the for-profit enterprise may be found.
- Incubation Model: It consists of a combination of internal and external innovation aiming at transforming the selected ideas into pilot projects, which can regenerate the core business of the enterprise.
- Strategic Partnership Model: Corporate structures, such as the sustainability/ CSR's unit, establish a partnership with an already existing social enterprise in order to cooperate, share the risk, and foster mechanisms of hybridisation between organisational dynamics.

The three models require an approach to the territory implying a kind of partnership, sometimes not so recognisable at a contractual level, where new variable becomes important, in addition to the traditional "financial risk", namely the variable of "trust" between partners. It is a concrete value, not a mere financial one, a positive impact guaranteed for the community, the Public Administration, and the direct beneficiaries of the supplied product or service (Arena et al., 2016).

Therefore, impact investing represents an approach aimed at overcoming the segmentation of concepts on which social and productive systems were based until now and looking for a new correlation between enterprise, community and sociality to generate economies based on the intentional request for "spill-over" effects. On the other hand, giving these financial tools and their political-cultural approach such a relevant weight is likely to create colonisation effects from mainstream finance, thus generating isomorphism phenomena at multiple levels: in defining territorial development policies; in determining priorities of collective interest services and their beneficiaries; and in redesigning organisational mechanisms and even the mission of entrepreneurial organisations with a social goal (Roy et al., 2017). In this sense, social regeneration of real estate goods and public spaces contributes to showing the genuine nature of impact investing, in terms of both opportunities and ambivalences. In fact, these initiatives are characterised by a evident investment dimension in terms of the necessary financial resources and the need to make explicit all those social impact elements that can be generated through such initiatives by negotiating them with a plurality of stakeholder actors, needs, and resources. To sum up, the field of social regeneration can unveil whether impact investing acts as a "wolf in sheep's clothing" or as a new way to create social value within chains of production incorporating elements of mainstream economy in an equilibrated and sustainable way (McHugh et al., 2013). In the following paragraph, we will present a case of potential application of these tools with reference to the regeneration of Italian railway assets as common goods.

## The Case of Railway Community Assets

Besides the railway network, Ferrovie dello Stato—a holding company entirely owned by the Italian State—also manages important property assets which are nowadays excessive with respect to the real needs of its mission (i.e. managing the rail transport of both passengers and goods). This led to a medium-long-term restructuring strategy aimed at "demobilising" and "attributing value" to properties of different nature and dimensions owned by the firm. This strategy was largely implemented through market initiatives: assets alienation and the change in their intended use so that they could host commercial business activities, especially in railway stations.

An important strategic project also concerns the regeneration of unattended stations and railway lines by entrusting their management to public local authorities and third-sector organisations for public interest purposes. There are more than 1,700 unattended stations across the entire Italian territory, particularly in rural areas, of which 345 stations have already been assigned to host social activities. In the case of unused railway lines, of the almost 3,000 km, 325 km have already been transformed into "greenways": cycle paths, green itineraries, etc. The use of these assets for activities of collective interest was made possible thanks to an agreement between the owner and important networks that are represented and coordinated by local public authorities, the third sector, and the cooperative movement (Torella and Coltellese, 1999).

Some recent surveys on unattended railway stations (Jona Lasinio, 2014; Zandonai, 2014) allow for an update in the knowledge framework, particularly with reference to the possibility of analysing the effects of this strategy in terms of the evolution of CSR towards a model of production of shared value in the paradigm of common goods. In this sense, research results[1] outline a process oriented in this direction, but not completely realised, since the elements qualifying social regeneration of property assets as commons were only partially identifiable (Sacconi and Ottone, 2015).

- First of all, there is no systematic way of involving local communities, and especially beneficiaries, in defining the new intended use of railway assets, e.g., through testing the temporary reuse of unattended stations, or through service design sessions targeted on users' needs.
- Secondly, it was difficult to retrieve the existence of external economies capable of strengthening the productive and entrepreneurial dimension, in particular with regards to the abandoned stations. These stations are often regenerated as the mere headquarters of charity organisations, and only in few cases were they assigned to host activities belonging to the real social economy (in agricultural, cultural, social, touristic fields, etc.), thus affirming themselves as a "community hub" that enhance processes of participation and co-production of collective-interest goods and services (Locality, 2015).
- Finally, in most cases, the governance of community assets appears to be rather simplified. It would focus only on the actor managing the structure and feature a weak involvement of other stakeholders, institutional interlocutors, informal groups, and citizens.

In view of a strategic model that has a strong structure but is still incomplete in terms of social impact, it is possible to enhance the role of the financial resources especially targeted to increasing the impact dimension, in a phase when these structures were even more stimulated by the amount of problems they were called upon to face. As presented in Table 4.1, the process of social regeneration is articulated in different steps and puts at stake multiple variables of a strategic and managerial nature (Borzaga and Zandonai, 2013). In the first phase, donative resources prevail (both economic and in kind) and are allocated to identify and test the new intended use of the building by emphasising its features that are of a general interest for the community. The subsequent opening of a regeneration construction site, even in structural terms, critically depends on financial resources, which have to be repaid thanks to the launch of a social business activity. In any case, regardless of the nature of the resource, what is prevalent in the whole process of social regeneration is an investment dimension recalling some typical entrepreneurial dimensions, such as the assumption of risk, a prospective change, and the ability to repay the resource flow (Social Investment) in multiple ways.

*Table 4.1* The Process of Social Regeneration: Stages, Variables, Resources

| Stages | Variables | Resources |
|---|---|---|
| *Trigger* | How the asset is of general interest | In kind to promote a call to action on the new intended use |
| *Assetholder* | Effective convergence of the holders of needs and resources | Pro bono and institutional grant in order to foster community building paths |
| *Testing* | Structural and functional tests through "transition contracts" towards the new intended use | Institutional grant, civic fundraising, European Structural Funds |
| *Governance* | Participation of different stakeholders with a positioning of the entrepreneurial activity | Shareholdership (community shareholdership and venture institutional investors) |
| *Sustainability of the process* | Regeneration construction as a project supported by a mix of resources | Financial debt resources with interests mixed with donative resources |
| *Sustainability of the regenerated structure* | Business and scaling model to repay financial costs | Market transactions within economies that convey social and environmental value |

Nowadays, the space of impact investing is just potential within regeneration projects of railway assets. However, the implementation of a targeted ecosystem of financial resources (European Commission, 2016) may play a relevant role in "upgrading" these initiatives by acting on the following factors:

- The overall improvement of the project, with a particular focus on the development of entrepreneurial initiatives targeted at the economic sustainability, but also at the promotion of social inclusion that acts on beneficiaries' and local communities' empowerment;
- A more efficient analysis of the socio-economic context in which railway assets are located, through due diligence tools capable of measuring their potential social impact and within those local production chains that can endorse the characteristic features of the territory;
- Recognising social assets as a fundamental part of wider projects of regeneration of railway assets in order to foster the spread of these initiatives not just as philanthropic activities, but rather as a structural component of a renewed business model that considers social engagement as an element of creation of social value and not as a mere reparatory intervention.

## Beyond CSR in the Field of Social Regeneration

To win social regeneration challenges, it is necessary to resort to management and governance mechanisms based on new principles which can offer many enterprises, not only non-profit ones, the opportunity to re-consider the meaning and the content of their relations with the territory, beyond the boundaries of traditional CSR approaches. The latter, usually considered as a reputational investment in the domain of business strategies (and, for this reason, included within business communication and marketing strategies) (Crane et al., 2014), may be interpreted in the light of the common goods paradigm. The fact of establishing and strengthening relations with territorial—and even social—stakeholders may result, under certain conditions, in a potentially strategic investment for the enterprise, even with a business perspective. Following the discussion on common goods, the social dimension of the territory is now connected not only to a whole set of unsatisfied needs and physical, environmental, and cultural resources to be protected, but also and, most importantly, to resilience processes with respect to social and economic changes that have (or may have) direct or indirect relations with the business of the enterprise. From this point of view, sustainable development of the territory may become a strategic objective that the enterprise and other actors have in common. Creating long-term perspectives, in which the enterprise itself can play a new and different role in the territory, capable of producing positive social impacts, may offer the testing ground to implement social responsibility initiatives in the short term, as opportunities to reformulate and test these "alternative" business models.

There are different ways in which each enterprise can accept and meet this new challenge: they are different in terms of both involvement of the enterprise in creating the specific content of project initiatives (ranging from the original idea to co-funding, and from the allocation of specific competences to the creation of strategic partnerships aimed at realising certain initiatives), as well as in terms of the level of integration between the content of projects and the business objectives of the enterprise.

The regeneration role of the enterprise in the territory is characterised by some essential elements that can be included within the paradigm of common goods:

- The search for new ways of involving the community, which usually leads to trying new solutions, even temporary ones, concerning the use and the function of unused or abandoned properties.
- The construction of new market areas or new production chains, which include the social dimension and which may, therefore, influence the core business of the enterprise.
- Multi-stakeholder governance, where it is possible to involve multiple actors in the process of value creation and where territory becomes the testing ground to build new relations.

- The search for new investment opportunities, not as an appendix of some extemporary project, but rather as a strategic approach based on the will to create a social impact on the territory.

An important step marking a change in the approach is the possibility to embark on a journey where it is possible to measure the produced social value and the change that is yet to be produced in particular, as far as the intended use of abandoned or underused real estate goods is concerned. Not only does this path allow us to develop a vision of long-term objectives, but it also prioritises strategies and actions which support change and may influence the core activity of the enterprise through the adopted practices. Innovating usually means opening up to the territory and supporting co-production processes with other actors, on the condition that one's own interests are no longer determinant, and that one has to be open to a re-definition by adjusting them to the suggestions of other interested actors (mutual adjustment; see Lindblom, 1990). In this sense, through the process of co-production, the enterprise becomes an actor and is intentionally available to interact with other actors, on the basis of a predefined strategy, knowing that convergence is not a predefined outcome and that it will probably be induced to redefine its own roadmap.

Therefore, before acting on the territory, the enterprise does not apply as an actor (Crosta, 2010), and for this reason, territory becomes a system of common resources that needs to be recombined in order to generate collective benefits. In this sense, social regeneration is a field of different interventions where multiple resources for the production of common goods are available and where impact investing leads the enterprise to consider itself in a different perspective and to play a role as a territorial actor. Through the co-production of common goods and the creation of a link between the enterprise and the territory, new modes of action and new organisations can be generated, which will mark the development model of contemporary society. This has enhanced the emergence of new institutional aggregates which are different from the dominant ones, namely public, private, and non-profit, and whose constituency will focus on making value production and redistribution mechanisms converge and combine under common goals (Bullock and James, 2014).

## Note

1. A first illustration of the results of this survey was proposed in Battistoni and Zandonai (2017).

## References

Arena, M., Bengo, I., Calderini, M., and V. Chiodo. 2016. "Social Impact Bonds: Blockbuster or Flash in a Pan?" *International Journal of Public Administration*, 39(12): 927–939.

Arvidsson, A. 2008. "The Ethical Economy of Customer Coproduction." *Journal of Macromarketing*, 28(4): 326–338.

Arvidsson, A., and A. Giordano. 2013. *Societing Reloaded. Pubblici produttivi e innovazione sociale.* Milano: Egea.

Austin, J., Stevenson, H., and J. Wei-Skillern. 2006. "Social and Commercial Entrepreneurship: Same, Different, or Both?" *Entrepreneurship Theory and Practice*, 30(1): 1–22.

Battistoni, F., and F. Zandonai. 2017. "La rigenerazione sociale nel dominio dei *commons*: gestione e governo dei *community asset ferroviari.*" *Territorio* (forthcoming).

Benkler Y. 2016. "Peer production, the commons, and the future of the firm". In *Strategic Organizations*, 15(2): 264–274.

Billis, D., ed. 2010. *Hybrid Organizations in the Third Sector: Challenges of Practice, Policy and Theory.* Basingstoke: Palgrave Macmillan.

Boiardi, P., and A. Gianoncelli. 2016. *The State of Venture Philanthropy and Social Investment (VP/SI) in Europe: The EVPA Survey 2015/2016.* European Venture Philanthropy Association.

Borzaga, C., and G. Galera. 2016. "Innovating the Provision of Welfare Services Through Collective Action: The Case of Italian Social Cooperatives." *International Review of Sociology*, 26: 31–47.

Borzaga, C., and F. Zandonai. 2009. "L'impresa sociale nelle metamorfosi dei mercati." In *Impresa sociale e capitalismo contemporaneo*, edited by Jean-Louis Laville and Michele La Rosa, 175–195. Milano: Edizioni Sapere 2000.

Borzaga, C., and F. Zandonai. 2013. "Il riuso di strutture ferroviarie a scopo sociale. Caso studio e indicazioni per la gestione." *Euricse Research Report*, No. 9. Trento.

Bruni, L., and S. Zamagni, eds. 2013. *Handbook on the Economics of Reciprocity and Social Enterprise.* Cheltenham: Edward Elgar.

Bullock, G., and L. James. 2014. *The Convergence Continuum: Towards a "4th Sector" in Global Development?* Accenture.

Cellamare, C. 2012. "Pratiche di progettazione. Introduzione." In *Tracce urbane. Alla ricerca della città*, edited by Adriano Cancellieri and Giuseppe Scandurra, 189–196. Milano: Franco Angeli.

Colucci, A., and P. Cottino. 2015. "The Shock Must Go On: territori e comunità di fronte all'impresa della resilienza sociale." *Impresa Sociale*, 5: 36–43.

Conaty, P., and D. Bollier, eds. 2014. "Toward an Open Cooperativism: A New Social Economy Based on Open Platforms, Cooperative Models, and Commons." *A Report on a Commons Strategies Group Workshop*. Berlin.

Cottino, P. 2009. *Competenze possibili. Sfera pubblica e potenziali sociali nella città.* Milano: Jaca Book.

Crane, A., Palazzo, G., Spence, L. J., and D. Matten. 2014. "Contesting the Value of 'Creating Shared Value'." *California Management Review*, 56(2): 130–153.

Crosta, P. L. 2010. *Pratiche. Il territorio 'è l'uso che se ne fa'.* Milan: Franco Angeli.

Daggers, J., and A. Nicholls. 2016. *The Landscape of Social Impact Investment Research: Trends and Opportunities.* Oxford: Said Business School, University of Oxford.

Dardot, P., and C. Laval. 2014. *Commun. Essai sur la révolution au XXIe siècle.* Paris: Editions La Découverte.

Daskalaki, M., Hjorth, D., and J. Mair. 2015. "Are Entrepreneurship, Communities and Social Transformation Related?" *Journal of Management Inquiry*, 5: 1–5.

Deaton, A. 2013. *The Great Escape: Health, Whealth, and the Origins of Inequality.* Princeton: Princeton University Press.

Donolo, C. 2007. *Sostenere lo sviluppo. Ragioni e speranze oltre la crescita.* Milano: Mondadori.

European Commission. 2016. *Social Enterprises and their Eco-systems: Developments in Europe*. Authors: Carlo Borzaga and Giulia Galera.

Fondazione Symbola. 2014. *Coesione è competizione. Nuove geografie della produzione del valore in Italia*. Roma: I Quaderni di Symbola.

Foss, N. J., ed. 2000. *The Theory of the Firm: Critical Perspectives on Business and Management*. New York and London: Routledge.

Galison, P. 1999. "Trading Zone: Coordinating Action and Belief." In *The Science Studies Reader*, edited by Mario Biagioli, 137–160. New York and London: Routledge.

Garriga, E., and D. Melé. 2004. "Corporate Social Responsibility Theories: Mapping the Territory." *Journal of Business Ethics*, 53: 51–71.

Grandori, A. 2015. *Epistemic Economics and Organization: Forms of Rationality and Governance for a Wiser Economy*. New York and London: Routledge.

Guida, M. F., and R. Maiolini. 2014. "Social Innovation, Actors, Contexts and Trends. Opening the Black Box." In *Enabling Social Innovation Ecosystems for Community-led Territorial Development*, edited by F. Sgaragli. Quaderni della Fondazione Giacomo Brodolini, "Studi e ricerche" Series, 49, 13–20.

Honeyman, R. 2014. *The B Corp Handbook: How to Use Business as a Force for Good*. Oakland: Barrett-Koehler Publishers.

International Finance Corporation. 2012. "Impact." *Annual Report 2012*. Washington, DC.

Jona Lasino, L. 2014. "Ricerca sulle stazioni impresenziate assegnate per scopi sociali, turistici e culturali." In *Stazioni Ferroviarie: come rigenerare un patrimonio*, edited by Ferrovie dello Stato, 8–75. Roma.

Lindblom, C. E. 1990. *Inquiry and Change*. New Haven: Yale University Press.

Locality. 2015. *Community Hubs: How to Set Up, Run and Sustain a Community Hub to Transform Local Service Provision*. Accessed from mycommunity.org.uk.

Mäntysalo, R., Balducci, A., and J. Kangasoja. 2011. "Planning as Agonistic Communication in a Trading Zone: Re-examining Lindblom's Partisan Mutual Adjustment." *Planning Theory*, 10: 1–16.

Manzini, E. 2015. *Design, When Everybody Designs: An Introduction to Design for Social Innovation*. Cambridge, MA: The MIT Press.

McHugh, N., Sinclair, S., Roy, M., Huckfield, L., and C. Donaldson. 2013. "Social Impact Bonds: A Wolf in Sheep's Clothing?" *Journal of Poverty and Social Justice*, 21(3): 247–257.

Mori, P. A. 2017. "Community Cooperatives and Cooperatives Providing Public Services: Facts and Prospects." In *The Oxford Handbook of Mutual, Cooperative, and Coowned Business*, edited by Jonathan Michie, Joseph Blasi and Carlo Borzaga, 184–194. Oxford: Oxford University Press.

Mulgan, G. 2010. "Measuring Social Value." *Stanford Social Innovation Review* (Summer): 38–43.

Nyssens, M. 2006. *Social Enterprise: At the Crossroads of Market, Public Policies and Civil Society*. New York and London: Routledge.

Pais, I., and G. Provasi. 2015. "Sharing Economy: A Step Towards the Re-Embeddedness of the Economy?" *Stato e Mercato*, 3: 347–378.

Polanyi, K. 1971. *The Great Transformation: The Political and Economic Origins of Our Time*. Boston, MA: Beacon Press.

Porter, M. E., and M. R. Kramer. 2006. "Strategy and Society: The Link Between Competitive Advantage and Corporate Social Responsibility." *Harvard Business Review* December: 78–93.

Putnam, R. D., Leonardi, R., and R. Y. Nanetti. 1993. *Making Democracy Work: Civic Traditions in Modern Italy*. Princeton: Princeton University Press.

Rockefeller Foundation. 2012. *Accelerating Impact: Achievements Challenges and What's Next in Building the Impact Investing Industry.* New York: Rockefeller Foundation.

Rodin, J., and M. Brandenburg. 2014. *The Power of Impact Investing: Putting Markets to Work for Profit and Global Good.* Wharton Digital Press.

Roy, M. J., McHugh, N., and Sinclair, S. 2017. "Social Impact Bonds—Evidence-based Policy or Ideology? In *Handbook of Social Policy Evaluation*, edited by Bent Greve, 263–277. Cheltenham: Edward Elgar.

Sacconi, L., and S. Ottone. 2015. *Beni comuni e cooperazione.* Bologna: Il Mulino.

Salzano, E. 2009. *La città bene comune.* Ogni uomo è tutti gli uomini Edizioni.

Social Impact Investment Taskforce, ed. 2014. "Impact Investment: The Invisible Hearth of Markets. Harnessing the Power of Entrepreneurship, Innovation and Capital for Public Good." *Report of Social Impact Investment Taskforce.* Accessed from http://www.socialimpactinvestment.org/reports/Impact%20 Investment%20Report%20FINAL[3].pdf

Torella, F., and T. Coltellese, eds. 1999. "Le stazioni impresenziate sulla rete ferroviaria italiana. Definire il fenomeno per definire le opportunità." *Research Report.* Roma.

United Nations Global Compact. 2012. *A Framework for Action: Social Enterprise & Impact Investing.* New York: The Rockefeller Foundation.

Venturi, P., and F. Zandonai. 2014. *Ibridi organizzativi. L'innovazione sociale generata dal Gruppo cooperativo CGM.* Bologna: Il Mulino.

Vitale, E. 2013. *Contro I beni comuni. Una critica illuminista.* Bari: Laterza.

Warren, S., and P. Jones. 2015. *Creative Economies, Creative Communities: Rethinking Place, Policy and Practice.* New York and London: Routledge.

Zandonai, F. 2014. "L'impatto della rigenerazione. Gestione e accountability delle stazioni impresenziate affidate da RFI a soggetti non profit." In *Stazioni Ferroviarie: come rigenerare un patrimonio*, edited by Ferrovie dello Stato, 76–97. Roma.

# 5 Cooperative Leadership

## Social and Spatial Regeneration in Rural Western Canada

*Darcy Overland*

## Introduction

Rural communities in western Canada are different from their urban coun-terparts. In general, urbanisation and changing economies mean there are fewer people living in these communities and there are fewer goods and services available locally. Community members want to find ways to rein-vigorate their communities and ensure their continuance in the current economy. The cooperative model, which balances both business and asso-ciative capacity, can succeed where other business models or government provision aren't practicable and can form an important part of regeneration in these communities. However, all development, and particularly coopera-tive development, needs leadership.

Cooperatives represent a business model that exists in the landscape between traditional investor owned firms, not-for-profit organisations, and public organisations. Leadership has been studied from many lenses. However, the leadership attributes and styles looked for in traditional entrepreneurs, or non-profit leaders are not sufficient measures for the requirements of cooperative leadership. As cooperatives are a unique model of organising, it takes leaders with a unique set of attributes to start and sustain cooperatives. Through a series of interviews with experi-enced cooperative developers, commitment to the community and shared leadership, possession of business acumen and controlled energy, knowl-edge of the community and group dynamics, and an ability to put a proj-ect over politics were identified as attributes that successful cooperative leaders possess.

## Background and Methodology

The information from this chapter comes from data collected, and analysis conducted, as part of the Cooperative Innovation Project (CIP),[1] a research project carried out by the Centre for the Study of Cooperatives at the University of Saskatchewan. CIP was undertaken between 2014 and 2016. It attempted to determine if the cooperative model was a viable option to meet community need in rural and Indigenous communities in western Canada. While there are many regulatory and other external factors that impact the development of cooperatives, CIP was focused primarily on those internal to the community.

The study focused on 1,200 rural and 500 Indigenous communities spread throughout a land mass of 2.7 million km squared. Data was collected through five different methods: an in-depth statistical review at the community level; a broad-based telephone survey with 2,025 respondents; a web-based community administrator survey with 359 respondents; seven interviews with cooperative development experts; and 26 community based meetings involving 13 Indigenous communities and 50 rural communities.

This chapter uses data collected from the interviews as previously reported in the CIP final report. Between March and June 2015, seven interviews totaling over 400 pages of transcript were conducted by CIP. These interviews were with provincial cooperative developers from the four western Canadian provincial cooperative associations (Manitoba Cooperative Association, Saskatchewan Cooperative Association, Alberta Community and Cooperative Association, and BC Cooperative Association) and one from a private cooperative development company.

The interviews were open coded with NVivo, a qualitative programme that supports interview analysis. Using this programme, the interviews were analysed in a number of ways, including identifying key words, top references, and ideas that receive the most attention. One of the ideas that coded strongly was discussion of the role and characteristics of leaders in cooperative development. Segments of the interviews that were coded to leadership were then re-coded to bring out common themes on the characteristics, knowledge, and style of cooperative leaders. While CIP focused on both rural and Indigenous communities and the leaders in these communities, it is important to note that the discussion in this chapter is generalised. Indigenous peoples in Canada have unique cultures, histories, experiences, and communities. It is inappropriate to apply the general findings of this chapter, which include non-Indigenous voices and perspectives, to Indigenous contexts. Describing Indigenous cooperative leaders requires further initiatives, such as focused consultation, conversation, and study with, and by, Indigenous people.

## Cooperatives and Social and Spatial Regeneration

Cooperatives in western Canada are simultaneously a well-known business model and an unthought-of solution to contemporary gaps in service or goods provision. People can easily identify the local credit union, cooperative food store, or gas station that has been in town for 50 or more years. More challenging is the ability to imagine a cooperative business model as a solution to a current lack of service or need a community might be facing (CIP, 2016, Overview, 7).

Most simply, a cooperative is "an autonomous association of persons united voluntarily to meet their common economic, social and cultural needs and aspirations through a jointly-owned and democratically-controlled enterprise" (ICA, 2017). Users of the cooperative are then member-owners, interested equally in ensuring the goods/services are provided in their community and in ensuring the return they may receive as owners. As a result of this dual focus, where traditional markets or government have not or may not be able to provide service, cooperative models can be more successful (Fairbairn, 2000, 42).

Rural communities in western Canada have changed. At one time, rural communities were the economic centre of western Canada. However, urbanisation and a shift away from agriculture-based economies have altered the role these communities play in the larger system. The effects of rural depopulation and changing demographics, shifting economies and changes in technology, and the impacts of centralisation, amalgamation, jurisdictional boundary changes, and greater accountability requirements for government funds meant to assist rural communities have increased the demands on communities, while depleting their resources (CIP, 2016, Conclusion, 3–4).

Much of the policy and economic development conversations do not adequately address the local situation in the rural context. The people in these communities were clear. They live in these communities not because they do not have a choice, but because they believe in their community, they value the lifestyle, and they want to see it carried on (CIP, 2016, Community Capacity, 14). These communities are looking for ways to build resilience and sustainability in their new context. Community members recognise that the ability to attract outside business to their community to meet their needs is limited because of their small market size. Also, they feel they do not carry enough political weight for government to adequately meet their needs (CIP, 2016, Community Capacity, 7–11). When CIP asked community members who they felt would be most likely to meet their needs, they usually answered themselves.

Each community has different strengths, challenges, and history. While the needs in each community are unique, overall, CIP found that the primary community needs are in areas such as health care (mental health services in particular), housing, support services, business development, overcoming community barriers, services for senior's transportation, volunteerism, recreation, infrastructure, and youth. (CIP, 2016, Needs, 5–15). While cooperatives are not the right model in all situations in all communities, cooperative models have proven effective at delivering a good number of the goods or services communities are lacking.

However, new cooperatives have not been forming in great numbers where they could pose a real solution to the multiple needs faced in western Canadian communities. While structural, economic, and political changes have impacted all development and service provision activities within communities, the development of cooperatives, which may be uniquely suited to meeting these needs, have additional challenges.

CIP found that there are a number of reasons why there may be a lack of cooperative development. There is limited knowledge among the general public of what the cooperative model is, how it works, and how it can be leveraged as a useful community development tool (CIP, 2016, Executive Summary, 3). Without knowledge of the model, it is unlikely that cooperatives will be created to fill needs in the community, or, in-depth training in the model will have to be provided first. Organisations that do provide cooperative training often have limited capacity and reach and may require interested individuals to proactively seek out the information. However, people will not often seek out something they do not know about. Additionally, starting a cooperative can be a lengthy process requiring ongoing support from knowledgeable individuals, who are limited in supply.

Any development in a community can have both political and cultural implications as the creation of new entities or services interacts with power dynamics in a community. Cooperatives have a great deal of disruption potential, as by creating a cooperative, community members take control of the provision of a particular good or service (CIP, 2016, Executive Summary, 4). If the potential area of cooperative business in an area that is of limited interest to the existing political structures, then it would be unlikely to create a great deal of local disruption. However, if the area of business is one that is typically undertaken by the public sphere, or in direct competition to initiatives undertaken by existing governments or individuals of power in a community, it may require much greater initiative to create and ensure it is supported.

In order for cooperatives to retain their competitive advantage in markets which would not support traditional business, their community must be fully engaged. The members of the community should have both social (or associative) capacity and business capacity. People must have a certain level of trust so they can work together to a common purpose, or they must be assisted to build that trust. Additionally, they must have the collective business sense required to run and operate a business. Not only that, but there must be a willingness of a core number of dedicated community members to volunteer, not only in the development process, but also in an ongoing manner to serve on the board of cooperative.

Cooperatives could form an important component of regeneration in rural and Indigenous communities that have faced economic exclusion due to their geographic location and small populations. They offer opportunities to build the social capacity of communities by having them support and/or work together on a common project. They offer opportunities to increase the capacity of local community members through governing and operating local businesses. Perhaps most importantly, they offer opportunities for communities to identify and meet their needs for goods and service provision.

However, it is necessary to have local community catalysts and leaders to spearhead cooperative development. The cooperative model does not work well when it is imposed on communities. The level of engagement required of community members to both support the cooperative through using its services and to participate in the development and governance of the cooperative means there has to be a great deal of local engagement in the model. It has to be a ground-up solution driven from within a community to meet the needs of the community. Additionally, there must be local leaders ready to take on and champion the cause. Without these local leaders, the cooperative will not be able to generate and sustain momentum through the development and early stages, manoeuvre the political culture, get buy-in, and maintain support from the community. (CIP, 2016, Executive Summary, 3–7).

## Cooperative Leadership

Whether a group that is interested in starting a cooperative gets help from a developer or forges ahead on their own, there is usually a core group of individuals that builds support for the idea, advances the work in between meetings, works out logistics and details, and acts as guides and mediators throughout the process. One developer stated, "You don't have what strikes me as a coop leadership personality . . . your idea is good, you need it, but I would say go for a different model. Go for a social enterprise model, or a standard business model or a non-profit". Without the right leadership, cooperatives stand less of a chance of successfully starting, and if they are able to start, less chance of being sustainable.

In the CIP interviews with cooperative developers, it became clear that there are a set of characteristics developers associate with successful leaders in new cooperative ventures, some identified in the entrepreneurial leadership literature, and some unique to the situations they were describing. The literature on leadership is extensive and diverse. Dinh et al. (2014) identified 21 distinct established or emerging leadership theories. However, there is relatively little that is written specifically to what leadership looks like in a cooperative context or in a cooperative development context. Developing any new organisation is an entrepreneurial activity and a cooperative is no different, except that the development of cooperatives can be conceived of as group entrepreneurship. As such, entrepreneurial leadership theory lends itself well to examining leadership in cooperative development contexts.

Entrepreneurial leadership either focuses on the intersection of entrepreneurship and leadership studies, examines psychological components of leadership, or examines places where entrepreneurial leadership is required. Cogliser and Brigham (2004) identify four main areas where leadership theory and entrepreneurship theory intersect: vision, influence, leadership of individuals, and planning. Leaders in cooperatives are never a heroic leader. The difference with cooperatives is that by their definition, they are group entrepreneurship endeavours, and they have to share leadership. As such, leaders in cooperative development have to have vision, and yet be willing to share responsibility for the vision and have it altered. They have to influence others to be involved in the endeavour, and yet not take control of the endeavour. They have to identify and encourage other leaders to drive different aspects of development rather than directly lead others, and they have to plan, but not own the plan and be willing for the plan to change based on the input of others.

Psychological components of leadership focus on traits or styles of leaders. J. M. Burns (1978) differentiated between transactional leadership, in which power is granted to the leader and enforced through the bureaucratic structures that exist, and transformational leadership, in which charismatic visionaries inspire and energise others into following them. Ensley et al. (2006) identify the importance of both transactional and transformational leadership in new ventures and the importance of shared leadership in start-up teams. Gupta et al. (2004) identify behaviours and roles of entrepreneurial leaders: framing the challenge, absorbing uncertainty, path-clearing, building commitment, and specifying limits. Cooperative leaders have to balance transactional and transformational leadership styles. They have to know their groups and group dynamics and have a strong business acumen to know when to use different styles of leadership for different tasks required at different points in the development. It is knowledge of and commitment to the community, possessing controlled energy through long development timelines, and an ability to put the project first that differentiate cooperative leaders.

The following categories are presented as identified by members of the CIP research team by open coding the interview transcripts. All the quotes provided come from those interviews as previously reported in the CIP final report.

### Commitment to Community

It is, without question, helpful for cooperative leaders to have some connection to, or knowledge of, the cooperative model. At the start of development, leaders do not have to be experts in the cooperative model. At the same time, being committed to the cooperative idea alone is not generally their primary motivation. When developers "find [the leader's] primary motivation to get the coop going and it's not just to have a coop, it's to meet a real community need". Leaders in these communities aren't merely trying to create a cooperative. They are trying to improve life in their community, not only for themselves, but for their whole community.

Having an in-depth understanding of the community and its needs is crucial for these leaders. Not only do they have to understand the need, "[t]hey have to have a passion for the idea. . . . They have to feel that this is something worth doing". They need to know that the idea is something that will work in their community, and they need to know their community well enough to know that the community will support the idea or know enough of the inner functioning of the community to build support for the idea. Leaders need to be aware of the strengths in their communities and how to leverage these strengths to come together collectively. Perhaps most importantly, it has to be enough of a passion area for the leaders that they will persevere through what can be a long development process filled with obstacles.

In order for a cooperative to survive where other models may not, the community has to be invested in the cooperative. Reciprocally, the individuals starting the cooperative have to be heavily invested in their communities. Rural and Indigenous communities in western Canada are populated for the most part by people who are from there. In 2011, 74% of people in rural western Canadian communities were the third generation or greater living in that community, and in Indigenous communities, that number is 98% (CIP, 2016, By the Numbers, 5). However, being from a place alone doesn't mean a person is invested in that place. Whether a person is originally from a community or are a not, some people look for personal gain for their efforts, and some have a different motivation. For cooperative leaders, "there's a personal connection to the community, and they talk community very strongly. It's 'our community', 'our business', it's 'we'. There's a strong sense of collectiveness around that". While other models may be options to meet a need in a particular community, cooperative leaders are motived by a sense of collective benefit that could be achieved if a cooperative is successful.

For individuals interested in creating an organisation to meet a need in their community, knowledge of their community is essential. However, for those that want to build a cooperative model, "there's got to be a strong commitment to the community. People who want their community to survive and thrive". Cooperative leaders are those who believe that when their community succeeds, they will succeed.

### Shared Leadership

In many groups, it is easy to spot the leader. It is the person that everyone looks to when a decision needs to be made. It is the person that is in charge and the person that is ultimately responsible. All entrepreneurs have to have an idea and a vision of what they are trying to build. However, cooperative leaders are different because cooperatives are meant to be democratic in nature, and democracy means shared decision-making. While a strong business leader may have the knowledge on the business end of a cooperative, "your traditional tech entrepreneur or new start-up entrepreneur may not get the democracy aspect of a coop". Without a willingness of individuals to share the vision and the decision-making, a new cooperative runs the risk of becoming too reliant on a single individual.

Additionally, in cooperatives, both the end product and the eventual success or failure of the venture belong to the whole group, "and that sharing amongst the members of the responsibilities for the success of the cooperatives is something that isn't present in every entrepreneur". Good business leaders do not necessarily make good cooperative leaders. In cooperatives, the decisions that are made may not align with the original idea the leader had and may in fact go against what the leader thinks is a good idea, and the leader has to be prepared to accept this outcome.

Individuals that want to use the cooperative model understand that "by working together . . . you have much better success". The success for many new cooperatives in rural or Indigenous communities lies in the commitment the members have to the cooperative. In the cooperative ". . . model, it's a shared ownership, a shared leadership piece. You have to feel part of it". Cooperatives require investment and dedication from the members, and one of the ways to build those feelings is by including all members in the decision-making process. In order to achieve this outcome, a cooperative leader "leads from the middle".

Leading from the middle is ". . . a different kind of leadership, because you're . . . giving up some of your power as leader to those on the ground". Anyone familiar with group work recognises that not all group members are equally equipped for all tasks. The leader must be able to leverage the right people to the right jobs to ensure the project moves forward, while still enabling group decision-making. For a leader that "want[s] to start an enterprise like a coop, you have to be able to identify who those other leaders are and what it is that you're looking for". The leader must identify other leaders to ensure the venture moves forward and empower all members of the group to be part of the decision-making process to build early feelings of ownership. They need to find "who can lead a meeting well, who can do a set of minutes, who can keep the books, who's good at putting together communication pieces. You have to find those people and get them together".

As a result, it is not always possible to immediately spot the leader in the room when doing cooperative development. "They're often the quiet ones who are in the background, they've seen the work, they're not there for the ego, coops are not the best [places] for ego leaders". A developer speaking of a failed cooperative indicated "it was a perfect business model but it failed because of internal politics, with one who had been the 'natural born' leader of the organisation, and some challenges with the democratisation of that". Although the model was correct, and the business sound, a lack of shared leadership led to the eventual downfall of the cooperative.

### Business Acumen

At heart, cooperatives are businesses. They may be set up as for-profit or not-for-profit, but they have to have a strong and sustainable business plan. If cooperative leaders do not "have that business background and can't speak intelligently and with confidence about the business plan, then it's very hard for [them] to represent, and convince people to go to the next step". While people have to have input into the decisions and directions the cooperative will take, in many rural and Indigenous communities, people first need to be convinced that the idea has merit. Many of these communities have seen initiatives and ideas come and go and require a convincing case that this time is different before they get involved.

While many ideas may have been tried to solve a need in a community, it is unlikely that a cooperative model will have been tried. Cooperative leaders should be able to explain why cooperatives are different and why they may succeed where other models can not. One developer stated, "the most successful ones I work with are folks who understand other business models, [and] who understand coops". Having knowledge of multiple models make cooperative leaders more able to explain to others why a cooperative is the right model and why this initiative may work where others have failed.

However, cooperative leaders do not own the cooperative development process, nor are they usually experts in a field. Just like they share leadership, they share responsibility. "They're kind of jack of all trades. . . . They know enough to know it, and they know where to ask if they don't know it".

### Controlled Energy

Cooperative leaders have to be committed to the long-term vision for the cooperative and be able to guide and motivate the people they are working with through the entire process. The leader of a new cooperative initiative is often "someone who has the energy and the experience and the capacity and the excitement to build up a cooperative. They're bringing their colleagues who are also interested in this along, but one person is very often the source of the energy". Leaders act as motivators and as a source of energy for the entire group because generally they ". . . are the most committed. They're the ones who generally had the idea to start out with and they go in it realistically". Getting and keeping people excited about an idea and keeping their expectations realistic are part of the balance cooperative leaders need to strike.

Developing a cooperative is often, but not always, a long process. Cooperatives require not only solid business planning, but also member engagement, buy-in, and contribution. As a result, development can be a two-steps-forward, one-step-back dance, and "it's not unheard of for it to take two to three years before you're even incorporated, just because it takes that long to hammer [the details] out". Individuals that get very excited about a project but do not have the perseverance to see it through until the end are great to have involved for bursts of energy, but leaders have to control their energy throughout the process, from inception to incorporation to operations, to help the group move through each stage. Leaders have to display ". . . a good mix of idealism and sometimes shear bullheadedness", and they have to be able to display both at the right time to help their group.

Apart from controlling their energy to ensure they have enough reserves to motivate their group, successful cooperative leaders generally display a wide range of personal traits, and they are astute enough to know when each is needed. While in no way predictive or comprehensive, developers used a common set of words to describe these traits in the interviews: confident, self-motivated, strong, independent, persistent, patient, adaptable, committed, and realistic. Leaders are able to utilise these traits to help their groups through the development of the cooperative.

## Knowing the Community

Leaders of any new venture in a community need to be aware not only of their own strengths and capacities, but also those of their community. They need to know its history, its current strengths, and which needs can realistically be met by the community and which are out of reach or will require additional partnerships. Cooperatives are "reliant on the local support for their coop to succeed", so leaders of new cooperatives need to deeply understand their community to understand if a cooperative might be a fit.

Communities all have identities that have been established over generations, and cooperatives may not be a good fit in some of these communities (CIP, 2016, Community Capacity, 15). In describing characteristics of communities where new cooperatives have been successful, a developer stated, "there's some capacity of independence, there's some capacity for self-help, there's some capacity for a protagonsim in a way, where people will see themselves as 'the' actors that can start to address a pressing need in their community".

Leaders need to understand the unique identity of the community within which they are working. If a community does not believe it has not only the capacity to solve its problems, but the right to do so, a strong cooperative leader will not be able to successfully start the initiative. A developer spoke of a cooperative that was unlikely to succeed, but did succeed. This cooperative "developed in part because the geographic community was really supportive and really wanted to make it happen". An attitude of support for new initiatives is needed. In some communities, individuals are able to build on a series of successful past initiatives. Other communities may not have recent successes to build upon, but people can be motivated if "they've seen the loss in their community. They recognise that their business, their futures will not survive". Leaders need to know which category their community fits into. Each cooperative development project is different, so leaders need to determine if there are enough dedicated, passionate, and skilled community members that believe they can bring positive change to their community to work together on building the cooperative.

Cooperative leaders need to know that the members of the community are able to continue to put in work with little immediate return while focusing on longer-term, shared rewards. A developer identified that "people are more and more focused on short-term gain and rewards. So often, the rewards of developing a coop can take a while to get there. People have to be able to delay that gratification". Leaders can only take a group so far. The group must be willing to work with each other and the leader. The longer the initiative takes, the harder it is to keep the group motivation. Cooperative leaders should have a sense of the support they will receive and the willingness of their community to become engaged in new initiatives prior to beginning development.

Cooperative development is in many ways an inherently political act. Starting a cooperative "is local politics. It's where you put your nexus of power. . . . You're making a decision of where you're going to place your time, where you're going to place your money, where you're going to shop, and that's a small 'p' political act". When a new cooperative is addressing a need that is in a true gap area, where there is no provision or history of provision, and there is no power imbalance connected, it is unlikely to create disquiet in the community. However, where the cooperative could be seen as a direct threat to an existing organisation or to an existing power balance, the cooperative may face direct opposition. Leaders must be aware of these situations and be prepared to navigate them within their community. A leader that does not know the community they are working in can inadvertently cause a great deal of harm.

### Knowing Group Dynamics

In order for there to be a cooperative, there has to be a group of interested people coalesced around a similar desire to meet a need in the community, who are willing to be involved in the venture and to stay involved. A big part of cooperative leadership is "helping people ask the questions they need about [coops] and end up with a list of people that you could go to and approach them and see if they want to get involved in that group". The CIP programme found that community members in rural and Indigenous communities in western Canada are stretched, and the people in the community face volunteer burn-out, but they will contribute if there is a leader they trust driving the project forward (CIP, 2016, Community Capacity, 10). Once there is a group established, however, it is necessary to manage the group, especially in the shared leadership and decision-making system inherent to cooperatives.

While some groups are able to access the use of cooperative development specialists that can assist with managing group dynamics, it is not the case for every group. Even groups that use development specialists need to have leaders from within the group that can manage the unique dynamics of their group of which an outside developer may not be aware. To start the development process and to make decisions that include everyone, cooperative leaders need to "get people talking together. You get people animated and having conversations all around you in which you're included". They do not lead the conversation, but they lead the process to make sure each individual's voice is heard and that the group is able to work together.

People have differing opinions. In rural and Indigenous communities, there will be members of a group that have a common interest in meeting a need in the community, but may have very different ideas, backgrounds, and roles in the community. Cooperative leaders ". . . have to have a lot of respect for people, in the sense that they have respect for the players at the table and knowledge of them and make sure they're balanced in how people are contributing to the organisation". The value that locally embedded leaders bring is that they know their neighbours, and they recognise and are able to help the group navigate potential problem areas.

The idea of respecting people and ensuring that all members are treated equally is important from the beginning of the venture to ensure sustainability. In order for the cooperative to belong to everyone, everyone's voice must be heard. The delicate balance between helping people work together and taking over the room is challenging. Coop leaders ". . . don't try and be the person in the room that everybody looks at". They do not want to do all the talking, and they do not want to have all the answers. Rather, "they have to have the quality of getting people to speak up and stand up". Not only is this trait important in building group dynamics, it is crucial for creating shared leadership in a cooperative.

Differences of opinion will arise at all times in a cooperative. However, cooperative leaders embrace differences of opinion as it allows members to resolve their differences of opinion and move forward together. A developer stated, "It's not about putting conflict down, it's bringing conflict up. That's the attitude you need to have as a coop leader. Because that's the most important part". Members of cooperative groups need to understand how to raise and manage conflict, and cooperative leaders need to be able to mediate this process if members are not able to do so on their own. In the long run, even if "the business model . . . is sound, then the biggest problem that the group is going to face will probably be the cooperative side of things. Because the social and the member relations and the internal governance will all impact the business and enterprise model in some way or another". Good cooperative leaders understand the importance of group dynamics and how to build good dynamics in their groups.

Perhaps the most crucial component for leaders of managing group dynamics is being able to ensure that the group stays unified. Cooperatives that do not stay unified are likely to lose their way. Members will have different ideas on how to approach planning, obstacles, and decisions, often informed by their individual previous experiences. Some of these ideas will work well with the cooperative model, and others won't. Cooperative leaders have to be able to make sure that all voices are heard and have to help ". . . them thread the links between the various capacities and needs you have for other approaches to business development or local development, with the coop identity". Being able to leverage strengths, divergent ideas, and keeping a group centred around a common purpose are all necessary for successful cooperative leadership.

### Putting the Project Over Politics

Often people assume that cooperatives are a left-of-centre solution and that people involved in cooperatives are politically aligned on the left. However, as put by a developer, "Coops are never a right-wing solution or a left-wing solution, it's an up solution". Regardless of the political affiliation of the membership, cooperatives can provide necessary goods and services to all members of a community. Very strong affiliation with political ideology among the leaders may minimise the success of the cooperative to reach all members of the community. Cooperative leaders are able to put their own political ideology to the side in order to successfully launch their project.

A developer stated, "the ones who do it [lead development of a cooperative] the best are not the ones who are not in politics. . . . It can happen, but, when you get into the politics, that's a different style of leadership, election and process". Elected leaders utilise a different leadership style, engage with people in a different way, and want to carry out change in a different way than cooperative leaders. The community will recognise the inherent leadership in cooperative leaders, and they are the "ones who've probably been asked by a number of different parties to run for election and they've said no". Cooperative leaders would rather use their leadership to leadership to help their communities by undertaking tangible action and ensuring others are involved in the change.

Nevertheless, cooperative leaders need to work with, and around, politics. The act of joining a cooperative, grounded in democratic values, is a political act. Those who want to form or join cooperatives tend to believe in democracy. They tend to believe that people should have a level of control over their lives and that people are capable of enacting change in their communities. These are many of the same ideals that drive politicians. Successful cooperative leaders "want to work behind the scenes, they just want to make it happen in the community". Cooperative leaders are interested in ensuring the whole community gains with them, not because of them. At the same time, they must be aware of the political implications and subtleties in their communities to ensure their project advances.

## Conclusion

Rural and Indigenous communities in western Canada have faced significant changes over the past 30 years which have resulted in decreased economic opportunities for many communities. People living in these communities want to see their communities regain their economic sustainability and offer a high quality of life to community members. Traditional businesses will often not establish in smaller market areas, using volunteers is not a sustainable model, and government service provision is more and more centralised to large urban centres. The cooperative business model allows communities to use knowledge of their community, its needs and its strengths, to create local solutions to meet its needs. The model combines social and business capacity, and requires large community buy-in, increasing chances of sustainability and also increasing the skills of community members.

Cooperatives do not work well as an imposed model; they must be a community-driven solution. A key component of community-based cooperative development is local leaders. The correct people need to be at the table to develop a cooperative, and having individuals with the right attributes to lead this work is crucial. Entrepreneurial leadership theory can provide some guidance to determine these attributes, which the research has identified as: commitment to the community and shared leadership, possession of business acumen and controlled energy, knowing the community and group dynamics, and putting the project over politics. It is knowledge of and commitment to the community, possessing controlled energy through long development timelines and an ability to put the project first that differentiate cooperative leaders from other entrepreneurial leaders.

Most communities undertaking this work cannot lose the large amounts of energy put into development if it leads to an unsuccessful venture. In many cases, this is more damaging than trying nothing at all. Cooperatives can be an exciting part of regeneration for those communities and those individuals willing to take on the challenge of developing one.

Further work focused specifically on the attributes and style of cooperative leaders, both at the initial development stage and throughout operations of the cooperative, are needed to verify and expand the attributes identified in this research. Additionally, while CIP included research on Indigenous communities and cooperatives, consultation with Indigenous people is required prior to ascribing the attributes described in this article to Indigenous contexts.

## Note

1. The full results of the CIP project can be found on the project site: https://coopinnovation.wordpress.com. This chapter would not be possible without the contributions of the entire CIP team and, in particular, Merle Massie.

## References

Burns, MacGregor J. 1978. *Leadership*. New York: Harper and Row.
CIP. 2016. *Final Report*. Saskatoon: Centre for the Study of Cooperatives. Accessed from https://coopinnovation.wordpress.com/final-report/.
Cogliser, C. C., and K. H. Brigham. 2004. "The Intersection of Leadership and Entrepreneurship: Mutual Lessons to Be Learned." *The Leadership Quarterly*, 15(6): 771–799.

Dinh, J. E., Lord, R. G., Gardner, W. L., Meuser, J. D., Liden, R. C., and J. Hu. 2014. "Leadership Theory and Research in the New Millennium: Current Theoretical Trends and Changing Perspectives." *The Leadership Quarterly*, 25(1): 36–62.

Ensley, M. D., Hmieleski, K. M., and C. L. Pearce. 2006. "The Importance of Vertical and Shared Leadership Within New Venture Top Management Teams: Implications for the Performance of Startups." *The Leadership Quarterly*, 17(3): 217–231.

Fairbairn, B. 2000. *Cooperative Development and the State: Case Studies and Analysis*. Saskatoon, CA: Centre for the Study of Cooperatives.

Gupta, V., MacMillan, I., and G. Surie. 2004. "Entrepreneurial Leadership: Developing and Measuring a Cross-cultural Construct." *Journal of Business Venturing*, 19: 241–260.

ICA. 2017. *What Is a Cooperative?* Accessed from https://ica.coop/en/what-cooperative.

# 6 The Social Regeneration of Mafia Assets in the Land of Gomorrah

## The Role of Social Cooperatives

*Michele Mosca*[1]

## Introduction

The economic crises of the last decade and the consequent transformation of social and economic relationships make us rethink the possible ways of increasing people's well-being and the types of entrepreneurship that favour sustainable development. In fact, social exclusion, new forms of poverty, and marginalisation of disadvantaged people that resulted from the crisis boosted require new policies that will be able to provide more effective solutions.

These phenomena are more intense in territories that had suffered the domination of the mafia. These territories have embarked on perverse development paths and witness the deterioration of the endowment of social capital. Social capital is transformed into "mafia's social capital", that is, into a network of relationships that allows the mafia to gain advantages and play the false role of a common market operator (Sciarrone, 2011). In other words, the mafia generates or relays on fiduciary ties and dominates social and commercial relationships, sustaining and generating illegal behaviours. Criminal organisations build ties and networks among individuals and between individuals and institutions by flaunting strength and power and spreading the myth of invincibility and the ability to produce wealth for their members. In fact, criminal organisations count on a system of strong relationships which allows them to sustain the social consensus that helps them dominate territories. Therefore, this social consensus is the basic element for their creation and existence. However, it is formed and strengthened by destroying trust among individuals and towards public institutions.

The mafia destroys diffused trust and social norms. Trust, as it is stressed in the economic literature, is fundamental for economic growth and strengthening civicness (Putnam, 2000; Bruni and Zamagni, 2007). Trust and reputation are components of social capital, which represents a fundamental input for the emancipation and freedom of people. A greater quantity and quality of social capital increase economic and social wealth. It is not by chance that criminal organisations find fertile land to pursue their activities and establish themselves in territories with a lower level of social capital.

For these reasons, it is crucial to act on more generalised forms of "social capital" in order to neutralise the strength of the mafia. By targeting social ties and networks and proposing alternative social principles and behaviours, we challenge the main strategic resource that the mafia uses to achieve its aims, that is, its social capital. Social capital regeneration may result in a different allocation of resources and opportunities in the territory by re-orienting social capital towards the promotion of the substantial freedoms of people and the general interests of a democratic community (Baldascino and Mosca, 2012).

The contribution of this chapter is to reflect on the kinds of policies that should be designed to combat mafias[2] and on the kinds of institutions and production organisations that can sustain development in these territories. The chapter also focuses on the Italian experience of the fight against organised crime, which complements conventional tools of repression and relies on social cohesion actions that support the social reuse of confiscated assets from organised crime. It discusses the opportunity granted by the Italian legal system, through Law 109/1996 and the Legislative Decree 159/2011, to third sector organisations, particularly to social cooperatives, to become privileged concessionaires in the assignment of confiscated properties.

The chapter uses available data on the Italian phenomenon of confiscated assets. It shows that the seizure and confiscation of the illegally acquired assets, combined with suitable policies for the development of social cooperatives and non-profit organisations, such as social cooperatives, which assume an important role in the labour market, can have a direct impact on the choices of individuals by reducing the incentive for illegal activity, strengthening emancipation and promoting community development.

After analysing the mafia's action by usurping the social capital, the chapter presents the Italian experience in the fight against the mafia illustrating the results that the confiscation of illicitly acquired assets has produced in Italy. The chapter continues by proposing policies to combat the mafia that are complementary to repressive ones such as those that can be built by the role of the social economy that can function as an antidote to the criminal economy. It is investigated the role played by social cooperatives that, thanks to the social re-use of confiscated assets, are regenerating social capital. The chapter ends with some concluding remarks

## The Usurpation of Social Capital

Mafia-style[3] criminal organisations build networks among affiliates, politicians, and individuals to rule in territories. In fact, criminal organisations accumulate considerable financial resources by using violence, crime, and illegal activities that increase their power and thus put the yoke on people and territories and condition the legal economy. They obtain this strength by using their capacity to take away, directly or indirectly, the management and control of the economic activities of enterprises and by influencing public administration activities (Parliamentary Commission of Enquiry on Mafia-style Organised Crime, 2007, 3). The evolution of this phenomenon and its transnational dimensions should push countries to formulate uniform combat policies that prevent criminal behaviour.

In fact, mafia-style criminal organisations have taken, over the years, a transnational dimension[4] through which criminal organisations "act as economic operators in the markets, distorting their proper mechanisms, with the use of massive economic and financial resources gathered from the exercise of a multiplicity of illegal activities, ranging from drug trafficking to contraband dealings, from property speculation to tendering for public works, from racketeering to extortion—carried out also abroad, and often in synergy with foreign criminal groups" (Parliamentary Commission of Enquiry on Mafia-style Organised Crime, 2007, 6).

But what confers greater strength to mafia-style criminal organisations is the ability to use social ties and networks to construct a social consensus which allows them to produce, uncontested, illegal wealth for their affiliates. These organisations usurp social capital by controlling all dimensions of civic life that influence trust, values, and social norms (Putnam et al., 1993; Fukuyama, 1995), as well as social relations and networks (Bourdieu, 1986; Coleman, 1988). In this manner, criminal organisations achieve illegal gains and generate a vicious cycle of social and cultural impoverishment and the consolidation of an economy sustained by crime.

In fact, the mafia represents a complex phenomenon. In the territories where it operates, the mafia employs (physical and symbolic) violence to construct a social consensus and present a dominant cultural model to economically and socially "fragile" young generations, shaping their values and behaviours in order to serve its purposes. The mafia uses symbols to show how successful it is in choosing and supporting its activities and to recruit new affiliates. Among the symbols used as bait to attract new members are villas, apartments, luxury cars, jewellery, etc., assets which mafias accumulate massively. These goods exert a double function; not only do they increase the utility and the economic wealth of their affiliates, but they also function as symbols of their power, which are used to signal their domination in the community and the territory where they act and to generate submission. The quantity and the quality of these assets publicly show the mafia's power and strength. They are similar to positional goods which confer utility by means of the status they grant to those who possess and consume these goods (Hirsch, 1976). Possession of these assets improves the consumers' own wealth and their relative status offering them a higher utility than the one they would have had if these assets were owned by others in the community. Moreover, the wealth status they confer raises the owner's position if other consumers' position falls and thus enables him/her to approach higher levels of the social pyramid. Criminal organisations accumulate goods for illegal aims to achieve a higher status level and to signal their force, strength, and capacity to generate wealth. This illegal accumulation takes away relevant resources from the territory, worsening the wealth position of other individuals.

The similarity between positional goods and criminal organisations helps us explain why mafias are interested in making territories poor, dredging them of economic resources and development opportunities. Both the economic and social impoverishment of territories facilitates criminal organisations to infiltrate and root in these territories. However, the mafia accumulates goods which cannot be considered similar to other goods for different reasons. Firstly, these assets are the products of illegal activities which take away economic resources from territories depriving them from individuals who operate legally. Secondly, these assets are obtained by terror and crime. The activities carried out by criminal organisations allow them to obtain goods through the usurpation of social capital. Through illegal activities, goods lose their neutral (Douglas and Isherwood, 1979) function, and they are used for "anti-social" objectives, because they create obstacles to economic and social development.

These interpretations help us understand why it is essential to remove illicitly acquired assets from criminal organisations and to re-assign them so they could be used to pursue social objectives in the communities that they were taken from. The social reuse of illicitly acquired assets can therefore represent an economic policy intervention able to restore and re-enforce trust among individuals and trust towards legal institutions. This idea is the basis of the Italian law on the social reuse of assets confiscated from criminal organisations (Law 109/1996 and Legislative Decree 159/2011). The social and economic development of territories sustained by initiatives that favour the accumulation of social capital for general purposes, such as those generated by the social economy, can prevent criminal organisations from continuing to gain the consensus of a large part of the population living in the territories in which they operate.

## The Italian Experience in the Fight Against Mafias

Mafia-type criminal organisations are complex phenomena, as they do not affect single economic activities, but attempt to infiltrate the legal economy. Most of their activities are carried out in a covert manner, weakening the effectiveness of repressive policies. In fact, to defeat mafia-style criminal organisations, it is necessary to combine repressive tools with preventive strategies and actions, which weaken and reconvert "the mafia's social capital". This kind of social capital represents the network of relationships that enables such organisations to "communicate" in a lucrative way with the economic and social context within which they operate, drawing further advantage from a position of intrinsic strength and assuming the false guise of a normal operator in the market (Sciarrone, 2011). The attack on "the mafia's social capital" can redirect social capital towards the promotion of the substantive freedom of people and the general interests of a democratic community (Baldascino and Mosca, 2012).

Therefore, it is necessary to develop new programmes for the empowerment and development of territories based on the supply and quality of social capital, which helps to promote respect for democratic rules, civil life and public institutions. These new programmes rely on planning procedures that involve a variety of local players, institutional (and non-institutional), which collaboratively pursue a common interest, namely the defeat of the mafia, and thus maximise the contribution of their resources.

Over the years, Italy has gained considerable experience in combatting the mafia by means of innovative legislation and the support of institutions capable of regenerating social capital by taking away the consensus that mafias have in territories. These policies aim at defeating the mafia consensus by acting on the social capital held by the mafia and re-orienting it towards genuinely social objectives. Traditional policy tools need to be associated with activities that can generate changes and create different opportunities for people and territories.

In fact, in order to defeat mafia, arrests, confiscation, and criminal trials are not sufficient, but social and cultural operation is essentially needed. Breaking the vicious cycle of social and cultural impoverishment and the perpetuation of an economic growth model based on crime requires the adoption of policies that impede the usurpation of the social consensus imposed by criminal organisations. These policies would contribute to combatting organised crime and promoting the socio-economic development of territories. In fact, they could stimulate the creation of social activities which would favour the accumulation of social capital for generalised interests.

Following these ideas, Italy has adopted effective repressive measures to combat criminal mafia-style organisations and the accumulation of illicit capital. Noteworthy among these are the measures for illegal wealth prevention (Section II of Legislative Decree No. 159 of 6 September 2011, known as the Anti-Mafia Code). These measures provide for the seizure and confiscation of assets for which no legitimate provenance has been demonstrated and which are found to be at the direct or indirect disposal of someone suspected of belonging to a mafia-style organisation. Thus, they are aimed at deterring persons deemed socially dangerous for committing crimes and are applied independently of a previous crime having been committed, so they are termed measures applicable *ante delictum* or *praeter delictum*. Such combat policies were implemented in Italy during the attacks on public institutions that caused the death of the prestigious magistrates who had taken on the "war" against the mafias.[5] However, actions combating mafia-style crime have increased thanks to the strengthening of the Italian legal statutes that allow authorities to adopt action against assets that were illegally acquired.[6]

The strategy for combating criminal organisations can be divided into two distinct stages. The first stage includes the identification, seizure, and confiscation of the wealth of criminal organisations, including current assets, real estate, and company assets; the second stage regards the re-allocation of assets and wealth to serve public aims. Possessions and wealth taken from mafia-style organisations are mainly returned to the community in order to be reused for social and institutional purposes.[7] This action differs from the illicit wealth confiscated in penal trials and which, once valued in monetary terms, ends up in the state cauldron, not designated for specific aims but utilised for general public expenditure.

The values and symbolic message underlying this trend in the legislation are extremely important: they demonstrate that the state is succeeding in targeting the wealth accumulated by criminal associations, thereby restoring or building trust in public institutions. The assets confiscated from mafia-style associations constitute a precious resource for local territories, providing an opportunity for community development that can help trigger and sustain the process of social and economic growth, guided by respect for the rules of law. To give further impetus to the utilisation of assets confiscated from mafia-style associations, and to improve the efficient management of these assets, the National Agency ANBSC was founded. ANBSC is the Italian acronym for the *National Agency for the Administration and Management of Assets Seized and Confiscated from Criminal Organisations.*[8] The Agency guarantees the effective administration and allocation of seized and confiscated assets that are the proceeds of organised crime, also through a stable accord between the judicial authorities and the Public Administrations concerned.

Among the juridical tools employed, the seizure and confiscation of assets that have been illegally obtained constitute the most effective measures in fighting criminal organisations. This is what organised crime fears the most, because it loses not only its economic wealth, but also the power to sustain the social consensus it uses for spreading a sense of invincibility in the territories. In fact, tools of seizure and confiscation deprive criminal assets of the characteristics that make them symbols of status.[9] From status goods that produce wealth through the exploitation and the impoverishment of the economic and civil resources of territories, they can be transformed into opportunities for economic and social development.

Through this metamorphosis, these assets re-acquire their neutral function and are used for social aims. This principle is ratified by Law 109/1996 and the Legislative Decree 159/2011, which allow for the reutilisation of assets belonging to organised crime by applying tools of seizure and confiscation. In particular, the law allows confiscated assets to be re-assigned to non-profit organisations and thus underlines the social role of these organisations and their ability to transform "illegal" goods into useful community activities. Strengthening the social economy can be an effective policy to remedy criminal economies. In fact, the social utility maximisation pursued by non-profit organisations can enhance social capital and social community. The development of social entrepreneurship can be an ideal mechanism capable of producing civil, social, and economic development in territories. The development of social entrepreneurship activities can increase job opportunities and wealth in these territories.[10] Seizure, confiscation, and, above all, the reutilisation of illegal assets for social aims can be used as indicators of the loss of power and influence of criminal organisations in territories. Therefore, the number of reutilised goods for social and institutional purposes and civic activities can be considered a proxy of the regeneration social capital in a territory and the levels of civil and social development. Overall, by returning assets illegally held by organised crime to the local community and reusing them for social purposes, we can create an effective strategy for re-allocating social capital to public interests.

## Social Economy as an Antidote to Criminal Economy

The issues illustrated in the previous sections help us to understand that mafias must also fight on all fronts in the economy they create. Therefore, it is necessary to build new paths of growth inspired by different features and values from those characterising the economy they exploit and abuse. The emergence of the social economy[11] as a grassroots, entrepreneurial sector which is based on democratic values and seeks to enhance the social, economic, and environmental conditions of communities, often with a focus on their disadvantaged members, can represent an antidote to the criminal economy (Mosca and Musella, 2013). Social economy and its organisations can be an interesting field of action to build a new basis to free territories of the burden of criminal organisations and restore growth and development by pursuing common aims: reducing poverty, providing affordable housing, and addressing environmental concerns through social, cultural, educational, employment, and lifestyle activities.

The social economy is characterised by the presence of organisations that pursue social aims while respecting the economic constraint and generating economic value through the services and goods they provide. Their activities are inspired by values of solidarity, autonomy, and citizenship and pursue finalities of general interest for the benefit of the community. They mainly provide services to members of the community through autonomous management and democratic decision-making processes generating the participation of citizens (Mook et al., 2007).

Among non-profit institutions, social enterprise represents the main productive organisation of the social economy that has recently demonstrated that it is possible to make an economy that pursues goals beyond profit, by reversing means with ends. The goal of for-profit organisations, namely profit, becomes for the social enterprise a tool to reach a broader objective, namely the social utility (Borzaga and Fazzi, 2011). The Italian experience shows that the social cooperative represents a specific kind of social enterprise that is able to combine social and economic goals by responding to the needs of disadvantaged people and communities (Borzaga and Santuari,

2001) and contributing to local development and job creation. Furthermore, these cooperatives are one of the most characteristic manifestations of the propensity to create relationships and trust that underpins social capital (Evers, 2001; Sabatini et al., 2014). The social enterprise comprises a particular type of enterprise that has "the purpose of pursuing the general interest of the community in human promotion and the social integration of citizens" (Art.1 Law 381/1991).

Social cooperatives are, in fact, productive enterprises founded by private bottom-up initiatives to counter the social exclusion of disadvantaged people by generating virtuous development processes in the territories where they operate. This form of enterprise was introduced in the Italian legal system with Law 381/1991. The law identifies social enterprises with cooperatives that pursue the general interest of the community and promote the human and social integration of citizens by means of: a) managing health, educational and social services (A-type social cooperatives); and b) carrying out different activities—agricultural, industrial, commercial, or services—aimed at providing employment for disadvantaged people (B-type social cooperatives) (Article 1 of the Law 381/1991). According to the law, these organisations are considered as non-profit organisations, which, thanks to their multi-stakeholder governance and democratic participation, can attract resources to satisfy social needs (minors, elderly, disabled, unemployed, drug addicts, ex-prisoners, etc.) (Borzaga, 2002). In fact, they activate the direct participation of stakeholders such as workers, volunteers, financial partners, users, and institutions and incorporate them in decision-making processes, reinforcing relationships among the various stakeholders and positively affecting economic activity (Freeman, 1984; Clarkson, 1995).

As already mentioned, these organisations pursue aims of general interest such as people's health, social services, or re-integration of disadvantaged individuals into the workforce. Additionally, they can take part in the fight against the mafia. In this sense, they may be considered as a response to the exclusion of certain categories of people from economic and social life Social cooperatives can play an active role in producing goods, services and simultaneously preventing illegal behaviour, thanks to their capacity to build entrepreneurial pathways aimed at pursuing general interest aims, such as social cohesion. In fact, they build relationships different to those that criminal organisations have, and in doing so strengthen efforts for converting the "mafia's social capital" into "social capital" for general purposes.

The presence of productive organisations that have in their DNA different characteristics to sustain the development of territories does not guarantee the defeat of the mafia and its criminal behaviour. It is necessary to recapture the assets that criminal organisations have accumulated and return them to the community. This principle is enshrined in Law 109/1996 and in the Legislative Decree 159/2011, which stipulate that assets taken away from organised crime by seizure and confiscation must be reutilised for social and institutional aims. As part of their social reuse, the law has identified social cooperatives as entrepreneurial entities that can reconvert the use of assets that belonged to mafias.

Thanks to these laws, Italy has been the first country to give social cooperatives an active role in the fight against organised crime. Social cooperatives have the ability to combat social exclusion and to contribute to community development. In fact, non-profit organisations, and particularly social cooperatives that assume the structure of a social enterprise, can effectively and efficiently manage patrimonies, which can produce, if appropriately valorised and "revitalised", huge flows of wealth for the territories that were abused by criminal organisations. This would contribute to creating jobs and, at the same time, finding new paths to enhance social capital and build trust towards legal institutions. In fact, the mistrust of the community towards the latter is tightly connected to the possibility that, in a direct or indirect way (through, for example, the role of dummy companies or figurehead individuals), criminal organisations continue to operate without being contested. The profit-budget constraint and the multi-stakeholder governance model of non-profit organisations enable individuals in both the public and private spheres to share the management of non-profit organisations. Thus, they potentially provide suitable mechanisms to prevent criminal organisations from re-appropriating assets that have been seized and confiscated and to increase trust towards the state and its institutions. Furthermore, the multi-stakeholder nature of non-profit organisations enables them to successfully prevent criminal organisations from repurchasing confiscated assets and thus to break the vicious cycle which produces mistrust and hinders economic development in territories (Mosca and Villani, 2013, 2015).

The tools of seizure and confiscation of illegally acquired assets and their reutilisation by social enterprises for social and institutional purposes could represent a juridical measure which, if well implemented, can develop an important deterrent to illegal behaviour. The high symbolic value of the reutilisation of assets for social and institutional purposes can contribute in a positive and effective way to breaking the yoke put on territories by criminal organisations that create "illegal" social networks and criminal activities. Furthermore, the possibility for social cooperatives to manage the former properties of criminal organisations and to utilise them for the creation of socially useful activities can, in a direct way, produce wealth for the territory through the production of goods and services and the creation of job opportunities.

Greater support to the development of social enterprises, in combination with a simplification of the administrative procedures concerning the assignment of confiscated assets, would directly and indirectly increase the levels of wealth. Social enterprises produce and sustain components of social capital (such as trust, respect for the civil rules, and the empowerment of active citizenship); that is, they provide the building blocks for increasing respect for the law and thus improving the quality of life of individuals. By managing assets that formerly belonged to criminal organisations, social cooperatives directly contribute to the creation of the wealth in the territory through the production of goods and services and the creation of employment opportunities perhaps in more effective ways than private for-profit organisations and the public sector. Moreover, the promotion of social initiatives, typical of a social cooperative, can trigger mechanisms capable of pushing individuals to prefer legal activities from illegal activities.

The social reuse of properties belonging to criminal organisations can, therefore, contribute positively and effectively to breaking the vicious cycle that is set up by "illegal" social networks and criminal activities, especially in areas with a long history of weak social ties and civic values. In particular, removing assets from criminal organisations and re-assigning them to the community can help restore and strengthen trust among individuals and towards public institutions. Consequently, social cooperatives turn illegal assets into community goods. The social use of confiscated properties can also become an indicator of community growth in contrast to the "community" that criminal organisations try to impose through their practices and culture. This means that it can be used as a proxy variable of the change process taking in place in the 'mafia lands'. Furthermore, it can function as an indicator of how local authorities and institutions can support and encourage the regeneration of social capital and sense of civicness in their territories. Finally, it can be employed as an indicator to assess the process of re-appropriation and transformation of the social capital usurped by the mafia. We return to these issues in the following section, where we present our empirical study.

Through the social regeneration of confiscated assets, social cooperatives support social innovation processes which start from the bottom and convey human and financial resources to the social and economic development of territories. There is a common thread running across the various social innovation processes which can be activated in the territory and demonstrate its ability to propose innovative solutions to social problems and needs by providing new goods and services and creating new organisational forms which increase people's well-being.

The Italian experience shows that social cooperatives are one of the most important expressions of social entrepreneurship and make a significant contribution to the community by combating social exclusion through the creation of social innovation (Bygrave and Hofer, 1991; Churchill and Muzyka, 1994). Adding to this, social cooperatives can contribute to the fight against organised crime (Frigerio, 2009) and the development of local communities (Mosca and Villani, 2013; Fondazione Libera Informazione, 2009; Picciotto, 2012).

To initiate these paths of transformation, it is necessary to sustain new production organisations that are inspired by different principles and practices to generate healthy growth and development. The social enterprise, which has been operating in countries across the globe for some time now, is capable of implementing such policies by mobilising bottom-up initiatives and relations among people and re-orienting activities towards social problems. In fact, the social economy contributes to developing a social cohesion-generating economy by forming new mentalities within the local socio-economic environment (Matei et al., 2015).

## Typologies and Consistency of Confiscated Goods

Law 109/1996 and Legislative Decree 159/2011 define assets confiscated from mafias as: current assets (sums of money, state bonds, personal accruals, jewellery, etc); registered current assets (cars, motorcycles, boats, aeroplanes, etc.); non-current assets in the form of property (villas, apartments, farm buildings, retail premises, lands, etc.); and company assets (company quotas, shares, factories, industrial premises, manufacturing plant, commercial activities, etc.). Such assets, once confiscated, must be transformed and transferred[12] for use in public interest aims. More precisely, for real estate, the law provides their social reuse by identifying privileged concessionaries within non-profit organisations that will relocate them back to the community. When local authorities do not directly intend to administer the property, they can assign the asset free of charge to communities, organisations, more representative associations of local authorities, voluntary organisations (Law 266/1991), social cooperatives (Law 381/1991), or therapeutic communities and centres for the recovery and treatment of drug addicts (DPR 309/1990), as well as recognised environmental protection organisations (Law 349/1986).[13]

Table 6.1 summarises the overall picture of the number of confiscated assets in Italy and their distribution at the territorial level.[14] The consistency of confiscated assets depends on two factors: 1) the number of seizures and confiscations; and 2) the time it takes to re-assign assets by the National Agency ANBSC after the verdict of judicial proceedings is issued.

The data show that the total number of confiscated assets in 2015 exceeded 20,000 units. This accounts to a large amount of resources that need to be re-allocated to avoid further costs to the community. Approximately 80% of confiscated assets were located in the four southern regions (Sicily 38%, Calabria 13%, Campania 15%, and Puglia, 9%), which also record the highest crime rates. Among the northern regions, Lombardia had a significant amount of confiscated assets (7.4%). The other regions of the North with a significant supply of confiscated goods are Piemonte (1.5%), Emilia Romagna, and Veneto (1%).

Table 6.1 shows that confiscated assets from organised crime cover the entire national territory and concern even northern regions, such as Valle d'Aosta, which recorded one of the lowest regional crime rates. The data also show a concentration of confiscated goods mainly in the southern regions. However, when we analyse data in relation to type of assets, Lombardia, which is located in the North and constitutes one of the most industrial and

*Table 6.1* The Consistency of the Confiscated Assets in Italy (December 2015)

| | Firms | (%) | Real estate | (%) | Total | (%) |
|---|---|---|---|---|---|---|
| Abruzzo | 6 | 0.21 | 261 | 1.30 | 267 | 1.16 |
| Basilicata | 6 | 0.21 | 25 | 0.12 | 31 | 0.13 |
| Calabria | 335 | 11.58 | 2,738 | 13.62 | 3,073 | 13.37 |
| Campania | 637 | 22.03 | 2,793 | 13.90 | 3,430 | 14.92 |
| Emilia-Romagna | 49 | 1.69 | 255 | 1.27 | 304 | 1.32 |
| Friuli Venezia Giulia | 2 | 0.07 | 40 | 0.20 | 42 | 0.18 |
| Lazio | 380 | 13.14 | 1,455 | 7.24 | 1835 | 7.98 |
| Liguria | 17 | 0.59 | 74 | 0.37 | 91 | 0.40 |
| Lombardia/Lombardy | 276 | 9.54 | 1,430 | 7.12 | 1,706 | 7.42 |
| Marche | 6 | 0.21 | 52 | 0.26 | 58 | 0.25 |
| Molise | 0 | 0.00 | 5 | 0.02 | 5 | 0.02 |
| Piemonte/Piedmont | 31 | 1.07 | 320 | 1.59 | 351 | 1.53 |
| Puglia | 217 | 7.50 | 1,984 | 9.87 | 2,201 | 9.57 |
| Sardegna/Sardinia | 12 | 0.41 | 245 | 1.22 | 257 | 1.12 |
| Sicilia/Sicily | 885 | 30.60 | 7,976 | 39.69 | 8,861 | 38.54 |
| Toscana/Tuscany | 22 | 0.76 | 178 | 0.89 | 200 | 0.87 |
| Trentino-Alto Adige/Südtirol | 1 | 0.03 | 17 | 0.08 | 18 | 0.08 |
| Umbria | 4 | 0.14 | 70 | 0.35 | 74 | 0.32 |
| Valle D'Aosta/Valle D'Aoste | 0 | 0.00 | 6 | 0.03 | 6 | 0.03 |
| Veneto | 6 | 0.21 | 174 | 0.87 | 180 | 0.78 |
| Total | 2892 | 100.00 | 20,098 | 100.00 | 2,2990 | 100.00 |

Source: Author's elaboration on ANBSC data

productive Italian regions, registers the highest level of confiscated firms (9.5 %). This finding highlights the tendency of criminal organisations to expand into richer territories, such as those of Northern Italy (Figure 6.1).

The data provide a picture of the phenomenon of confiscated assets in Italy and show the penetration capacity that criminal organisations use to conquest markets. Their presence in Northern Italy and the incidence with which this phenomenon is increasing exposes national and international territories to infiltration by mafia-style criminal organisations. This implies that the mafia needs to be fought with innovative tools and with repressive and preventive action that requires the collaboration of international law enforcement agencies.

The data provided by the ANBSC is limited to the destination of assets for institutional and social purposes, but they do not offer structured and comparable information on the real condition and use of such goods. The first field research that attempted to overcome this gap was conducted by Libera in 2013.[15] This study undertakes the mapping of 524 concessionaries of confiscated assets in 16 out of 20 regions in Italy. Lombardia is the first region in Italy to reuse confiscated assets (124). In this region, only 30% of

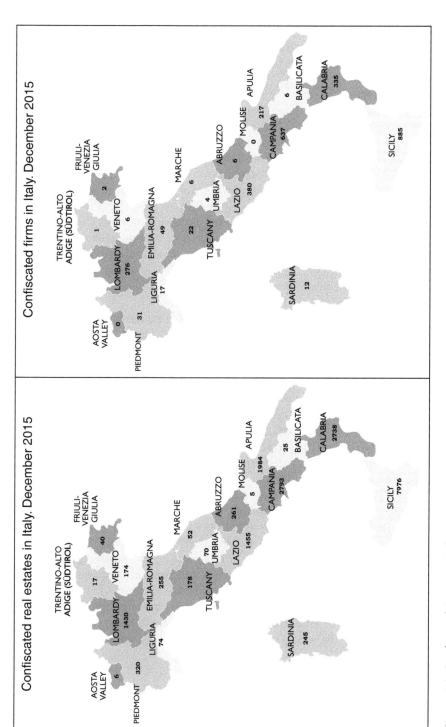

*Figure 6.1* Confiscated Assets in Italy. December 2015

Source: Author's elaboration

confiscated goods are not reused. Sicily (116), Campania (78), and Calabria (77) are the other Italian regions reporting the highest number of reutilised confiscated assets. In relation to the legal form of the concessionaries, this study finds that associations (284), social cooperatives (131), but also dioceses and parishes (22) mainly manage apartments (167), villas, buildings, and, in general, real estate, land (56), commercial and industrial units (82), but also tourist facilities and beach resorts. With an ad hoc online questionnaire to 105 social concessionaries, the study investigates the impact of reutilised goods in the local markets. There are interesting results regarding the human capital mobilised for activities of social reuse. In a sample of 70 concessionaries, there are 403 employees, 1,421 volunteers, and 25,368 beneficiaries. These results may appear quantitatively irrelevant from an entrepreneurial point of view; however, they are very important to the community because they may have the capacity to be able to respond to the needs of the area. In fact, the study highlights important activities in the field of: voluntary activities and the third sector (51); education for citizenship (41); cultural promotion and aggregation (38); and combatting social disadvantage and the integration of disabilities (30).

This research also raises critical issues. Apparently, it takes, on average, ten years to assign assets after they have been confiscated. Properties suffer further damage as a result of retaliation from criminal organisations, deterioration, and time. In 53 out of 76 cases, it turned out that assets were in poor condition when they were finally transferred (for more details, see Falcone et al., 2016). These drawbacks should be remedied by implementing rapid administrative procedures so as to allow a greater number of organisations to apply for confiscated assets and thus trigger a new way of doing economy, namely the social economy.

The social reuse of confiscated assets by non-profit organisations, and in particular by social cooperatives, is a policy tool that is producing interesting results on the front of the fight against the mafia. However, the mafia has shown over the years the capacity to "shed skin" and infiltrate into public and private institutions by conditioning their performance. In order to prevent them from adapting to the social enterprise model of cooperatives, the governance of these organisations must be implemented through active community participation mechanisms and shared transparency rules communicated to all potential stakeholders in the territory. This is a further challenge that the world of non-profit organisations can also grasp thanks to its ability to innovate in the forms of governance, products, and processes, which we have observed over the years at the international level.

## Concluding Remarks

This chapter has envisaged the role of social enterprises in the process of transforming 'the mafia's social capital'. This role is granted by Italian law to non-profit organisations, including social cooperatives. This particular type of social enterprise pursues the general interest by offering job opportunities to disadvantaged people. Furthermore, social cooperatives are, for the Italian law, privileged concessionaires in the process of re-assigning confiscated assets, and they are called upon to reuse these assets in the territories that have suffered the yoke of organised crime. If appropriately valued through the social re-conversion of their use, confiscated assets from criminal organisations can provide not just the legal background to reconstruct the cultural fabric and civic consciousness of territories, but also a development model capable of generating a different economy, that of the social economy.

The Italian experience related to the re-conversion of confiscated assets by social cooperatives for social aims contributes to generating social and economic growth in the territories where mafias have reigned. The Italian experience of combatting organised crime shows that it is being fought with repressive and preventive tools. While the repressive tools are designed and implemented by public institutions, preventive tools need partners and organisations that are able to rebuild aspirations and trusting relations among people who have long been overwhelmed by criminal organisations. Therefore, it is necessary to stress the possibility of building vigorous development paths from bottom-up initiatives, which bring people closer to institutions enforcing the regeneration of social capital. The social reuse of confiscated assets generated by social cooperatives increases the number of reused assets, generates jobs for disadvantaged people, and gives back what has been taken away from people and territories enmeshed in organised crime.

The social reuse of confiscated assets, which gives young people the opportunity to work in social cooperatives and to undertake pathways for the inclusion of disadvantaged people, are good practices to be supported and reproduced with more effective and active policies and tools beyond the sale or the lucrative use of these goods. Not only do these experiences have high symbolic value, they are better at regenerating and reconverting for general purposes both the economic resources and the social capital that mafias have dredged.

The large amount of confiscated assets in Italy represents an interesting field of action for social enterprises, such as social cooperatives, to reuse these assets and promote development projects capable of pursuing general interest objectives in favour of territories and communities where confiscated assets are concentrated. The data shows that although the social use of confiscated assets was introduced in Italy more than 20 years ago, there are factors that negatively affect the demand of such goods by other social cooperatives, such as: the delays in administrative procedures for the assignment of goods; the conditions in which confiscated assets are often found; and the short period of time granted to concession of confiscated property.

As this chapter has tried to highlight, the number of confiscated assets can be used as a proxy of how territories and people succeed in converting mafia-based social capital into social capital for general purposes by getting rid of criminal pressures. That is, it can be employed as an indicator of the process of transformation of the free and healthy communities, which local authorities and institutions can use to assess and compare the effectiveness of policies for generating social capital and civicness in different territories. In particular, removing assets from criminal organisations and re-assigning them to the community can help to restore and strengthen trust among individuals and towards public institutions, allowing goods to re-acquire their neutral function and become community goods through the action of social cooperatives.

## Acknowledgements

This research was carried out within the STAR Programme and was financially supported by UniNA and Compagnia di San Paolo'.

## Notes

1. *The author wishes to thank Asimina Christoforou and Silvia Sacchetti for their comments and suggestions that have improved earlier versions.*
2. Hereafter, we use the term *mafias* for the different types of criminal organisations using the same methods of intimidation.
3. Criminal association of the mafia type is a crime covered by Art. 416 b of the Italian Penal Code, introduced by Law No. 646 of 13 September 1982 and subsequent amendments and additions. The law states that "Association is of the Mafia type when those who belong to it use group-inspired intimidation and adhere to a vow of silence to commit crimes, in order to obtain, directly or indirectly, the management or in some way the control of economic activities, concessions, authorisations, tenders and public services or to impede or hamper the free exercise of the right to vote or to solicit votes for oneself or others during elections".
4. The Naples Political Declaration and Global Action Plan against Organised Transnational Crime, which was approved by the United Nations during the General Assembly on 23 December 1994, is the first official document envisaging the transnational dimension and the dangers of mafia-type criminal organisations. For details, see Turone (2007).
5. Just to name a few, we refer to the massacre era that led to the assassinations of Judges Falcone and Borsellino.
6. On this point, see Books I and II of the "Code of Anti-Mafia laws and measures of prevention", known as the Anti-Mafia Code, approved on 6 September 2011.
7. The reuse of confiscated assets was introduced in Italy by Law No. 109 of 7 March 1996. The law grew out of a popular initiative promoted by "Libera: Associations, names and numbers against Mafias", which gathered more than a million signatures.
8. The ANBSC has been constituted in Italy by Law 50/2010. The Agency guarantees the effective administration and allocation of seized and confiscated assets that are the proceeds of organised crime.
9. In particular, they deprive criminal organisations of economic wealth and, therefore, of the financial capability to bribe judges, prosecutors, witnesses, politicians, entrepreneurs, professional men or women, and all other subjects with whom the Mafia forms its "shadow alliances".
10. The contribution of social economy to the creation of jobs and innovative models of industrial relation is discussed by Borzaga and Tortia (2007).

11. There are many definitions of the social economy. Many of these can be found on the websites of the Social Economy Hub, the Chantier de l'économie sociale and l'Alliance de recherche universités-communautés en économie sociale (ARUC-ÉS) www.msvu.ca/socialeconomyatlantic/English/whatisE.asp.
12. The ANBSC decrees the destination of assets.
13. See in particular Art. 48 of the Legislative Decree 159/2011.
14. The table demonstrates the consistency of the phenomenon for the year 2015, the last update provided by the ANBSC.
15. "Libera. Associations, names and numbers against mafias" was founded on 25 March 1995 with the purpose of involving and supporting all those who are interested in the fight against mafias and organised crime.

## References

Baldascino, M., and M. Mosca. 2012. "La Gestione dei Beni Confiscati: Un'occasione Perduta per le Imprese Sociali?" In *L'Impresa Sociale in Italia. Pluralità dei Modelli e Contributo alla Ripresa*, edited by P. Venturi and F. Zandonai, 213–236. Milan: Altreconomia.

Borzaga, C. 2002. "Sull'Impresa Sociale." *Working Paper*, No. 19. Università degli Studi di Trento: Istituto Studi Sviluppo Aziende Non Profit.

Borzaga, C., and J. Defourny. 2001. *The Emergence of Social Enterprise*. London and New York: Routledge.

Borzaga, C., and L. Fazzi. 2011. *Le Imprese Sociali*. Rome: Carocci.

Borzaga, C., and A. Santuari. 2001. "Italy: From Traditional Cooperatives to Innovative Social Enterprises." In *The Emergence of Social Enterprise*, edited by C. Borzaga and J. Defourny, 166–181. London and New York: Routledge.

Borzaga, C., and E. Tortia. 2007. "Social Economy Organisations in the Theory of the Firm." In *The Social Economy: Building Inclusive Economies*, edited by A. Noya and E. Clearence. Paris: OECD.

Bourdieu, P. 1986. "The Forms of Capital." In *Handbook of Theory and Research for the Sociology of Education*, edited by J. Richardson, 249–262. Westport, CT: Greenwood Press.

Bruni, L., and S. Zamagni. 2007. *Civil Economy. Efficiency, Equity, Public Happiness*. Oxford and Bern: Peter Lang.

Caulier-Grice, J., Davies, A., Patrick, R., and W. Norman. 2012. "Defining Social Innovation. A Deliverable of the Project: The Theoretical, Empirical and Policy Foundations for Building Social Innovation in Europe (TEPSIE)." In *European Commission—7th Framework Programme*. Brussels: European Commission, DG Research.

Churchill, N. C., and D. F. Muzyka. 1994. "Defining and Conceptualising Entrepreneurship: A Process Approach." In *Marketing and Entrepreneurship: Research Ideas and Opportunities*, edited by G. E. Hills, 11–23. Westport, CT: Quorum Books.

Clarkson, M. B. E. 1995. "A Stakeholder Framework for Analysing and Evaluating Corporate Social Performance." *Academy of Management Review*, 20(1): 92–117.

Coleman, L. S. 1988. "Social Capital in the Creation of Human Capital." *The American Journal of Sociology*, 94: S95–S120.

Douglas, M., and B. Isherwood. 1979. *The World of Goods*. New York: Basic Books.

Evers, A. 2001. "The significance of social capital in the multiple goal and resource structure of social enterprises." In *The Emergence of Social Enterprise*, edited by C. Borzaga and J. Defourny, 296–311. London and New York: Routledge.

Falcone, R. C., Giannone, T., and F. Iandolo. 2016. "BeneItalia Economia, Welfare, Cultura, Etica: la Generazione di Valori nell'Uso Sociale dei Beni Confiscati alle

Mafie." In *Quaderni di Libera con Narcomafie*, edited by R. C. Falcone, T. Giannone and F. Iandolo, 1–152. Torino: Edizioni Gruppo Abele.

Fondazione Libera Informazione. 2009. "Beni Confiscati alle Mafie: il Potere dei Segni." In *Viaggio nel Paese Reale tra Riutilizzo Sociale Impegno e Responsabilità*, edited by Agenzia per le Organizzazioni Non Lucrative di Utilità Sociale. Milan: Fondazione Libera Informazione.

Freeman, R. E. 1984. *Strategic Management: A Stakeholder Approach.* Boston: Pitman.

Frigerio, L. 2009. "I Beni Confiscati alle Mafie per lo Sviluppo Sociale e Produttivo." In *Impresa Sociale Innovazione e Legalità*, edited by P. Iorio. Roma: Ediesse.

Fukuyama, F. 1995. *Trust: The Social Virtues and the Creation of Prosperity.* New York: Free Press.

Hirsch, F. 1976. *The Social Limit to Growth.* Cambridge, MA: Harvard University Press.

Matei, A., and A. D. Dorobantu. 2015. "Social Economy—Added Value for Local Development and Social Cohesion." *Procedia Economics and Finance*, 26: 490–494.

Mook, L., Quarter, J., and B. J. Richmond. 2007. *What Counts: Social Accounting for Nonprofits and Cooperatives*, 2nd edition. London: Sigel Press.

Mosca, M., and M. Musella. 2013. "L'Economia Sociale come Antidoto all'Economia Criminale." *Rassegna Economica, Rivista Internazionale di Economia e Territorio*, 1: 97–108.

Mosca, M., and S. Villani. 2013. "Reuse for Social Aims of Illegal Assets and the Competition Policy. A New Network Strategy to Defeat Organised Crime." In *Polish International Yearbook of Law & Economics*, edited by J. Bełdowski, K. Metelska-Szaniawska and L. Visscher, vol. 3. Poland: Warszawa.

Mosca, M., and S. Villani. 2015. "Good and Bad Networks. The Role of Social Enterprises in the Fight Against Organised Crime." In *Cooperative Enterprises in Australia and Italy: Comparative Analysis and Theoretical Insights*, edited by A. Jensen, G. Patmore and E. Tortia, 245–264. Florence: University of Florence Press.

Parliamentary Commission of Enquiry on Mafia-style Organised Crime. 2007. *Report on the State of Implementation of the Regulation and of Practices to Implement It as Regards Seizures, Confiscations and Allocations of the Proceeds of Organised Crime.* Accessed from http://legislature.camera.it/_dati/leg15/lavori/documentiparlamentari/indiceetesti/023/007/INTERO.pdf

Picciotto, L. 2012. "Turismo Responsabile e Valorizzazione dei Beni Confiscati alla Mafia: Opportunità di Sviluppo Umano e Territoriale. Il Caso di Libera Terra Mediterraneo." In *Atti della IV Riunione Scientifica della Società Italiana di Scienze del Turismo (SISTUR)*, edited by M. Ruisi and L. Picciotto, 447–481. Rome: Aracne Editrice.

Political Declaration and Global Action Plan Against Organised Transnational Crime. 1994. *United Nations General Assembly*, 23 December. Accessed from http://www.un.org/documents/ga/res/49/a49r159.htm

Putnam, R. D., Leonardi, R., and R. Y. Nanetti. 1993. *Making Democracy Work: Civic Traditions in Modern Italy.* New York: Princeton University Press.

Reuse of Confiscated Assets for Social Purposes (RO2013_C5.2_17). 2015. *The Centre of Legal Resources.* Editura Hamngiu. Accessed from http://www.crj.ro/wp-content/uploads/2015/10/Reutilizarea-bunurilor-confiscate-EN.pdf

Sabatini, F., Modena, F., and E. Tortia. 2014. "Do Cooperative Enterprises Create Social Trust?" *Small Business Economics*, 42(3): 621–641.

Sciarrone, R. 2011. *Alleanze nell'Ombra. Mafie ed Economie Locali in Sicilia e nel Mezzogiorno.* Rome: Donzelli.

Turone, G. 2007. "Legal Frameworks and Investigative Tools for Combating Organised Transnational Crime in the Italian Experience." *UNAFEI*, Fuchu, Tokyo, Japan, December.

# 7 Territorial Governance and the Social Economy in Migrants' Reception

## The Case of Romagna Faentina in Central Italy

*Massimo Caroli and Ermanno Tortia*[1]

## Introduction

The phenomenon of the migrant poor, as well as that of war and political refugees, has been growing steadily in recent years, especially in Southern Europe, and it is likely to increase further or remain at a critical level in the years to come (Saraceno et al., 2013). Therefore, the reception of economic migrants, asylum seekers, war and political refugees in European countries is becoming a paramount social and political phenomenon (Impagliazzo, 2012, 2015). Substantial parts of electoral campaigns are played around issues of migration and related themes. Given the conplexity and extent of the migration problem, in our chapter we do not aim at providing an exhaustive discussion and at examining its far-reaching socio-political implications. Rather, we focus on one specific theme regarding the patterns and governance of social inclusion vis-a-vis exclusion, led by public authorities and third sector organisations at the local level. To this end, we introduce the case of the territory surrounding the municipality of Faenza (Province of Ravenna), which extends from North Eastern to Central Italy. Localities and their actors became crucial players in the process of migrants' reception in Italy, where they are in charge of managing national funds to implement reception schemes and programmes, to find suitable structures, and to involve civil society operators and organisations.[2] They are also in charge of evaluating the achieved results in satisfying basic needs and inclusion of migrants, as well as supervising the external effects (both positive and negative) of migration inflows.

We strive to identify the elements of migration flows that can lead to social regeneration, as opposed to marginalisation and exclusion. Social regeneration is seen as a process of inclusion and cooperation aiming at improving peoples' lives through democratic empowerment and the involvement of beneficiaries and other stakeholders (Sen, 2002; as Sacchetti and Borzaga, 2017, Chapter 1 in this volume). Within Europe's Net4Society, socio-economic research develops "new forms of organisations and interactions to respond to societal challenges" in order to determine and satisfy community needs (NET4SOCIETY, 2014, 21). Our contribution is in line with this goal. The aim is to analyse the local governance of relations and understand which governance solutions are able to lead to virtuous results. Social regeneration, in our approach, is the upshot of suitable sets of rules, resources, and actors. Local resources, especially social capital, are employed by actors in public institutions and the social economy to achieve the integration of immigrants.

We analyse cooperative and collaborative solutions at several levels (individuals, organisations, networks, local authorities), which are applied to different dimensions of the migration issue. Social regeneration in terms of the socio-economic integration migrants requires the creation of a context where opportunities and capabilities for migrants and local communities can be developed. Social enterprises emerged historically to incorporate these elements, since they are characterised by a social objective, cooperation, and inclusive governance (Borzaga and Defourny, 2001, Borzaga and Galera, 2016; European Commission, 2016). Specific policy solutions require elements of public leadership that recognise the desirability of processes based on deliberative democracy and civic engagement in the management of migration flows, which entail the necessity of cooperation and inclusion within a multi-stakeholder context characterized by potential conflict and emergency (Campbell and Sacchetti, 2014).

The introduction to the chapter is followed by the definition of the conceptual frame and by a snapshot of the number and management of migration flows and migrants' reception in Italy. We then proceed to analyse the case of migrants' reception and integration in the territory of Romagna Faentina in Central Italy and to provide an initial evaluation of the impacts of the management of migration flows in this territory. The pivotal role of the ASP, the public Agency for Personal Services (*Azienda per i Servizi alla Persona*) in Faenza is evidenced, especially in relation to the governance of strategic and operational activities. Finally, we analyse the involvement of other local actors, especially third sector organisations and social enterprises. We conclude with a final discussion.

## Refugees and Asylum Seekers in Italy

The problem of migrants' reception is complex, multifaceted, and multilayered. At least four dominant dimensions can be singled out: (i) initial reception and survival, which includes the most pressing initial aid and dislocation at the local level; (ii) integration in economic and social activities to convert the presence of migrants from passive receptors of aid to active participants in local systems; (iii) the interaction between the presence of migrants and the local context in terms of direct impacts (creation/destruction of wealth and welfare) and indirect impacts (positive/negative external effects on social regeneration or degradation); and (iv) intra-relations within migrants' communities, which can be both homogeneous and/or heterogeneous in ethnic and cultural terms. The risk of internal dispute needs to be carefully considered and guarded against. In the second and third dimensions, the intervention of local actors is most crucial, since the management of migration flows and their integration within local systems requires dedicated actors (local authorities, volunteers, third sector organisations, enterprises, etc.) steering the process in appropriate ways to eschew the risk of degeneration. Apart from the intrinsic difficulties that always characterise migrants' integration, exclusionary and maladapted patterns can be due to several causes, such as the insufficiency of dedicated resources; the bureaucratisation and costs of the integration process; and the less then optimal and opportunistic behaviour of involved organisations, which may pursue private appropriation instead of social benefit. As mentioned earlier, the presence of local resources, such as civic culture, social capital, and leadership, and the construction of governance including appropriate rules, balances, checks, and sanctions become necessary ingredients to eschew vicious social processes and outcomes.

Resources and actors interact fruitfully in the presence of correct governance. Beyond formalised relations set by law, each locality needs to develop its own governance structure on the basis of available resources and organisations. The establishment of suitable governance does not rely on predefined solutions, but depends on contextual elements, among which the features of the actors involved (e.g., whether there is one single pivotal actor playing a leadership role, or an heterarchical plurality of equally positioned actors, etc.) (Ostrom, 1990; Poteete, Janssen and Ostrom, 2010). The temporal aspect and direction of the process is also crucial: governance can evolve through time passing from centralised to decentralised structures or from exclusive to inclusive ones, etc. Ideally, inclusive and decentralised structures always represent the best solutions. However, centralisation and strong leadership may be necessary conditions to kick-start the process, which needs to be observed in real, historical time. Path dependency is crucial in most cases, since initial conditions very often influence the whole process. However, patterns can be modified through appropriate intervention, and this is especially true in emergency situations.

Governance solutions providing decision-making patterns for the achievement of well-being through social regeneration have been theorised in the work of institutionalist scholars, such as Elinor Ostrom (1990), who studied the evolution and self-governed management of common-pool natural resources by local actors through the self-production of governance rules (Ostrom, 2010; Sacchetti and Sugden, 2009). 'Participatory and cooperative forms of interaction and decision-making can activate transformative answers to valued problems' (Sacchetti, Christoforou and Mosca, 2017, p. 4). These solutions, as social economy scholars have remarked, go beyond the use of material resources and the production of monetary outcomes, and involve the use and production of relational goods (Gui, 2000), or behavioural norms of reciprocity and cooperation (as in Borzaga and Tortia, 2017). Social economy organisations and other interacting contextual factors can achieve social regeneration and promote development and welfare not only for the existing population, but also for immigrants, refugees, and asylum seekers. In the latter case, difficulties are severely heightened by the emergency nature of relevant parts of migration flows and by the need to create integration schemes in the presence of strongly heterogeneous socio-cultural and institutional factors. In this sense, the study of migration flows represents a distinctive and sensitive social issue in contemporary political science. Whilst conflict is often the result of exclusion and heterogeneity, patterns of inclusion are difficult to imagine, devise, and accomplish. Marginalisation, or even exclusion and rejection, represent dangers that can never be ignored and must guide proactive policy and intervention. On the other hand, inclusion represents a necessary direction to follow in advanced societies and a unique occasion for social regeneration, given the high social potential attached to cultural diversity and interaction. The potential for positive economic impacts is large as well, especially in those advanced countries, such as Italy, that are characterised by the aging of the population and by the need to restructure the labour market. The conspicuous and stringent inter-temporal effects, spanning many years to come, require understanding, analysis, intervention, management of direct effects and understanding of indirect or external ones.

## The Reception System in Italy

Immigration policy in Italy has been perceived as an emotionally charged and contradictory issue, and thus regulated and managed as a security or emergency concern, at least in the first phase of the migration crisis. On the other hand, immigration is also perceived as a way to meet the economic and demographic needs of the country.[3] The Italian reception system is based on the authority of the Ministry of Interior to manage reception. Temporary reception (first aid) is organised on the basis of hotspots (CARA, Reception Centres for Asylum Seekers) and directly delivered by the central government. Medium- to long-term reception (on average 12 months) can be: (i) emergency-led and directed by local prefectures and is then directly contracted out to private providers (CAS, Extraordinary Reception Centres); or (ii) coordinated by municipalities or consortia of municipalities and delivered, in most cases, in cooperation with local third sector organisations (SPRAR,[4] Protection System for Asylum Seekers and Refugees).

The impact of reception services is substantially different when different instruments are considered. The SPRAR system represents the most virtuous example in terms of range and quality of services to immigrants. However, it is highly bureaucratised as a result of the need to monitor the process. On the other hand, the best examples of CAS show a strong inclination towards innovation and entrepreneurship to face first aid. However, since they are less regulated, more often than SPRAR services, they are haunted by many cases of bad practice. As we shall see, what is likely to make the difference in terms of quality of services is the "maturity" and local anchorage of the managing entity. Maturity is mainly affected by the extent to which the community engages with reception initiatives and by the ability of the managing entity to steer the asylum challenge so as to generate social and territorial innovation and development.

### The Number of Recent Migration Flows

In recent years, Italy has increasingly become the destination of new migration flows, mainly composed of war-torn people, or people connected to natural disasters or intolerable socio-political and economic conditions. As of 1 January 2015, in Italy, there were 3,929,916 regular non-EU citizens (Ministry of Interior data). According to the United Nations High Commissioner for Refugees (UNHCR), in 2015, more than 150,000 migrants landed on Italian shores, and almost 90,000 asylum applications were received. Among these new arrivals, there is a surge in demand for refugee status.[5] According to ISTAT, as of 1 January 2015, the immigrants present in Italy with a regular residence permit issued for humanitarian reasons, asylum, or protection were 117,820,[6] but in October of 2016, the overall estimate rose to over 150,000 (Galera, 2016; Membretti and Galera, 2017).

Unlike other European countries, the Italian reception system of asylum seekers sees a strong involvement of private organisations, which take on the task of operating as bodies responsible for managing refugee flows by virtue of contracts agreed directly with the prefectures. This is according to an emergency logic or within the SPRAR circuit, which presupposes a partnership relationship with the local authority. This system requires the promotion of a micro hospitality model, spread across the territory by highly rooted management bodies at the community level and marked by wide participation of different stakeholders as members (Galera, 2016; Membretti and Galera, 2017). This is the reason why our contribution focuses on the role of local actors and the interaction between local public authorities and third sector organisations in the deployment of hospitality measures. A system of bilateral relations emerges in which central policies, funding, and directives are promoted and complemented, via the principle of subsidiarity, by civil society initiatives, which exploit local social capital (as substantiated, for example, by volunteer organisations and financial and in kind donations), production capabilities, and information to pursue objectives of inclusion, regeneration, and development. We now consider the case of the system of immigrants' reception and integration in Romagna Faentina in Central Italy.

## Immigrants' Reception and Integration in Faenza: The Role of the ASP Public Agency

In 2016, the municipality of Faenza in the Province of Ravenna was populated by slightly less than 60,000 residents. This small town is located in Romagna,[7] between North Eastern and Central Italy. It is at the heart of the so called "Third Italy", which is characterised by the highest levels of socio-economic development and social capital in the country.

The existing pattern of immigrants' reception and integration emerged in recent years as the result of: (i) the policies and regulation of the central government; (ii) the spontaneous initiatives of civil society, which in some cases date some decades back, towards the end of last century, when immigration became a relevant phenomenon in Italy; and (iii) the emergency situation caused in recent years by the exponential growth of migration flows due to the uprising, revolution, and war in North Africa and the Middle East. To counteract the mounting challenge, the Union of six Municipalities of Romagna Faentina[8] (*Unione Romagna Faentina*) developed its own system following central regulation and specific local experience. This system conjugates funding from the central government, which is monitored and contracted out (through tenders and public procurement) by local authorities and is coupled by the active intervention of civil society and third sector organisations. These factors are producing, *in fieri*, a new local system of reception and integration, which has been evaluated by privileged referees in Faenza as a well-functioning one. We now turn to depict the way the system emerged and describe its main features.

### Bird's-Eye Overview of the Faenza System and the Role of the ASP

The reception system of the Union of Romagna Faentina was built around the Union's ASP, which addresses the problems of the most fragile persons in its territory by offering aid, support, and medical attention. Its local and social embeddedness enables the development of a network of integrated and innovative services, making it the ideal agency to detect emerging social fragilities and to deliver services in a flexible and speedy manner (Sacchetti and Tortia, 2017). The ASP's experience and networking are founded on principles and practices of horizontal subsidiarity and participation, transparency, and shared values, as well as direct interactions with the community and its social actors.

Given the continuous increase of migration inflows, and especially of political refugees and asylum seekers, at the national level, the territory of Faenza developed its own receptive capacity within the provincial governance and hospitality planning scheme of the prefecture of Faenza. The ASP was singled out by the municipalities of the Union as an exemplary operational instrument able to build an experimental model of hospitality made of small nuclei structured in the form of apartment groups (which were first introduced in the municipalities of Solarolo and Casola Valsenio).

The agreement between the ASP and the Union was ameliorated in late 2015. At the same time, the prefecture manifested the need to increase its receptive capacity to 80 more beds in shared rooms for foreigners applying for international protection. The Union, represented mainly by the mayors of its municipalities, faced this emergency in a coordinated and unitary way, which enabled it to achieve effectiveness and to plan services for secondary hospitality that start after migrants obtain the international protection status, exit reception facilities, and thus receive a long-term residence permit.[9] Following agreements with the Union and the prefecture, the ASP is now in charge of directly managing hospitality facilities and coordinating the reception process in the Union's territory.[10]

For the year 2017, the territorial coordination system will guarantee the availability of 353 beds in shared rooms; 252 of these beds derive from requests for increased availability originally guaranteed by the 2015 convention between the Ravenna Prefecture and the ASP. The remaining 101 beds have been integrated into the territorial coordination system, though facilities and beds are still managed by the original operators.

The ASP delineated the management of sleeping accommodation in 2016. That is when it started to search for subjects that would guarantee the delivery of reception services in their facilities. The aim was to cover all the accommodation that the territory had committed to. Though seven private social operators responded to the public announcement, they gave insufficient attention to the public disclosure procedure and to its requirements, so that ASP had to take up a dominant role in the direct management of several facilities and shared rooms.

### The Management of Hospitality by the ASP

The strategic provision of a much needed, yet unplanned, service, in an imminent and sustainable manner, has necessarily been progressive. From the outset, the organisational model of widespread hospitality and apartment groups was carried out in four to ten 12-person housing units managed by the ASP with its own staff, which was supported by educational and linguistic-cultural mediation activities provided by qualified external operators.

Therefore, a medium-sized structure delivering up to 40 beds in shared rooms was established. It was characterised as a territorial mini hub functioning as a place of first acquaintance and subsequent transit to other structures. The structure is managed and supported by ASP personnel. Educational, linguistic-cultural mediation and garrison of the 24-hours-a-day structure is offered by qualified service providers. A complete restructuring is under way, with the aim to set up 20 reception places inside a farm owned by the ASP. The objective here is to organise training courses in the agricultural sector in synergy with other social farming projects which were designed to target the elderly and the under-aged.

In June 2016, just before the time of the year when new massive arrivals are at greater risk, the ASP was deploying what had actually been characterised as a new, more structured and unified business service with concrete prospects to serve more needs and more people. It undertook the direct management of reception activities. Such an intervention in the organisational structure of the ASP would allow not only the use of competences already present in this new field of activity, but also the simultaneous reconnaissance of specialised skills, which were not present within the corporate body or were acquired from external sources.

The direct management of reception services (in addition to the services required by the relevant legislation, such as administrative management services, hotel services, integration services, etc.) implied taking care of various groups of people, which were from time to time assigned to the territory and had different nationalities, ethnicities, languages, and cultures. It was therefore necessary, in order to build an ASP reception service, to find out who was able to take responsibility for these people, to speak with them in their language or dialect, to teach them the Italian language, to orient them in the rules of reception and coexistence in Italy, and to work on their life plan. There was also the need to relate to the applicants hosted in other institutions and associations, and interact with the various components of the civil society undertaking integration projects and socially useful activities, which are key components of reception processes.

For these reasons, the ASP has been moving in the direction of acquiring specific coordination skills capable of intercepting and understanding the needs of applicants. It sought among those linguistic-cultural mediation figures with whom collaboration had already started, especially for the construction and preparation work of the personal memories and records to be presented to the territorial commissions.

Eventually, after several months of informed exchanges, the ASP chose a Senegalese university graduate with 15 years of experience in the field and maturing skills as a teacher in training courses in regional vocational training programmes funded by the European Social Fund. This person has been joined by another Italian practitioner who has been active for ten years now in social affairs related to immigrant people in the Union of Romagna Faentina. In this way, the ASP acquired the missing skills it needed to build the project's operational coordination in close relationship with its management and staff.

### The Implementation of the Territorial Coordination Model

The territorial coordination model pivoted by the ASP methodologically refers to the content and guidelines resulting from the National Framework Agreement "Charter of Good Reception of Migrant People", initiated by the Department of Civil Liberties and Immigration of the Ministry of Interior, the ANCI, the National Association of Italian Municipalities, and the Alliance of Italian Social Cooperatives. This model is directed towards actions which, during the reception phase, pre-constitute tools aimed at facilitating the exit from "assisted" reception and the conscious and active entrance in civil society.

The coordinating functions of the ASP have thus evolved from the management of the initial emergency phase to a more complex activity which, already at the initial reception stage, provides for the creation of conditions and opportunities to facilitate immigrants' integration paths. In particular, the coordination and integration of macro functions throughout the territory of Romagna Faentina are founded upon:

1. The in-depth knowledge of the personal, social, educational, and professional stories of international protection applicants in order to acquire all the information useful to a subsequent individual and/or group planning of life paths that will then have to be retrieved, mapped, and recorded in specific databases.
2. The in-depth mapping of all the actors and organisations present in the territory of Romagna Faentina, able to provide resources and opportunities for the development of individual and/or group integration pathways as related to: (i) professional training and retraining; and (ii) orientating and accompanying to work placement, housing, and social inclusion.
3. The networking, with strategic orientation, of all public and private social interventions in the territory related to the SPRAR, in order to: (i) plan and coordinate action; (ii) avoid as much as possible waste of energy and resources; and (iii) identify funding channels for the development of the post-reception phase.
4. The consolidation of a centralised information system for optimising and simplifying the international protection applicants' database for permits, demographics, health records, CVs, etc.

Thanks to the organisational and operational structure of the ASP, it has been possible to initiate and develop a coordinated and integrated intervention, which cuts across the aforementioned macro functions and involves all of the actors engaged with and coordinated by the ASP. This has been an effective response both to the need to directly manage the hosting service and to the territorial coordination function.

## The Local Embeddedness of the Hospitality System in Faenza: The Role of Civil Society Organisations

The decision of the municipality of Faenza to put the ASP in charge of the hospitality measures has been followed by the spontaneous emergence of a partnership between public authorities and third sector organisations, which are taking a leadership role in the process. We consider in some depth the experience of three main cases: the Penny Wirton School of Italian Language; the Teranga Social Cooperative; and the Without Borders Project by the Two Worlds Theatre.

## The Penny Wirton School of Italian Language

Teaching the Italian language to migrants is compulsory and included in the agreement between the ASP and the prefecture of the Province of Ravenna. Under the prefecture's requirements, the Italian School for Immigrants Penny Wirton[11] was singled out by the ASP as the institution that will carry out this duty. The school has been created to teach Italian to foreigners that intend to reside in the country. Faenza hosts one of the main branches of the school, while its centre is in Rome. Students from high schools, the linguistic lyceum, volunteer to accumulate competencies in teaching the Italian language and to help in the welcoming and linguistic inclusion of migrants. The school has been successful in teaching Italian, given its informal style and the involvement of migrants both in teaching and extra-teaching activities.

Penny Wirton is an association founded in Rome in 2008 by Eraldo Affinati and Anna Luce Lenzi. To this day, it counts 20 administratively autonomous and independent schools nation-wide, from Calabria to Lombardy.[12] All affiliated schools recognise the basic and indispensable principles of the Charter of Intellectual Property, whose Article 1 states that the school is "free, apolitical and a-confessional" and always welcomes everyone by teaching "one by one, or by small groups" (Article 3). The school's operation depends on beneficent donations and the volunteer work of teachers and tutors, who are often high school students. The didactic approach is based on human relationships. Meetings are not conceived as teachers lecturing to a group of students, but as interactions between people, who have the knowledge, values, and skills to share the aims of the school. These elements convinced volunteers in Faenza to create the 21st Associated Penny Wirton School in Italy. The ASP gave space and instruments to the school to carry out its activities: a photocopier and the foyer of a theatre to teach Italian lessons twice a week. The total amount of time migrants spend with the volunteers is four hours per week. The school also intends to ensure openness throughout the solar year and not just for the school year in order to avoid summer breaks that interrupt friendship relations and the learning process.

The experience began with the involvement of four teachers in humanities and English language and 28 students from the third class of the local Linguistic Lyceum who, initially involved in a completely voluntary way, then obtained that their activity was recognised as part of the work-school alternation framework for high school students.[13] The school started its operations on 12 January 2017 with the participation of 14 asylum seekers, selected by the ASP, seven of whom are from Côte d'Ivoire and six from Afghanistan. In March 2017, the school had over 20 participants coming from Pakistan, Gambia, New Guinea, Nigeria, Senegal, and Morocco. Most participants are asylum seekers. The prevailing gender is male, but one Nigerian girl and an asylum seeker from Morocco are well placed in the group.

Lessons begin with the preparation of the space. Immigrants are grouped by volunteers according to their linguistic levels: basic (illiterate or just literate), medium, and advanced. It is not always possible to guarantee the continuity of teaching. Most of the students (only two volunteers are male) are carrying out the service once a week, so migrants are looked after by different people, not just students, but also volunteer adults who gradually joined the four "founding" teachers. These are people from civil society; not all of them are teachers. They work alongside female students whose English and French language skills allow for effective language mediation. Lessons are aimed at acquiring survival language skills and the practical use of language in the most common everyday communication. Regardless of their different pace of learning, migrants are strongly motivated to take an active part, because being tutored individually or in small groups allows for the personalisation of learning that has value from both the educational and the human point of view. Migrants feel that each volunteer tries to teach them what they most need and, in turn, volunteers obtain a concrete perception of ways to meet their "students'" needs, while their linguistic skills gain practical relevance. From a human point of view, the most striking and exciting aspect is the spontaneity with which, especially young students, find themselves in the new situation of being literate teachers, leaving tangible signs, thanks to the gratuity they make available to their own "students". The atmosphere is, as testified by several attending persons, one in which it is unclear "who teaches and who learns", based on a logic of a spontaneous and reciprocal exchange of skills and cultural abilities.

### Teranga Social Cooperative

The Teranga Social Cooperative[14] was created in November 2015 when people with different skills and knowledge and different geographical, educational, and work backgrounds were brought together. In particular, it was borne out of the experience of an association created in 2004 by a group of Senegalese migrants who reside in Ravenna. The group was formed several years ago in Italy by Senegalese with university education. The group founded the Global Solidarity Association to provide support to and accompany newcomers from Africa. Given the extreme complexity of Italian bureaucracy, especially when compared to most African countries, the association helped migrants by delivering good administrative practice in the renewal of residence permits, access to territorial services, etc. The volunteers of the association thus allowed their fellow countrymen and the general population to gain access to their fundamental rights. Another goal of the association was to promote the Senegalese culture in Italy through the gastronomic experience. The association has participated in several events and festivals sharing its own dishes and flavours with the native Italian population. Among the members of the association there are cultural mediators: key professional figures who work as a bridge between two cultures, in addition to pursuing linguistic mediation, which is a small part of the integration path and of inclusion of foreign citizens in Italy.

In 2014, the association's mediators began collaborating with the Ravenna Prefecture in linguistic and cultural mediation, given the important numbers of international protection seekers who came from the Libyan coasts and were then deployed throughout the Italian territory. In November 2014, the association, under the pressure and in recognition of the emergency, created a CAS centre on the outskirts of Ravenna, under the mandate of the prefecture. The CAS offered capabilities and expertise in terms of mediation and foreign population management.

Some members of the association and some Italian citizens, with experience in managing foreign populations in countries like France and Argentina, met in 2015. They decided to combine their skills and knowledge to create a new organisation responding to the needs of international protection seekers at this precise historical moment. This led to the genesis of Cooperativa Teranga, a multicultural cooperative with intercultural skills whose purpose is to support and accompany the foreign population in Italy. Its main aim is to contribute to the integration of the foreign community and the local population, understanding integration not as a unilateral process concealing the culture of the immigrant community, but as a movement that unites two cultural phenomena and thus creates a new intercultural reality.

Teranga is a term drawn from the native Wolof idiom, the most widespread language in Senegal and Gambia. It can be translated as "hospitality", but it actually expresses a lot more: welcome, attention, respect, kindness, cheerfulness, and the pleasure of receiving a guest in your house. An action Teranga is experiencing and promoting now is the "Amalg-aimiamoci" ("Let's interact with love") project, which has as its objective the intercultural exchange and the reciprocal knowledge of protection seekers with the resident citizens. This is put into effect through convivial moments where the asylum seeker is welcomed in the family for a snack, lunch, or dinner in private or public places, such as gardens, bars, and clubs.

The aim is to try to break down the wall of distrust through mutual knowledge between the local community and the host structure. The guests are given the opportunity to know and understand Italian culture throughout the day, for example having a coffee at the bar, eating Italian food and spending some time with members of the community. For the local community, it can be an opportunity to widen its cultural reach and understanding by interacting with distant social, political, and cultural contexts. Informal encounters, which are not included in events or activities that were organised in advance, make it possible to establish connections that can develop into sincere and positive relations and friendship.

## *Without Borders Project (Participative Theatre "Due Mondi")*

The Two Worlds Theatre (*Teatro Due Mondi*) is an association that was born in 1979 as a "group theatre" and is still engaged in continuous artistic research, which is the basis for its daily practice of self-pedagogy.[15] It performed its shows all over the world, from Northern Europe to South America, from Taiwan to Eastern Europe.

The theatrical practice follows two main directions: street theatre and social engagement, mostly linked to pedagogical projects. Choosing to operate "in the street" has led theatre associates to meet cultural and social realities far from the official circuits and outside the commercial theatrical performance. On the artistic side, it has led to developing a theatrical technique that focuses on the use of the body and non-verbal communication in order to get in touch with the heterogeneous and casual audience with whom associates want to interact. The latest developments in the project work of the Theatre have seen the intensification of social engagement especially with migrants. A "Refugee" project has been developed with the refugees in the territory of Faenza.

The Theatre has been developing workshops aimed at the social inclusion of refugees for about six years now. The workshops allowed for the refinement of the competence to mediate between the different cultures. This helps the various groups of participants to slowly relate to one another, overcoming initial mutual distrust and thus recreating a solidarity community. The theatre work of Teatro Due Mondi, therefore, becomes a social inclusion vehicle. Projects with "non-actors" also aim at "giving voice" to the weaker or marginalised social groups, for which the theatre becomes a social communication vehicle and at the same time an affective and effective empowerment tool.

In 2012, the participative theatre workshop "Without Borders" was initiated. It targets the community of reference, the citizens of the area, and hosted migrants, with the aim to build street actions on issues that affect people's lives as citizens of the world. Theatrical activity, in this case, can be a tangible and incisive way to communicate with the city on topical issues and becomes an effective exchange means among individuals: it offers people the opportunity to meet the other and stimulates them to open up, knock down barriers and prejudices, and commit themselves to these values. It has been defined as "participative" theatre, since the aim is to share content, reflections, and goals with everyone who wants to do so, without forgetting fun, irony, and curiosity.

Street actions are interpreted as social and cultural exchanges between participants (whether they are actors or non-actors) and create the possibility—boundless and therefore without limits—to express their identity, their own visions, their dreams. The workshop sets one rendezvous per week and is open to all. No entry fee is imposed, and there are no age limits. From the outset, the idea was to activate laboratories that would work together with Italian citizens and asylum seekers, thus inserting this activity into an inclusive and participatory perspective that promotes mutual encounters and knowledge among different people and ethnic and national groups, accepting each with its own peculiarities. Difference becomes so widespread and dominant that it implies a high potential to build on it and create something new and fruitful. Working together eliminates the risk of creating ad hoc structures in favour of specific subjects, leading to the ghettoisation of the marginalised. The linguistic "problem" is overcome by explaining each exercise in the required languages, coherently with the composition of the group.

Over the years, the laboratory has produced a number of street actions. Being able to take advantage of the various opportunities offered and to go down to the street as often as possible proved very important to continue to raise citizens' awareness against the construction of the walls and barriers implemented in recent months by some European countries to block the flows of migrants. Street action can therefore be defined as a theatrical happening halfway between the show and the event. The event shares the strong political will to support a cause. Not by chance, many of the people involved are non-actors, driven by the will to do something together and express their opinion on a given theme and take it out in open places, which are testimonies of large crowds of people in the street, on the street, or in the heart of the city. The show shares a structured form with a well-defined schedule and a strong stage presence of participants, with the will to meet and relate with anyone who stops and pays attention. Street action has the ability to deal with current and strong themes by presenting personal visions, which immediately acquire broader appeal and become the object of dialogue with the rest of the world. This is also because the actions, mostly simple and everyday, are repeated by a large group of different people, and gain meanings that eliminate any joke or rhetoric and transcend the daily to become universal poetic language.

## Discussion and Conclusion

The social issue of the reception and integration of migrants, war refugees, and asylum seekers became all the more pressing in recent years, especially in countries such as Italy, which neighbours war and unrest areas and faces strong migration flows along its borders. Italy, along with several other European countries, faces migration flows as a dual phenomenon: both as a danger and as an opportunity for development.

In countries characterised by the aging of the population and the need to regenerate wide urban and rural areas, migrants represent resources that need to be empowered and included actively in the fabric of society. Social regeneration is a key issue that sharply separates integration and inclusion from marginalisation and exclusion patterns. The explosion of the problem of asylum seeking, starting from the "Arab Spring" in 2011, forced governments, local authorities, and civil society across countries to take or reinforce action. Italy is no exception: over the last few years migrants' reception and integration became, necessarily, a dominant political, social, and cultural issue. The central government intervened by guaranteeing financial coverage for life rescue and for fulfilling the most pressing needs of migrants.[16] The organisation of hospitality has been decentralised to local authorities and prefectures, which are in charge of finding suitable shelters and implementing integration policies. Most municipalities in Italy accepted to be involved in reception and hospitality activities. Different patterns clearly emerged: at the extremes of the hospitality spectrum, some municipalities used public resources to guarantee minimal services, without any effort to achieve integration, thus generating ghettoisation and refusal by local communities; other municipalities, instead, took integration and social regeneration as opportunities and as polar stars or pathways for development and regeneration. Positive and far-reaching external effects can be envisaged, starting from purely economic ones in terms of support to local and marginalised areas and the creation of new jobs. Beyond economic effects, social regeneration can play its positive role in terms of the creation of a multicultural, open, and variegated society, which can complement and renew the traditional Italian culture. Also, the study of the Italian landscape clearly shows that hospitality is work in progress: local authorities, municipalities, and civil society are building the road as they travel along it. New initiatives are added to face emergency. Push-and-pull social processes are clearly at work, whereby the needs of migrants stimulate the accomplishment of new and creative solutions, while organisations and public agencies are also able to figure out new services through their own experience and imagination.

The Union of Municipalities of Romagna Faentina in Central Italy represents a virtuous case in which local authorities and civil society organisations collaborate in implementing new social patterns that are geared to overcome exclusion and to generate positive social effects. The governance of the hospitality system in Faenza can be interpreted as a hub in which public authorities, as represented by the ASP, play a pivotal role. The ASP of Romagna Faentina has been implementing the bulk of necessary hospitality measures: it directly provides most sleeping accommodation and other necessary goods and services. Interestingly, public structures favour migrants' inclusion also through self-catering and self-managed cooking facilities. On the other hand, public tenders, calls, and procurement have been used to include several civil society organisations, whose operations are most of the time guaranteed by volunteers. The interaction between civil society and local authorities is two-way and does not appear to be hierarchical. Civil society organisations take action in implementing activities and services much needed to migrants and to the community of reference. On the other hand, local authorities have shown themselves to be ready to recognise and also to stimulate the virtues of civil society intervention and creative initiative. It may be possible to imagine that governance will be further decentralised over time through more substantive delegation of activities and strategic decisions to local actors in the third sector. However, our study clearly highlights a strong pattern in which the leadership role of public agencies is necessary to create and run the whole system. Identification of suitable public agencies and local actors appears to be an unavoidable feature of public policy if the integration of migrants and social regeneration are to be achieved.

## Notes

1. The authors thank Giulia Galera for precious comments and suggestions. We also thank volunteer teachers and tutors at the Penny Wirton School and Alberto Grilli at Teatro Due Mondi, who agreed to be interviewed. Usual discalimers apply.
2. The Department of Civil Liberties and Immigration of the Ministry of Interior manages foreign integration policy through the network of Territorial Councils for Immigration: structures operating at provincial level, under the direction of prefects (Art. 57 of the DPR 31.8.1999 n. 394; Montefusco, 2012). The Territorial Councils are made up of representatives of all relevant immigration and asylum subjects at the local level and deal with, inter alia, the analysis of needs, as well as the programming and implementation of social integration policies for immigrants. The coordination promoted by the Ministry is aimed at providing the necessary link between centre and periphery and the implementation of homogeneous placements in immigration interventions within the territory. The Ministry of Labour, in addition to regulating inputs for work, promotes inclusion policies and social cohesion of foreign citizens, such as cultural mediation activities, linguistic literacy, civic formation, etc. The existing legislation on social integration of immigrants attributes to the 20 regions of the Italian state a crucial role in defining the fundamental features of local autonomy in this type of social policy. This dates back to the '90s, when Law 39/1990 delegated matters of reception, employment, and social integration of immigrants and refugees at the regional level. Regional laws concerning social policy for immigrants soon followed.
3. The new law on immigration, Law 46/2017, concerns "Urgent provisions for the acceleration of international protection proceedings and measures to counter illegal immigration". The most relevant innovations included in the law are two: the speeding up of the procedures for accepting or rejecting cases of asylum seekers; and the strengthening and speeding up of the procedures for the expulsion of irregular migrants.
4. SPRAR was institutionalised in 2002 by Law 189/2002 following an agreement between the Department of Civil Liberties and Immigration of the Italian Ministry of Interior, the ANCI, and the UNHCR to establish a "National Asylum Programme". The SPRAR system, funded by the National Fund for Asylum Policies and Services, is constituted by the network of local authorities which, with the support of third sector organisations, guarantee "integrated reception" interventions for the construction of individual paths of socio-occupational integration.
5. The refugee status is granted by the Territorial Commission for the Recognition of International Protection, which consists of four members, two of which belong to the Ministry of Interior, one representative of the local authorities, and one representative of UNHCR.

6. 100,138 males and 17,682 females, excluding subjects with long-term permits and residence cards and unaccompanied minors.
7. Romagna is the South Eastern, maritime part of the Emilia-Romagna region, whose capital is Bologna. It includes the three provinces of Forli-Cesena, Ravenna (in which Faenza and the surrounding municipalities are located), and Rimini.
8. The Union includes also, besides the capital city Faenza, the municipalities of Brisighella, Casola Valsenio, Castelbolognese, Riolo Terme, and Solarolo in the Apennine Piedmont. It counts a total population of about 85,000 inhabitants.
9. The new programming and coordination model has been defined in 2015 by: the decision of the Union; the resolution of the Assembly of the Members of the ASP Romagna Faentina; the resolution of the Board of the ASP itself; and the agreement between the prefecture and the ASP, as representative of the Union.
10. At the beginning of 2016, the sleeping accommodation directly managed by the ASP rose to 30 beds, which were distributed between five reception facilities in three different municipalities.
11. The name of the school was conceived after the title of the novel by Silvio D'Arzo "*Penny Wirton and his Mother*".
12. One collective interview was carried out in April 2017 with two volunteer teachers from the school and two students from the linguistic lyceum volunteering to teach in the school.
13. The "work-school alternation" framework is promoted by the Union of the Municipalities of Romagna Faentina in collaboration with ASP and the schools in Faenza.
14. The social cooperative is, in Italy, a special kind of cooperative enterprise, in which mutual benefit is conjugated with an explicit social aim, the non-profit distribution constraint, the socialisation of the firm assets, and multi-stakeholder governance, as provided by Law 381/1991.
15. One in-depth interview was conducted in April 2017 with Alberto Grilli, founder and representative of the Two Worlds Theatre.
16. The Italian government helps each migrant financially by giving a daily allowance of 2.5 Euros and about 30 Euros to assisting organisations.

## References

Borzaga, C., and J. Defourny. 2001. *The Emergence of Social Enterprise*. London: Routledge.
Borzaga, C., and G. Galera. 2016. "Innovating the Provision of Welfare Services Through Collective Action: The Case of Italian Social Cooperatives." *International Review of Sociology*, 26(1): 31–47.
Borzaga, C., and S. Sacchetti. 2015. "Social Regeneration and Cooperative Institutions". In *Social Regeneration and Local Development Cooperation, Social Economy and Public Participation*, edited by Silvia Sacchetti, Asimina Christoforou, and Michele Mosca, 21–42. London: Routledge.
Borzaga, C., and E. C. Tortia. 2017. "Cooperation as Coordination Mechanism: A New Approach to the Economics of Cooperative Enterprises." In *The Oxford Handbook of Mutual, Cooperative, and Coowned Business*, edited by J. Michie, J. Blasi, and C. Borzaga. Oxford: Oxford University Press.
Campbell, C., and S. Sacchetti. 2014. "Social Enterprise Networks and Social Capital: A Case Study in Scotland/UK." In *Social Capital and Economics: Social Values, Power, and Social Identity*, edited by A. Christoforou and J. B. Davis, 215–236. London: Routledge.

European Commission. 2016. *Social Enterprise and their Eco-systems: Developments in Europe.* Accessed on 17 June 2017 from ec.europa.eu/social/BlobServle t?docId=16376&langId=en

Galera, G. 2016. "Verso l'inclusione sociale: dall'accoglienza all'autonomia." *Welfare Oggi*, 3: 32–37.

Gui, B. 2000. "Beyond Transactions: On the Interpersonal Dimension of Economic Reality." *Annals of Public and Cooperative Economics*, 71(2): 139–169.

Impagliazzo, M. 2012. "'Mare Nostrum'? Storia, Culture, Migrazioni." In *Mediterraneo: crocevia di popoli*, edited by F. Baggio and A. Skoda Pashkja, 13–23. Vatican City: Urbaniana University Press.

Impagliazzo, M. 2015. "Bergoglio, l'Europa, i migrant." *Italianieuropei*, 6: 77–83.

Membretti, A., and G. Galera. 2017. "Accoglienza dei migranti e turismo sostenibile nelle Alpi: il ruolo dell'impresa sociale." *Rivista di Antropologia Pubblica* (forthcoming).

Montefusco, C. 2012. *Analisi delle Buone Prassi Esistenti a Livello Europeo per lo Sviluppo delle Politiche relative all'Accoglienza e all'Integrazione degli Immigrati ed in Particolare delle Categorie più Vulnerabili.* Rome. Accessed on 29 August 2017 from http://www.socialelazio.it/binary/prtl_socialelazio/tbl_pubblicazioni/ INDIVIDUAZIONE_E_ANALISI_DELLE_BUONE_PRASSI_ESISTENTI_A_ LIVELLO_NAZIONALE_ED_EUROPEO.pdf

Net4Society. 2014. *Opportunities for Researchers From the Socio-economic Sciences and Humanities (SSH)*, October. Accessed from www.net4society.eu

Ostrom, E. 1990. *Governing the Commons: The Evolution of Institutions for Collective Action.* Cambridge, MA: Cambridge University Press.

Ostrom, E. 2010. "Revising Theory in Light of Experimental Findings." *Journal of Economic Behavior and Organisation*, 73(1): 68–72.

Poteete, A. R. Janssen, M. A., and E. Ostrom, eds. 2010. *Working Together: Collective Action, the Commons, and Multiple Methods in Practice.* Princeton, NJ: Princeton University Press.

Sacchetti, S., Christoforou, A., and M. Mosca. 2017. Introduction. In *Social Regeneration and Local Development: Cooperation, Social Economy and Public Participation*, 1–17. London: Routledge.

Sacchetti, S., and R. Sugden. 2009. "The Organisation of Production and Its Publics: Mental Proximity, Market and Hierarchies." *Review of Social Economy*, 67(3): 289–311.

Sacchetti, S., and E. C. Tortia. 2017. "The Notion of Social Responsibility Across Different Types of Nonprofit and for Profit Organizations." *Econometica Working Paper*, No. 61/17. Accessed on 17 June 2017 from www.econometica.it/wp/ wp61.pdf

Saraceno, C., Sartor, N., and G. Sciortino, eds. 2013. *Stranieri e diseguali. Le disuguaglianze nei diritti e nelle condizioni di vita degli immigrati.* Bologna: Il Mulino.

Sen, A. 2002. "Why Health Equity?" *Health Economics*, 11: 659–666.

# Part III

# Contextual Elements for Social Regeneration

# 8 Deliberative Participation
## Bringing the Citizens Back In

*Rudolf Lewanski*

> "The multitude is more wise and steady than the Prince".
>
> N. Machiavelli, *Discorsi sopra la prima deca di Tito Livio*, ch. 58

> "The democratic model born after World War II today is in crisis . . . if it is to survive, democracy must be able to reinvent itself".
>
> M. Gauchet

## Introduction

Social regeneration is tightly interconnected with political regeneration and revitalisation of democratic regimes. The situation of representative democracy in the contemporary world appears somewhat paradoxical: on one hand, since the late '80s, it has apparently become hegemonic, winning the competition with other forms of political regimes; at the same time, it is affected by a deep legitimation crisis. Even more importantly, the locus of decisions has shifted away from the political and public sphere to arenas over which the (supposedly sovereign) people exert no influence or control at all.

Assuming that democracy ensures its members values that are normatively desirable (such as political rights and protection against arbitrary exercise of coercion), what can be done to tackle its present difficulties? Perhaps the answer lies "simply" in the root of the word and meaning of democracy: bringing the people back into the processes by which collective decisions are made and giving some of the power (*kratos*) back to the *demos*, i.e. "participation". The problem is that citizen participation, as it is usually practiced, is hardly meaningful or credible; furthermore, even the two fundamental channels of citizen engagement within representative democracy—voting and parties—have lost much of their appeal.

Over the last half decade, an innovative form of citizen engagement has been developed and put into practice in many parts of the world: *deliberative* participation. After discussing the malaise affecting contemporary representative democracy, this chapter singles out and examines six distinctive features of deliberative participation that distinguish it from other more traditional forms of engagement: inclusion; information; dialogue and deliberation; consensus; empowerment. It then proceeds to answer the question of what can be the added value for society generated by such deliberative processes, focusing in particular on its capability to contribute to better decision-making and to social capital regeneration. Finally, it briefly addresses another critical issue, i.e. whether deliberative participation should be institutionalised, and how that might be done. Though the chapter focuses on the polity, similar considerations can apply also to the public and collective sphere more broadly, including the varied forms of aggregations of society, that could use this approach in their internal decision-making, as well as promoting this form of involvement in public decision-making in their respective fields of action.

## The Malaise of Representation: An Opportunity to Rethink Democracy

Since the '70s, citizens of many Western countries have become "more skeptical about government, more distrustful of politicians, and are more cynical about the workings of the democratic process" (Dalton, 2004); they have lost trust in the capabilities and intentions of political élites, parties, and institutions (Barber, 1984; Norris, 1999; Held, 1996; Rosanvallon, 2008; Gauchet, 2009). If in 2004 only one-third (precisely 34%) of Europeans trusted their governments, by 2016, trust further decreased to approximately one fourth of the population (27%). The loss of trust is not limited to present institutions and élites, but involves the political regime itself; according to the World Values Survey (Wave 6, 2010–14), on average, only slightly more than 42% of citizens of democratic countries consider democracy "absolutely important"; in the first modern democracy, the United States (along with other countries, ranging from Holland to Brazil to Spain), the figure is lower than 50%; in the largest democracy on the planet, India, the figure is less than 30%.

In a way, this is paradoxical, as representative democracy, at the same time, has become the hegemonic form of political regime worldwide. Whereas electoral democracies represented 41% of all countries in 1989 (the year that marked the end of Soviet regimes), by 2013 they had become 61% of the total (112 countries out of 195 considered) (Freedom House, 2014).

This scepticism might well be explained by the fact that citizens sense that the actual locus of decision-making is no longer in the hands of representative institutions, but has shifted in time to actors—interest groups, media, bureaucracies, international finance, IT companies, and even organised criminality—that hold no popular mandate; it has become a post-political world in which the exercise of power is invisible (Bobbio, 1991). If this is correct, what we call democracy is actually in the process of becoming a post-democracy (Crouch, 2004): apparently, the external democratic layer is still in place, but in fact, the substance has been hollowed out (Zakaria, 2003).

However acute, a crisis may well represent an opportunity (Urbinati, 2013) to introduce innovations capable of revitalising and deepening democracy and the public sphere more broadly (Fung and Wright, 2003; Pruitt and Thomas, 2007; Smith, 2009). In this respect, the recipe is relatively "simple" and under our eyes: rediscover the essence of democracy since its origins by bringing the *demos*, the (sovereign) people back into the processes by which collective decisions are decided. The "democratic ideal prospers when there are major opportunities for the mass of ordinary people actively to participate, through discussion and autonomous organisations, in shaping the agenda of public life" (Crouch, 2004, 2).

More than two centuries since it was first introduced in modern times, democratic institutions and processes are in need of a serious tuneup. In the face of a decline of political participation in many Western countries (Torcal and Montero, 2006), James Fishkin (1995) rightly asks, "When is it that the people express their voice?" A *vital* democratic regime needs to give voice to its citizens, not only on election days, and pay heed to it. Part of the crisis discussed above also affects just the two fundamental channels of citizen engagement even within the most minimal conception of representative democracy: voting and parties (Mair, 2013). On the other hand, the forms of citizen involvement used by authorities often are too episodic and superficial to be credible or useful. So the question the crisis poses is whether it is possible to effectively involve citizens in a meaningful and practicable way.

## Deliberative Participation

Also in connection with the malaise of representative democracy and its institutions, there has been growing interest in new modes of citizen engagement; particularly deliberative participation has attracted increasing attention from many quarters[1] over recent years.

Deliberative democracy has by now become a social and political movement resulting from a "global laboratory" in which, since the '70s, field experiences and a vast theoretical and empirical literature from three diverse political cultures (South America, the Anglo-Saxon world, and Northern European countries) aimed at upgrading the quality of citizen participation have spread and interwoven (see, for example, Sintomer and Allegretti, 2009; Hartz-Karp, 2007). New approaches have been proposed, tested, and developed by professionals, political leaders, public administrations, academics, civil society organisations, and ordinary citizens alike, often fruitfully collaborating in the endeavour.

Deliberative participation is not a political utopia: hundreds of real-world cases have been carried out over the last half century; in some cases, it has evolved into "a normal way to contribute to political choices" (Font et al., 2014, 2). Citizen engagement inspired by deliberative theory has been applied to a variety of fields as well as at all levels of government, from local to regional national and even international:[2] Citizen Juries were introduced in the U.S. in the early '70s (at the same time Germany was experimenting with very similar *Plannungszelle*); Consensus Conferences were used by the Danish Board of Technology since the mid-'80s; other methods, such as the Deliberative Polls and the 21st-century Town Meetings, started to spread in the '90s. In the following decade, the deliberative approach was used to tackle major issues, such as the reform of the electoral system by the British Columbia Citizens' Assembly (2002), or the reform of the Constitution itself, as in the cases of Iceland (2012) and Ireland[3] (2013) (Gastil, 2013). The first regional law incorporating the principles of deliberative democracy was passed by Tuscany (Italy) in 2007. Several large-scale deliberative processes have also been activated bottom-up by civil society, such as the Australian *Citizens' Parliament* in 2009 or the Belgian G1000 two years later. Interestingly, deliberative participation has also been fruitfully coupled with direct democracy as in the case of the Citizens' Initiative Review (CIR) process introduced by the State of Oregon in 2010.

These experiences demonstrate that, in appropriate and not excessively cumbersome conditions, deliberative democracy is doable, useful, and capable of producing significant outcomes (Landemore, 2013; Elstub and McLaverty, 2014). It represents the new paradigm of democratic participation and could well become the "next form of democracy" (Leighninger, 2006).

## The Distinctive Traits of Deliberative Participation

Deliberative participation constitutes a "deeper" form of involvement, much more promising and relevant as compared to traditional forms of participation. Broadly speaking, deliberative participation consists in a democratic social process that "puts talk and communication at the center of democracy" (Dryzek and Niemeyer, 2008, 484) within the context of non-biased procedural conditions ensuring that participants are, and feel, as free and equal as possible; the process is aimed at generating a careful reflection by "expanding their perspectives and learn about unforeseen consequences" (Bächtiger and Wegemann, 2014, 120) and at producing a shared decision on a relevant collective issue (Gastil, 2013, 216; Setälä, 2014) through "symmetric" cooperation by which participants "collectively exercise their best civic judgement to reach a mutually acceptable decision" (Fuji Johnson, 2009, 682).

The degree of innovativeness of this approach to citizen engagement can be fully appreciated by examining its distinctive traits in relation to six dimensions: inclusion; information; dialogue and deliberation; consensus; and influence.

## *Inclusion—Representativeness Rather than Representation*

"Inclusion", a term widely used nowadays in a variety of meanings, in this context indicates the possibility for all relevant "voices"—opinions, arguments, and discourses—to be expressed as well as *to be heard* (Dryzek and Niemeyer, 2008); deliberative democracy is about *political* inclusion:[4] the right of all—with special attention to the weak and disadvantaged—interested in and affected *by* a decision to express their voice and exert influence on it (Setälä, 2014).

Traditionally, "who participates" all too often represents an aspect taken for granted or simply ignored; yet it constitutes a "meta-decision" of crucial relevance: *who* the participants are and *how* they are "recruited" influences the subsequent process, its outcome as well as its credibility and legitimacy in the eyes of society and polity alike.

Democracy, since its first appearance in ancient Greece, is connected to ideas of autonomy, equality, political rights, and citizenship of each individual who is the primary political actor; the protagonist of participatory processes should be the "common citizen" representing—and speaking—only him/herself (Neisser, 2006, 2)[5] (rather than representatives of interest groups, common in consultation processes).

This in turn raises the issue: which citizens? However easy to state, to take inclusion literally and translate the principle into practice encounters an evident hurdle: it's common sense that it would be simply impossible to gather *all* the citizens and involve them *all* in a conversation, even in small communities (Parkinson, 2006) for simple, yet decisive, logistic, and time reasons.[6] In other words, citizen engagement must face a serious problem of scale; if this is true for the traditional "assembly"-type participation, in which many listen and few speak, it is even more the case of deliberative participation aiming at an authentic dialogue among participants.

Thus, assuming that participation of *all* citizens in contemporary societies[7] is not a viable option, there are three ways to go about participant recruitment:

1) invitation;
2) self-selection according to the "open doors" principle: processes and specific meetings are publicised and are open to anyone interested;
3) random selection of stratified samples of inhabitants (Sintomer, 2007) on the basis of certain social and demographic features so to ensure that participants are a descriptively representative microcosm or "minipopulus" (Dahl, 1989)[8] of the broader affected "universe" (Fishkin, 1995).

Participants recruited by invitation may well represent relevant segments of society, but can hardly be representative of society as a whole; typically, this system is used in consultations of stakeholders, though it is sometimes used in combination with other modes to ensure the presence of minorities and marginal groups. In a similar fashion, the "open doors" attracts "active citizens" and those who are strongly affected (usually, negatively) by the decision at hand (for example in project siting decisions). In both cases, participants hold pre-defined preferences, hardly a condition appropriate for dialogue, deliberation and the search for consensus.

Random stratified sampling, on the opposite, offers a number of advantages:

- (a guarantee of) impartiality and equality: each and every citizen has the same probability of being selected; furthermore, choice by lottery makes power circulate amongst members of society (Urbinati, 2013);
- the presence of diversity of opinions, a societal resource essential in tackling common issues and generating innovation (Gutmann and Thompson, 1996). "Bridging" diversities (Putnam, 2000) makes "good decisions" possible in a complex and heterogeneous society, as discussed below (whereas "open doors" favour "bonding" within groups and adversarial dynamics between groups);
- representativeness of participants (rather than delegated representation).

### The Quest for Informed Opinions

Democratic aggregation of preferences (i.e. voting), traditional participation and opinion polls all share the common assumption that citizens have a clear knowledge about their preferences; citizens' opinions are taken for granted, however "raw" they might be. In stark contrast, deliberative participation aims at offering participants the possibility of attaining a well-informed opinion on the issue at hand by taking into consideration available relevant information and knowledge.

As deliberative participation considers social acceptability alongside with other dimensions, it aims at fostering opinions based not only on "objective" or technical grounds, but also on "subjective" information, i.e. values, preferences, ideas, and interests that attribute social meaning to reality (Funtowicz and Ravetz, 1993). Even the definition of issues as problematic and the precise way in which they are framed represent social constructs (Fischer, 1993).

In this perspective, deliberative processes make balanced or, when possible, neutral information accessible to participants (limiting the cognitive asymmetries existing among them) through a variety of channels.

First of all, participants themselves contribute and share their arguments, knowledge, values and experiences. "Discussion is a way to combine information and broaden the range of arguments . . . *considered* judgements are simply those rendered under conditions favourable to the exercise of the sense of justice; the criteria that identify these judgements are not arbitrary"; such judgements have a positive effect, in time, on the issues at hand (Rawls, 1971, 47 and 359).

Deliberative processes typically include also stakeholders (i.e. interest groups), but in the role of "testimonies" (*not* as participants) so that their standpoints, problems and values may enrich the aspects in consideration (Hartz-Karp, 2007).[9]

Experts also have an important role in this respect, as they can offer information and knowledge that are useful and relevant for deciding on public matters. However, deliberative processes must be careful in avoiding undue influence on participants; experts don't have all the (right) answers, especially when it comes to issues laden with value, ethical, or political implications (Gutmann and Thompson, 1996; Pielke, 2005); expert opinions are inevitably filtered through their personal prejudices and dogmatic assumptions (Urbinati, 2013).

Contemporary society has to take "tough" decisions on the basis of "soft" evidence (Funtowicz and Ravetz, 1993) within a context featuring high degrees of uncertainty, not only cognitive and scientific (Fischer, 2000; Hajer and Wagenaar, 2003). In fact, the scientific community often has divergent opinions on many matters. During deliberative processes, participants should therefore have the possibility to hear and clarify opposing expert positions.

On the other hand, deliberative participation avoids using expert knowledge and information instrumentally according to the adversarial and partisan pattern of political struggle to support pre-defined positions. Instead, it offers a significative contribution towards increasing the epistemic quality of public decisions by incorporating both expert *and* lay knowledge and by creating 'bridges' between them. In the contemporary world, nobody has the monopoly of relevant knowledge; everybody has something to learn (Forester, 2007). Even ordinary citizens are experts, first of all of "everyday life" (Porsborg et al., 2007) and of their own needs; they can also be experts of solutions as they possess knowledge related to the specific context that specialists often lack (Fung and Wright, 2003; Hartz-Karp, 2007). Furthermore, they bring plain ordinary knowledge and common sense, which also has "an important role to play" (Fischer, 2000, 193). "Collective intelligence" mobilised by deliberative processes can generate better choices than those of experts "in isolation" (Landemore, 2013). Good decisions, as will be further discussed below, in a complex society require that they weigh and incorporate all types of information and knowledge alongside with preferences and values.

Available empirical evidence suggests that ordinary citizens involved in deliberative processes, if provided with adequate and balanced information, in fact are capable of understanding and discussing with competence public issues, even those presenting a high degree of technical and scientific complexity (Fischer, 2000; Pincock, 2012; Landemore, 2013). The experience of the previously mentioned Danish Consensus Conferences concerning a wide range of complex technical and scientific issues since the mid-'80s demonstrates that ordinary citizens, interacting with experts, are able to appreciate and decide even on such sophisticated matters (Kluver, 1995).

### Dialogue and Deliberation: Deep Reasoning, Deep Listening

Two other distinctive features are tightly linked and are therefore discussed jointly: dialogue and deliberation.

Deliberation, broadly speaking, can (or should) occur in many collective arenas, public and private (Bessette, 1994; Steiner et al., 2004; Parkinson, 2006); representative institutions such as parliaments (from the French *parler*, to speak) were originally meant to be deliberative fora, i.e. "government by discussion" (Manin, 2010).

Instead, the common dynamics of social and political discussion feature rigidly pre-defined, instrumental, polarised, "adversarial" positions, prone to specific interests (Mansbridge, 1983; Fishkin, 1995); there exists only one "right answer" and the aim is to "beat the other completely" (the literal meaning of the word "debate"). Incidentally, many meetings and assemblies labeled as citizen participation follow this type of discursive interaction.

Dialogue is not just any conversation, discussion, or debate (Dryzek, 2009). Instead, it implies significative interpersonal communication (Holman, 2007) in which interactions (usually face-to-face, but at least in theory, they could also take place online) occur within a context of mutual respect, of "deep listening" (Gastil and Black, 2008), of opinions and ideas, as well as of the meanings behind them, however diverse. Dialogue recognises the legitimacy of all opinions and the right to express them; even in conditions of conflict, it allows for the "humanisation" of the other (Steiner, 2012).

The specifically deliberative trait of these processes consists in the authentic (as opposed to strategic) and reciprocal exchange of reasons of arguments, reasons, and information in order to "weigh" them (Landemore, 2013). "Communicative action" (as opposed to strategic rationality based on instrumental utilitarian considerations) allows participants to reach an informed opinion thanks to the "non-coercive force of the best argument" (Habermas, 1984, 25). The intent of deliberative dialogue is to reach an effective decision on a specific issue by "weighing" possible options and their implications, the distribution of costs and benefits for individuals and groups, the constraints and opportunities, the *trade-offs* involved (Fishkin, 1995). To this end, reciprocal and public[10] justification of arguments used is the basic rule of deliberative discussion (Rawls, 1993; Gutmann and Thompson, 1996), which is about persuasion, rather than pressure or power (Mansbridge et al., 2011) (or, for that matter, even negotiation, based the exchange of stakes according to a purely self-interested mode). Deliberative interactions exploit the powerful "civilising force of hypocrisy" (Elster, 1993, 127) as they induce participants to use socially acceptable, logical, and coherent arguments, thus "compressing", to some extent at least, egoistic interests and allowing more general ones to emerge.[11]

It clearly emerges from these elements that the idea of deliberation features a strong rational component; rational arguments produce rational opinions and decisions "in the light of reason"; deliberation is the "moderate voice of reason" (Bessette, 1994).[12] However, in order to avoid becoming the domain only of privileged groups and individuals (who are used to rational modes of communication), deliberative dialogue hosts different communication styles and practices (Young, 2000). The meaning of "*dia logos*" ("word between" persons in ancient Greek), in the light of field experience, must be expanded so to include verbal as well as non-verbal interpersonal communication; furthermore, values, preferences, interests, and conflicts emerge not only through rational arguments, but also through other modes, such as storylines and personal anecdotes, and can also be expressed by means of emotional repertoires (Pruitt and Thomas, 2007; Gastil and Black, 2008; Elstub and McLaverty, 2014).

Dialogue and deliberation rarely rise spontaneously; conversations tend to reproduce the hierarchies of power present in everyday life; freedom of speech, however precious, does not suffice. Their chances of occurring can be greatly favoured by an appropriately structured context that is perceived by participants to be safe, guaranteed, and neutral. To this end, deliberative processes typically create "highly artificial" settings (Fung, 2003), with predefined agendas and for a limited period of time (that go under the name of "minipublics"). Ad hoc methods or techniques[13] based on rules and procedures and managed by professional facilitators are commonly used to proactively foster dialogue and deliberation (Pincock, 2012; Weiksner et al., 2012). For example, many such methods alternate plenary moments with phases of discussion in small groups.[14]

However useful, several aspects should be kept in mind in connection with such methods. Firstly, contrary to how it is sometimes unfortunately practiced, deliberative participation is a process in itself; it is not just a one-shot event. Also, it is part of a broader decision-making process, often long and complex. Finally, these methods cannot be applied "mechanically" to all cases and contexts; instead, they need to be carefully tailored to fit each specific context and type of issue, as well as the specific goals of the process.

### The Quest for Consensual Decisions

Dialogue allows participants to explore and discover innovative and possibly shared options (Pruitt and Thomas, 2007); however, talking per se does not constitute a decision-making device; rather, it is the "filter" through which proposals are sifted to gather sufficient consensus to be approved; it's consensus that makes public decisions (Manin, 2010).

Deliberative participation is a social process of transformative learning (Forester, 1999; Neisser, 2006) in which participants, exposed to dialogue and information, "are encouraged to reflect on their positions" (Dryzek, 2000, 79) so to form and/or modify them. As compared to other forms of verbal interaction, its distinctive trait is that deliberative dialogue enhances a posture of enquiry and learning (Pruitt and Thomas, 2007). By exploring different opinions as well as the assumptions behind them, it aims at enhancing reciprocal understanding, in turn favouring a shift towards balanced opinions.

As mentioned, opinions and practices are socially constructed and therefore can be socially formed and transformed by dialogic-deliberative practices (Dryzek, 2000; Pincock, 2012; Gastil and Black, 2008). If opinions can be transformed, this opens the way to the possibility that participants find common reasons and reach consensual decisions (Goodin, 2005). Consensus need not be necessarily "total", but even partial agreement, the discovery of shared terrains (Neisser, 2006) or a meta-consensus—on the nature of the issue if not on the solution to be adopted (Niemeyer and Dryzek, 2007)— are in any case useful to discover a "common map" that in turn can be the beginning of the quest for broader consensus.

## Empowering Citizens

Empowerment of participants and processes is more than just one more distinctive trait of deliberative participation (Fung, 2003; Avritzer, 2009); the other features mentioned above—inclusion, information, dialogue, deliberation, and search for consensus—are all aimed in the end towards one goal: making a *decision* (Gastil, 2013); real participation implies that decision-making power is transferred (returned) to citizens (Pateman, 1970).

The well-known "ladder of participation" proposed more than four decades ago by Sherry Arnstein (1969) is useful to clarify this point (Table 8.1). It distinguishes among various forms of participation according to the degree of influence exerted.[15] At the lowest rungs, Arnstein puts manipulation and therapy, which actually are not even to be considered as genuine forms of participation at all.

Information, consultation, and placation are considered forms of tokenism in which citizens "may indeed hear and be heard" . . . maybe even advise, but "lack the power to insure that their views will be heeded by the powerful". "Participation" is traditionally often meant simply as the top-down provision of information on decisions essentially already taken.

*Table 8.1* The Eight Rungs of the 'Ladder of Citizen Participation' Proposed by S. Arnstein (1969)

| | |
|---|---|
| *Citizen control* | *Citizen power* |
| Delegated power | |
| Partnership | |
| Placation | Tokenism |
| Consultation | |
| Informing | |
| Therapy | Non-participation |
| Manipulation | |

In consultation, decision-makers are squarely in control of the scope of the outcome: they are willing to listen, but there is no commitment as far as acceptance of proposals or requests is concerned.

In these cases, even the administrations that activate processes that they label as participatory, in fact are not willing to share their power (Wainwright, 2003). Only the last three rungs of the ladder—partnership, delegated power or citizen control—represent forms of participation that actually exert at least some degree of influence on decisions.

So, real participation is the possibility for citizens to influence political decisions that concern them (Avritzer, 2009; Pruitt and Thomas, 2007); it is not, as mentioned, an isolated event, but part of the broader decision-making process. Also, participants are empowered only if the issues under consideration are of some relevance and salience (Parkinson, 2006). Finally, empowerment also implies not only that the policy makers accept the indications emerging from citizen participation, but that this also has a "demonstration effect" (Bussu and Bartels, 2011, 15), exerting some type of actual impact on the situation or issue at hand (Rowe and Frewer, 2000). The UN Brisbane Declaration of 2005, for example, indicates that processes are influential when "their impact is evident".

The relevance of this feature cannot be stressed enough. The degree of empowerment (that must be evaluated case by case) represents the main factor that allows to distinguish between significative and, on the opposite, merely symbolic forms of engagement. If no power is involved in the process, it is not participation, and it's not worth the effort; actually, "bad engagement is worse than none at all" (Andersson et al., 2013).

Furthermore, the expectation of being able to exert actual influence on decisions constitutes an important motivational factor: citizens are willing to contribute their time, energy, and intelligence to participatory processes, provided their opinions will play a role and that the process will be implemented and have an impact (Fung and Wright, 2003) (whereas if this does not occur, they will lose trust and become sceptical of future attempts to involve them). To this end, process conveners should always stipulate a clear contract with citizens about the process and its influence.[16]

Summing up: deliberative participation aims at reinforcing the voice of the citizens, but also at promoting the willingness of institutions to listen to that "voice" (Carson, 1999) in the formation of collective decisions (Parkinson, 2006).

## The Added Values of Deliberative Participation

The previous pages highlight the specific features that differentiate deliberative participation from other—more traditional—modes of engagement. But this per se does not justify the adoption of such processes. The questions that should be critically asked are: why bother at all? What's the added value for society generated by such processes?

Literature, both theoretical and based on empirical research, claims that the added values of deliberation are numerous, ranging from increasing popular trust in decisions and authorities to reducing chances that decisions be "captured" by interest groups, from improving bureaucratic performance to developing a sense of ownership of public decisions, just to name a few. Here the discussion focuses on two major interwoven aspects that deliberative participation claims to contribute to: better decisions and social capital regeneration.

## Better Decisions

Deliberative participation, as discussed above, has an epistemic function insofar as it enhances well informed public judgement and decisions (Mansbridge et al., 2011). Through the *systematic* quest for the reasons of all involved, it allows an issue to be examined thoroughly, identifying and considering a broad range of preferences, opinions, interests, values, needs, and opportunities involved. By incorporating knowledge, as well as social values and preferences, deliberative participation contributes to wiser public decisions and increases policy capacity. Also, public judgement produces responsible choices because it considers a wide array of factors and implications, weighing options also in the light of ethical values (Yankelovich, 1991).

The nature of many of the issues that contemporary—highly sophisticated—society is called to tackle appears to be intrinsically "wicked", intractable, and persistent: technically, socially, and ethically (Fischer, 2000). The adoption of new technologies (such as Genetically Modified Organisms in food), ethical issues (divisive issues as gay marriage), and siting of impacting projects are all examples of such difficult decisions.

Furthermore, choices must be made in conditions of uncertainty, conflict, and complexity due to the constantly changing heterogeneity of interests, diversity of opinions, and plurality of identities and cultures cutting across the public sphere of contemporary societies (Benhabib, 1996; Rosanvallon, 2008; Manin, 2010).

Deliberative participation offers an innovative and effective path to making public decisions appropriate for societies with such features (Kies, 2010) while reducing uncertainty: by including a plurality of voices, it enhances the capability to perceive and judge implications of choices. It is through "democratic reason" resulting from the contributions, discussions, and interactions of many that society can hope to tackle the challenge of complexity (Landemore, 2013).[17]

By mobilising collective intelligence, deliberative participation can produce better—i.e. more effective, more efficient, and more equitable—collective choices as compared to alternative modes of decision-making. Furthermore, the features of deliberation, based on rationally and socially acceptable arguments, favour the consideration of general interests as compared to processes based on representation; in other words, deliberative participation enhances pro-social rather than egoistic, pro-self attitudes (Mansbridge, 1983).

## Social Capital and Regeneration

The notion of social capital[18] refers to the features of "social organisation such as trust, norms and networks" (Putnam, 1993), both "horizontally"—between members of a community—and "vertically"—between the latter and those by whom they are governed—(Pincock, 2012). Social capital is akin to social regeneration, as it increases community cohesion and builds its capacity and resilience in dealing with collective issues (Weiksner et al., 2012). There can be no real social regeneration if members of society are alienated from politics and excluded from collective choices.

Deliberative participation contributes to (re)generating social capital and represents an answer to its present decline (Putnam, 2000; Warren, 2002), as it increases trust in others and in democratic institutions along with decision ownership, greater sense of responsibility, solidarity with others, and community belonging.

Deliberative participation also develops individual assets relevant for social capital as it acts as a "school of democracy" making citizens more active, aware, responsible, competent, and informed (Fung and Wright, 2003; Parkinson, 2006; Weiksner et al., 2012) and contributes to the development of a sense of "political effectiveness" among citizens.[19] As J. S. Mill indicated already in the mid-1800s, a vital democracy requires active citizens; in turn, the practice of democracy itself has an educative function (Dewey, 1927; Bobbio, N., 1991; Landemore, 2013). Civic engagement in particular "educates individuals how to think publicly. . . . Politics becomes its own university, citizenship its own training ground, and participation its tutor" (Barber, 1984, 152). Following Aristoteles, by governing and being governed in turns, citizens become accustomed and familiar with both roles and with the complexity of the process of governing (Held, 1996; Parkinson, 2006).

## Institutionalising Participation: The Way Forward

A relevant question is whether deliberative participation should be institutionalised, and how that might be done. Broadly speaking, institutions are procedures, routines, norms, both formal and informal, "embedded in the organisational structure of the political system" (Hall and Taylor, 1996, 949). Institutionalisation gives "value and stability" to procedures and organisations. To institutionalise participation, in particular, means that it becomes a systematic practice "incorporating it in the way public decisions are made" (Fagotto and Fung, 2009).

Participation institutionalisation has been carried out on different scales, from cities (e.g., Montreal)[20] to regions (e.g., Catalunya)[21] and nations (e.g., Denmark, mentioned above, or the Brazilian "national conferences"). The creation of ad hoc offices, departments, or independent authorities (such as the French *Commission Nationale du Débat Publique*, CNDP),[22] often—albeit not always—is symptomatic of some degree of institutionalisation. Participatory budgeting is perhaps the most widely spread case of institutionalisation of empowered citizen engagement as a routine practice.

Though there have been many successful experiences of *deliberative* participation, there are few examples of its institutionalisation as a routine practice. An interesting example is represented by Law no. 69 passed in 2007 by the Region of Tuscany (Italy). The Law is remarkable as it aims at pro-actively promoting citizen involvement "as an ordinary form of administration and government . . . in all sectors and at all levels" and pursues this goal by enhancing features explicitly derived from deliberative theory[23] (Lewanski, 2013).

Institutionalisation of public involvement, on the basis of opposite arguments that appear to mirror each other, is favoured by some as a positive development and feared by others as a serious risk.

From the first perspective, rules and procedures can cause participation to become a sclerotic and ritualised exercise suffocating societal spontaneity, "encapsulated" and controlled, if not manipulated, by authorities. Furthermore, it is feared that regulated participation only reproduces and strengthens the inequalities of power already in society. However, spontaneous bottom-up participation, though a legitimate form of mobilisation (though practicable for limited periods of time), does not appear to be a way to systematically make decisions, as the experience of social movements— from the late '60s to 'Occupy Wall Street'—seem to confirm.

The opposite argument is that only systematic—rather than episodic— forms of democratic involvement allow citizens to (re)gain political power (Rosanvallon, 2008); in this perspective, institutionalisation is crucial for innovating democracy (Budge, 2000) because it:

- creates a "structure of opportunity" (Kitschelt, 1986, 58) enhancing participation;
- attributes legitimacy and effectiveness to participatory processes making them "normatively acceptable" (Bächtiger and Wegemann, 2014, 121);
- upgrades opportunities to exert actual influence on choices and policies;
- promotes the inclusion of disadvantaged and marginal social groups and individuals;
- subtracts participation from the discretion of decision-makers as well as from interest groups that might attempt to "capture" them, thus increasing its chances of survival and growth in time (Fung and Wright, 2003);
- offers guarantees against distortions and manipulations; in this respect, participatory processes must be perceived as impartial by both participants and society at large; in general, processes are perceived as legitimate insofar as they are fair and impartial (Dahl, 1956); to this end, institutionalisation can provide devices guaranteeing neutrality and thus fostering credibility (such as ad hoc independent authorities responsible for process management, as in the case of Tuscany or of the French CNDP).

All in all, if deliberative participation is to become politically and socially relevant, its institutionalisation as a routine practice, though not without risks, represents a necessary requisite.

## Conclusions

Society and polity are obviously tightly interwoven: a vital society promotes a vital democracy, and vice versa; at present, society appears to be affected by a decline in social capital and the polity by an increasing democratic deficit. The challenge—and the opportunity—is to invert the vicious downwards circle into a virtuous one. Deliberative participation is not the absolute remedy but certainly has the potential to generate a meaningful contribution in this direction.

Deliberative participation aims at deepening and strengthening democracy, a positive normative value that many cherish. But, perhaps even more relevant, it is also appropriate for a complex, plural, and sophisticated society making collective action possible thanks to its capability to mobilise collective intelligence by incorporating different forms of knowledge and preferences through cooperation amongst individuals, thus generating better, and more shared, decisions.

Of course, deliberative democracy must prove its worth on the field and its claims must be tested; over the last four decades or so, a number of promising real-life experiences have demonstrated that deliberative participation is doable, useful, and capable of producing meaningful outcomes. The recent Irish constitutional reform process that coupled an original deliberative participation process with direct democracy (referenda) is perhaps one of the most interesting and fruitful examples of this form of democratic innovation.

A caveat, however, is in order: there is a risk that the deliberative idea becomes fashionable whereby the "form"—rich and pleasant small group conversations assisted by facilitators—becomes widespread, without actually being relevant or influential. Mere 'appearance' would not be fruitful in addressing the present democratic deficit nor the decay in social capital. If it is to develop its potential and deliver its promises, deliberative democracy requires at least some degree of participant empowerment and that outcomes actually exert some influence on decisions and policies.

Finally, deliberative democracy is not a *revolution*, but it does represent a substantive *evolution* of democracy aiming at revitalising it in the face of clear symptoms of decay and *involution*. The balance of the political system today leans too heavily towards representation and needs to be re-adjusted. Such 'soft' change requires a polity that realises the crisis of legitimation and that is willing to modify its role by giving up, albeit in part, temporarily and on specific topics, its "power to decide according to the standard procedures of representative democracy, and choose to play a different role, that of promoters of a discussion and guarantors of its fairness" (Bobbio, L., 2005). In return, both decisions and policy makers gain in legitimacy. Deliberative participation is not meant to be an antagonist of traditional representation; instead, participation integrates and enriches the democratic process.

## Notes

1. See, for example, UN documents such as Millennium Declaration point V.25 www.un.org/millennium/declaration/ares552e.htm or the Brisbane Declaration www.ncdd.org/exchange/files/docs/brisbane_declaration.pdf.
2. WWViews on Global Warming in 2009 took place in 36 countries across the planet; see http://wwviews.org.
3. www.constitution.ie
4. Political inclusion is not only a democratic value; it is also, as Acemoğlu and Robinson have shown, an essential factor of economic growth: ". . . the quality of economic institutions depends on politics and political institutions" (2012, 53).
5. The "ideal" citizen, Norman Rockwell, is portrayed in "*Freedom of Speech*" (1943), showing a man speaking among his peers in a traditional New England *Town Meeting*.
6. Though it can certainly usefully complement face-to-face participation, the potential of online participation in ensuring an actual dialogue among millions of citizens is still to be explored and proven.
7. This did not occur even in a relatively small polity in which democratic feelings were strong as ancient Athens: the Pnix, the assembly, had only 6,000 places *vis-a-vis* some 30 to 60,000 citizens.
8. Interestingly, John Stuart Mill in his book *On Liberty* already proposed something similar with the "Congress of ideas" in mid-1800s.
9. Their involvement is also important for the success of the process and subsequent implementation of its outcomes.
10. In this deliberation differs from other forms of participation, such as voting, which typically is secret (Parkinson, 2006).
11. Elster's consideration appears to be relevant in an individualist context as that of contemporary societies, though it does not exclude that a more civic culture develops in time also thanks to the spread of deliberative participation.
12. Thus, deliberative participation considers citizens as reasonable agents, quite the opposite of the "irrational mob" feared by the élites, including James Madison and other "founding fathers" of the United States (Weiksner et al., 2012).
13. Literally hundreds of such methods have been developed over recent years; see www.participedia.net or www.iaf-methods.org.
14. The "magic number" should be big enough to ensure diversity of opinions and small enough to ensure dialogue, i.e. less than 50, more likely in the range between ten and 20 (Fung, 2003), or even less (Parkinson, 2006).
15. A simplified version of S. Arnsteins's ladder is the "Public Participation Spectrum" adopted by the International Association of Public Participation (IAP2) www.iap2.org/associations/4748/files/IAP2%20Spectrum_vertical.pdf.
16. An original, balanced, and workable example of how this can be accomplished in practice is offered by Law no. 69 of 2007 adopted by the Tuscany Region; Regional support is subordinated to an exchange, by which the Region requests local authorities to sign an inter-institutional *entente* agreement in which the authorities are required to declare officially that they will take into serious consideration the results of the participation process. Should they deem the outcomes less than acceptable (for example, opposing community interests or their electoral mandate), they can override the outcomes only on the condition that they publicly provide the reasons for their deferral. In this way, the autonomy

of local administrations is fully respected; the responsibility of the final decision remains in the hands of the competent administration.

17. Groups, according to social psychology, can develop better solutions than single individuals (Gastil, 2000).

18. For a discussion of the wide variety of meanings the term has acquired, see Ferragina (2012).

19. The public is often perceived by decision-makers as incompetent and irrational, a hurdle rather than a resource. Even if one considers this vision to be true, it should be considered whether this depends also on representation that attributes a marginal role to citizens; after all, decision-makers prefer "docile/meek or indifferent subjects" (Bobbio, N., 1991).

20. *Office de Consultation Publique;* www.ville.montreal.qc.ca/consultation.

21. www.gencat.cat/drep.

22. On the CNDP, see: www.débatpublic.fr.

23. According to Carson and Lewanski (2008), the Law incorporates the four core principles of the Brisbane Declaration, considered a best practice description of deliberative democracy: integrity, inclusion, deliberation, influence.

## References

Acemoğlu, D., and J. Robinson. 2012. *Why Nations Fail: The Origins of Power, Prosperity, and Poverty.* New York: Crown Publishing.

Andersson, E., McLean, S., Parlak, M., and G. Melvin. 2013. *From Fairy Tale to Reality: Dispelling the Myths Around Citizen Engagement.* London: Involve.

Arnstein, S. 1969. "A Ladder of Citizen Participation." *Journal of American Institute of Planners,* 35(4): 216–224.

Avritzer, L. 2009. *Participatory Institutions in Democratic Brazil.* Baltimore: Johns Hopkins University Press.

Bächtiger, A., and A. Wegemann. 2014. "'Scaling up' deliberation." In *Deliberative Democracy: Issues and Cases,* edited by Stephen Elstub and Peter McLaverty, 118–135. Edinburgh: Edinburgh University Press.

Barber, B. 1984. *Strong Democracy.* Berkeley: University of California Press.

Benhabib, S., ed. 1996. *Democracy and Difference: Contesting the Boundaries of the Political.* Princeton: Princeton University Press.

Bessette, J. 1994. *The Moderate Voice of Reason: Deliberative Democracy & American National Government.* Chicago: The University of Chicago Press.

Bobbio, L. 2005. "La democrazia deliberativa nella pratica." *Stato e mercato,* 73(April): 67–88.

Bobbio, N. 1991. *Il futuro della democrazia.* Turin: Einaudi.

Budge, I. 2000. "Deliberative Democracy Versus Direct Democracy—Plus Political Parties." In *Democratic Innovation: Deliberation, Representation and Association,* edited by Michael Saward, 195–209. London: Routledge.

Bussu, S. and K. Bartels. 2011. "Facilitative Leaders in Collaborative Governance: Windows of Opportunity and Window Dressing in Italy." Paper presented at *PSA Conference PSA,* London, 19–21 April.

Carson, L. 1999. *Random Selection: Achieving Representation in Planning.* Alison Burton Memorial Lecture, Royal Australian Planning Institute, Canberra.

Carson, L. and Lewanski, R. 2008. "Fostering Citizen Participation Top-Down." *International Journal of Public Participation,* 2(1): 72–83.

Crouch, C. 2004. *Post-Democracy.* Cambridge: Polity Press.

Dahl, R. 1956. *A Preface To Democratic Theory.* Chicago: University of Chicago Press.

Dahl, R. 1989. *Democracy and Its Critics.* New Haven: Yale University Press.

Dalton, R. 2004. *Democratic Challenges, Democratic Choices: The Erosion of Political Support in Advanced Industrial Democracies.* Oxford: Oxford University Press.

Dewey, J. 1927. *The Public and Its Problem: An Essay in Political Inquiry.* New York: Henry Holt.

Dryzek, J. 2000. "Discoursive Democracy vs. Liberal Constitutionalism." In *Democratic Innovation: Deliberation, Representation and Association,* edited by Michael Saward, 78–89. London: Routledge.

Dryzek, J. 2009. "The Australian Citizens' Parliament: A World First." *Journal of Public Deliberation,* 5(1), Article 9.

Dryzek, J., and S. Niemeyer. 2008. "Discoursive Representation." *American Political Science Review,* 102(4): 481–493.

Elster, J. 1993. *Argomentare e negoziare.* Milan: Bruno Mondadori.

Elstub, S., and P. McLaverty. 2014. "Introduction: Issues and Cases in Deliberative Democracy." In *Deliberative Democracy: Issues and Cases,* edited by Stephen Elstub and Peter McLaverty, 1–16. Edinburgh: Edinburgh University Press.

Fagotto, E. and A. Fung. 2009. "Sustaining Public Engagement. Embedded Deliberation in Local Communities." *An Occasional Research Paper by Everyday Democracy and the Kettering Foundation.*

Ferragina, E. 2012. *Social Capital in Europe. A Comparative Regional Analysis.* Cheltenham: E. Elgar.

Fischer, F. 1993. "Citizen Participation and the Democratization of Policy Expertise: From Theoretical Inquiry to Practical Cases." *Policy Sciences,* 26: 165–187.

Fischer, F. 2000. *Citizens, Experts and the Environment: Politics of Local Knowledge.* Durham: Duke University Press.

Fishkin, J. 1995. *The Voice of the People: Public Opinion and Democracy.* New Haven: Yale University Press.

Font, J., Della Porta, D., and Y. Sintomer. 2014. "Introduction." In *Participatory Democracy in Southern Europe: Causes, Characteristics and Consequences,* edited by Joan Font, Donatella Della Porta, and Yves Sintomer, 1–20. London: Rowman & Littlefield.

Forester, J. 1999. *The Deliberative Practitioner: Encouraging Participatory Planning Processes.* Cambridge, MA: MIT Press.

Forester, J. 2007. "Public Participation as Mediated Negotiation: Entangled Promises and Practices." *International Journal of Public Participation,* 1(1).

Freedom House. 2014. *Freedom in the World.* Accessed from www.freedomhouse.org.

Fuji, J. G. September 2009. "Deliberative Democratic Practices in Canada: An Analysis of Institutional Empowerment in Three Cases." *Canadian Journal of Political Science,* 42(3): 679–703.

Fung, A. 2003. "Survey Article: Recipes for Public Spheres: Eight Institutional Design Choices and Their Consequences." *The Journal of Political Philosophy,* 11(3): 338–367.

Fung, A., and E. O. Wright, eds. 2003. *Deepening Democracy: Institutional Innovations in Empowered Participatory Governance.* London: Verso.

Funtowicz, S., and J. Ravetz. 1993. "Science for the Post-Normal Age." *Futures* (September): 739–755.

Gastil, J. 2000. *By Popular Demand: Revitalizing Representative Democracy Through Deliberative Elections.* Berkeley: University of California Press.

Gastil, J. 2013. "A Comparison of Deliberative Designs and Policy Impact in the EU and Across the Globe." In *Is Europe Listening to Us? Successes and Failures of EU Citizen Consultations,* edited by Rapael Kies and Patrizia Nanz, 217–237. Farnham, UK: Ashgate.

Gastil, J., and L. Black. 2008. "Public Deliberation as the Organizing Principle of Political Communication Research." *Journal of Public Deliberation,* 4(1), Article 3.

Gauchet, M. 2009. *La democrazia da una crisi all'altra*. Sant'Angelo in Formis, Italy: Ipermedium.

Goodin, R. 2005. "Sequencing Deliberative Moments." *Acta Politica*, 40: 182–196.

Gutmann, A., and D. Thompson. 1996. *Democracy and Disagreement*. Cambridge, MA and London: Belknap Press of Harvard University Press.

Habermas, J. 1984. *Theory of Communicative Action*. Boston: Beacon Press.

Hajer, M., and H. Wagenaar. 2003. *Deliberative Policy Analysis*. Cambridge: Cambridge University Press.

Hall, P., and R. Taylor. 1996. "Political Science and the Three New Institutionalisms." *Political Studies*, 44: 936–957.

Hartz-Karp, J. December 2007. "Understanding Deliberativeness: Bridging Theory and Practice." *The International Journal of Public Participation*, 1(2).

Held, D. 1996. *Models of Democracy*. Cambridge: Polity Press.

Holman, P. 2007. "Preparing to Mix and Match Methods." In *The Change Handbook*, 2nd edition, edited by Peggy Holman, Tom Devane and Steven Cady, 44–58. San Francisco: Berrett-Koehler.

Kies, R. 2010. *Promises and Limits of the Web-deliberation*. London: Palgrave MacMillan.

Kitschelt, H. January 1986. "Political Opportunity Structures and Political Protest: Anti-Nuclear Movements in Four Democracies." *British Journal of Political Science*, 16(1): 57–85.

Kluver, L. 1995. "Consensus Conferences of the Danish Board of Technology." In *Public Participation in Science: The Role of Consensus Conferences in Europe*, edited by Simon Joss and John Durant, 41–52. London: Science Museum.

Landemore, H. 2013. *Democratic Reason: Politics, Collective Intelligence and the Rule of the Many*. Princeton: Princeton University Press.

Leighninger, M. 2006. *The Next Form of Democracy*. Nashville: Vanderbilt University Press.

Lewanski, R. 2013. "Institutionalizing Deliberative Democracy: The 'Tuscany Laboratory'." *Journal of Public Deliberation*, 9(1), Article 10.

Mair, P. 2013. *Ruling the Void: The Hollowing of Western Democracy*. London: Verso.

Manin, B. 2010. *Principi del governo rappresentativo*. Bologna: Il Mulino.

Mansbridge, J. 1983. *Beyond Adversary Democracy*. Chicago: University of Chicago Press.

Mansbridge, J., Bohman, J., Chambers, S., Christiano, C. T., Fung, A., Parkinson, J., Thompson, D. F. and M. E. Warren. 2011. "A Systemic Approach to Deliberative Democracy." Paper presented at *ECPR Joint Session of Workshops*, St. Gallen.

Neisser, P. 2006. "Political Polarization as Disagreement Failure." *Journal of Public Deliberation*, 2(1), Article 9.

Niemeyer, S. and J. Dryzek. 2007. "Using Interpersonal Consistency as a Measure of Deliberative Quality." Paper presented at *ECPR Joint Sessions*, Helsinki, May.

Norris, P. 1999. "Introduction: The Growth of Critical Citizens?" In *Critical Citizens: Global Support for Democratic Governance*, edited by Pippa Norris, 1–29. Oxford: Oxford University Press.

Parkinson, J. 2006. *Deliberating in the Real World*. Oxford: Oxford University Press.

Pateman, C. 1970. *Participation and Democratic Theory*. Cambridge: Cambridge University Press.

Pielke, R. 2005. *Scienza e Politica*. Bari: Laterza.

Pincock, H. 2012. "Does Deliberation Make Better Citizens?" In *Democracy in Motion: Evaluating the Practice and Impact of Deliberative Civic Engagement*, edited by Tina Nabatchi, John Gastil, Michael Weiksner and Matt Leighninger, 135–162. Oxford: Oxford University Press.

Porsborg, A., Lassen, J., and P. Sandoe. 2007. "Democracy at Its Best? The Consensus Conference in a Cross-National Perspective." *Journal of Agricultural and Environmental Ethics*, 20: 13–35.

Pruitt, B., and P. Thomas. 2007. *Democratic Dialogue—A Handbook for Practitioners*. International IDEA, CIDA, OAS and UNDP.

Putnam, R. 1993. *Making Democracy Work: Civic Traditions in Modern Italy*. Princeton: Princeton University Press.

Putnam, R. 2000. *Bowling Alone: The Collapse and Revival of American Community*. New York: Simon & Schuster.

Rawls, J. 1971. *A Theory of Justice*. Oxford: Oxford University Press.

Rawls, J. 1993. *Political Liberalism*. New York: Columbia University Press.

Rosanvallon, P. 2008. *La légitimité démocratique: impartialité, réflexivité, proximité*. Paris: Seuil.

Rowe, G., and L. Frewer. Winter 2000. "Public Participation Methods: A Framework for Evaluation." *Science, Technology and Human Values*, 25(1): 3–29.

Setälä, M. 2014. "The Public Sphere as a Site of Deliberation: An Analysis of Problems of Inclusion." In *Deliberative Democracy: Issues and Cases*, edited by Stephen Elstub and Peter McLaverty, 149–165. Edinburgh: Edinburgh University Press.

Sintomer, Y. 2007. *Le pouvoir au peuple. Jurys citoyens, triage au sort et démocratie participative*. Paris: la Decouverte.

Sintomer, Y., and G. Allegretti. 2009. *I bilanci partecipativi in Europa. Nuove esperienze democratiche nel vecchio continente*. Rome: Ediesse.

Smith, G. 2009. *Democratic Innovations: Designing Institutions for Citizen Participation*. Cambridge: Cambridge University Press.

Steiner, J. 2012. *The Foundations of Deliberative Democracy*. Cambridge: Cambridge University Press.

Steiner, J., Bächtiger, A., Spörndli, M., and M. Steenbergen. 2004. *Deliberative Politics in Action: Analysing Parliamentary Discourse*. Cambridge: Cambridge University Press.

Torcal, M., and J. R. Montero, eds. 2006. *Political Disaffection in Contemporary Democracies: Social Capital, Institutions, and Politics*. London: Routledge.

Urbinati, N. 2013. *Democrazia in diretta. Le nuove sfide della rappresentanza*. Milan: Feltrinelli.

Wainwright, H. 2003. *Reclaim the State: Experiments in Popular Democracy*. London: Verso.

Warren, M. 2002. "What Can Democratic Participation Mean Today?" *Political Theory*, 30(2): 677–701.

Weiksner, M., Gastil, J., Nabatchi, T., and M. Leighninger. 2012. "Advancing Theory and Practice of Deliberative Civic Engagement. A Secular Hymnal." In *Democracy in Motion: Evaluating the Practice and Impact of Deliberative Civic Engagement*, edited by Tina Nabatchi, John Gastil, Michael Weiksner and Matt Leighninger, 261–273. Oxford: Oxford University Press.

World Values Survey, Wave 6. 2010–14. Accessed from www.worrldavaluesseries.org.

Yankelovich, D. 1991. *Coming to Public Judgment: Making Democracy Work in a Complex World*. Syracuse: Syracuse University Press.

Young, I. M. 2000. *Inclusion and Democracy*. Oxford: Oxford University Press.

Zakaria, F. 2003. *The Future of Freedom: Illiberal Democracy at Home and Abroad*. New York: Norton.

# 9  City Leadership and Social Regeneration

## The Potential of Community Leadership and the New Roles for Public Managers and Politicians

*Alessandro Sancino and Leslie Budd*

## Introduction

The concept of regeneration, particularly in urban areas, has underwritten the discourse of urban development and renewal in the advanced economies in the immediate decades after World War II (WWII) and increasingly in the emerging economies[1] in the last two decades. Regeneration becomes often conflated with renewal, development, and gentrification, all with the prefix urban. But what they share is a set of underlying forces about the material and representational nature of space.[2] Particularly, in our contemporary turbulent and changing times, the complexity of places[3] goes beyond economic imperatives and does include the manifold socio-economic, cultural, and environmental dynamics. According to Sacchetti and Borzaga in this volume, "social regeneration is about the transformative processes which, through institutional choices that embody cooperation and inclusion, develop opportunities and capabilities for multiple categories of actors, and especially weak categories, leading to societal benefits and community resilience".

In this chapter, we aim to give a contribution discussing what types of city leadership can contribute towards promoting social regeneration of communities focusing in particular on the roles of public managers and politicians. The structure of the chapter is as follows: the second section sets out a fold-four classification of city leadership; the third section analyses the applicability of this framework in regard to social regeneration; the fourth section discusses the new functions for local governments and the new roles for public managers and politicians to enhance social regeneration of communities; the fifth section concludes with a summary of our main arguments.

## City Leadership: Agency and Structure for Social Regeneration

Since the middle of the 20th century, cities and their hinterlands have become the engines of economic development in the advanced and in many of the emerging economies (Glaeser, 2011). The United Nations estimates that over two-thirds of the world's population will be living in urban areas by 2050 (United Nations 2015).

However, the rapid growth of urbanisation is accompanied by socio-economic and political wicked problems that traditional forms of public policy no longer seem to address. Therefore, in an increasingly fragmented and individualised network society (e.g., Castells, 2004), the leadership to convene actors for activating social and organisational networks and self-adaptive systems becomes all the more important in order to cope with complex contemporary wicked and/or societal challenges (the latter including challenges that are not necessarily wicked: examples of contemporary wicked problems could be managing migration, climate change, and terrorism; examples of societal challenges could be the Sustainable Development Goals spearheaded by the United Nations).

City leadership is here defined as the capacity of people and/or organisations that are in the position—both formally and informally—to activate and lead processes where city and citizens' inputs, energies, and resources are mobilised for the accomplishment of relevant societal challenges (Sancino, 2017). In particular, drawing upon previous studies (Hambleton, 2015; Hambleton and Howard, 2013; Hartley, 2002) as well as upon our previous work (Budd and Sancino, 2016; Budd et al., 2017), we can identify four forms of city leadership:

- *Managerial leadership*, which deals with the public services (e.g., housing, health care, education, regeneration, leisure, etc.) delivered within a city;
- *Political leadership*, which deals with the democratic processes and decisions affecting a city and its citizens;
- *Community leadership*, which deals with all the community processes provided by the community and its actors operating outside the traditional realm of the public and private sector;
- *Business leadership*, which deals with the processes of (co-)creation of value provided by the private sector.

Within this classification, we can identify four elements of city leadership (Grint, 2000; Huxham and Vangen, 2005; Bryson et al., 2015):

- *Actors:* individuals, groups of individuals, but also an organisation and/ or a group of organisations which play a key leadership role in the life of the city;
- *Structures:* facilities, arrangements, and/or organisations that support and enable city leadership acting as conveners and/or catalysers— organisations are mentioned also here because they could be both actors and/or structures for city leadership;
- *Processes:* the way in which leaders build, activate, mobilise, and set directions for the followers;
- *Followership:* the nature and type(s) of followership that engage with the leaders and take part in the city leadership system (made up by leaders, structures, processes, and followers).

Forms and elements of city leadership establish patterns that vary according to the contexts, moments, and issues; indeed, as noted by Hambleton (2015, 11):

> Place-based leaders are not free agents able to do exactly as they choose. On the contrary, various powerful forces shape the context within which civic leaders operate. These forces do not disable local leadership. Rather they place limits on what urban leaders may be able to accomplish in particular places and at particular moments in time.

## What Types of City Leadership for Social Regeneration?

In this section, we discuss some key changing trends for each form of city leadership, and we discuss how they impact on social regeneration.

### Political Leadership and Social Regeneration

We can highlight the following as some of the most important trends in political leadership within cities across the Western countries:

- The trend towards the establishment of institutions that resemble the idea of the leader as a great man. Evidence of this can be found in the establishment of directly elected metro-mayors in the UK (see, for example, Gains, 2015) and more generally in the increasing interests towards the model of directly elected mayors (e.g., Hambleton, 2013; Sancino and Castellani, 2016);
- The declining role of political parties as structures for enacting political leadership at the local level (e.g., Copus, 2000);
- The increasing interactive and participatory nature of political processes (e.g., Edelenbos and Klijn, 2006; Fung, 2006; Torfing et al., 2012);

Against this backdrop, even if individual and centralised political leadership brings undoubtedly benefits in terms of public accountability, the nature of social regeneration seems more akin to individual and shared political leadership; in other words, the trend towards the social and institutional recognition of the individual leader should be rather transformed into the institutional establishment and social construction of multiple leaders (so going from the idea of a leader of the city to the idea of the leaders of the city) accountable to the public for specific societal challenges.

### Managerial Leadership and Social Regeneration

As indicated above, managerial leadership is about delivering public services within a city. In this respect, public services across all Western countries are currently characterised by the austerity measures implemented in many countries (e.g., Meneguzzo et al., 2013; Pollitt, 2010) and by the increasing role of the third and voluntary sectors in delivering public services (e.g., Osborne and McLaughlin, 2004). These trends create opportunities (such as the positive role that forms of community leadership can play in public services—see next paragraph), but also pose threats, such as the marketisation of public services that may lead to the socialisation of public costs and to the privatisation of public benefits. There is an increasing debate on which role should the public sector play in times of stagnating or recessive economies, with some pointing to a bigger and smarter role of public sector in the economy (for example, the Entrepreneurial State advocated by Mazzucato, 2013); in this respect, Box 9.1 below reports the example of municipal socialism implemented in the 1960s and 1970s in some cities in the UK and US and its positive impacts at that time on social regeneration.

---

### Box 9.1   "Municipal Socialism"

In the 1960s and 1970s, in the UK and US, coalitions of public and private actors organised themselves around the urban growth machine discourses and took on leadership roles in regenerating their towns and cities (e.g., Cox and Mair, 1989; Molotch, 1976): for example, with the construction of public housing on a large scale. In both these countries, these initiatives may be ascribed to the praxis of municipal socialism in the form of ownership of local public utilities and services, which began in the late 19th century, reaching its apogee at the start of World War I (WWI) in 1914 (Hunt, 2004; Sheldrake, 1989). This type of leadership acted as an intermediary of change that released many people from dwelling in slums.

Source: own elaboration.

---

### Community Leadership and Social Regeneration

The expansion of public needs and the retrenchment of the welfare state (e.g., Di Mascio and Natalini, 2015) have been filled by the emergence of a bigger society interested in the self-creation/peer production (Pestoff, 2012, 1104) and co-production with the public sector of the public value through inter-organisational collaboration (Huxham and Vangen, 2005) or through the engagement of individuals and communities of individuals (Bovaird, 2007). This means recognising that beyond the state, there are nowadays many more other actors that are contributing to the co-creation of public value (Bryson et al., 2017); as Benington and Hartley wrote (2015), "[the State and] public managers are an important part of public value creation, but public value can also be created by elected politicians, by community activists, by private companies, by the media and so on".

The experiences of co-creation (e.g., Bryson et al., 2017), co-production (e.g., Nabatchi et al., 2017), and social innovation (e.g., Brandsen et al., 2015) promoted by community actors are particularly important at the local level as the governmental level closer to citizen (OECD, 2011) and as the level where citizens feel that they make a real contribution to community building; the renewed sense of community is described by Nalbandian and Nalbandian (2003, 84) as follows:

> in a world that is increasingly interconnected through telecommunications, financial markets, and accessibility to technology, our personal connections to community are challenged as our sense of place and our sense of control over our lives erode, and as diversity in our population increases. The renewed sentiment for community signals an enduring desire for identity, grounding and tradition.

### Business Leadership and Social Regeneration

Business leadership and city leadership have been traditionally considered as a major driver of regeneration based upon real estate development interests. However, considering our focus here on social regeneration, we centre our attention on shared value as a concept and practice of business that recognise the importance of the relationship between business and place.

Specifically, the concept of shared value has been recently developed by Porter and Kramer (2011) and can be defined as policies and operating practices that enhance the competitiveness of a company while simultaneously advancing the economic and social conditions in the communities in which it operates. As written in Sancino (2016, 412), shared value can be considered a sub-segment of the overall private value produced by the private sector. A financial transaction may produce private value in the form of profit, but not necessarily shared value. To take an example, a shared value can be produced when a private firm opens a nursery for its employees. However, the issue becomes how to promote a business leadership committed to the creation of shared value as a pre-condition to enhance the social regeneration of the communities served and/or impacted by business.

## The Role of Local Governments

Sotarauta et al. (2017, 188) point out that "academic research and popular accounts of formal leadership experiences point to the need for a significant re-think of the meaning(s), dynamics and drivers of leadership in subnational development"; following their argument, in this section, we focus on the need for rethinking the function of local governments and the role of politicians and managers.

## New Challenges for Governing—Re-Imagining Local Governments

Politics and administration have been tremendously changing in the last two decades: on one hand, they are now taking place in new multi-governance levels and contexts; on the other hand, public policies and public services are in many cases co-created and/or co-produced not only by politicians and managers, but also by other actors (such as citizens and civil society organisations, as well as business organisations) with potentially multiple identities (for example, citizens may behave in the same process as clients and/or partners—see, for example, Thomas, 2013). Moreover, the development of new kinds of democracy (e.g., participatory democracy, deliberative democracy, online direct democracy, monitory democracy [Keane, 2011], etc.) is putting governments across Western countries—traditionally based on representative democracy—and their actors (politicians, public managers, and citizens) under pressures and tensions.

To enhance social regeneration, local governments should therefore understand their new functions in the current new public governance era (see, for example, Bingham et al., 2005; Osborne, 2006). Today as never before, local governments should be oriented toward a sustainable growth strategy for their territories and communities. Core stakeholders in the local system should take part in designing, implementing, and assessing policies and public services. In addition, various stakeholders and different organisational networks should move beyond the mindset of fragmentation and partiality; this is necessary in order to build a community, one with its own vision and identity (Putnam, 2005; Sancino, 2010). In this respect, according to Nalbandian et al. (2013), there are three main leadership challenges in local governments: working more actively at the intersection between political and administrative arenas; synchronising city and county boundaries with problems that have no jurisdictional homes; and connecting engagement initiatives to traditional political values.

### New Roles for Public Managers

The crisis of representation in political parties (Copus, 2000) is giving public managers a more political role in terms of community building and facilitating democracy (Nalbandian, 1999). Feldman and Khademian (2007) argue that the challenge for public managers today is not to build a distinct venue where the public can participate, but rather to do core tasks which create a community of participation where local- and experience-based ways of knowing problems engage with political and technical ways in order to move toward alternative ways of knowing and addressing problems. Overall, the recent literature on the role of public managers has particularly emphasised their role as creators of communities of participation (Feldman and Khademian, 2007). In particular, in order to meet the challenges of modernising the organisation and building communities, public managers are asked to develop political skills in order to fill the gaps that exist among elected officials and professional staff; among public, private, and non-profit organisations; among departments within local government; and among managers and citizens (Nalbandian and Nalbandian, 2003, 87).

Nabatchi (2010, 2012) has asserted that public managers should address the democracy deficit working collaboratively and horizontally with citizens and infusing government decision-making with reasoned discussions and the collective judgement of citizens. On this point, similarly, Feldman and Khademian (2007, 319) have argued that public managers should undertake two main kinds of work in practicing inclusive management: the informational work and the relational work. The first one is directed toward the goal of informed decision-making, while the second one is directed toward the goal of creating connections that allow people to use that information to deliberate.

### New Roles for Politicians

Sørensen (2006) has extensively written about the implications of new public governance processes (Bingham et al., 2005; Osborne, 2006) on the roles of politicians, arguing how the role of politicians should evolve towards a meta-governance role. Though this shift could undermine representative democracy in its traditional forms, it does not necessarily undermine representative democracy as such: in fact, meta-governance may open the door for the development of a new, strong model of representative democracy (Sørensen, 2006, 99). In particular, Sørensen defines meta-governance as a way of enhancing coordinated governance in a fragmented political system based on a high degree of autonomy for a plurality of self-governing networks and institutions (Ibid., 100). Meta-governance may be exercised by four main strategies by: 1) framing political, organisational, and financial contexts within which self-governance takes place; 2) using storytelling for sense-making and sense-giving; 3) offering support and facilitation to self-governing actors; and 4) participating as meta-governor in processes of self-governance, that is, acting as one of a number of actors who negotiate collective solutions to shared problems.

The role of politicians in governance processes has also been addressed by Hansen (2001). He has described elected councillors as participant co-governors contributing to public-oriented interactions between the many institutions and actors in local governance. According to this author, the traditional vertical political relations and interactions from above and below between elected councillors and voting citizens must be supplemented with lateral relations and interactions among institutions, professionals and users. Therefore, councillors must participate and engage in public deliberations about common concerns of the municipality, ensuring that all citizens get an opportunity to voice their opinion and interests and that the plurality of voices is taken into account at various levels and in various fields of local decision- and policy-making (Hansen, 2001, 122).

## Summary

This chapter focused on the relationship between city leadership and the social regeneration of communities. We highlighted forms and elements of city leadership and we discussed some contemporary trends on the four main forms of city leadership and their impacts on social regeneration. Finally, we focused specifically on the functions of local governments and on the new, further roles that public managers and politicians should play to enhance social regeneration of communities.

We believe that social regeneration can be achieved by more than one ways, through a number of paths with varying configurations of factors (patterns) that are related to different societal challenges. For example, dealing with an aging population is a different societal challenge from ensuring community safety and integration within a poor neighbourhood.

However, our main argument is that social regeneration could be triggered by patterns of collective (not individual) community leadership promoted by public managers and politicians through the establishment of new democratic structures open to citizens and communities of citizens and characterised by interactivity, participation, social justice, social innovation, and, in some cases, by public deliberation.

Examples of these new democratic structures could be arenas for co-commissioning, co-designing, co-delivering, and co-assessing public services (see, for example, Nabatchi et al., 2017) and systems for self-governance of the commons within cities (such as neighbourhood committees established for managing public parks) that include logics of interactivity, participation, social justice, social innovation, and possibly deliberation.

Of course, our main argument here solely refers to a kind of democratic procedural condition that enhances social regeneration. However, this condition should be complemented by a substantial condition of social regeneration, which could only be achieved by a more sustainable and responsible business; by a smarter and more resilient government able to rapidly adapt to the changing circumstances and able to focus on the democratic priorities; and by the progressive establishment of a federalist global governance that is able to recognise the possibility of self-governance at the community level but at the same time is able to guarantee basic rights for all human beings on a global scale.

## Notes

1. For example, as China moved from emerging to advanced economy status, its development path was conditioned by applications of stage-growth pole and central-place theories to urban renewal and regeneration (Gottdiener et al., 2017).

2. Henri Lefebvre, the French philosopher and sociologist, distinguishes three types of representation in his thesis of the *Right to the City* within the social production of space (Lefebvre, 1996/1967). They are:

- Spatial practice: the basic set of characteristics of a locale in which its inhabitants enjoy coherence and continuity in their daily experience.
- Representations of Space: this encompasses the codes by which a place is able to function based upon the way in which its production and reproduction provide some order to these codes.
- Representational Spaces: These involve the complex symbolism of how a place is known to its inhabitants including the publicly unseen subterranean practices and events.

3. Here we focus on the city broadly defined at all levels of analysis ranging from neighbours to city-regions and global mega-cities.

## References

Benington, J., and J. Hartley. 2015. "Personal Views on the Future of Public Value Management Research and Theory." Paper presented for the *International Seminar "The Value of Public Value"*, Utrecht University, Utrecht, Netherlands, 17–19 May.

Bingham, L. B., Nabatchi, T., and R. O'Leary. 2005. "The New Governance: Practices and Processes for Stakeholder and Citizen Participation in the Work of Government." *Public Administration Review*, 65(5): 547–558.

Bovaird, T. 2007. "Beyond Engagement and Participation: User and Community Co-production of Public Services." *Public Administration Review*, 67(5): 846–860.

Brandsen, T., Cattacin, S., Evers, A., and A. Zimmer. 2015. *Social Innovations in the Urban Context*. Heidelberg: Springer International Publishing. doi:10.1007/978-3-319-21551-8.

Bryson, J. M., Crosby, B. C., and M. M. Stone. 2015. "Designing and Implementing Cross-Sector Collaborations: Needed and Challenging." *Public Administration Review*, 75(5): 647–663.

Bryson, J. M., Sancino, A., Benington, J., and E. Sorensen. 2017. "Toward a Multi-actor Theory of Public Value Co-creation." *Public Management Review*, 19(5): 640–654.

Budd, L., and A. Sancino. 2016. "A Framework for City Leadership in Multilevel Governance Settings: The Comparative Contexts of Italy and the UK." *Regional Studies, Regional Science*, 3(1): 129–145.

Budd, L., Sancino, A., Pagani, M., Kristmundsson, Ó., Roncevic, B., and M. Steiner. 2017. "Sport as a Complex Adaptive System for Place Leadership: Comparing Five European Cities With Different Administrative and Socio-Cultural Traditions." *Local Economy*, 32(4): 316–335.

Castells, M. 2004. *The Network Society – A Cross-Cultural Perspective*. Cheltenham: Edward Elgar.

Copus, C. 2000. "Community, Party and the Crisis of Representation." In *Representation and Community in Western Democracies*, edited by N. Rao, 93–133. Basingstoke: MacMillan.

Cox, K. R., and A. Mair. 1989. "Urban Growth Machines and the Politics of Local Economic Development." *International Journal of Urban and Regional Research*, 13: 137–146.

Di Mascio, F., and A. Natalini. 2015. "Fiscal Retrenchment in Southern Europe: Changing Patterns of Public Management in Greece, Italy, Portugal and Spain." *Public Management Review*, 17(1): 129–148.

Edelenbos, J., and E. H. Klijn. 2006. "Managing Stakeholder Involvement in Decision-making: A Comparative Analysis of Six Interactive Processes in the Netherlands." *Journal of Public Administration Research and Theory*, 16(3): 417–446.

Feldman, M. S., and A. M. Khademian. 2007. "The Role of the Public Manager in Inclusion." *Governance*, 20(2): 305–324.

Fung, A. 2006. "Varieties of Participation in Complex Governance." *Public Administration Review*, 66(1): 66–75.

Gains, F. 2015. "Metro Mayors: Devolution, Democracy and the Importance of Getting the 'Devo Manc' Design Right." *Representation*, 51(4): 425–437.

Glaeser, E. 2011. *Triumph of the City*. New York: Penguin Press.

Gottdiener, M., Budd, L., and P. Lehtovuori. 2017. *Key Concepts in Urban Studies*. London: Sage Publications.

Grint, K. 2000. *The Arts of Leadership*. Oxford: Oxford University Press.

Hambleton, R. 2013. "Elected Mayors: An International Rising Tide?" *Policy and Politics*, 41(1): 125–128.

Hambleton, R. 2015. "Place-based Leadership: A New Perspective on Urban Regeneration." *Journal of Urban Regeneration and Renewal*, 9(1): 10–24.

Hambleton, R., and J. Howard. 2013. "Place-Based Leadership and Public Service Innovation." *Local Government Studies,* 39(1): 47–70.

Hansen, K. 2001. "Local Councillors: Between Local Government and Local Governance." *Public Administration*, 79(1): 105–123.

Hartley, J. 2002. "Leading Communities: Capabilities and Cultures." *Leadership and Organization Development Journal*, 23(8): 419–429.

Hunt, T. 2004. *Building Jerusalem: The Rise and Fall of the Victorian City*. London: Wiedenfeld and Nicolson.

Huxham, C., and S. Vangen. 2005. *Managing to Collaborate: The Theory and Practice of Collaborative Advantage*. London and New York: Routledge.

Keane, J. 2011. "Monitory Democracy." In *The Future of Representative Democracy*, edited by S. Alonso, J. Keane, and W. Merkel, 212–235. Cambridge: Cambridge University Press.

Lefebvre, H. 1996 [1967]. "The Right to the City." In *Writings on Cities*, edited by E. Kofman and E. Lebas, 63–184. London: Blackwell.

Mazzucato, M. 2013. *The Entrepreneurial State: Debunking Public vs Private Sector Myths*. London: Anthem Press.

Meneguzzo, M., Sancino, A., Guenon, M., and G. Fiorani. 2013. "New development: The crisis and European local government reforms." *Public Money & Management*, 33(6): 459–462.

Molotch, H. 1976. "The City as a Growth Machine: Toward a Political Economy of Place." *American Journal of Sociology*, 82: 309–332.

Nabatchi, T. 2010. "Addressing the Citizenship and Democratic Deficits: The Potential of Deliberative Democracy for Public Administration." *American Review of Public Administration*, 40(4): 376–399.

Nabatchi, T. 2012. *A Manager's Guide to Evaluating Citizen Participation*. Fostering Transparency and Democracy Series. Washington, DC: IBM Centre for the Business of Government.

Nabatchi, T., Sancino, A., and M. Sicilia. 2017. "Varieties of Participation in Public Services: The Who, When and What of Coproduction." *Public Administration Review*, 77(5): 766–776.

Nalbandian, J. 1999. "Facilitating Community, Enabling Democracy: New Roles for Local Government Managers." *Public Administration Review*, 59(3): 187–197.

Nalbandian, J., and C. Nalbandian. 2003. "Contemporary Challenges in Local Government." *National Civic Review*, 92(1): 83–91.

Nalbandian, J., O'Neill, R., Wilkes, J. M., and A. Kaufman. 2013. "Contemporary Challenges in Local Government: Evolving Roles and Responsibilities, Structures, and Processes." *Public Administration Review*, 73(4): 567–574.

OECD (Organisation for Economic Cooperation and Development). 2011. *Together for Better Public Services: Partnering with Citizens and Civil Society*. Paris: OECD Public Governance Reviews, OECD Publishing.

Osborne, S. P. 2006. "The New Public Governance?" *Public Management Review*, 8(3): 377–387.

Osborne, S. P., and K. McLaughlin. 2004. "The Cross-Cutting Review of the Voluntary Sector: Where Next for Local Government—Voluntary Sector Relationships?" *Regional Studies*, 38(5): 571–580.

Pestoff, V. 2012. "Co-production and Third Sector Social Services in Europe: Some Concepts and Evidence." *Voluntas*, 23(4): 1102–1118.

Pollitt, C. 2010. "Cuts and Reforms: Public Services as We Move Into a New Era." *Society and Economy*, 32(1): 17–31.

Porter, M., and M. Kramer. 2011. "Creating Shared Value: How to Reinvent Capitalism and Unleash a Wave of Innovation and Growth." *Harvard Business Review* (January–February): 1–17.

Putnam, R. 2005. "A New Movement for Civic Renewal." *Public Management*, 87(6): 7–10.

Sancino, A. 2010. "Community Governance as a Response to Economic Crisis." *Public Money and Management*, 30(2): 117–118.

Sancino, A. 2016. "The Meta Coproduction of Community Outcomes: Towards a Citizens' Capabilities Approach." *VOLUNTAS: International Journal of Voluntary and Non Profit Organizations*, 27(1): 409–424.

Sancino, A. 2017. "Conceptualizing Forms and Elements of City Leadership: A Research and a Practice Agenda." Paper presented at the *International Leadership Conference*, Brussels, 12–15 October 2017.

Sancino, A., and L. Castellani. 2016. "New Development: Directly Elected Mayors in Italy: Creating a Strong Leader Doesn't Always Mean Creating Strong Leadership." *Public Money and Management*, 36(2): 153–156.

Sancino, A., Rees, J., and I. Schindele. 2017. "Coordinating the Common Good Through Cross-Sector Collaborations: Re-Imagining the Role of Public Sector." In *From Austerity to Abundance? Creative Approaches to Coordinating the Common Good*. Critical Perspectives on International Public Sector Management, Vol. 6, edited by M. Stout. Bingley: Emerald (forthcoming).

Sheldrake, J. 1989. *Municipal Socialism*. Aldershot: Avebury.

Sicilia, M., Guarini, E., Sancino, A., Andreani, M., and R. Ruffini. 2016. "Public Services Management and Co-production in Multi-level Governance Settings." *International Review of Administrative Sciences*, 82(1): 8–27.

Sørensen, E. 2006. "Meta-governance: The Changing Role of Politicians in the Process of Democratic Governance." *American Review of Public Administration*, 36(1): 98–114.

Sotarauta, M., Beer, A., and J. Gibney. 2017. "Making Sense of Leadership in Urban and Regional Development." *Regional Studies*, 51(2): 187–193.

Thomas, J. C. 2013. "Citizen, Customer, Partner: Rethinking the Place of the Public in Public Management." *Public Administration Review*, 73: 786–796.

Torfing, J., Peters, B. G., Pierre, J., and E. Sørensen. 2012. *Interactive Governance: Advancing the Paradigm*. Oxford: Oxford University Press.

# 10 Digital Technology as a Tool for Social Regeneration

## Web 2.0's Intended and Unintended Outcomes Within a Society

*Andres Morales and Sara Calvo*

*"If technology is the answer what was the question?"*

Cedric Price

## Introduction

Entering the end of the second decade of the 21st century, a different global society is emerging within what is acknowledged as the age of information, whereby communities and individuals are virtually connected by a ubiquitous system known as *Digital Technology* that is perpetuated by the vast use of Information and Communication Technologies (ICTs). The development and the expansion of digital technology within socio-economic, political, and cultural life on a global scale illustrates the sort of society the world is moving towards, a society blended, interconnected, and grounded virtually by the World Wide Web (the Web). ICTs have transformed the way society lives, works, communicates, informs itself, engages in social relationships, forms values, tackles political problems, and so on (Fuchs, 2011). Thus, moving away from a traditional economy and crawling gradually into a more digital one, ICTs are presented as participative, inclusive and universal-accessible tools that will enable a better society (Narula, 2014). In the same fashion, earlier in the century, forecasts in relation to a fairer, more inclusive, and egalitarian society had been suggested. However, globalisation processes, nurtured by neoliberal ideas in which privatisation, free-market, decentralised-statism, and trickle-down economics (or Reaganomics) presented as the panacea for all global issues, appear to have failed. In fact, they have reconfigured and reproduced the same socio-economic and political inequality of the last century, but with the aggravation of environmental distresses that have conditioned society to set back such linear 'progress' towards achieving the internationally agreed development goals (the Sustainable Development Goals—SDGs) by diverse economic institutions to re-design national, regional, and local development agendas and to transform and enhance society seeking for a better future.

That said, and acknowledging the far-reaching impact of digital technology, there is rising concern about the emergencies of new equalities (Wessells, in Fuchs, 2011) and therefore a need for a more critical approach in relation to digital technology as an instrument for socio-economic, political, and cultural transformation. This is especially important because of the fragility of economic recovery and uneven progress in major economies, in which social conditions are not only expected to recover slowly, but also to encounter societal distresses beyond the economic dimension such as political, social, environmental, and trust crises. Trump, Brexit, the Syrian war and the refugee crisis, post-Arab Spring, the Yemen civil war, and the Chinese environmental meltdown, amongst others, depict the need for societal reconstruction and wider citizen participation and empowerment. As the United Nations suggested in 2011, increased levels of poverty, hunger, and unemployment will continue to affect billions for years to come. Therefore, within such an obscure, vague, and not very promising scenario, '*brand-new*' e-based strategies and actions for social, rural, and urban regeneration are emerging with innovative and more contemporary approaches for socio-economic, political, and environmental transformation. In this respect, digital technology appears to be a really sensible ally to achieve societal regeneration.

For the purpose of this chapter, digital technology will only look into the prism of social regeneration. *Regeneration* is an indicator to represent a movement that consists of various actions and strategies concentrating on mitigation and provision treatments for a better future and usually refers to urban development and urban ecosystems transformed into more inclusive and fairer urban environments in which aesthetics play an important part (Roberts, 2008. *Social regeneration*, in particular, can be seen as a transformative process of improvement of an individual/ community/ neighbourhood/region/area/country that develops equal opportunities and capabilities for everyone (Lees, 2008). Generally speaking, social regeneration focuses on themes of health, education, community participation, arts and culture, and community well-being.

The main objective of this chapter is therefore to explore the role played by digital technology with the example of the *Web 2.0* invention as a tool for social regeneration. With the emergence of *Web 2.0* platforms and internet access growth worldwide in the so-called information age, *Web 2.0* generation seems to offer a practical digital mechanism that may enable social transformation and enhancement through more inclusive, participatory and collaborative e-actions and e-strategies to deliver opportunities, capabilities, and citizen participation (Mrabet, 2016). *Web 2.0* technology is diversely designed and implemented with a variety of tools and codes, from finance and business sectors with e-Commerce or e-Business (i.e. Amazon, Yahoo, and Google) to education, media, and health sectors with e-Education, e-News, and e-Health (i.e. MOOCs, Blogs, and Health Forums). Nevertheless, beyond the boom of digital technology on a global scale, the *Web 2.0* technology phenomenon must be explored critically as the existing literature on the concept tends to be over-positive, optimistic, and hopeful. Hence, there is a need to examine both the intended and the unintended outcomes generated by the *Web 2.0* generation, looking through the positive and the negative aspects of its implementation and practice onto and within society. On the one hand, good practices are included (a Social Enterprise MOOC and two video case studies, the Citizens Foundation and Million Kitchen) to illustrate the importance of digital technology when aiming to generate social and environmental change and therefore social regeneration through participatory, collaborative, and inclusive processes. The chapter also introduces basic theoretical discussions and debates about digital division 2.0 and attempts to explain the role of *Web 2.0* technology amongst different groups and how far-reaching digital technology serves the purpose of access for all and its use and knowledge-implementation amongst the global communities.

## Web Generations: The Past (1.0), the Present (2.0), and the Future (3.0)

*Web 2.0* technology is defined as the second generation of web technology that enables users to interact, collaborate, and participate freely and online in an open way. It is, in essence, a web application facilitating participatory information sharing, interoperability, a user-centred design, and collaboration on the Web that allows users to interact and collaborate with each other through different channels. Hence, *Web 2.0* operators work as prosumers,[1] in which users generate their own content in a virtual community but are simultaneously online consumers of the product created by themselves or by other members of the e-community (Henry et al., 2014). But to start with, it is important to understand what *Web 1.0* is. In contrast with *Web 2.0*, *Web 1.0* platforms, the first generation, are designed to provide information unidirectionally, whereby users (consumers) are limited to passive viewing of content that was created for them (Te Velde and Plomp, 2011). That means that *Web 1.0* platforms are designed for a two-dimensional interaction between *producer* and *consumer*, in which the *producer* (i.e. web designers, IT engineers, or web masters) designs and creates a *read-only* piece of information, and the user-role is completely passive and merely for passive consumption (Best, 2006).

Web 1.0 platforms are considered more business-oriented, in which firms/entities/organisations advertise, trade, or provide information about themselves to the users through unilateral information digital channels. Corporate websites, e-advert agencies, web directories, web catalogues, and personal websites exemplified the *Web 1.0* generation. Having said that, *Web 2.0* is the transition from the internet-enabled delivery of content to participatory-based internet communities. Thus, *Web 2.0* is assimilated to web tools which, rather than working as a forum to divulge information to a passive, receptive audience, invite users to comment, collaborate, contribute, and edit information, constructing a more inclusive, power-distributed form of authority in which the limits between producer (site creator) and consumer (user) are indistinct (Adebanjo and Michaelides, 2010).

In sum, *Web 2.0* is characterised by a more multidirectional relationship between *producer* and *consumer*. In fact, users have become producers and the generation from the unidirectional relationship has become a multidirectional one, in which the passive user becomes a prosumer; hence, *Web 2.0* enables users to interact actively and generate content which, in web jargon, is synthesised as user-generated content (UGC) and is any type of content created by users through online systems or service such as blogs, wikis, or discussion forums (Balasubramaniam, 2009). An interesting aspect of *Web 2.0* is that users are able to install and administer applications that were previously the prerogative of large, centralised organisations. Examples include comprehensive knowledge management systems known as *wikis* (i.e. Wikipedia or WikiLeaks), press offices (blogs), TV stations (YouTube), and telephone exchanges (microblogs such as Twitter and Yammer). *Web 2.0* operates both as a platform for communication, which is the exchange of messages with a focus on the people who exchange messages (i.e. Twitter), and as a platform of a knowledge-sharing facilitator, which is the exchange of content with a focus on the content itself (i.e. Wikipedia) (O'Reilly, 2007). To conclude, the past, the present, and the future *Web 2.0* are conditioned by the past legacy of working as a read-only *Web 1.0*, the present of a read-write-publish *Web 2.0*, and moving towards to the read-write-execute *Web 3.0* (Hendler, 2009).

## The Intended and the Unintended Outcome: Technology, Organisations, and Community

It has been discussed by different scholars that there is an antagonistic relationship between technology and nature, and the outcome of such a turbulent relationship has caused numerous ecological distresses. It has been argued that modern technologies have delivered unforeseen consequences that could have been avoided. For instance, environmental problems from chemical pollution to global warming were not actually anticipated. Also, it has been claimed that Digital Technology has also contributed to such negative effects, especially as Digital Technology is perpetrated by ICTs such as mobile phones, laptops, tablets, and so on that in the process of being manufactured may cause irremediable ecological harm (Fuchs, 2006). However, the aim of this chapter is not to understand the unanticipated consequences of *Web 2.0* from an environmental point of view (which is important indeed and is one of the roots of criticism). On the contrary, the authors are keen on exploring the intended and unintended outcomes from the technological, organisational, and community perspectives. Hence, they draw on Merton's (1936) analysis of unintended consequences of deliberate acts, which are intended to cause social change and of the emergence of outcomes, which are not foreseen and intended by a purposeful action. The authors will examine *Web 2.0* from the perspective of the intended, the unintended, or the hybrid form of both.

## *Web 2.0 from a Technological Point of View*

*Web 2.0* technology intends to offer a more autonomous and independent system for the user. These platforms are mainly characterised by openness and freedom on the Web. Its operability allows the user to interact easily as it is built on user-friendly systems. *Web 2.0's* operational system is designed upon an architectural participatory system, in which users are fundamental contributors in taking part in the construction of it. Particularly, the interactive and read-write-publish nature of the users' participation facilitates the creation of virtual communities and many collaborative societies simultaneously, and therefore such participation generates a wider e-learning experience from each other's cultures, religions, beliefs, traditions, and views of contemporary issues (Alexander, 2006).

Another interesting point is the fact that *Web 2.0s* are decentralised from the initial producer, as there is a sharable knowledge experience that enables users to also be contributors (*prosumers*). Likewise, an additional important aspect is the way that data are produced and reproduced and are enabled to be remixable, recyclable, and transformative; users are able to recreate and reproduce data already online. For instance, *memes* that are usually images, videos, texts that are supposed to be comical in nature, which are copied and spread rapidly by internet users, often with slight adaptations, exemplified how data that are already produced can be recreated again for different purposes. Actually, the management of big and freely available data that were intended to be useful in nature may cause harm when negatively practised (see the example of girls' "pain memes" on YouTube in Dobson, 2015). Different from detrimental experience, data produced by users are also available for consumption in different platforms, mostly for free. For instance, free stock video footages and audio loops are available for free use on different platforms to enrich video or music producers; e-portals such as *VideoBlocks.com or audioblocks.com* are *Web 2.0* platforms that are allowed for both consumer and producer to interact and share their work freely (Fuchs, 2011).

ICTs are fundamental tools generated by *Web 2.0* platforms. *Web 2.0* platforms of communication can be interfaces such as Facebook, LinkedIn, and Twitter, by which users are enabled to communicate freely with others and interact with each other. The users generate their own content and share and interact with others based on their own interests (O'Reilly, 2007). *Web 2.0* platforms of information are based on generating content to be shared freely and openly with other users, enabling the creation of an online library of knowledge. One of the best examples are the *wikis*,[2] in which people create information and share knowledge. Similarly, YouTube is a very useful platform of information, as users upload their own videos and generate their own information channels (i.e. entertainment, sports, news, tutorials, and so on) (O'Reilly, 2007); yet in some literature, *YouTube* is not considered a *Web 2.0* platform, as videos are restricted for users to be downloaded (Te Velde and Plomp, 2011). Another intended feature of *Web 2.0* is the possibility for users to promote their own brands and become their "own-brand", and by doing this, *Web 2.0* enables long tail sales or knowledge transfer amongst prosumers who hold their own brands, offering products, services, news, information, and even education (i.e. tutorials, MOOC platforms, and so on). Users empowered by *Web 2.0* technology are able to create their own channels of information to promote and advertise their own brands, and by brands, the authors refer to the inseparable form between *brand* and *product/service* (Klein, 2000). The participatory structure of *Web 2.0* technology allows users to develop their own brand-product/service popularity through the review system; products and services' own labels are widely available (O'Reilly, 2005).

## The Unintended Benefit and Drawback Paradox as a Tool for Social Regeneration

Drawing on Merton's (1936) analysis, *Web 2.0* has delivered different outcomes which are embodied in intended participatory, inclusive, freely accessible, and fair action purposes, have and led to unforeseen consequences. Especially in the current transition from a traditional to a digital economy, there have been industries that were severely damaged and others that have substantially benefited from the Digital Technology (Elder-Vass, 2016). The music and the film industries, the latter less dramatically, have not been able to recover from the emergence of *Web 2.0* technology that has enabled a wider global participation in the production and distribution of music and films. The fact that users can freely share music and films at almost zero cost (there is a cost that users pay to the mobile/internet or broadband companies) has diminished their sectors.

Such *phenomena* are illuminated by the *Zero Marginal Cost* concept developed by Rifkin (2014), in which the emergence of new technologies, combined with a socio-economic and environmental global consciousness, has led to the production of products or the provision of services at nearly zero cost. For instance, large firms of music production have faded away, and it seems that they will not be able to recover unless their business models are transformed (for instance, with the appearance of *Napster*). Another example is the appearance of online platforms such as *The Pirate Bay* and *Kickasstorrents*, in which millions of *feeders* (providers) and *seeders* (receivers) share movies, music, and software for free. It can be claimed that distribution is accessible for wider audiences, especially for those users who cannot afford to purchase certain products (i.e. software, music, or films).

Although such online platforms are claimed to be illegal as they breach copyright law, they were made to widen distribution and reach those who do not have access to products and services.

Similar platforms seem to be invading the news, magazine, and book publishing industries or even perhaps the film and TV industry. In fact, industry architecture and business models in the broadcasting industry are being increasingly transformed by digitisation and convergence (Evens, 2010). Consumer choice has become more diverse and widely available with online streaming. With the help of YouTube or Netflix, the audience is not only able to choose and schedule their own TV programmes and films, but they are also able to produce their own entertainment, and, in some cases, it can be very profitable. According to YouTube's statistics, there are approximately 8,000+ YouTube partners (YouTubers) that have produced over 10,000 videos which have generated over one billion views and 70+ million hours of watch time. YouTube has paid out $2 billion to rights-holders who have chosen to monetise claims.[3]

## *Web 2.0 Regeneration from an Organisational Level*

Equally important, *Web 2.0* generation has also delivered unintended consequences at the organisational level. Needless to say, *Web 2.0* digital architecture encourages access, inclusiveness, and participation amongst users; hence, members belonging to any organisation are subjected to new forms and dynamics to interact and cooperate internally and externally at the organisational level. The more often organisations seek improvements in networking, innovation, emerging markets, e-marketing, and disruptive technology embracing ICTs, the more room there is for *Web 2.0* technologies to become indispensable (Christensen, 2013). In the existing literature on *Web 2.0* technology, ICTs are seen as enablers for organisational transformation; thus, online principles such as e-commerce, e-banking, e-democracy, e-government, or e-health are more frequently used by organisations (Mrabet, 2016).

Arguably, the focal objective of *Web 2.0* generation was to generate a societal transformation or enhance society in socio-economic and cultural terms. However, unanticipated benefits emerged by numerous organisations from its usage. As an example of this, the implementation of *Web 2.0* technology by organisations related to the solidarity sector, illustrates that *Web 2.0*'s rationale may offer new opportunities for the development and growth of these kind of firms or organisations (i.e. Charities, NGOs, Social Enterprises, Associations, or Social Cooperatives). This conclusion emerged from the exploration of 12 different organisations that have implemented peer to peer systems and e-banking. Their findings suggested that advantages from *Web 2.0* platforms, with big, freely available data, helped to develop organisational strategies to address social issues as well as enhance their networking and develop alliances and partnerships with other organisations within the same sector (Morales-Gutiérrez and Ariza-Montes, 2010).

In the same fashion, there are two concepts that enlighten *Web 2.0* technology at the organisational level, e-democracy and e-government, and both can be seen to carry implicit elements of social regeneration as wider citizen participation, inclusion, decentralised control, and non-hierarchical relationships are encouraged by both concepts. E-democracy is defined as the exercise and practice of democracy online through ICTs. By following *Web 2.0* principles, e-democracy pursues wider citizen participation and inclusiveness and is also diversely practised by democratic sectors from the private, media, government, and third sectors, as well as by political groups, and is claimed to be a filter for e-government (Lindner et al., 2016). Likewise, e-government also has an online component and is defined as a governmental structure that seeks to enhance citizen participation, transparency, and accountability and meet the public will by using ICTs. The intention of e-democracy, in theory, is to improve the scenario in which people can participate in the political decision-making, and, related to socioeconomic and environmental decisions, e-government is meant to be the organisational structure that can legitimate and assure this intention.[4]

*Figure 10.1* 'Talking with the Cofounders of Citizens Foundation', Sara Calvo, One of the Researchers, Interviewing the Cofounders of the Citizens Foundation in Reykjavik, Iceland

©2014, Living in Minca.

SEE VIDEO-CLIP: *Citizens Foundation:* www.youtube.com/watch?v=8WxQjljN7JU

In practice, it can be argued that there are fundamental components in implementing *Web 2.0* technology that may lead to a radical change in the organisational culture of different public and private institutions and organisations. The fact that *Web 2.0*, by definition, is built by a flat, transparent, and demand-driven component, illustrates that its application may lead to a more transparent, flat, and horizontal organisational structure in some organisations. An example from Iceland, Citizens Foundation's platform, illustrates the benefit of the utilisation of *Web 2.0* technology, followed by the principles of e-democracy. The platform is built on *Web 2.0* technology, in which citizens and the government of the city have the opportunity to e-meet and practise e-democracy directly; for *Citizens Foundation*, there is no effective democracy without participation.

## *The Community and Web 2.0 Regeneration*

*Web 2.0* technology has also played an important role in enriching community interaction promoting sharing, collaboration, and participation and enabling users to evolve from the static to the dynamic *Web 2.0* technologies. It is argued that it may offer an opportunity to create virtual communities, but it can also hamper social cohesion (Carter et al., 2015). The interactive and read-write characteristics of *Web 2.0* technologies may accelerate user participation that builds user-centred virtual community and participatory societies at the same time. Community e-gatherings are therefore generated by the online opportunity of learning about each other's interest (Alexander, 2006), on the one hand, and, on the other, of having the opportunity to create data shared by other users (O'Reilly, 2005), as *Web 2.0* platforms are designed to be continually updated though user interaction. Similarly, *Web 2.0* platforms are often described as e-hub spaces, where online communities e-meet, by consequence of sharing a common interest, and are reinforced by communicating through electronic mailing lists, chat rooms, internet user groups, or any other social media interface (Mrabet, 2016).

There are other studies, however, that argue that being involved in virtual communities may generate weak ties, as users are involved anonymously online and interact with others without affiliation, and there is no contact outside of the online space (Kozinets, 2002). Interpersonal relations tend to be weaker than face to face (strong ties) relations. This point in the context of social regeneration is actually important because having weak ties do not hinder social cohesion and may enable a virtual community to develop collective actions to solve societal issues. If weak ties are seen through Granovetter's (1983) work on the *strength of weak ties*, then they can constitute the interactions that connect individuals who belong to distant areas of the social graph and are brought together by an online space that in the long-term brings more benefits to the user. In this way, *Web 2.0* technology seems to be the sensible tool that enables community to come together for a collective purpose or interest. Having a wide range of acquaintances is supposed to be better than a few close-knit relationships. For instance, weak ties can be very useful for activists who need to mobilise large protests or action groups, and the correlation between social media and collective action can be very effective. In the study by Segerberg and Bennett (2011), two Twitter hashtags were examined to analyse how such technologies infuse specific protest ecologies and how there was a substantial response enabled by Twitter. Even though there was no direct relationship between participants (strong ties), the immediate response was mediated by Twitter as an online space for people to be aware of the protest. Thus, social media interfaces serve as tools for collective action and therefore social cohesion.

Users are bound to interactions between a close-knit group or acquaintances within *social networks*. Social networks are constituted by the interaction of nodes (users) and edges (between users with a relationship), and such interaction is facilitated by bridges (*Web 2.0 technology*). Hence, bridges allow diffusion of information and communication between otherwise disconnected users, creating virtual communities. That is to say, online bridges bring otherwise distant communities together (Granovetter, 1983). Hence, *Web 2.0* technology juxtaposes what Anderson (2006) calls "imagined communities", as a community evolved from an imaginary scenario to a virtual reality, where individuals know each other and interact through weak ties for a common interest or purpose. *Web 2.0* appears as the tool that enables social interactions to encourage social cohesion within a *network society*, which is what Castells (2005) describes as the society whose social structure is made up of social networks powered by ICTs and is referred to as social, cultural, economic, and cultural changes caused by the interrelation of the participants of the network. *Web 2.0* platforms enable informal information flows and the Web's relationships within society, which differ from hierarchical relationships.

### Does Web 2.0 Technology Transform Education? MOOCs as Disruptive Technologies for Free and Open Access to e-Education

A Massive Open Online Course (MOOC) is defined as an online-based course designed to reach a large number of users operating within a *Web 2.0* and characterised by their openness, inclusiveness, scalability, partitioning, and free accessibility to all users (as long as they have an internet connection) (Rabanal, 2017). MOOCs are created to enable users to generate knowledge through peer-to-peer review assessments (P2P), online discussions, and debates. They differ from traditional course materials as they provide not only filmed lectures, readings, and problem sets, but also offer interactive user forums to support community interactions amongst learners. The MOOC system is built on participatory-based architecture and its user-friendly system. The role of the educators is scarce and supposed to be minimal (De Waard et al., 2011).

MOOCs can be considered a disruptive digital technology, as they are transforming education and creating a totally different experience for learners (users) and are exercised by different institutions, organisations, and e-communities and all have different financial streams to reach financial sustainability (Rabanal, 2017). Examples of MOOC platforms are HOME, OpenupEd, ECO, SCORE2020, BizMOOC, MOONLITE, Coursera, and FutureLearn. One of the key features of MOOCs is free-access; hence, in societies in which education is either limited or exclusive for certain socio-economic groups, MOOCs seem to be a feasible alternative way of learning for vulnerable groups (Liyanagunawardena et al., 2014). The notion of MOOCs as a disruptive digital technological tool for education may create a social regeneration as a transformative practice that embodies collectiveness, cooperation, and inclusion that develop opportunities and capabilities to their learners.

As an example, a Social Enterprise MOOC Programme created by Middlesex University, Living in Minca, and the Jindal Centre for Social Innovation and Entrepreneurship (JSiEin) has given the opportunity to multiple learners from all over the world to learn, discuss, debate, and network through the FutureLearn platform. In the first round of the Social Enterprise Programme,[5] 20,000 participants from 177 countries participated and both intended and unintended outcomes have been delivered. For instance, as part of the course, the co-founder of Arusha Women Entrepreneur (AWE), a social enterprise located in Tanzania, had the opportunity to share AWE's challenges through a P2P assessment named *Acting as a business advisor*. The intended objective of the exercise was that the learners were meant to give feedback to AWE based on their own experience and on the content thought in the MOOC. AWE addressed five different questions to grow/scale up its business. Interestingly, more than 80 feedback/comments were given, and, according to the cofounder, some partnerships emerged from the exercise (see Figure 10.2 with comments from some participants). Currently, AWE is running a crowdfunding campaign to scale up its business and carry on with its social and environmental objective, as was suggested by a few of the learners from the programme. During a period of three months in early 2017, the British Council offered 10,000 free course certificates to MOOC users from 36 developing countries. The second course, named *Turning Ideas into Action* from the Social Enterprise programme, gave out 170 free-of-charge certificates. Interestingly, some of the learners came from deprived areas. As an example, *The Butterfly Project*, a school for social entrepreneurs located in a slum from Kampala called Acholi Quarters in Uganda, took advantage of this opportunity. Two of the Butterfly Project's Alumni claimed that the MOOC was very useful and benefitted them vastly (see Figure 10.3).

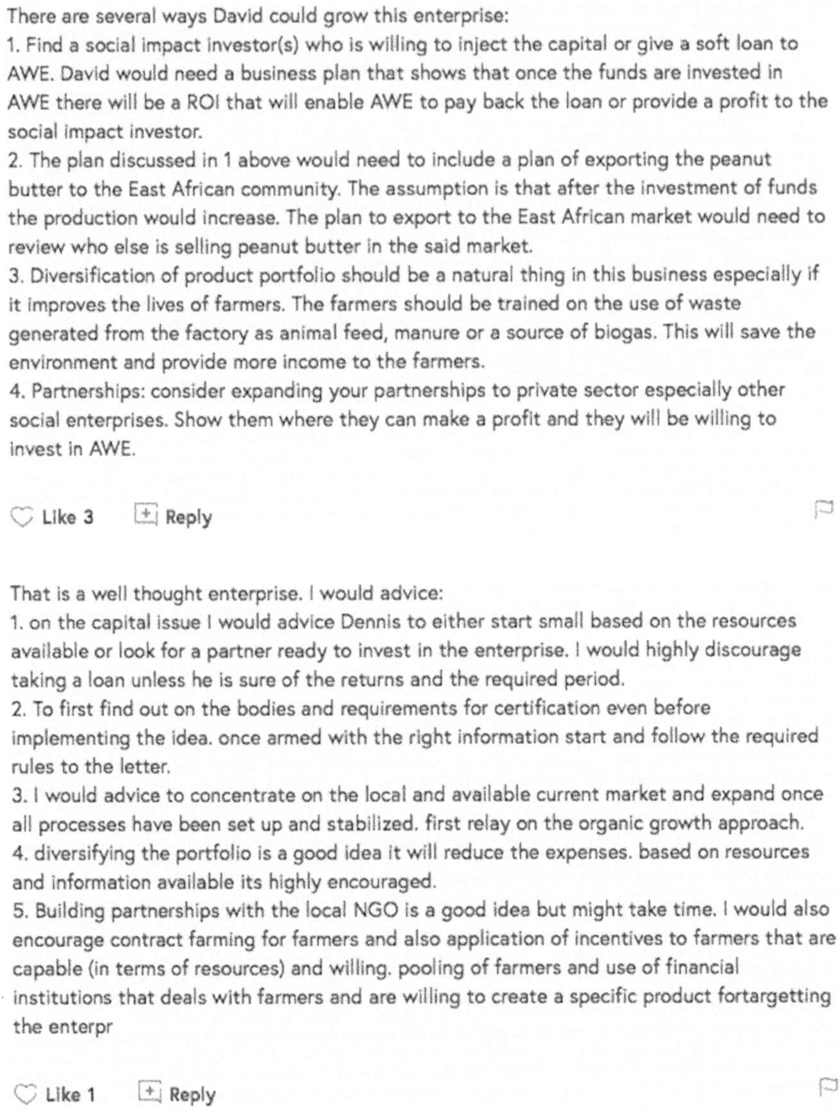

There are several ways David could grow this enterprise:
1. Find a social impact investor(s) who is willing to inject the capital or give a soft loan to AWE. David would need a business plan that shows that once the funds are invested in AWE there will be a ROI that will enable AWE to pay back the loan or provide a profit to the social impact investor.
2. The plan discussed in 1 above would need to include a plan of exporting the peanut butter to the East African community. The assumption is that after the investment of funds the production would increase. The plan to export to the East African market would need to review who else is selling peanut butter in the said market.
3. Diversification of product portfolio should be a natural thing in this business especially if it improves the lives of farmers. The farmers should be trained on the use of waste generated from the factory as animal feed, manure or a source of biogas. This will save the environment and provide more income to the farmers.
4. Partnerships: consider expanding your partnerships to private sector especially other social enterprises. Show them where they can make a profit and they will be willing to invest in AWE.

♡ Like 3      + Reply

That is a well thought enterprise. I would advice:
1. on the capital issue I would advice Dennis to either start small based on the resources available or look for a partner ready to invest in the enterprise. I would highly discourage taking a loan unless he is sure of the returns and the required period.
2. To first find out on the bodies and requirements for certification even before implementing the idea. once armed with the right information start and follow the required rules to the letter.
3. I would advice to concentrate on the local and available current market and expand once all processes have been set up and stabilized. first relay on the organic growth approach.
4. diversifying the portfolio is a good idea it will reduce the expenses. based on resources and information available its highly encouraged.
5. Building partnerships with the local NGO is a good idea but might take time. I would also encourage contract farming for farmers and also application of incentives to farmers that are capable (in terms of resources) and willing. pooling of farmers and use of financial institutions that deals with farmers and are willing to create a specific product fortargetting the enterpr

♡ Like 1      + Reply

*Figure 10.2* 'Comments about the MOOC', Two of the Members of the Butterfly
         Project Commenting on the MOOC
©2016, FutureLearn.

### Grassroots and the Case of Million Kitchen

Harnessing digital technology to reach social regeneration is in many ways very helpful to grassroots organisations[6] to be more effective and impactful. On the basis of the *Web 2.0*'s rationale of inclusiveness, participation, and

There are several ways David could grow this enterprise:

1. Find a social impact investor(s) who is willing to inject the capital or give a soft loan to AWE. David would need a business plan that shows that once the funds are invested in AWE there will be a ROI that will enable AWE to pay back the loan or provide a profit to the social impact investor.

2. The plan discussed in 1 above would need to include a plan of exporting the peanut butter to the East African community. The assumption is that after the investment of funds the production would increase. The plan to export to the East African market would need to review who else is selling peanut butter in the said market.

3. Diversification of product portfolio should be a natural thing in this business especially if it improves the lives of farmers. The farmers should be trained on the use of waste generated from the factory as animal feed, manure or a source of biogas. This will save the environment and provide more income to the farmers.

4. Partnerships: consider expanding your partnerships to private sector especially other social enterprises. Show them where they can make a profit and they will be willing to invest in AWE.

♡ Like 3     ⊞ Reply                                                        ⏳

That is a well thought enterprise. I would advice:

1. on the capital issue I would advice Dennis to either start small based on the resources available or look for a partner ready to invest in the enterprise. I would highly discourage taking a loan unless he is sure of the returns and the required period.

2. To first find out on the bodies and requirements for certification even before implementing the idea. once armed with the right information start and follow the required rules to the letter.

3. I would advice to concentrate on the local and available current market and expand once all processes have been set up and stabilized. first relay on the organic growth approach.

4. diversifying the portfolio is a good idea it will reduce the expenses. based on resources and information available its highly encouraged.

5. Building partnerships with the local NGO is a good idea but might take time. I would also encourage contract farming for farmers and also application of incentives to farmers that are capable (in terms of resources) and willing. pooling of farmers and use of financial institutions that deals with farmers and are willing to create a specific product fortargetting the enterpr

♡ Like 1     ⊞ Reply                                                        ⏳

*Figure 10.3* 'Comments about the MOOC', Two of the Members of the Butterfly Project Commenting on the MOOC

©2016, FutureLearn.

accessibility, grassroots organisations may be empowered and take advantage of the existing ICT tools available. As an illustration, *Million Kitchen*, a mobile app and web-based aggregating platform that empowers home-based kitchen women to provide healthy, affordable, and homemade food

*Figure 10.4* 'Interviewing the Cofounder of Million Kitchen', Sara Calvo, One of
the Researchers, Interviewing the Cofounder of Million Kitchen in New
Delhi, India

©2015, Living in Minca.

SEE VIDEO-CLIP: *Million Kitchen:* www.youtube.com/watch?v=SZOBGq_989w

to people in New Delhi, represents an interesting example of how grassroots
organisations can be empowered by *Web 2.0* technology in their intended
objective of transforming society. According to the co-founder, in early
2015, *Million Kitchen* had about 5,500 app downloads and had received so
far between 150 and 180 orders on a weekly basis.

### Digital Division: Challenges from Web 2.0 Technology

Unintended consequences must also be considered in the study of *Web 2.0*
technology. In examining the existing literature, there seems to be an optimistic and exaggerated positive understanding of implementing *Web 2.0*
within the technological scenario and in its use for social regeneration
(Mrabet, 2016). A more critical approach is needed in the study of digital technology, especially as society is moving towards to a more digital
economy. Although in the study of *Web 2.0* technology, there are innovative, interesting, and 'break-through' examples, the overall analysis tends
to claim that there are only advantages of implementing *Web 2.0* technology and these have a very positive influence in the contemporary culture
(Fuchs, 2011, 269). The literature leaves the impression that *Web 2.0*
emerges throughout an age of information and access (see Rifkin, 2001,
2000) as a digital tool to empower its users, through promoting creativity,
democratising information and production, and empowering communities,

rather than institutions (see O'Reilly, 2007), as it is built upon an inclusive, participation-based, and accessible system. Some scholars strongly emphasise the non-hierarchical approach of *Web 2.0* technology, in which power-decentralisation, openness, democratic inclusive discussions and activities, and individual participation and contribution seem to be the advantages acquired through its implementation (Nemer, 2016). This is also true for scholars that emphasise the empowerment of communities and society through the exercise of *Web 2.0* technology for the benefit of social and/or environmental change (Mrabet, 2016). That being said, *Web 2.0* literature generally tends to overlook the distribution, ownership, management, and knowledge of *Web 2.0* technology both globally and amongst social groups within countries (Ragnedda and Muschert, 2013).

Therefore, one of the key questions that arises from the conceptual analysis of *Web 2.0* technology is whether society benefits equally from it and whether the *access to*, *use of*, and *impact of Web 2.0* technology is fairly distributed at a global level. These questions are explicitly explored and discussed in the *Digital Divide* (DD) studies. DD is defined as the unequal (i) *access to*, (ii) *use of*, and (iii) *impact of ICTs*. In other words, it is the study of the socio-economic inequality in the digital sphere (Ragnedda and Muschert, 2013). Such digital division is also exhibited at global level, known in the literature as the *Global Digital Divide* (GDD), which refers to the division amongst countries in relation to digital inequalities between individuals, households, businesses, and geographic areas, usually at socio-economic and demographic levels (Ragnedda and Muschert, 2013). According to some studies, there is an explicit technological gap between countries, and in recent years, technology is considered the latest abstraction to global socio-economic inequality (Fuchs, 2010a). For instance, in the work led by Ragnedda and Muschert (2013), in which scholars from all over the world try to analyse empirically and theoretically such DD by bringing examples from their own context to illustrate the contemporary nature of the socio-economic inequalities projected in the digital scenario, they demonstrate that a critical approach is needed while looking at digital technology and in this case, *Web 2.0* technology. In effect, it is fundamental to explore the unintended consequences of the *Web 2.0* generation by looking briefly at the studies of DD in the light of understanding the role of *Web 2.0* technology enabling social regeneration.

DD is a research field that needs more than a section to be understood as a consequence of its complexity within an information age. In its simplistic sense, it cannot be solely explored, as it was initially, as the gap between those who have vis-a-vis those who have no *access to* ICTs (Hilbert and López, 2011). DD must be examined from a multidimensional perspective and beyond the "*access to*" phenomenon, particularly if it is a global-based evaluation (i.e. see the work of Fuchs, 2010a, 2010b). It is argued here that the analysis should be explored and conceptualised on the basis of a multi-variable function (see Figure 10.5 below), which defines the digital technology relationship (connection) from different dimensions.

$$f(w, x, y, z) = w + x + y + z$$

*Figure 10.5* Digital Divide Function
Source: Compiled by Authors

Variable $w$ represents who is/are the *subject(s)* that connect(s) with the digital domain. The *subject* refers to the type of *user* who is behind the connection and includes individuals, organisations, enterprises, political institutions, countries, or regions (Hargittai, 2002). Variable $x$ denotes the types, characteristics, or attributes of division the *subject* is subjected to. In other words, variable $x$ explores the reasons why the *user* is constrained in using ICTs effectively. Elements such as *income, age, geography, location*, and *motivation* should be taken into account for the analysis (Ragnedda and Muschert, 2013). Variable $y$ is also important to complement the analysis, as it indicates the type of usage that the *user* performs and whether or not the type of usage is sophisticated. Aspects from the *user* perspective such as innovation in their contribution, intensive versus extensive usage, level of interactivity, online information retrieval, and simply mere access must be taken into account to determine the level of connection of *users*. Finally, variable $z$ implies the means of connectivity by the *users* and whether *users* are connected to a broadband Internet or telephony, Digital TV or Fixed, or mobile phones (Hilbert and López, 2011).

As suggested by the authors, the DD must be analysed at a multidimensional level, and it should be seen as the summation of different variables that may compound the same subject. The unintended consequences of the implementation of digital technology at a global level have been explored from different perspectives. For instance, there are some studies that try to simplify the analysis to fewer variables using statistical methods (see modelling income-related structural challenges for ICT diffusion in Latin America, in Hilbert, 2010), or the study of DD based on Kbits consumption per capita to calculate the *bandwidth* (data transfer rate) per individual (Hilbert and López, 2011). Additionally, DD has also been explored through classical sociologists, like Marx, Weber, and Durkheim, in order to understand the dynamics of stratification, power, status, and division of labour within a global context of the digital sphere (see the work of Ragnedda and Muschert, 2013). Other analysis has focused on skills and digital literacy, arguing that DD is more than having *access to* ICTs and cannot be alleviated merely by providing the necessary equipment, but rather by looking at ICT accessibility, utilisation, and receptiveness. That said, users need to have a more proficient knowledge of ICT tools once these are introduced within a community/region/country/school. With this in mind, differences in digital knowledge may create new inequalities and links to the study that authors have called *Digital Divide 2.0*. The *Digital Divide 2.0* is defined in the literature as *the second level digital divide*, in which *Web 2.0* technology is implemented the most (see the work of Gui and Argentin, 2011). Namely, it is the (authors') intention to turn *Web 2.0* technology into an enabler of social regeneration.

## Digital Divide 2.0: The Second Level Digital Divide (2LDD)

The key characteristic to describe the DD is the gap that separates the users from the *access to*, the *use of* and the *impact of* ICTs within an e-society. Such a gap should be examined at multi-variable level. However, such examination is just the first layer of the DD studies; the second-level digital divide (2LDD) is defined as the transition from the conceptual analysis about the user in relation to gaps in the *access, type of division, knowledge, type of usage*, and *the means of connectivity*, which are generated by the given digital technology setting of society, towards the analysis of gaps that separates the *prosumers* on the internet (Graham, 2011) and even appear amongst *prosumers* themselves (as *prosumers* are encouraged and enabled by the conditions given in their own context). The rapid development and the pervasiveness of the digital technology across the globe and the use of ICTs at different levels (socio-economic, political, environmental, and cultural life) which, at the same time, is introduced and implemented unequally, with no planning and strategy to society, raises the concern whether at the second level of digital production new inequalities and their reproduction are emerging (see Wessels Chapter 1, in Ragnedda and Muschert, 2013).

The Second Level Digital Divide is also enlightened by the work of Fuchs (2011), who analyses the existing data and statistics of *Web 2.0* platforms in the context of the USA. He raises awareness about the shallow approach on the topic still adopted in the academic theoretical and empirical research, due to the absence of many elements in the *Web 2.0* equation, such as *ownership, free labour*, and *internet users' exploitation* and *ICT knowledge for its creation*. Thus, in a way, the work of Fuchs not only illustrates the self-contradictory elements of using *Web 2.0* in terms of participation, but also escalates the analysis towards the benefits of this "*supposedly participatory-advantage*". Interestingly, based on his empirical study, he found that 92.3% of the most frequently used *Web 2.0* platforms and 87.4% of monthly unique *Web 2.0* usages in the USA are corporate based, which shows that the vast majority of popular *Web 2.0* platforms are mainly interested in generating monetary profits and that the corporate *Web 2.0* is much more popular than the non-corporate *Web 2.0* (Fuchs, 2011, 272). That said, *ownership* is an important variable while examining the *Web 2.0* equation, as *Web 2.0* is mostly built by user interaction and participation (*Prosumers*). Thus, ultimately, the content generated by them enriches both: on the one hand, the interactivity of the *Web 2.0* platform ensures online status (*more users and more popularity leads to more financial reward*) and, on the other hand, the financial surplus to the owners of the *Web 2.0* corporate platforms is enhanced (*platforms that are generally owned by very few and the users hardly share the financial reward*), as most *Web 2.0* profit-oriented corporations accumulate financial capital by online advertising and, in some cases, by selling special services through it (Fuchs, 2011, 278). Needless to say, it seems that the *Web 2.0* corporate platforms are taking advantage of the so-called "*professional or creative precariat*" necessity to generate wealth within an illusionary platform of 'possibilities' in a very competitive market, in which free labour is the key to success (Fuchs, 2011). Additionally, and in coherence with the definition of 2LDD, Fuchs concludes that *Web 2.0* is stratified by age, income, and education, as well as being shaped by information inequalities. Although everyone can easily produce and diffuse information, in principle, with the help of the internet, because it is a global, decentralised, many-to-many and one-to-many communication system, not all information is visible to the same degree and gets the same attention. Furthermore, not everybody has the same ICT knowledge to produce or generate content (Fuchs, 2011).

That said, and drawing on DD theoretical frameworks, differences in motivation, access, skills, and usage that appear to underlie and perpetuate differences in online content creation practices between social groups appear to be obvious (Graham, 2011). Thus, the multi-variable function stated above that specifies the DD has to be augmented and complemented by additional variables determined by what type of subject is behind the digital connections. By doing this, the *Augmented Digital Divide Function* incorporates the 2LDD. In this case, 2LDD is determined by its own multi-variable function (thus *w* is replaced by *f(a)*), so the *augmented* DD function is determined by the addition of the new incorporated function and the other variables (see Figure 10.6). Thus, in practice, the authors suggest

$$f(w, x, y, z) = f(a) + x + y + z$$

$$if$$

$$w = f(a)$$

$$f(a) = b + c + d$$

$w = $ *Who is the subject that connects with the digital domain*

$a = $ *What type of subject is the one that connects with the digital domain*

$b = $ *Ownership of the Subject*

$c = $ *Whether or not is free labour*

$d = $ *Level of ICT knowledge*

*Figure 10.6* Augmented Digital Divide Function
Source: Compiled by Authors

to integrate $f(a)$ that denotes not only the subject that is/are connected to the digital domain, but also the subject that participates and generates content. As suggested above, *prosumers* are not only subjected to the gaps that separate them from the *access to, use of*, and *impact from* ICTs, but also are subjected to the ownership status $(b)$, free labour or users' exploitation $(c)$, or the level of ICT knowledge $(d)$ Thus, the authors suggest that is important to determine what type of subject is the one that tries to connect with the digital domain $(a)$, whereas variable $w$ denominates only the user subject. In sum, with the *Augmented Digital Divide Function*, the authors intend to highlight the relationship or expression of the 2LDD involving more variables.

## Concluding Remarks

Digital Technology, and in particular *Web 2.0* as an example of it, must be critically explored and analysed. The contrast between intended and unintended consequences illustrates that scholars need to conduct an in-depth analysis to examine Digital Technology as a solution for societal transformation. Although there are clear, and to some extent inspiring, examples of *Web 2.0 technology* enabling social regeneration, it remains to be seen whether *Web 2.0* really has enhanced inclusion, participation and accessibility on a large scale. Studies on the Digital Divide have shown that *Web 2.0* goes beyond digital technology and has become a new form of socioeconomic inequality, and, despite its intention to innovate in technology and develop a non-hierarchical, participative and free-accessible tool, unintended positive and negative consequences were delivered.

The authors have described the unforeseen consequences of *Web 2.0* technology. On the one hand, they are drawing from organisational and community perspectives by bringing diverse examples that include MOOCs as a disruptive tool for education, the practice of e-Democracy and e-Government in Iceland with *Citizens Foundation* and the empowerment of grassroots organisations with *Million Kitchen* in New Delhi, India. On the other hand, the authors have discussed and briefly examined the studies on the Digital Divide. They suggest that although the implementation of *Web 2.0* technology may deliver positive and hopeful outcomes, a multi-variable function must be considered to evaluate its eventual impact. Different dimensions should be contemplated when analysing *Web 2.0* technology within a Digital Divide framework.

The authors not only acknowledge that the success of effectively implementing *Web 2.0* technology for social transformation relies on the goodwill of its participants, as the platform is built-on a participation-based, inclusive, and accessible system, but also that the use of *Web 2.0* platforms may enable social transformation by developing equal opportunities and capabilities for different actors. However, beyond misanthropy, the conversation about Digital Divide was addressed to raise the question whether all societal actors play by the same rules in the Digital Technology sphere and whether the transition from a traditional to a digital economy will reproduce the same socio-economic and environmental distresses that society is trying to move away from. Hence, if *Web 2.0* technology is supposed to be the answer, what was the question that was formulated then?

## Notes

1. A consumer who becomes involved with designing or customising products for their own needs (producer = consumer simultaneously).
2. A website or database developed collaboratively by a community of users, allowing any user to add and edit content.
3. See YouTube statistics on www.youtube.com/yt/press/en-GB/statistics.html (Accessed on 29/12/2016).
4. There are a few countries (e.g., the United Kingdom and Canada) that have already started to explore e-democracy and moving towards an e-governmental organisational structure. Please check: www.consultingcanadians.gc.ca and http://forums.e-democracy.org.
5. See the full programme at www.futurelearn.com/programs/social-enterprise
6. The authors refer to those who, by using self-organisation, encourage community members to contribute by taking responsibility and action for their community.

## References

Adebanjo, D., and R. Michaelides. 2010. "Analysis of Web 2.0 Enabled-Clusters: A Case Study." *Technovation*, 30(1): 238–248.
Alexander, B. 2006. *Web 2.0—A New Wave of Innovation in Teaching-Learning.* Accessed on 15 April 2017 from www.net.educause.edu/ir/library/pdf/ERM0621.pdf.
Anderson, B. 2006. *Imagined Communities: Reflections on the Origin and Spread of Nationalism.* London: Verso Books.
Balasubramaniam, N. 2009. "User-Generated Content (UGC)." *Proceedings of Business Aspects of the Internet of Things*, Zurich ETH, 1: 28–33.
Best, D. 2006. *Web 2.0: Next Big Thing or Next Big Internet Bubble.* Eindhoven, Netherlands: Technische Universiteit Eindhoven.
Carter, R., Thok, S., O'Rourke, V., and T. Pearce. 2015. "Sustainable Tourism and Its Use as a Development Strategy in Cambodia: A Systematic Literature Review." *Journal of Sustainable Tourism*, 23(5): 797–818.
Castells, M. 2005. *Manuel Castells' Network Society.* Accessed on 12 April 2017 from www.geof.net/research/2005/castells-network-society.
Christensen, C. 2013. *The Innovator's Dilemma: When New Technologies Cause Great Firms to Fail.* Boston, MA: Harvard Business Review Press.
De Waard, I., Abajian, S., Gallagher, M. S., Hogue, R., Keskin, N., Koutropoulos, A., and O. C. Rodriguez. 2011. "Using mLearning and MOOCs to Understand Chaos, Emergence, and Complexity in Education." *The International Review of Research in Open and Distributed Learning*, 12(7): 94–115.
Dobson, A. S. 2015. "Girls' 'Pain Memes' on YouTube: The Production of Pain and Femininity in a Digital Network." *Youth Cultures and Subcultures: Australian Perspectives*, 1: 173–182.
Elder-Vass, D. 2016. *Profit and Gift in the Digital Economy.* Cambridge, UK: Cambridge University Press.

Evens, T. 2010. "Value Networks and Changing Business Models for the Digital Television Industry." *Journal of Media Business Studies*, 7(4): 41–58.

Fuchs, C. 2006. "The Dialectic of the Nature-Society-System, Triple C: Communication, Capitalism & Critique." *Open Access Journal for a Global Sustainable Information Society*, 4(1): 1–39.

Fuchs, C. 2010a. "Class, Knowledge and New Media." *Media, Culture, and Society*, 32(1): 141.

Fuchs, C. 2010b. "Labor in Informational Capitalism and on the Internet." *The Information Society*, 26(3): 179–196. doi:10.1080/01972241003712215

Fuchs, C. 2011. *Foundations of Critical Media and Information Studies*. London, UK: Taylor & Francis.

Graham, M. 2011. "Time Machines and Virtual Portals: The Spatialities of the Digital Divide." *Progress in Development Studies*, 11(3): 211–227. doi:10.1177/146499341001100303

Granovetter, M. 1983. "The Strength of Weak Ties: A Network Theory Revisited." *American Journal of Sociology*, 78(6): 1360–1380.

Gui, M., and G. Argentin. 2011. "Digital Skills of the Internet Natives: Differences of Digital Literacy in a Random Sample of Northern Italian High School Students." *New Media and Society*, 2(17): 1–18.

Hargittai, E. 2002. "Second-Level Digital Divide: Mapping Differences in People's Online Skills." *First Monday*, 7(4): 1–23.

Hendler, J. 2009. "Web 3.0 Emerging." *Computer*, 42(1): 111–113.

Henry, S., Abou-Zahra, S., and L. Brewer. 2014. "The Role of Accessibility in a Universal Web." Presented at the *Proceedings of the 11th Web for All Conference*, Seoul, Republic of Korea: ACM, 17–27.

Hilbert, M. 2010. "When Is Cheap, Cheap Enough to Bridge the Digital Divide? Modeling Income Related Structural Challenges of Technology Diffusion in Latin America." *World Development*, 38(5): 756–770. doi:10.1016/j.worlddev.2009.11.019

Hilbert, M., and P. López. 2011. "The World's Technological Capacity to Store, Communicate, and Compute Information." *Science*, 332(6025): 60–65.

Klein, N. 2000. *No Logo*. London: Flamingo.

Kozinets, R. V. 2002. "The Field Behind the Screen: Using Ethnography for Marketing Research in Online Communities." *Journal of Marketing Research*, 39(1): 72–82.

Lees, L. 2008. "Gentrification and Social Mixing: Towards an Inclusive Urban Renaissance?" *Urban Studies*, 45: 2449–2470.

Lindner, R., Aichholzer, G., and L. Hennen. 2016. *Electronic Democracy in Europe: Prospects and Challenges of E-Publics, E-Participation and E-Voting*. New York, NY: Springer.

Liyanagunawardena, T. R., Williams, S., and A. A. Adams. 2014. "The Impact and Reach of MOOCs: A Developing Countries' Perspective." *eLearning Papers*, 1: 38–46.

Merton, R. K. 1936. "The Unanticipated Consequences of Purposive Social Action." *American Sociological Review*, 1(6): 894–904.

Morales-Gutiérrez, A., and J. Ariza-Montes. 2010. *E-Social Entrepreneurship and Social Innovation: The Case of On-line Giving Markets in E-Entrepreneurship and ICT Ventures: Strategy, Organization and Technology*. Hershey, PA: IGI Publishing.

Mrabet, R. 2016. "Web 2.0 as a New Channel for Innovation Diffusion: The Case Study of Renewable Energy Products." *IJI Journal*, 4(2): 1–10. doi:10.5585/iji.v4i2.100

Narula, R. 2014. *Globalization and Technology: Interdependence, Innovation Systems and Industrial Policy*. Sussex, NJ: John Wiley & Sons.

Nemer, D. 2016. "Online Favela: The Use of Social Media by the Marginalized in Brazil." *Information Technology for Development*, 22(1): 364–379. doi:10.108 0/02681102.2015.1011598

O'Reilly, T. 2005. *What Is Web 2.0": Design Patterns and Business Models for the Next Generation of Software.* Web 2.0. Accessed on 26 March 2017 from www. oreilly.com/pub/a/web2/archive/what-is-web-20.html.

O'Reilly, T. 2007. "What Is Web 2.0: Design Patterns and Business Models for the Next Generation of Software." *Communications and Strategies*, 65(1): 17–37.

Rabanal, N. 2017. "Cursos MOOC: Un Enfoque desde la Economía." *RIED Revista Iberoamericana de Educación a Distancia*, 20(1): 145–160.

Ragnedda, M., and Muschert. G. W. 2013. "The Digital Divide: The Internet and Social Inequality." *International Perspective*, Vol. 73. London: Routledge.

Rifkin, J. 2000. "The New Capitalism Is About Turning Culture Into Commerce." *Los Angeles Times.* Accessed on 15 February 2017 from www.uni-muenster.de/PeaCon/dgs-mills/mills-texte/Rifkin-Hypercapitalism.htm.

Rifkin, J. 2001. *The Age of Access: The New Culture of Hypercapitalism: Where All of Life Is a Paid-For Experience.* New York: Tarcher.

Rifkin, J. 2014. *The Zero Marginal Cost Society: The Internet of Things, the Collaborative Commons, and the Eclipse of Capitalism.* London: Palgrave Macmillan.

Roberts, P. 2008. "The Evolution, Definition and Purpose of Urban Regeneration." In *Urban Regeneration: A Handbook*, edited by P. Roberts and H. Sykes, 9–36. London: SAGE Publications.

Segerberg, A., and W. L. Bennett. 2011. "Social Media and the Organization of Collective Action: Using Twitter to Explore the Ecologies of Two Climate Change Protests." *The Communication Review*, 14(3): 197–215. doi:10.1080/1071442 1.2011.597250

Te Velde, R. A., and M. G. Plomp. 2011. "Web 2.0 as a Megatrend in eGovernment: An Empirical Analysis of Its Preconditions and Outcomes." *European of ePractice*, 13(1): 94–108.

# 11 Immigration Policies, Public Decision-Making Processes, and Urban Regeneration

## The Italian Case

*Luigi Ferrara and Salvatore Villani*

## Introduction

Through the implementation of adequate immigration and urban regeneration policies, several cities and regions in the world have gradually succeeded in breaking the chains of path dependence[1] and in rising again, like a phoenix, from their own ashes. From steel and pollution capitals, they have become a symbol of innovation, sustainability, and socio-economic regeneration, achieving the successful coexistence between the advanced techniques of industrial manufacturing and a quality of life. The examples that we can mention are numerous: the city of Malmö, which was one of Scandinavia's first major manufacturing and trading centres, and the main urban centre of Southern Sweden, is now experiencing a transition period from an industrial past toward a future of integration of immigrants in the inner city and the creation of universities and research centres of the highest level; Pittsburgh, which already in the nineteenth century was considered 'the world capital of steel', has also experienced a revival as a great centre of excellence in research, health care, nanotechnology, and robotics; the Canadian city of Hamilton, Ontario, once centre to an important steel plant with significant adverse effects on the environment and the quality of life of its citizens until the early 1990s is now committed to promoting smart, sustainable, and inclusive growth through the implementation of environmental redevelopment strategies and the promotion of the integration of immigrants into the labour market.

In Italy, however, any attempt to exploit and convert early industrialisation areas has tragically failed because of the lack of a national strategy for developing and strengthening interconnections between urban areas of the country. This failure has had, moreover, serious effects on the territory, especially in the metropolitan areas of Southern Italy, in which it is possible to see every day the implications of: the absence of a specific funding system of local agencies for the management of extended areas (Provinces and Metropolitan Cities); an ineffective policy of prevention and prediction of environmental risks; an inoculated spatial planning; and an increase in inequalities in income and standard of living, leading to the exclusion and the marginalisation of a growing number of citizens.

In Italy, the real factors that prevent the regeneration of urban and suburban areas, or lead to abandoned industrial areas, are not only economic, but also political, considering the acknowledged current inconclusiveness of public decision-making processes. In fact, reflecting on urban regeneration raises issues related to the multi-level governance of these processes by various public subjects. Governance structures are determined by the system of subsidiarity shared among the State, Regions, and Local Governments and regulated by Articles 117 and 118 of the Italian Constitution in the areas of environmental protection, crisis management and industrial reconversion, urban planning and territorial governance, infrastructural networks, reorganisation of local public services, and economic and social welfare systems (social protection and inclusion, education, and training). In all these competence areas, the institutional players move among constraints set by expenditure evaluation, public procurement, and opportunities in the shared internal ownership of a wide variety of European funds (including policies of regional cohesion, urban planning policies, integration and cultural policies, industrial crisis management policies, and immigration policies).

The complexity of coordinating these subsidiarity systems and heterogeneous policies is well evident in legislative reforms and in case law (Constitutional Court case law and criminal, bankruptcy, and administrative courts case law), which mark the beginning of the rehabilitation of polluted sites and the urban regeneration processes in Taranto and in Bagnoli. At the same time, however, since the 90's, a new regulatory season started to answer the irreversible crisis of the traditional urban planning instruments. It was marked by the experimentation of new routes of intervention and new programming practices. This new regulatory season has led to the elaboration of juridical tools, such as the so-called "complex" or "complex urban programmes" ("Programmi Urbani Integrati" o "complessi"), which address urban planning through an integrated reading of territorial regeneration, social development, and environmental sustainability, which often aim at the realisation of social and immaterial instances. An articulated and heterogeneous legal framework has gradually formed, in Italy. Currently, prospects and procedures of urban regeneration, in the broadest sense of the word, depend on this framework. These tools include, in fact, even those procedures which tend to carry out contextual actions involving the territory, or the economy and the society of certain territories or regions, with particular attention to the fight against marginalisation and social exclusion.

This chapter aims at contributing to the ongoing debate between urban planners and regional scientists about the most appropriate techniques for managing urban regeneration processes and fostering the economic and social exploitation of territories, as well as the human development of people living in the areas concerned. For this purpose, we will try to identify the role which can be played in this context by the management policies of migratory flows, whose strategic value is today underrated, and by a greater openness of public decision-making processes, which are scarcely transparent and inclusive of citizens' interests.

In particular, this section of the chapter aims at verifying whether and to what extent ethnic and cultural diversity can be considered as a resource, that is, as a benefit to the social and economic development of a region, rather than as a problem. The third section of the chapter reconstructs the complex Italian legal framework governing the matter of urban regeneration and the most important current issues. The fourth section of the chapter also contains a reflection on the use of complex urban programmes and the results obtained through these new regeneration tools aimed at achieving, at the same time, objectives related to the economic and social development and to the environmental sustainability. In particular, the analysis of the case study of the Barriera district ("quartiere Barriera") of Turin will show how a wise management of integration policies and a greater involvement of all stakeholders in the planned regeneration could favour the economic and social enhancement of the territory, as well as the human development of populations resident in deprived urban areas. Finally, the fourth section deals with the cases of the urban regeneration of the Bagnoli and Coroglio sites, which incarnate the failure of the policies pursued, without any continuity, by the local governments that have ruled so far and reveal their inability to involve external elements (for example, immigrants or non-institutional actors) in the urban regeneration process of the above mentioned dismantled industrial area (Frascani, 2017). In the fifth section, we will set out our conclusive remarks on the Italian experience of urban regeneration analysed in the paper.

## Migration Policies and Cultural Diversity

International migration is a global phenomenon which is rapidly growing. Figures 11.1 and 11.2 can help us understand its characteristics and how it has developed over time. They show the evolution of the migratory phenomenon in some or most of the advanced countries of the 'old' and the 'new' world (see, in particular, Figure 11.1 for Europe and Figure 11.2 for the Americas and Oceania) in just over half a century.

The figures clearly show that, in all countries analysed, during the 1960–2015 period, there has been a remarkable increase in migratory pressures. Despite the diversity of starting points and trajectories, the figures show a clear upward trend in migration flows. Figure 11.3 also enables us to rank by geopolitical areas which are most under pressure. Though the European Union ranks third, with a rate of 10.7%, following Oceania (20.6%) and North America (15.2%), in the past decade (2000–2015), it has witnessed an intense and progressive growth in migration flows (+51.8%). This raises some concerns about the consequences it might have on social cohesion and the sustainability of national welfare systems.[2]

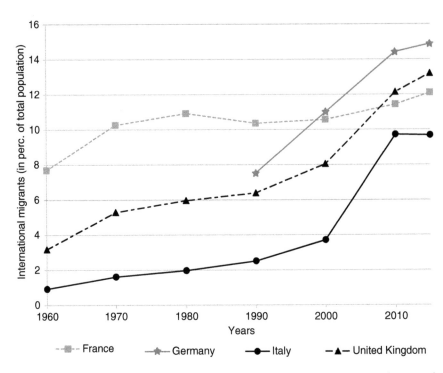

*Figure 11.1* The Evolution of the Migratory Phenomenon in Europe in the Period 1960–2015

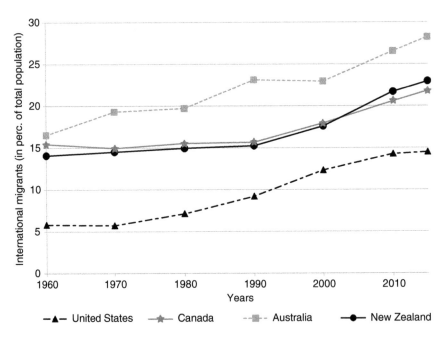

*Figure 11.2* The Evolution of the Migratory Phenomenon in the Americas and Oceania in the Period 1960–2015

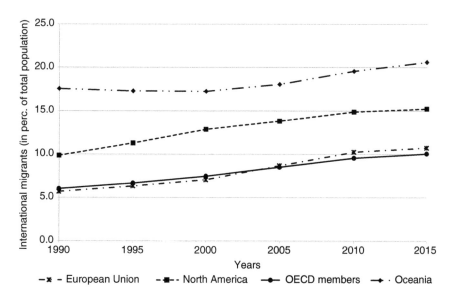

*Figure 11.3* The International Migratory Pressure in the Main Geopolitical Areas of the World in the Period 1990–2015

It is almost impossible to stop the phenomenon of migration described above. Migrants, especially smugglers, have been shown to be able to continually change their strategies to adapt themselves to obstacles (walls and other types of barriers, physical or regulatory) introduced from time to time by single countries. Some recent studies (Wayne, 2007; Didiot, 2013) show that anti-immigration walls and barriers are certainly an effective way to reduce the number of migrants trying to cross the physical boundaries of nations. However, they fail to completely stop, or at least to contain, the new waves of immigrants. They can only divert them to the borders of those countries that are less organised or less prepared to address the problem, like Italy. In fact, some of these countries may be incapable of handling the complex phenomenon of migration.

As migratory flows intensify, heterogeneity and complexity of contemporary societies strongly increase. In this way, governments around the world are forced to face increasingly difficult and uncertain challenges. Many of these challenges mainly concern metropolitan areas and big cities, where most people currently live (see Figure 11. 4). In fact, it appears that after the urban population surpassed the rural one in 2007, the twenty-first century became with full rights the 'century of cities' (ANCI The European House Ambrosetti, IntesaSanpaolo 2016).

According to forecasts of the United Nations' Department of Economic and Social Affairs, these urbanisation processes should particularly affect the least developed and developing countries by 2050 (Figure 11. 5), though we

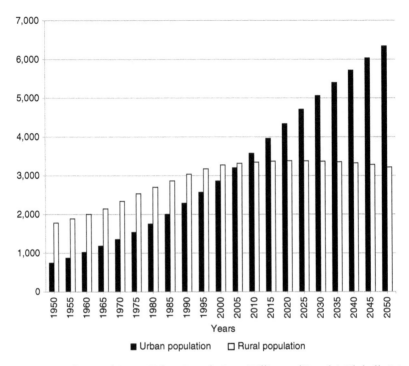

*Figure 11.4* Urban and Extra-Urban Populations (Billions of People) Globally Measured in the Period 1990–2050

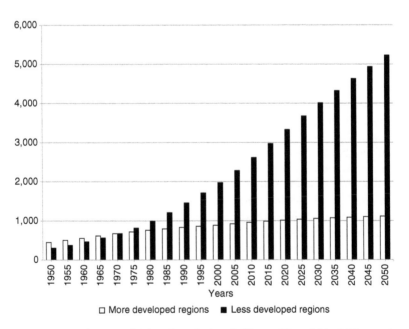

*Figure 11.5* Distribution of Urban Population (Billions of People) in Different Areas of the World Characterised by Different Levels of Economic Development During the Period 1990–2050

cannot rule out that this phenomenon will also occur in the most advanced countries. It is most likely that advanced countries will not be able to avoid many challenges posed by this problem.

Among these challenges, the biggest, but perhaps even the most difficult to face, is the need to manage the economic and social consequences of turmoil, such as the growth of marginality (Wacquant, 2008; Maloutas, 2009), inequality, and poverty (Berube and Holmes, 2016) leading to the progressive consolidation of a logic of exclusion and/or expulsion (Sassen, 2014). With this logic, social groups and individuals become not only unequal or marginal, but above all useless and redundant, regardless of whether they live in rich or poor countries.

According to common perception, it is now imperative that governments address these issues, and do not underestimate them. In fact, if these phenomena were properly managed, they could be transformed into opportunities, and migration policies could become an effective means of economic and social regeneration of the territories affected by the processes of socio-economic turmoil. Recent studies that analyse the effects of cultural and religious differences between natives and immigrants, have evidenced that "from the economic point of view a multi-ethnic society can work very well" (Alesina and Giavazzi, 2015) and that cultural diversity can stimulate innovation, productivity, and entrepreneurship, bringing huge benefits to both national and local economies (Alesina and Giavazzi, 2015; Alesina and La Ferrara, 2005; Kemeny, 2013).

Cultural diversity is not necessarily a source of violence and conflict, as often claimed. Clearly, in the short-medium term, migration can have a negative impact on social solidarity and social capital because it promotes dissolution of social ties and a falling the collective level of trust. Initially, there is what Putnam (2007) called the 'turtle effect': as the number of immigrants increases within a community, mutual levels of cooperation and trust diminish, not only between immigrants and indigenous peoples, but also between immigrants themselves and members of the indigenous community. However, in the medium-long term, this process can also reverse its course. Migration and the development of a multi-ethnic society can, in fact, contribute to overcome social fragmentation and to create a new model of solidarity within the community (*e pluribus unum*) by building new cultures and new identities.

Therefore, it is important to recognise and assess the potential benefits as well as the social costs produced in a country by enhancing cultural diversity. The effect of this on economic performance will depend, on the one hand, on the ability of governments and institutions to predict and anticipate these assessments and, secondly, on their ability to create a climate of trust and mutual consideration which could encourage cooperation and the integration of immigrants into the host society. Consequently, the task of migration policy should be, first of all, to find the degree of sustainable diversity in a particular economic and social system and then calibrate to this degree the effectiveness of immigration controls and the speed of the integration process.

A simple model, borrowed in part by Collier (2013), can be useful to illustrate how, in our opinion, migration policies could be used to improve the performance of the economy and, at the same time, to increase the efficiency of regeneration processes in regions affected by the phenomenon of urbanisation. Figure 11.6 depicts two functions: the first, which we might call the 'performance function', shows how a greater degree of cultural diversity

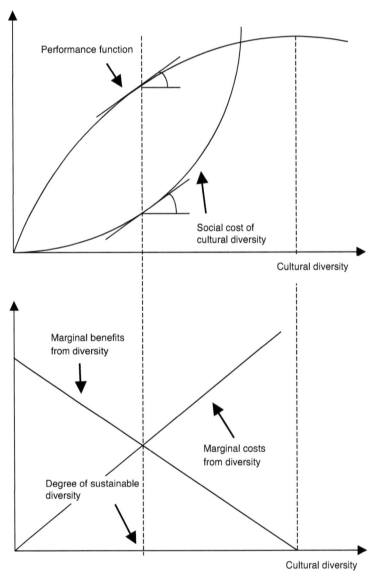

*Figure 11.6* Determination of the 'Sustainable Diversity Degree'

can have a positive impact on the productivity of the economic system; the second function represents the so-called 'social cost of cultural diversity', i.e. the negative effect produced by the migratory flows on the levels of cooperation and social capital. The intersection between the two functions will allow us to find the aforementioned 'level of sustainable cultural diversity'. Substantially, institutions and governments must balance the costs and the benefits of diversity to determine this level. The benefits arising from diversity will conceivably generate diminishing returns, as observed with any form of variety. Conversely, the social costs of diversity will increase progressively, probably exponentially. In this way, we can find the appropriate degree of cultural diversity for the economic system under consideration by comparing the benefits and marginal costs that result from it.

Figure 11.7 shows the model used to explain the nature of the problems which the governments of the host countries are forced to deal with in the acceleration phases of migration. Even in this case, the functions we have to consider are two: the 'migratory function', which represents the positive and constant relationship between the diaspora and the migratory flow; the 'diaspora curve', which shows the diaspora and migration combinations in which the number of immigrants entering the diaspora is equivalent to that of those who come out of it, because they are able to integrate into the society of the host country. To get the 'right' level of diversity, it is necessary to employ the appropriate mix of selective measures (border control) and integration policies: the former will change the slope and shape of the

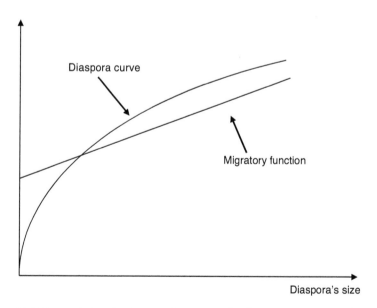

*Figure 11.7* Determining the Appropriate Mix of Selective Measures and Integration Policies

migratory function; the latter will act on the diaspora curve, accentuating or moderating its concavity and turning it clockwise or counter-clockwise. However, it becomes evident that there is no advantageous migration policy for all countries and for all historical periods. Each country will adopt the policy that best suits it according to its characteristics.

## Current Legal Issues in the Emergence of Urban Regeneration as a Legal Concept in the Italian Legal Framework

The constitutional rationale of the Italian legal framework for planning could be found in the general principles of: a) functionalisation of public and private property (Art. 42 Italian Constitution, which also includes the rule of law in statutory powers to limit property rights); b) protection of cultural heritage and landscape (Art. 9 of the Italian Constitution); and c) subsidiarity in protection of local government powers (Art. 5 and 118 of the Italian Constitution). The Art. 117.3 of the Italian Constitution sets out the multilevel governance of regulation and management in urban planning. It foresees that general principles about land-use planning will have to be established by national statutes, while regional laws provide for specific and implementation rules (Simonati, 2011). The rulemaking process is carried out by local authorities' byelaws. The national legal rules concerning general land-use planning are still expressed in Law No. 1150/1942 ("Legge Urbanistica", urban planning law) and in the Consolidated Building Law No. 380/2001 ("Testo Unico sull'Edilizia"). As anticipated, the Italian planning legal framework is characterised by multilevel rulemaking in several administrative sectors and, in the original legal design, by the central role of general masterplans (PRG) adopted by municipal authorities (the communes), by incorporating together both urban development and land-use policies. It is based on the concept of zoning to define uses and limits (and the main public interest to be protected) across the local government area. The main command-and-control measures of urban planning management were identified in discretionary building permits and compulsory purchase orders. From its inception and even to this day, we notice several issues. On the one hand, the main body of urban planning law does not include urban regeneration main rules; on the other hand, several general principles and detailed rules on urban regeneration policies (mainly on regional and district/metropolitan strategic planning, land consumption, public participation, and polluted sites rehabilitation) are located in different bodies of law: Cultural heritage and landscape Code (Legislative Decree No. 42/2004); Environmental Code (Legislative Decree No. 42/2004); and Consolidated Local Government Law (Legislative Decree No. 267/2000). In recent years, only rulemaking by Regions tried to introduce comprehensive regional regulations on urban regeneration.

Towards the end of the 1970s, the first regulation on urban renewal (routine maintenance, extraordinary maintenance, restoration building and urban redevelopment) was provided by Law No. 457/1978, which also introduced the recovery plans that were intended to address the management of the transformation of existing built-up areas. During the 1980s, the legal framework was integrated within the new statutes on environmental protection, landscape protection, and water and soil consumption (Laws No. 431/1985, 349/86 and 183/1989). It introduced the so-called Landscape Plans, which are legislative measures at the strategic regional and district level in urban planning. In 1990, the local government reform (Law No. 142/90) introduced metropolitan cities and provided new district strategic plans.

In the 1990s, Laws No. 179/1992 and 493/1993 introduced the *integrated programmes*, the *urban renewal programmes* (Art. 3) and the *urban regeneration programmes* (Art. 2) (PRU). This was the first attempt at overcoming rigid command-and-control zoning, towards a more reactive planning based on Public-Private Partnerships (PPP)in urban planning. The PRU was not designed on the basis of strategic and highly operative local government planning by communes (approved and financed by the Italian Government) for declining industrial zones. Another relevant issue was the introduction of procedures of burden and advantages sharing resulting from the changes among the property owners involved in the transformations designed in programmes (the so-called "equalisation").

Trends to redesign the urban planning law in a "reactive" perspective led to Law No. 127/1997, which provided within the regeneration legal framework the so-called *urban regeneration company* (STU, now provided in the Consolidated Local Government Law, Art. 120). The STU was designed as an in-house scheme company, which was set up by local authorities with powers of urban regeneration and sold shares to the private sector. Local authorities were fitted with powers to buy, regenerate and resell properties and to adopt Equal Opportunities Committee (CPO), but they did not update the local masterplan (Passalacqua, 2010). In recent years, the case law has clarified that they may be subject to bankruptcy proceedings, just like in the Bagnoli case (Macchiarulo, 2015).

To strengthen local democracy in the proceedings of urban regeneration we need to test several types of planning agreements (*urbanistica negoziata* or *contrattata*). These agreements were introduced in the Italian planning law in the 1990s and were designed to promote a process of negotiation of local interests and to replace command-and-control planning tools with innovative planning agreements. Scholars observed that in Italy, these tools have proved to be more efficient in strengthening the PPP with enterprises rather than enhancing transparency and participatory democracy to involve citizens and associations in the decision-making processes (Cento Bull, 2005).

As a complement to PPP with the private sector, scholars analysed the rise of new schemes of "Pacts of management of commons" in Italian local government byelaws, within the local government rulemaking on urban regeneration. These "pacts" are classified as public law agreements in the light of Art. 11 of the Italian Administrative Proceeding Act of 1990 (Giglioni, 2016).

In 1998 the Ministerial Order No. 1169 updated the urban regeneration legal framework by introducing the *urban regeneration and land sustainable development programmes* (PRUSST). These programmes provided a useful tool for supra-local and district urban regeneration planning in broader areas in order to promote the inter-local cooperation and agreement within communes and, in certain cases, within district and regional authorities. They are promoted by one or more local authorities to develop associations between them and, in certain cases, with other private and public stakeholders. Once again, approval and financing by the Italian Government are required, before all partners can arrive to an operative administrative agreement (Damonte, 2001).

However, scholars underline that both PRU and PRUSST will continue to be measures of subsidiary-local urban planning, which must be coherent with the local general masterplan PRG. Above all, it should be stressed that the legal framework about PRU and PRUSST remains detached from the legal frameworks on soil consumption and polluted sites rehabilitation provided by the 2006 Environmental Code.

Art. 239–253 of the Environmental Code provide two routes for the rehabilitation of polluted sites. The ordinary route designates that the regional authority manages rehabilitation procedures by safeguarding powers of local authorities (of the communes where the polluted site is located). Thus, local authorities are involved in agency meetings (*conferenza di servizi*) to prepare soil rehabilitation planning and in the administrative agreement on rehabilitation (*accordo di programma*). Finally, they will directly handle the rehabilitation measures (in the absence of a liable polluter).

Art. 252 of the Environmental Code provides an alternative route for the rehabilitation of polluted sites of "strategic interest". Reformed in 2012 and 2013, the route provided for "strategic interest" sites is fully handled by the national authority (Environment Minister), and only marginally involves local authorities. Both these routes do not mention urban regeneration measures. The 2013 reform provides the rehabilitation of polluted brownfield of "strategic interest" (Art. 252bis of the Environmental Code) by means of the new *industrial restructuring and redevelopment projects* (PRRI). Thus, for the first time, the Italian Environmental Code links rehabilitation to urban regeneration.

In this updated route, national and regional authorities may involve in PRRI agency meetings and PRRI public agreements the owners of polluted sites and "other interested subjects". Local authorities are involved in PRRI agency meetings and public agreements, but the management of PRRI rehabilitation and regeneration is entrusted to a Ministerial in-house company. Scholars stressed that the new PRRI may conflict with PRUSST and local urban regeneration planning. In any case, it seems to be a tool that may contribute to the fragmentation of urban regeneration planning (Pulvirenti, 2015).

Finally, it may be stressed that all these measures show that administrative proceedings to achieve them are not able to provide all standards of transparency and public participation required by the Aarhus Convention. When the approach to urban regeneration planning is concretised in subsidiary site-specific planning, often the planning and management of regeneration measures eludes the minimum limits to apply SEA and EIA proceedings and participation safeguards. In such cases, it comes to support only regional rulemaking by redesigning transparency and public participation schemes.

Furthermore, all these tools seem to constitute a body of laws that are "disconnected" from other legal frameworks provided for social policies (related to the future of urban regeneration planning), particularly the legal framework of local integration policies of regular migrants (long-term residents and refugees and admitted to humanitarian protection), provided in the Consolidated Act on Immigration (T.U. No. 286/1998). We should recall that the priorities of the "EU 2020 strategy for smart, sustainable, and inclusive growth" consider the integration of migration policies within urban regeneration planning.

In recent years, scholars stressed that in the field of constitutional rights and duties for individuals, it seems possible to identify for third-country nationals the fundamental rights of a 'constitutional' or 'administrative' citizenship. After constitutional reform in 2001, some Regions and local authorities began to admit foreigners into regional welfare systems, in contrast with the national Immigration Act (Biondi Dal Monte, 2013; Ronchetti, 2012). Case law has given rise to debate about this 'administrative' citizenship. With Italian Constitutional Court case law, we would propose that the legal basis of this administrative citizenship should be found in a participatory democracy perspective (Palma, 1971; Grosso, 2010), following from common constitutional duties for citizens and migrants. Constitutional positive deontology in the post-WWII-era European Constitutions shows that the protection of fundamental human rights requires that public powers let all individuals in the Republic, like citizens, be able to fulfil "the fundamental duties of political, economic and social solidarity" (Art. 2 of the Italian Constitution) and that "every citizen has the duty, according to personal potential and individual choice, to perform an activity or a function that contributes to the material or spiritual progress of society" (Art. 4 of the Italian Constitution).

Furthermore, local authorities take part in the Italian Protection system for asylum seekers and refugees (SPRAR system) for the reception and national relocation of refugees. It is also clear that the planning choices of SPRAR centres in urban areas may become part of future strategic metropolitan urban regeneration planning. According to our economic analysis of links between urban development and integration policies and the phenomena of path dependencies, we would like to stress that it is necessary to analyse the legal issues that arise when connecting local integration policies with urban regeneration policy reforms.

On 13 May 2017, the draft of Law No. 2039 (that was submitted in 2014) on "Containment of soil consumption and reusing" was endorsed by the Senate and currently is pending before the first Chamber of Parliament. In Art. 1, urban regeneration is defined as a general principle of planning law. In Art. 4 and 5, the general model of administrative proceedings for urban regeneration is set out. The delegated legislation and the regional legislation will have to harmonise the several current legal frameworks involved in urban regeneration. Scholars underline that the draft law provides the 'general clause' on soil consumption, which shall be allowed only where there are no viable alternatives to urban regeneration, after EIA proceedings.

For the first time, a national law provides the legal definition of urban regeneration: a coordinated set of urban, building, and socio-economic interventions in urban areas, which pursues the objectives of replacing, reusing and reclaiming the soil in the context of environmental sustainability and the containment of soil and water consumption. This is a legal meaning different from the traditional urban landscape planning measures provided by the urban law (integrated intervention programmes recovery plans provided by the 2001 urban planning Code, regional or district landscape plans provided by the 2004 Code for the protection of cultural heritage and landscape goods). The legal meaning includes complex actions for urban, environmental, and social rehabilitation of degraded urban areas to pursue complex social goals (Dipace, 2014). But above all, while traditional programmes for urban renewal provided by the several current, different legal frameworks (the urban planning 2001 Code, the 2004 cultural heritage Code) are implementing tools of the city land-use masterplan, urban regeneration planning should now go to the next level: to the level of metropolitan strategic plans (Dipace, 2014; De Lucia, 2016), provided by the recent reform of Metropolitan Areas government (Art. 44, Law No. 56 of 2014), which should also coordinate the rules provided by the 2006 environmental protection Code. Law No. 56 of 2014 provides for the "core" functions of Metropolitan Cities, and foresees that Metropolitan Cities shall annually adopt and update the three-year strategic plan of the metropolitan territory, which governs the actions of all local authorities in the metropolitan territory (Marzuoli, 2015).

## Integrated Strategic Planning and Integration Policies: The Case of Turin

The "Integrated Strategic Planning" was born in Italy in the early 1990s of the last century with the establishment by the so-called "Botta-Ferrarini Act" (Law no. 179, issued on 17 February 1992) of the "Integrated Intervention Programmes" (IIPs), territorial governance tools specially designed to re-qualify the buildings and environment of towns. The use of these tools marks the beginning of a new phase in the evolution of urban planning, determined by a different approach to urban and territorial policies, aimed at integrating a variety of functions and types of intervention within a single planning tool, which contemplates for the first time the possibility of involving private operators and resources for the realisation of infrastructure and services of public interests.

The IIPs have since evolved and were immediately accompanied by other spatial planning instruments with different characteristics and complementary at the same time: from the Urban Renewal Programmes, to those for the re-qualification, both at the municipal and the territorial scale, up to the Urban Regeneration Programmes. All of these tools differ from their original model as they have a richer declination of the involved public and private actors and include different types of intervention.

In a few years, more generations of Complex Programmes have followed each other:

a)  the first generation consists of experiences that, to a greater or lesser extent, aim at redefining urban planning policies, putting the focus of interventions on the territory;
b)  the second is that of the "Negotiated Programming Tools" and includes experiences focusing on economic-productive goals, from which they start in order to define local development strategies that also affect the territory and/or institutional practices related to it;
c)  the third generation includes "Urban Regeneration Programmes" and all those policies which combine contextual actions on the building heritage and on the economic and social system, with particular attention to the fight against social exclusion.

The transition from the first to the next generations of complex programmes also shows a significant evolution of the innovative content of these tools towards an accentuation of the integration of actors involved in the definition and implementation of the agreed programme.

The rapid consensus acquired by these instruments produced quickly the maturation of potential characteristics initially just sketched to the point that, in the most recent regional legislation, they acquired the contents and the nature of tools for the implementation or the replacement of the traditional urban planning tools. To the typical characteristics of traditional urban plans (excessive structural rigidity, institutional and administrative fragmentation, uncertainty and length of implementation time, top-down nature of decision-making and reduced financial capacity of public investment) these urban regeneration programmes oppose, in fact, a reorganisation of the territory based on concerted and partnership practices, streamlining of procedures and administrative simplifications, the integration of public funds with private financial resources and the possibility of an easier access to public funding. For these reasons, through the regional legislation, there has been a wide and rapid spread of the described approach to urban and territorial policies. Very significant forms of experimentations have been launched in Puglia (with the Regional Law 29 July 2008, No. 21, *Provisions on the urban regeneration*), in Tuscany (with the Regional

Law 10 November 2014, No. 65, *Provisions concerning the government of territory*), in Lombardy (with Regional Law 28 November 2014, No. 31, *Provisions on the reduction of soil consumption and regeneration of deteriorated grounds*), in Umbria (with Regional Law No. 21 of January 21, 2015, *Consolidated text of the laws on the government of territory and related matters*), and, more recently, also in Emilia Romagna (with the Regional Bill No. 422/2017, which regulates the protection and the uses of the territory). In our opinion, however, a case study is particularly significant. The experience of "Barriera di Milano" district in Turin deserves to be mentioned because it allows us to show how a wise management of integration policies and a greater involvement of all stakeholders in the implementation of urban regeneration plans could favour economic and social enhancement of the territory (and therefore its economic and social regeneration) and human development of people living in the interested areas.

This experience is particularly interesting, because it demonstrates in a very effective way the great potential of the above mentioned complex programming tools, realised by the provision of integration strategies (of the multi-ethnic communities inhabiting the Barriera district) connected to the traditional procedures of urban regeneration.

The city of Turin, since the second post-war period to date, has been the target of substantial migratory flows: first, from the South of Italy, given the employment opportunities offered by the greatest industrial development of Northern Italy at the time of the "economic boom" and then, in recent decades, from the countries of the so-called "South of the world".[3] The "Barriera di Milano" district, often called simply "Barrier", is an old "working class neighbourhood" of Turin, officially born in 1853, with the first boundary walls, erected in order to ensure customs control over goods entering the town. In this district, already after the early sixties of the last century, was localised the major industrial facilities of the city and, for this reason, it became a zone of particular industrial and economic interests, in the same way as South Mirafiori district, in the south of Turin, where is located the Fiat's headquarters. In fact, the first important factories settled there as early as the late nineteenth century, with Fiat Grandi Motori (the historic GM brand, 1905) and several textile industries, including Fratelli Piacenza in Via Bologna, as well as the industry of CEAT tires, in Via Leoncavallo, opened in 1939 and whose production ceased in 1979, with definitive closure in 1982.

The reconversion and regeneration of this area lasted many years and also allowed for the recovery of a large green zone in the central courtyard, with its playground, recently inaugurated (September 10, 2012) and titled to the former President of the Republic Giuseppe Saragat. Currently, Barrier is inhabited by a multiethnic community. It is one of the most attractive neighbourhoods for foreign communities, thanks to favourable conditions for their settlement (including affordable housing and good public services), obtained through the implementation of effective integration policies. These policies were implemented on the basis of complex urban programmes governed by the regional legislation of Piemonte (see Regional Law No. 18/1996, No. 3/2013 and No. 17/2013). Among them, in particular, it is worth mentioning the Integrated Urban Development Programme "Urban Barrier of Milan", by which the Municipal Administration of Turin has been able to realise the economic and social regeneration of the area.

The "Urban-Barrier of Milan" is a plan of 34 coordinated and integrated interventions, financed through the use of public and private resources, and is structured on three strategic axes of intervention: Axis 1, "physical environment" on the redevelopment of public space; Axis 2, "economic-occupational", concerning the local economic system and, in particular, improving the employability conditions of communities in the neighbourhood; and, finally, Axis 3, "socio-cultural" on the strengthening of the cultural offer and social cohesion within the neighbourhood.

The peculiarity of the intervention is represented by the recognition of the neighbourhood immigrant community as strategic to boost local economic development. The programme aimed at exploiting cultural diversity and promoting greater participation among immigrants in local socio-economic processes by providing them with a more competitive and structured professional background to access the labour market and to have active voice in local government decisions.

## A Case Study: The Rehabilitation of Polluted Sites and the Urban Regeneration Processes in Bagnoli

In 1992, after an age-old industrial history, the ILVA steelworks planted in Bagnoli (borough in Naples) ceased all activities. The Italian Government launched the brownfield rehabilitation by a statutory order of the Government Committee for economic planning CIPE on 20.12.94. Laws No. 582/1996 and No. 388/2000 established provisions for financing this project by supporting the regeneration of ILVA area for non-industrial purposes. The reassessment of the city of Naples masterplan (*Variante di Piano per l'area occidentale di Napoli*) was proposed in Naples City Council in December 1994 and approved in January 1996. The revised masterplan provided the brownfield renewal for non-industrial activities (including the marina, the conference centre, the cultural centre "Città della Scienza", the redevelopment of some steelworks buildings, as an example of "industrial archaeology", housing, parks, tourism services, small traditional businesses).

The National Government set up the national in-house scheme company "BagnoliSpA" in April 1996 and transferred to it the brownfield ownership to start the rehabilitation. After several brownfield rehabilitation interventions by the national company "BagnoliSpA" were criticised, the City Council set up in 2002 the *urban regeneration company* (STU) "BagnoliFuturaS.p.A.", local authority in-house scheme company, and started purchasing and transferring the land to the STU (the transfer of ownership was completed in some years). After much delay, in 2013, the State's Attorney in Naples started a judicial inquiry against the company board for maladministration and ordered the seizure of assets. On 29 May 2014, the Civil Court of Naples delivered the judgement declaring bankruptcy. Scholars stressed that in this judgement, the predominant case law about the exclusion of bankruptcy in in-house schemes had been misapplied. In this specific case, the judgement excluded that the STU management was subject to the control similar to that which the local authority exercises in its own departments, as a result of the STU public agreement of rehabilitation and regeneration. Furthermore, in the STU, company assets could not be ordinarily spent for settling obligations towards creditors. In accordance with the "public nature" of the procedural steps that identified the assets and updated the PRG masterplan, the assets remain permanently linked with rehabilitation and regeneration planning purposes (Macchiarulo, 2015).

In 2014, after the bankruptcy judgement, the National Government provided a new emergency tool for brownfield rehabilitation and urban regeneration in Bagnoli, designed on PRRI model. Art. 33 of the Legislative Decree No. 133/2014 (updated several times, and integrated by Prime Ministerial Decree 15 October 2015) provides a specific law-measure ("legge-provvedimento", "Maßnamengesetz") on the environmental rehabilitation and the urban regeneration of the Bagnoli site.

First of all, Art. 33 states that the Bagnoli site is "of national interest" and clarifies that all paragraphs shall provide rules for the rehabilitation and regeneration of the Bagnoli site, stated "of general interest" in a short time, notwithstanding articles 252 and 252bis of the Environmental Code. Primary objectives are to ensure the programming, implementation, and management of environmental remediation and urban regeneration interventions in a short time. By mentioning the principles of subsidiarity and adequacy, the law authorises the State to complete the route by appointing an extraordinary Government Commissioner and thus safeguarding the local authorities' participation in land-use governance. Two entities, the Government Commissioner and the national in-house company InvitaliaSpA (called as "implementing body"), shall manage the whole procedure, starting from the development of the brownfield rehabilitation and urban regeneration planning. The brownfield rehabilitation and urban regeneration planning is discussed and approved in an agency meeting promoted by the Government Commissioner (that shall promote also the requested SEA and EIA), in which the regional and local authorities shall take part, in common with all other public authorities involved. After the agency meetings, the Government Commissioner shall adopt the brownfield rehabilitation and urban regeneration planning. The National Government shall adopt the brownfield rehabilitation and urban regeneration planning if the agency meeting fails. The programme approved shall replace all permits, licensees, orders, agreements, and opinions according to the current urban planning legal framework. It also constitutes an automatic update of the city masterplan and takes on the role of a CPO scheme. A Prime Ministerial Decree shall transfer the ownership of assets from BagnoliFuturaSpA (involved in bankruptcy proceeding) to InvitaliaSpA. InvitaliaSpA shall refund BagnoliFuturaSpA by means of financial instruments within 15 years. InvitaliaSpA shall handle the operational phase of rehabilitation and urban regeneration, under the control of the Government Commissioner and under the supervision of the "control room" established at the Prime Minister Office, which shall involve the regional and local authorities.

The new legislative action has generated litigation between national and local government, which has led to the judgements of the Administrative Regional Court (No. 1471/2016) and, in May 2017, of the Supreme Administrative Court (No. 2407/2017). The Supreme Administrative Court stated that the use of a specific law-measure in this case was legitimate and proportionate, due to the environmental emergency. It may be stressed that the CJEU pointed out in the judgement *Deutsche UmwelthilfeV* (Case C-515/11, *Deutsche UmwelthilfeV* v. *Bundesrepublik Deutschland*, 2013) that the feasibility of specific laws-measure should be restricted when it comes to environmental proceedings in the light of the Aarhus Convention regarding access to information, public participation in decision-making, and access to justice in environmental matters (Tinto, 2013).

Instead, the Supreme Administrative Court stated that the rules established with regard to the transfer of assets from BagnoliFuturaSpA to InvitaliaSpA should be understood as an unusual CPO scheme and may be in breach of the Constitution principles on CPO. Furthermore, the tools provided to involve regional and local authorities in the procedure may be in breach of the Constitution principles of subsidiarity and loyal cooperation. For both these profiles, the Supreme Administrative Court proposed a review of constitutionality before the Italian Constitutional Court.

## Conclusions

The gradual implementation of new rules, proceedings, and best practices of urban regeneration and the innovations in the actual national and regional legal framework on urban planning may lead in Italy to the emergence of a new 'law of cities', outlined by some scholars as the future urban planning law (Frug, 1980). Auby (2013) underlines that in the French (but we may also extend the scope to the Italian) legal approach, the several parts that constitute 'the legal functioning of cities' are "apprehended in a fragmented way, they are left to various categories of law—law on property, law on public contracts, law on local government, law on local public services, and so on—although one piece has tended to become dominant: planning law, or land use law". The "law of cities" may be understood as the law applicable to the "various essential dimensions of cities functioning: public and private spaces, infrastructure, land occupation, local economic development, local public services, local government, and so on". The "law of cities" approach shows that often local government powers and competencies do not fit with the real problems of contemporary urban bodies. The metropolitan government is often designed as a complex "multilevel governance" in a subsidiary organisation of public powers, in which governing constantly requires the cooperation of several centres of administrative decision, which share the duties of the involvement of stakeholders (citizens, resident foreigners, enterprises) in the decision-making process and in the organisation of public services in PPP (Giglioni, 2016).

The articles in the new metropolitan statutes, in the new regional laws on metropolitan functions, the metropolitan strategic plans (Art. 44, Law No. 56/2014) are the first field in which we analyse the harmonisation of urban regeneration, rehabilitation of polluted sites, development policies and social policies (in which the integration of migrant policies is included). Based on these considerations, we agree with scholars who suggest that policies and tools of "metropolitan autonomy" may be the future core of the new 'law of cities' and may redesign the urban regeneration planning to qualify it as general and strategic, reversing the relationship with the PRG and differentiating it from PRU and PRUSST specific planning (Dipace, 2014).

Furthermore, it must be stressed that the rethinking of urban regeneration legal framework is still compressed by the national legal framework on rehabilitation of polluted sites. In these fields of sectoral policies, we could often underline that the Italian Constitutional Court admits specific acts of legislation (the so called "leggi-provvedimento") in contrast to the CJEU that provided alternative routes in urban regeneration. The sectoral legislation often admits in these fields the subsidiary role of National Government based on "strategic national interest". In many cases, national specific acts of legislation are mixed with national special administrative proceedings, as it is happening in the case of the rehabilitation of the polluted area of "Bagnoli". It is clear that the route to update the current Italian legal framework on urban regeneration to the development trends proposed in the EU law still requires the resolution of very relevant legal issues.

The case of Turin shows, on the contrary, how the enhancement of cultural diversity, achieved by the strategic involvement of immigrants in productive activities and in the city's political life, can promote the economic and social regeneration of severely degraded areas. The adoption of effective integration policies and the wider opening of public decision-making processes to non-institutional actors can stimulate local economic development and promote social cohesion within the interested areas in certain contexts.

## Notes

1. The theory of path dependence, originally formulated by Arthur (1989) to explain the evolution of technology in modern economies, is now used by economic geographers (Martin and Sunley, 2006; Martin, 2010) to describe the dynamics of institutional change, assuming that the future behaviour of institutions is significantly influenced by their past behaviour. This theory, therefore, largely excludes

radical changes, only admitting incremental or marginal transformations with respect to the original 'institutional matrix'.
2. A number of different factors, such as the growing internationalisation of the economy and the aging of the population, have today revived the debate on sustainability and even on the legitimacy of welfare systems (Koch and Mont, 2016; Vouvaki and Xepapadeas, 2008; Esping-Andersen, 2006; Hediger, 2000).
3. See Sacchi and Viazzo (2003).

# References

Alesina, A., and F. Giavazzi. 2015. "Immigrati. La lezione americana." *Corriere della Sera*, 13 September. Accessed from www.corriere.it/editoriali/15_settembre_13/immigrati-lezione-americana-editoriale-dabcf5ac-59d5-11e5-b420-c9ba68e5c126.shtml.

Alesina, A., and E. La Ferrara. 2005. "Ethnic Diversity and Economic Performance." *Journal of Economic Literature*, 43: 762–800.

ANCI (National Association of Italian Municipalities), The European House Ambrosetti, IntesaSanpaolo. 2016. *White Paper: Metropolitan Cities—The Recovery Starts Here*. Firenze: ANCI.

Arthur, B. W. 1989. "Competing Technologies, Increasing Returns, and Lock-in by Historical Events." *The Economic Journal*, 99: 116–131.

Auby, J. F. 2013. "Droit de la Ville. An Introduction." *Italian Journal of Public Law*, 2: 302–306.

Berube, A., and N. Holmes. 2016. *City and Metropolitan Inequality on the Rise, Driven by Declining Incomes*. Washington: Brookings Institution.

Biondi Dal Monte, F. 2013. *Dai diritti sociali alla cittadinanza: La condizione giuridica dello straniero tra ordinamento italiano e prospettive sovranazionali*. Turin: Giappichelli Editore.

Cento Bull, A. 2005. "Democratic Renewal, Urban Planning and Civil Society: The Regeneration of Bagnoli, Naples." *South European Society and Politics*, 10(3): 391–410.

Collier, P. 2013. *Exodus: How Migration Is Changing Our World*. Oxford: Oxford University Press.

Damonte, R. 2001."Programmi di riqualificazione urbana e di sviluppo sostenibile del territorio (PRUSST) di cui al d.m. 8 ottobre 1998, n. 1169." *Rivista giuridica dell'edilizia*, 2(2): 33–41.

De Lucia, L. 2016. "Il contenimento del consumo di suolo e il futuro della pianificazione urbanistica e territoriale." In *A 150 anni dall'unificazione amministrativa italiana. La coesione politico-territoriale: vol. II*, edited by L. Ferrara, D. Sorace, G. De Giorgi Cezzi, and P. L. Portaluri, 299–318. Firenze: Firenze University Press.

Didiot, M. 2013. "Les barrières frontalières: archaïsmes inadaptés ou renforts du pouvoir étatique?" *L'Espace Politique. Revue en ligne de géographie politique et de géopolitique*, 20: 2013-2. Accessed from https://espacepolitique.revues.org/2626.

Dipace, R. 2014. "La rigenerazione urbana tra programmazione e pianificazione." *Rivistagiuridicadell'edilizia*, 5(2): 237–260.

Esping-Andersen, G. 2006."A Welfare State for the Twenty-first Century." *The Welfare State Reader*, 434–454.

Frascani, P. 2017. *Napoli: Viaggio nella città reale*. Bari-Roma: Laterza.

Frug, J. 1980. "The City as a Legal Concept." *Harvard Law Review*, 93: 1059–1154.

Giglioni, F. 2016."I regolamenti comunali per la gestione dei beni comuni urbani come laboratorio per un nuovo diritto delle città." *Munus*, 2: 271–314.

Grosso, E. 2010. "I doveri costituzionali." In *Lo statuto costituzionale del cittadino – Atti del XXIV Convegno annuale*, edited by AIC, 229–280. Napoli: Jovene.

Hediger, W. 2000. "Sustainable Development and Social Welfare." *Ecological Economics*, 32: 481–492.

Kemeny, T. 2013.*Immigrant Diversity and Economic Development in Cities: A Critical Review*. London: London School of Economics and Political Science, LSE Library.

Koch, M., and O. Mont, eds. 2016. *Sustainability and the Political Economy of Welfare*. London and New York: Routledge.

Macchiarulo, L. 2015. "Il fallimento di una società pubblica di trasformazione urbana: il caso "Bagnolifutura."*Il Dirittofallimentare e dellesocietàcommerciali*, 2(2): 328–349.

Maloutas, T. 2009. "Urban Outcasts: A Contextualised Outlook on Advanced Marginality." *International Journal of Urban and Regional Research*, 33: 828–834.

Martin, R. 2010. "Roepke Lecture in Economic Geography—Rethinking Regional Path Dependence: Beyond Lock-in to Evolution." *Economic Geography*, 86(1): 1–27.

Martin, R., and P. Sunley. 2006. "Path Dependence and Regional Economic Evolution." *Journal of EconomicGeography*, 6: 395–437.

Marzuoli, C. 2015. "Il piano strategico metropolitano: note introduttive." *Osservatorio sulle fonti*, 2: 1–6.

Palma, G. 1971. *Beni di interesse pubblico e contenuto della proprietà*. Napoli: Jovene.

Passalacqua, M. 2010. "La società di trasformazione urbana quale strumento di valorizzazione territoriale." *Urbanistica e appalti*,2: 133–143.

Pulvirenti, M. G. 2015. "La riconversione dei siti produttivi inquinati." *Rivistagiuri dicadell'edilizia*, 5(2): 251–274.

Putnam, R. D. 2007. "E pluribus unum: Diversity and Community in the Twenty-first Century the 2006 Johan Skytte Prize Lecture." *Scandinavian Politica lStudies*, 30(2): 137–174.

Ronchetti, L. 2012. "I diritti di cittadinanza degli immigrati e il ruolo delle regioni." In *I diritti di cittadinanza dei migranti. Il ruolo delle regioni*, edited by L. Ronchetti, 29–54. Milano: Giuffré.

Sacchi, P., and P. P. Viazzo, eds. 2003. *Più di un sud: studi antropologici sull'immigrazione a Torino*, Vol. 9. Milan: Franco Angeli.

Sassen, S. 2014. *Expulsions*. Cambridge: Harvard University Press.

Simonati, A. 2011. "The Urban Plans of Italian Towns." *Iuspublicum Network*: 1–18. Accessed from www.ius-publicum.com/repository/uploads/22_02_2012_12_23_SIMONATI_EN.pdf.

Tinto, V. 2013. "Legge provvedimento e strumenti di tutela derivanti dal diritto dell'Unione Europea." *Diritto del commerciointernazionale*, 1: 287–292.

Vouvaki, D., and A. Xepapadeas. 2008. "Changes in Social Welfare and Sustainability: Theoretical Issues and Empirical Evidence." *Ecological Economics*, 67: 473–484.

Wacquant, L. 2008. *Urban Outcasts: A Comparative Sociology of Advanced Marginality*. Cambridge: Polity Press.

Wayne, A.C. 2007. "Introduction: Does Border Enforcement Deter Unauthorized Immigration?" In *Impacts of Border Enforcement on Mexican Migration: The View From Sending Communities*, edited by A. C. Wayne and J. M. Lewis, Vol. 3, 1–15. San Diego CA: La Jolla, Center for comparative immigration studies, University of California.

# 12 Spatial Injustice and Social Capital

## The Wall Between East Jerusalem and the West Bank

*Safa H. Dhaher*

## Introduction

Close family ties play a crucial role in coping with political instability, the Israeli occupation, and the worsening of socio-economic conditions in the Occupied Palestinian Territories (OPT). Social capital provides a safety net for improving people's chances in their day-to-day survival efforts, especially after Israel had constructed a Wall to separate Israel and East Jerusalem from the West Bank. The current geopolitical context of the OPT is very complex due to the different sources of political hegemony over its components. The aim of the present chapter is to examine the role of social capital in these areas after the Wall was built and what this implies for social regeneration.

Section two presents the political events that had determined these differences over time starting from the occupation in 1967, the Oslo Accords in 1993 up to the construction of the Separation Wall that Israel started to build in 2002. Section three focuses on the Wall in East Jerusalem, explaining how and why it separates Palestinians, those who are considered to be of the West Bank, from those of East Jerusalem, highlighting the complexity on both sides of the Wall. Moreover, the section discusses the main aim behind the comprehensive explicit policies by the state authorities of Israel, which is to change the demographic balance in favour of the Israeli population in the city of Jerusalem. These policies cover areas like the "Permanent Resident" status, the allocation of the municipality budget, restrictions on building new houses, shortages in service delivery, and, finally, restrictions on free movement. The analysis highlights the Israeli authorities' comprehensive and specific policies for the Palestinian neighbourhoods starting from the Old City, the centre of East Jerusalem, and moving towards the three half rings around it: the first half ring covers the communities adjacent to the historic wall of the Old City, such as al-Musrara and Silwan; the second half ring covers the suburbs that are inside the municipality boundaries; and the third is outside these boundaries, which became separated from the centre by the Separation Wall. The analysis explains how the Wall designs a border leaving outside two Palestinian neighbourhoods that are part of East Jerusalem.

*Figure 12.1* The Separation Wall Between al-'Eizariyah (West Bank) and the Mount of Olives (East Jerusalem), 2016

Section four tackles the role of social capital in coping with this spatial injustice whether inside or outside the Wall, highlighting the enormous challenges which the suburbs in the West Bank areas are facing. The imprisonment inside the Wall had enforced social capital in all its manifestations at the individual, community, and the governmental levels in order to overcome problems related to education and health care services and the problem of the security vacuum in these areas due to their classification as Area B according to the Oslo Accords of 1993. For example, security was maintained by reinforcing the tribal law. The section also highlights the negative externalities of the strong bonding social capital, in addition to bridging and linking social capital. The conclusion summarises the political reality and highlights the capacity of social capital to sooth problems in that specific area. However, it is emphasised that without a concrete political solution the situation will move from bad to worse.

## Historical Background

Jerusalem is one of the most controversial issues in the Israel-Palestine conflict. It is holy for the three monotheistic religions; Judaism, Christianity, and Islam, triggering the exceptionally impulsive politics of the city (Hever, 2007). Therefore, and under the partition plan of 1947 of the United Nations General Assembly Resolution 181 (United Nations, 1947), Jerusalem was to be internationalised as a *corpus separatum*—a separated body—and placed under a special international regime to be administered by the United Nations Trusteeship Council (CCPRJ, 2011, 7). However, the fate of Jerusalem was determined through military subjugation (Derejko, 2009). As a result of the 1948 war that erupted after the creation of the state of Israel on the major part of Historic Palestine, Jerusalem was divided. The west side came under the control of Israel, while the East, like the rest of the West Bank, was under the control of Jordan. Nineteen years later, as a result of the 1967 War, Israel occupied the West Bank, including the other half of the city, as well as other areas.[1] The occupied territories fall under the Israeli military administration except for the former Jordanian municipality of

East Jerusalem and an additional 64 square km that were annexed directly to Israel, meaning that it came under the authority of the Israeli municipality of West Jerusalem (Hever, 2007). However, the international community has never recognised the annexation. It is noteworthy that the residents of East Jerusalem were not granted equal Israeli citizenship (Kimhi, 2006). Instead, "Permanent Resident" status (Blue ID) was given to the Palestinian Jerusalemites with some rights; it allowed them to move freely in Israel, enjoy health insurance and social welfare benefits (B'Tselem, 2006). However, this "Permanent Resident" status can be revoked if a Jerusalemite lives outside the municipality boundaries or leaves the city to live in another country for seven years or more (B'Tselem, 2009). For many observers, the new municipal boundaries were dictated by both strategic and demographic considerations in order to allow future expansion of the new Jewish communities (12 settlements) in the open space around the city (Allegra, 2012). The de facto annexation of East Jerusalem was formalised in 1980 when the Knesset (Israeli Parliament) enacted the 'Basic Law', which stated that 'Jerusalem, complete and united, is the capital of Israel'.

The Palestinians living in the West Bank and Gaza were given an Orange Colour ID without the rights that were given to the Jerusalemites; they needed permits to be able to enter Israel, including East Jerusalem, either for work, shopping, or entertainment. The Orange ID was replaced by a Green Colour ID after the creation of the Palestinian Authority in 1994. During the period from the occupation in 1967 till the Oslo Accords of 1993, Israel had taken control of hundreds of thousands of dunams[2] throughout the West Bank, with the objective of establishing settlements and providing reserves of land for their expansion. In doing so, and by using different methods, Israel practically has seized control of around 50% of the West Bank, excluding East Jerusalem (B'Tselem, 2002; 2012). Although these settlements are illegal according to the International Law (B'Tselem, 2002), they were taken into consideration when drafting the political agreements, as will be explained later in this section. Following the Oslo Accords, the West Bank, excluding the Jewish settlements and Israeli military locations, was supposed to be transferred to the Palestinians in phases under the arrangement of redeployment. To facilitate this process, the West Bank was divided into three areas: Area A with a full civil and security Palestinian control; Area B with a Palestinian civil control and joint Israeli-Palestinian security control; and Area C with a full Israeli civil and security control. This categorisation was built on the basis of Palestinian population density; all Palestinian cities with high population density were classified as Area A and were given to the Palestinian Authority with full civil and security control, such as Ramallah and Nablus, while most of the suburbs of these cities were categorised as Area B, with less authority for the Palestinians. The rest of the West Bank, which was mostly unpopulated and considered to be a natural reservoir for future Palestinian urban expansion, were classified as Area C with full Israeli control.[3]

The distribution of the areas was as follows. At the beginning of the establishment of the Palestinian National Authority (PNA) in 1994, Area A covered 3%, Area B covered 24%, and Area C covered 73% of the West Bank. This distribution was adjusted after many other agreements, so in the year 2000, Area A covered 18%, Area B covered 22%, while Area C covered 60% of the West Bank.[4] However, the implementation of the process came to a halt midway, and the West Bank has since remained divided into these three administrative areas (Jamal, 2007). Practically, the Palestinian Authority has full control only over areas that were classified as A, while Israel has full control over areas that were classified as C, which consist of the major part of the West Bank. As viewed in Figure 12.2, control over areas classified as B is divided between the PNA and Israel; the PNA is responsible for civil administration, that is, it delivers services such as health and education, among others,[5] while Israel controls security, that is, areas classified as B are not allowed to have Palestinian Police Forces. This classification of A, B, and C was supposed to be temporary. The plan was that Area C would be gradually transferred to Area B; then Area B was to become Area A. This process was supposed to be completed within 18 months until all the West Bank, except for Israeli military bases and settlements, would become Area A with full Palestinian control by the end of 1999. By then, a permanent agreement, including the status on East Jerusalem, would have also been reached (Shlaim, 2005). Now, and despite the fact that the Oslo Accords failed, the West Bank is still divided into these three areas and with no jurisdiction for the PNA over East Jerusalem. The holistic picture of the West Bank is that Areas A and B are scattered in the bigger Area C that is under the full Israeli control. This means that Israel controls the roads between the Palestinian cities and villages in the West Bank. For the Gaza Strip, and although Israel had withdrawn from it in 2005, the territory has been under Israeli siege since then. Israel maintains the control of Gaza Strip's borders and coastal territory; vital needs are mainly imported from Israel under strict conditions. Hence, the overarching logic of the Oslo Accords is what Gordon (2008, 35) has highlighted: "Israel transferred all responsibilities relating to the management of the population to the Palestinians themselves while preserving control of Palestinian space". Indeed, these areas, subject to different authorisations, developed into a complex "zone system" that fragmented the West Bank, in addition to the total separation from East Jerusalem, the supposed "Palestinian Capital".

Direct control over the Palestinian space became more sophisticated since the outbreak of the Second Intifada,[6] which erupted in 2000 as a response to the failure of the Oslo Accords. The apparatus of control includes a permit system, restricted roads, checkpoints, and roadblocks subjecting all people and vehicles to security inspection. In April 2002, a big shift occurred: the Israeli government decided to construct a Wall "to hinder, disrupt, and prevent the penetration of terrorist activity from Judea and Samaria[7] into

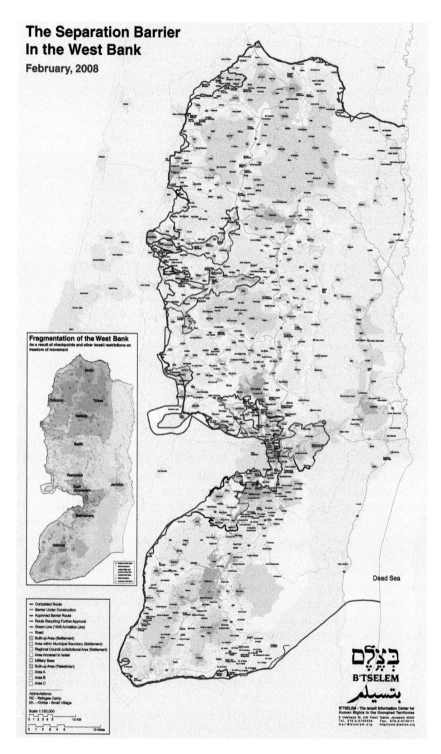

*Figure 12.2* The Separation Barrier in the West Bank (February 2008)

Israel".[8] This was the Israeli official declaration; "marking a border" is the human rights organisations view, so security was used as an excuse. Separation has been achieved via a six- to eight-metre-high concrete Wall in urban areas in general and electronic fence in some rural areas. The Wall has a convoluted route; this means it is longer than the border line itself (B'Tselem, 2012). In fact, it is double the length of the Green Line,[9] and it does not follow the pre-1967 boundaries. Thus, 85% of the Wall is located within the West Bank, snatching more land for Israel, especially those areas where the illegal Israeli settlements are located (Bimkom and B'Tselem, 2005). The length of the Wall, including parts that have already been built, are still under construction, or in planning, is 709 kilometres, fragmenting the West Bank into social and economic enclaves that are apart from each other (World Bank, 2010). Thirty-eight percent of the West Bank's populations (around 875,000 people) are being directly and undesirably affected by the Wall; over a quarter of them live in the East Jerusalem area (Müller, 2004; UN-OCHA, 2006; Aronson, 2008). At least 12% of the Palestinians are now living in a closed military zone, such as those of the Jordan Valley region, or encircled by the Wall, such as the city of Qalqilya, or isolated between the Wall and the Green Line (Grassroots Palestine, 2010).[10]

## The Wall in East Jerusalem

Prior to 1967, East Jerusalem functioned as the metropolitan hub for the West Bank; Palestinians could move freely between East Jerusalem and the surrounding areas. Strong socio-economic and cultural bonds extended throughout the entire West Bank. No obstacles blocked the movement of the Palestinian population, the trade of goods, or social interactions (B'Tselem, 2006). Since the first Intifada (1987), Israel started to impose restrictions on free movement from and to East Jerusalem; however, the Wall, as a physical barrier, started to be implemented in 2002. The separation was achieved by a wall that was approximately 90 kilometres long (Thawaba, 2011), with 12 official gates (checkpoints), only four of which are open to Palestinians.[11] Stage A of the six- to eight-meter-high concrete Wall was approved in June 2002. It includes two sections: one north of Jerusalem that extends from the Ofer Army Base in the west to the Qalandiya Checkpoint in the east; and the other section south of Jerusalem that runs from the Tunnels Road in the west to Beit Sahour in the east. The two sections were completed in July 2003, with a length of about 20 km for both (B'Tselem, 2011). A few months later, the "Jerusalem Envelope" plan was also approved to surround East Jerusalem with walls from the south, east, and the north (Hever, 2007).

The Wall in East Jerusalem cuts through a developed urban area, profoundly affecting the lives of schoolchildren, workers, families, and whole communities on a daily basis. The Wall had cut off the main, relatively

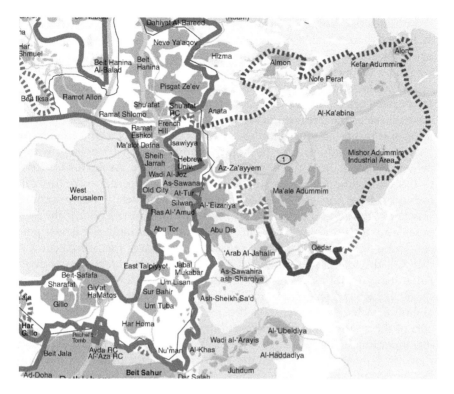

*Figure 12.3* The Separation Barrier in East Jerusalem

*Figure 12.4* The Section of the Wall in East Jerusalem that Separates Abu Dis on
One Side (West Bank) and Silwan (East Jerusalem) on the Other Side

short, roads that used to connect the East Jerusalem suburbs with the cities of Ramallah and Bethlehem through East Jerusalem. Now the long alternative bypass roads that Israel has constructed to these cities are much longer, so the cost and time of commuting was elevated. The disruption of the public transportation system, which connected these suburbs with their centre before the Wall, has also led to a rise in the number of private cars, as well as the diffusion of illegal unlicensed vehicles as a substitute for internal transportation within these areas. The Wall has restricted entry to East Jerusalem only to Blue ID holders and the Green ID holders with a permit, who can cross the border through the Wall's checkpoints.[12] Prior to the Wall, although (Green ID) holders without a permit were formally forbidden from entering Israel including East Jerusalem,[13] this restriction was not enforced as a general rule. However, the construction of the Wall poses now such restrictions (Amir, 2011). On the ground, the Israeli policies had divided the space many years ago, but it was the construction of the Wall that confirmed the division and reduced the interaction between Palestinians on both sides of the Wall to its minimum level. In other words, the Wall even redirected the social relations map. The ID categorisation's ability of inclusion or exclusion became visible, and the Wall became the core of the decision-making process of the residents on both of sides, affecting important decisions such as where to live, work, or study, and even who to marry (Dhaher, 2016). Since the Wall was built, the pattern of marriage has witnessed a fundamental change: people now tend to marry someone who has been issued the same ID to avoid a series of difficulties, such as family reunification activities and the registration of their children in the future (Ibid).

## The Special Injustice: The Three Rings

According to the Palestinian Central Bureau of Statistics, Palestinians in the Jerusalem metropolitan area are divided in two along the annexation line, regardless of the type of identification cards they obtain (Hever, 2007). The Palestinian population is estimated to be 240,000 inhabitants in the annexed area, and another 150,000 in the outlying communities which were not annexed to Israel (Ibid). Although there are differences in the civil status between the annexed East Jerusalem (Israel) and its West Bank suburbs, the distinction between neighbourhoods in and out of East Jerusalem was purely artificial. The social fabric of the residents did not correspond to this distinction. Often, members of the same family have different civil statuses: some hold Israeli "Permanent Resident" status (Blue ID), and others have a West Bank identification card (Green ID). These differences had influenced entitlement to services and other benefits in the past, but it had not split families apart (Amir, 2011).

Many political and social studies, as well as human and civil rights organisations reports, which focus on different bio-political conditions of the Palestinian people in East Jerusalem (Amir, 2011), "portray the unmistakable and consistent policies of negligence, discrimination and expropriation exercised by the Jerusalem municipality and the different Israeli governmental agencies" (Ibid, 770). The primary goal of Israeli authorities, since the annexation of East Jerusalem in 1967, has been to create demographic and geographic conditions that will prevent any future withdrawal from East Jerusalem. Indeed, the advisor on Arab Affairs to the former Israeli Mayor of Jerusalem, Amir Cheshin, declared that "Israel's leaders [. . .] adopted two basic principles in their rule of East Jerusalem. The first was to rapidly increase the Jewish population in East Jerusalem. The second was to hinder growth of the Arab population and to force Arab residents to make their homes elsewhere" (Cheshin et al., 1999, 10). Several steps have been implemented to achieve this goal, starting from the isolation of East Jerusalem from the rest of the West Bank, to land appropriation, to the policies that discriminate against the Palestinians in many aspects, especially in planning schemes and budget allocation.[14] Between 1968 and 1973, Israel has constructed 12 Jewish neighbourhoods[15] within the new municipal borders, populated by some 192,000 people (B'Tselem, 2006), while limiting and restricting the Palestinian neighbourhoods' growth to already built-up areas. Housing policy and urban planning have been used in a biased way to deploy and limit Palestinian demography and urban geography in East Jerusalem (Bollens, 2000). One-third of the annexed area was confiscated from Palestinian landlords to build Jewish settlements (B'Tselem, 2006), while Palestinians are only allowed to build in 13% of their city, often in current Palestinian localities. And, most likely, they will not acquire a building license to enlarge their homes and solve the shortage in housing. This has motivated many to build without license and live in anxiety of the possibility that their home will be demolished sometime in the future (UN-OCHA, 2009). Others moved to the outskirts, where the cost of housing is cheaper and obtaining a building license is easier (Allegra, 2011), even at the risk of losing their "Permanent Resident" status (Blue ID), given the regulations of Israeli authorities which could revoke the permanent residency status of those for whom Jerusalem ceases to be their "Centre of Life".

Israel made enormous and constant efforts to create a "reverse magnet" for the Jerusalemites (Hever, 2007). This was reached through two parallel actions: firstly, by providing incentives to those who wanted to leave, and, secondly, by creating many difficulties to those who wanted to stay and live there (Kimhi, 2006). Most of the policies of the Israeli state authorities were set to force the Jerusalemites to leave the city are comprehensive. However, there are also specific policies in some neighbourhoods, depending on their geopolitical location. To explain this diversity in policies, it would be helpful to visualise East Jerusalem as a half circle with the Old City in its centre, surrounded by half rings of neighbourhoods, each of which is characterised by specific problems. Generally, Israeli policies were built upon the concept of discrimination, which covers budget allocation and planning schemes between its residents, Palestinians and Israelis. Starting from the centre point, the Old City of East Jerusalem, the Muslim Quarter suffers from lack of maintenance, and restoration, while old private and public buildings and roads are always in need of continuous maintenance to be suitable for the people's use. And while Israel has spent annually almost half a million dollars on restoration work in the Jewish Quarter since the occupation, less than one-third of that amount was delegated to the Muslim Quarter of the City (Khatib, 1993, Chapter III-Part 1).

In the first half ring around the Old City, Palestinian neighbourhoods such as Musrara, Silwan, Mount Scopus, Wadi Al-Joz, and Sheikh Jarrah, in addition to communities inside the Old City,[16] were targeted by right-wing groups to create Jewish settlements based on ownership claims. Around 180 Palestinian families who live in those neighbourhoods have eviction cases filed against them; therefore, 818 Palestinians are at risk of displacement, including around 370 children.[17] All the Palestinian neighbourhoods and suburbs within the municipality boundaries are suffering from poor infrastructure and lack of municipal services, in shocking contrast to the well-maintained Jewish settlements around them. Israeli policies were set to restrict the Palestinians' growth to already built-up areas, while expanding the administrative boundaries of the settlements built on their land. It is almost impossible for Palestinian residents of East Jerusalem to obtain building permits, and "as families grow and children marry, there is an even greater demand on the limited housing available" (Dhaher, 2014, 118). Therefore, many moved to the suburbs, while others resorted to the only chance left for them, which was to build illegally, despite risks of having their home demolished or paying substantial fines (Paq, 2015). The second half ring around the Old City, which, among others, includes Al-Tur, Silwan, Jabal al-Mukaber, and Al-Issawiya, and constitutes land that was to be used for Palestinians' natural growth, was confiscated to build Jewish settlements and to construct the Separation Wall. As a result, there was no land left to expand horizontally, so the residents had to expand vertically. If there is no building permit, authorities can demolish the house for a floor or an apartment in a high-rise building by taking down the walls between rooms, or destroying and blocking the bathroom and kitchen. Another method used by authorities is pouring cement through the windows till the rooms are fully blocked. Israeli authorities usually ask the owner to demolish his own apartment within a fixed deadline, and if the job is not accomplished by the fixed date, they will proceed with the operation and then send the owner the invoice of the exact cost that he must pay them.[18] There are approximately 20,000 houses that do not have a building permit in East Jerusalem. In 2014, 98 structures were demolished, and 208 residents have been uprooted from their homes (ACRI, 2015). Demolishing the house is not the only problem, though. A house that was built without a permit cannot be connected to the official water and sewage network, according to Israeli law. Thus, thousands of residents living in these houses are obliged either to plagiarise connections or purchase water tanks and operate pumps. They usually dig cesspits in their own yard to solve the sewage problem, which creates an unhealthy environment and contributes to the spread of epidemics and diseases (Ibid).

Some of these suburbs in the second half ring around the Old City of Jerusalem were excluded from services provided by the municipality of Jerusalem when the Separation Wall route was determined, although they remained within Jerusalem boundaries. This is true for areas such as Kafr A'keb, Shua'fat refugee camp, and Dahyet al-Salam, which ended up inside the Separation Wall, so the municipality delivers public services only through subcontractors with the least supervision. These conditions led to extremely poor infrastructure; inadequate school buildings, health centres, streets, and sidewalks; and insufficient garbage collection (Dhaher, 2017). These areas also suffer from lack of urban planning. Therefore, many high-rise buildings that are poorly designed are relatively cheap, attracting those who are looking for cheap housing inside the municipality boundaries. They were constructed with the minimum safety qualifications and are often inhabited while they are still under construction to fulfil the growing need for housing. The unfinished parts are usually the entrance and the surroundings, which will be completed at a later stage. In reality, it might take years before the building is completely finished. The problem is that chaos is governing the general scene and becoming acceptable. This enforces an attitude of neglect towards the common space. Many analysts unfortunately attributed this attitude to the Palestinian culture, though it's a natural consequence of the absence of urban planning and adequate service delivery (Ibid). Neglect and discriminating policies enforce the "neighbourhood effect" in these areas, which implies that some behavioural, attitudinal, or psychological features of neighbourhoods affect their residents (Friedrichs et al., 2003). They are producing undesirable social problems, such as displacement, impoverishment, and social fragmentation. In addition to all of that, the residents of these areas have to cross the checkpoint on their way to Jerusalem (outside the Wall) for work, school, or any other activity. The negative psychological impact, especially on schoolchildren, is huge, as they are exposed to security inspections on a daily basis, apart from the time wasted at checkpoints. And although these areas were considered within the Jerusalem municipality boundaries, the Jerusalemites who live there started to doubt this fact after the Wall. Many believe that Israel excluded these areas for a territorial swap with Ma'ale Adummim, the Israeli settlement that is located outside the municipal boundaries of Jerusalem, in future negotiations with the Palestinian Authority when the position on East Jerusalem will be discussed.[19]

The third half ring consists of the East Jerusalem West Bank suburbs that were not annexed to Israel and are now separated from East Jerusalem by the Separation Wall. Areas such as al-'Eizariyah, Abu Dis, al-Sawahra, al Ram, and Anata have been severely affected: the Separation Wall has completely isolated them and prevents their residents from entering East Jerusalem, except those who have the Israeli identity card (Blue ID) or a Palestinian identity card (Green ID) with a permit only through controlled entrances (checkpoints). It never occurred to the residents of these areas that a physical separation could take place, even though Israel had previously declared the annexation of East Jerusalem. As long as the city was open, the people were not aware of the consequences (Yousef, 2011). Hence, they depended on East Jerusalem in almost all aspects of life, such as education, health care, shopping, entertainment, and other social activities. The separation affected the locals and those Jerusalemites, who moved out of the city, running from the housing crises in the past to settle down in these suburbs. The immediate impact of the Wall was the rise in the unemployment rate. Most of the residents who used to work in Jerusalem lost their jobs after the Wall because Israeli authorities did not grant them a "work permit". The health and education sectors were also the first to be affected. The hospitals in East Jerusalem, which were within walking distance, became out of reach, while the small clinics that were placed in these areas could not meet the needs of their residents. Pregnant women and patients requiring advanced medical care have to be treated by the next nearest municipal hospitals in the West Bank, usually in Jericho (half an hour drive), or Bethlehem (an hour drive), or Ramallah (an hour and a half drive). Similarly, in education, the schools in Jerusalem became out of reach, especially for students over the age of 16 who needed a permit to cross the checkpoint, while younger students changed schools to avoid security checks and the morning delays at the checkpoint. Although the Jerusalemites who live in these suburbs have the right to enter Jerusalem through the checkpoints, many of them moved back inside the municipality boundaries to avoid inspection and the long hours of waiting at the checkpoint and out of concern of losing their "Permanent Residency" status (Dhaher, 2017).

All East Jerusalem suburbs that were excluded and are considered part of the West Bank were classified according to the Oslo Accords as Area B. This means that they are under a Palestinian civil control and joint Israeli-Palestinian security control. However, there were different interpretations of the term security: for Israelis, it's their own security, not Palestinians' security. Israel interferes only when there is a threat to its own security, but not when it comes to the Palestinians' security (AbuZayyad,[20] October 20, 2016). Therefore, these areas are without National Security Forces (Palestinian Police). The Palestinian police that are allowed to be located only in Area A cannot move freely to Area B because they have first to coordinate with the Joint Security Coordination Office, which usually takes up to 48 hours to respond, and, of course, this is useless in case of emergency. In fact, the residents of these areas live with anarchism; they became a perfect place for outlaws and suffer from many social problems.

## Social Capital's Role in Coping with Spatial Injustice

Social capital was defined by Lin (1999, 35) as resources embedded in a social structure which are accessed and/or mobilised in purposive actions. From this perspective the Arab cultures, in general, and the Palestinian culture, in particular, enforce their social capital by strong family and extended family relations, and in order to maximise their assets. Thus they tend to increase their family members' numbers, especially males. The "preference for boys over girls was deep rooted because boys carried the family or tribal name, helped their fathers with their work and in their old age" (Aburish, 1991, 22); therefore, more male children means more men and more power in the future. However, the Arab culture is also rich with concepts like reciprocity, cooperation, and the power of unity between family members, and they are well represented in poetry, aphorism and everyday language. The social capital concept, especially in its bonding form, is close to the functions of the tribal law that promote solidarity between family and extended family members in general and during times of crisis in particular. However, it excludes women's roles, especially in solving social conflicts. Thus, and to avoid the argument regarding the similarities and differences between the concept of social capital and tribal law, the author refers to bonding social capital as the close family ties (strong ties) that play an important role in coping with the political turmoil and the Israeli occupation in the OPT. Social capital, in all its manifestations, whether bonding, bridging or linking forms provides a safety net, and it improves people's chances of day-to-day survival, especially after the construction of the Separation Wall. It is extremely important to highlight the fact that Israel annexed East Jerusalem, which is part of the Occupied Territories of 1967, and it came under Israeli jurisdiction. This means that different rules and different rights are implemented in an urban area that shares everything else. The Wall marked these differences and made them visible, creating a bold border between East Jerusalem and the West Bank. This physical shock that cut East Jerusalem from its West Bank suburbs forced the residents of the two territories to respond to all subsequent restrictions on a daily basis. These include restrictions on access to work, housing, health facilities, education, services, and family and social life. Those of East Jerusalem adapted to the new reality and reorganised their lives around the Wall. However, most of the Jerusalemites that live inside the Wall moved back, although they have the right to enter Jerusalem through the checkpoints. They chose to avoid passing through checkpoints inspection in addition to their concern over the possibility of losing their "Permanent Resident" status. This result, combined with restrictions on building in East Jerusalem, forced many to live in crowded, inhumane conditions with a growing feeling of discomfort. Many of those Jerusalemites are living with their relatives, sons, brothers, sisters or even with members of the extended family, mostly for economic reasons, because they cannot afford to buy or rent a house in East Jerusalem.

Others had to find other solutions, which disperse and waste their personal resources: for example, some had to have two houses, one in the suburbs and another house in East Jerusalem, in order to keep a legal presence in the city and thus keep their "Permanent Resident" status and businesses or other properties (UN-OCHA, 2009). The "Permanent Resident" status, unlike citizenship, is revocable (as explained below): if the Israeli Ministry of Interior discovers, by unexpected visits, that some residents are not actually living in the city and Jerusalem is not their "Centre of Life", their "Permanent Resident" status will be revoked, according to Israeli authority's regulation, and they will lose the set of rights that stem from it. Therefore, some families split themselves and live in both places (Dhaher, 2017).

The case is different for the Palestinians who live in the West Bank suburbs of East Jerusalem, inside the Wall. The majority holds a Green ID and has no choice but to stay inside the Wall; thus, they have normalised their existence with the Wall. They have accepted the fact that East Jerusalem is no longer the centre of their social and economic activities, and, with time, the Wall for them became invisible. Bridging and linking social capital are also at the heart of the means in confronting the hardships caused by the Separation Wall, such as its role in reserving security in the absence of law and order and in solving problems occurring because of the disruption of the education and health systems. Communities sought other solutions. The security vacuum was partially solved by reinforcing the traditional tribal justice law, and the Palestinian Authority had considered the role of the community leaders in parallel with the force of law to solve societal problems in these areas. For this purpose, the PNA reconstituted the "management of tribal affairs" to support the rule of law and the establishment of social peace.[21] The core of the traditional tribal justice law is the code of honour (mithaq al-sharaf) that is binding to all male members and ties them together. The Palestinian society, like other Mediterranean countries, shares the honour-shame social system, where members cannot easily violate this code because, by doing so, they dishonour themselves and their families (Ibid). The people are familiar with tribal justice in solving disputes and are particularly aware that its decisions are efficiently binding to all clan members. This is useful, especially in the absence of a functioning state that can provide public security (Robinson, 2008).

Due to the disruption of the education and health systems, linking social capital played an important role in soothing this problem. The Palestinian Ministry of Education had to provide the local schools in these areas with extra space (classes), teachers, and facilities, following the increase in demand after many students were denied entry to East Jerusalem. At the beginning, they solved the problem by absorbing more numbers of students in each class and by converting some activity spaces into class rooms. Later, they built extra classes in each school, in addition to new schools. For health care, it was not easy to overcome problems on the spot. However, in due course, professional individuals' initiatives, along with the Health Ministry's small clinics, mobilised to serve the community. The rise in people's awareness thereafter helped in soothing the problem. They became aware of the difficulties and the need for official medical referrals and special medical permits to be hospitalised in East Jerusalem's hospitals. Hence, they regularly follow up with the local clinics, which coordinate with the hospitals in East Jerusalem to get the medical referrals and permits on time. Women in labour, for example, will do all the bureaucratic procedures before the due date (WHO, 2013).

## Social Resilience, Negative Social Capital, and Local Development

Over time, since the construction of the Wall started in 2002, the general attitude of the population trapped inside the Wall has changed from complaining to adapting to the new socio-economic and political changes. According to many observers, these areas have quasi-recovered from the negative implications of their separation from the Centre. They have become self-sufficient regarding education and economic activities and partially in medical care as well, after being totally dependent on East Jerusalem in almost every aspect of life. Some of those who lost their jobs in East Jerusalem had established their own businesses that cover services and commerce, from mini-supermarkets, hardware, and furniture stores to private schools and medical centres (Dhaher, 2016). On the other side of the Wall, the streets of East Jerusalem are almost empty, they lost their customers from the suburbs. The Wall has totally isolated the city that once was overcrowded with its suburbs' daily visitors.

Although the previous section demonstrated the positive role of social capital in coping with such a complicated geopolitical situation, the consequences of social capital for local development are not always positive as argued by Trigilia (2001). Politics makes it "more difficult to distinguish under which conditions social capital can have a favourable impact for local development, instead of generating collusion, patronage, political dependence or even corruption and criminal economies" (Trigilia, 2008, 227). Indeed, in the Palestinian case, the hierarchical system that emerged when the Palestinian National Authority was created, "Yaser Arafat's time", favoured a system of vertical linkages between civil society organisations and the PNA (Jamal, 2007). These associations, in order to be recognised by the PNA and be able to work, were "likely to favour nepotisms and 'clientelism' between some associational leaders and public officers" as explained by Jamal (2007, 21). In this case, the civil society organisations that supported the PNA were treated differently than those who opposed it, and, thus, they enjoyed access to local resources, governmental protection, prestige, and legitimacy (Ibid).

After the Wall, there was vast economic recovery in certain areas related to all types of social capital. However, as Mr. Isam Faroon, the

*Figure 12.5* The Wall in East Jerusalem/Qalandia Checkpoint in March 2014

Mayor of al-'Eizariyah[22] points out, on the one hand, the political context was such that it had encouraged the diffusion of the informal economy. The fact that his town is in Area B in the middle and Area C is in the surroundings means that it is within the security vacuum area, so there are no Israeli or Palestinian Authority security forces. This attracts certain kinds of investments, turning the area more or less into what is known in economics as a 'free trade zone'. Therefore, tax evasion and criminal economies are present in these areas; the diffusion of arms trade, drugs, money laundering, and prostitution became notable. On the other hand, the complicity of the economic agreement of the Paris Protocol (1994) between the Palestinian Authority and Israel had determined certain Israeli channels for Palestinian economic activities. Therefore, local development in these areas, as a response to the separation from the centre, became limited to service provision and trade of everyday life necessities and was enforced by survival needs rather than an ideology of self-sufficiency or endogeneity. On the social level, and although the "tribal law" has helped in implementing security and solving disputes in the absence of law and order in Area B, it brought back some undesirable social norms such as gender inequality. On the political level, from a social capital perspective, the Wall had a negative impact on bridging social capital between Israelis and Palestinians. This type of bridging social capital had started to develop as a by-product of the economic activities between the two populations since the Israeli occupation in 1967. Now, not only the areas inside the Wall had lost their Israeli customers, but also the other way around.

## Conclusion

Space is a very important element of the Israel-Palestine conflict. Under the partition plan of the 1947 United Nations General Assembly Resolution 181 (United Nations, 1947), Historic Palestine was supposed to be split into two states, with almost the same dimensions for both. The Palestinians and the Arab countries refused the division and did not accept to build the Palestinian state on almost 50% of their land. By the Oslo Accords, 46 years later, the Palestinians not only recognised the State of Israel but also accepted to establish their State on only the 22% of their land. However, the status on East Jerusalem and the Israeli settlements in both East Jerusalem and the West Bank were the main obstacles to reaching a final agreement. These settlements with the land confiscated for their expansion had swallowed almost 70% of the 22% of Historic Palestine. Instead of reaching an agreement in 1999, according to the Oslo Accords timetable, negotiations followed an endless process, leading to dead end. East Jerusalem is still annexed to Israel; the West Bank is still full of Israeli settlements divided into Areas A, B, and C and circled by the Separation Wall; and the Gaza Strip is still under siege.

The Wall in Jerusalem fragmented the space. It succeeded in isolating Palestinians, those of East Jerusalem outside the Wall, and those of the West Bank inside the Wall, depriving them of their very basic need of free movement. They are imprisoned by the Wall no matter which side they are in and they lost the ability to plan for their future. Their actions are a reaction to Israeli policies, which inevitably disperse their personal resources while searching for solutions. Palestinians on both sides of the Wall are busy with problems in their everyday lives that vary according to the different legal statuses and different Israeli policies. This means they do not share the same problems and that separates them even more.

The Wall in Jerusalem marks the new border between Israel and the West Bank set by Israel when it annexed East Jerusalem, except for two Palestinian neighbourhoods: Kafr A'keb and the Shua'fat refugee camp.[23] Practically, the Wall separates between Palestinians of East Jerusalem and Palestinians of the West Bank; therefore, the Wall in this specific area has no security significance. The provocative question that has always been in my mind regarding the route of the Wall is how could the Palestinians of the West Bank represent a security threat to the State of Israel, while those of East Jerusalem do not? How could Israel deceive the world and justify its act in constructing a Wall around Palestinians "for security reasons", while the main aim is to grab more land for Israel? However, the Third Intifada, or uprising as many like to call it, which spontaneously irrupted in East Jerusalem in 2014 after years of discrimination against the Jerusalemites, expose Israeli authorities' implicit intentions.

The Jerusalemites feel abandoned; they are neither Israeli nor Palestinian citizens, they are worried about the future in light of the Israeli demographic policies to reduce their numbers, and the continuous efforts to suppress their resistance of the occupation. Israel succeeded in separating East Jerusalem from its suburbs; East Jerusalem's streets and shops are empty from its suburbs' visitors, the neighbourhoods inside the Wall swell, suffering from the growing population density in their limited space.

At first glance, the impact of the Wall on Palestinian social capital types was positive: bonding, bridging, and linking social capital became stronger. Family became a strategy of protection, and solidarity among immediate family members increased. Hardships that the many Jerusalemites had faced after the construction of the Wall forced families to literally "stick together" as they moved to live with each other in uncomfortable conditions. Although this reflects solidarity and solves many social and economic problems in the short run, it also creates some social problems in the long run. The problems that were created by discomfort will harm the relationship as the solutions that were temporary became long term or permanent. Many believe that this was deliberate by the Israeli authorities to engage the Palestinians in internal social disputes, fighting over resources in order to ignore the real reasons behind their misery. Social capital may play an important role in helping Palestinians cope with continuous hardships and deal with problems. However, it certainly has no power to eliminate them without a fair political solution. The spatial and social segregation created by the Wall enhanced Palestinian social capital. But it also had negative side effects or undesirable externalities. It destroyed bridging social capital that was developed between Israelis and Palestinians during the process of economic integration over the previous years, ending the possibility of creating a healthy atmosphere to implement just peace.

The question of what type of social capital and under what conditions it can become a tool to enhance co-existence between peoples and develop the power to eliminate physical and social walls in the future still remains. This could be a good question for future research.

## Notes

1. These include the Sinai Peninsula of Egypt and the Golan Heights of Syria.
2. Four dunams = 1 acre.
3. Most of the Israeli settlements, including the road network connecting Palestinian cities, are located in Area C. This means that Israel controls the road network that Palestinians use to move from one area to another.
4. The Agreements were Wye I, II, and III and Sharam I.
5. There is no Palestinian Police in these areas, not even for traffic control.
6. The second Intifada, unlike the first Intifada of 1987, was a wave of violence and counterviolence on both sides.
7. Judea and Samaria are the Hebrew names for the West Bank.
8. Ministerial Committee on National Security Affairs, Decision No. 64/B dated 14 April 2002.
9. The Green Line refers to the 1949 armistice line between Israel and the West Bank. The name derives from the green ink used to draw the line on the map.
10. The Israeli government also built 14 alternative "fabric of life" roads to facilitate movement of the Palestinians between their cities and towns. These roads are usually longer than the original roads, which makes commuting time-consuming and costly.
11. The rest are reserved for the settlers' use only (Aronson, 2008).
12. See http://farm8.staticflickr.com/7180/6905737015_6d91fd21d3_z.jpg

13. East Jerusalem is considered by Israelis as Part of Israel.
14. See www.btselem.org/topic/jerusalem
15. Under international law, these neighbourhoods have the same status as Israeli settlements built in other parts of the West Bank, and they are illegal.
16. Such as Burj Laqlaq, Burj Al Qirami, Aqbat as Saraya, and Aqbat al Khaldiya.
17. See the mapping study carried out by UN-OCHA at www.ochaopt.org/content/east-jerusalem-palestinians-risk-eviction.
18. It is noteworthy that demolishing a home as a collective punishment because one of the family members was accused of committing a "terror attack" is free of charge. This role of collective punishment was enforced by Israel during the Third Intifada that started in the fourth quarter of the year 2014.
19. If this plan is realised, it will serve the main aim of Israeli governments to reduce the number of Palestinians and increase the number of Israelis in Jerusalem. See Dhaher (2017).
20. Mr. Ziad AbuZayyad was an ex-minister for Jerusalem affairs, an ex-Legislative Council member of the Palestinian Authority, a lawyer and publisher and co-editor of a quarterly *Journal of Politics, Economics and Culture*. This is based on information from a personal conversation.
21. See the website "Tribal Justice in Palestine" at www.wafainfo.ps.
22. Al-"Eizaryah is one of the towns that was isolated by the Separation Wall.
23. These two neighbourhoods were included in the municipality boundaries when Israel annexed East Jerusalem but were excluded when the Wall route was determined.

# References

Aburish, Said K. 1991. *Children of Bethany: The Story of a Palestinian Family.* London: Bloomsbury Publishing Limited.

Allegra, M. 2011. "From Partition to Reunification to . . .? The Transformation of the Metropolitan Area of Jerusalem Since 1967". *Palestine-Israel Journal of Politics, Economics, and Culture*, 17(1 & 2): 12–20.

Allegra, M. 2012. "Settlement Policy in Israel. Transforming Jerusalem's Contested Metropolitan Landscape." *Metropolitics*. Accessed on 10 December 2016 from www.metropolitiques.eu/Settlement-policy-in-Israel.html.

Amir, M. 2011. "On the Border of Indeterminacy: The Separation Wall in East Jerusalem." *Geopolitics*, 16(4): 768–792.

Aronson, G. 2008. "Report on Israeli Settlements in the Occupied Territories." *Foundation for Middle East Peace*. Accessed from http://fmep.org/wp/wp-content/uploads/2015/01/18.6.pdf

Association for Civil Rights in Israel (ACRI). 2015. *East Jerusalem 2015: Facts and Figures.* Accessed on 20 November 2016 from www.acri.org.il/en/wp-content/uploads/2015/05/EJ-Facts-and-Figures-2015.pdf.

Bimkom and B'Tselem. 2005. *Under the Guise of Security. Routing the Separation Barrier to Enable the Expansion of Israeli Settlements in the West Bank.* Accessed on 25 October 2016 from www.btselem.org/sites/default/files2/publication/200512_under_the_guise_of_security_eng.pdf.

Bollens, Scott A. 2000. *On Narrow Ground: Urban Policy and Ethnic Conflict in Jerusalem and Belfast.* Albany, NY: SUNY Press.

B'Tselem. 2002. "Land Grab. Israel's Settlement Policy in the West Bank." *The Israeli Information Centre for Human Rights in the Occupied Territories*. Accessed on 25 November 2016 from www.btselem.org/download/200205_land_grab_eng.pdf.

B'Tselem. 2006. "A Wall in Jerusalem: Obstacles to Human Rights in the Holy City." *The Israeli Information Centre for Human Rights in the Occupied Territories.*

Accessed on 5 January 2017 from www.btselem.org/download/200607_a_wall_in_jerusalem.pdf.

B'Tselem. 2009. "The Hidden Agenda. The Establishment and Expansion Plans of Ma'ale Adummim and their Human Rights Ramifications." *The Israeli Information Centre for Human Rights in the Occupied Territories.* Accessed on 26 November 2016 from www.btselem.org/download/200912_maale_adummim_eng.pdf.

B'Tselem. 2011. "Separation Barrier, Route of the Barrier Around East Jerusalem." *The Israeli Information Centre for Human Rights in the Occupied Territories.* Accessed on 27 November 2016 from www.btselem.org/separation_barrier/jerusalem.

B'Tselem. 2012. "Arrested Development: The Long Term Impact of Israel's Separation Barrier in the West Bank." *The Israeli Information Centre for Human Rights in the Occupied Territories.* Accessed on 27 November 2016 from www.btselem.org/download/201210_arrested_development_eng.pdf.

Cheshin, Amir S., Hutman, Bill and Melamed, Avi. 1999. *Separate and Unequal: The Inside Story of Israeli Rule in East Jerusalem.* Cambridge: Harvard University Press.

The Civic Coalition for Palestinian Rights in Jerusalem (CCPRJ). 2011. *43 Years of Occupation*, 2nd edition. Accessed on 26 February 2017 from www.civiccoalition-jerusalem.org/uploads/9/3/6/8/93682182/ 43_years_of_occupation.pdf.

Derejko, N. 2009. "Aggressive Urbanism: Urban Planning and the Displacement of Palestinians Within and From Occupied East Jerusalem." *The Civic Coalition for Defending Palestinians' Rights in Jerusalem.* Accessed on December 2016 from http://civiccoalition-jerusalem.org/system/files/documents/aggressive_urbanism.pdf.

Dhaher, S. 2014. "Al-'Eizariya (Bethany) and the Wall: From the Quasi-Capital of Palestine to an Arab Ghetto." *Palestine-Israel Journal of Politics, Economics, and Culture,* 19(4) and 20(1): 113–123.

Dhaher, S. 2016. *Al-'Eizariyah and the Wall: From the Quasi-capital of Palestine to an Arab Ghetto. The Impact of the Separation Wall on the Social Capital of the Palestinians in East Jerusalem and the West Bank.* PhD Dissertation, University of Trento. Accessed from http://eprints-phd.biblio.unitn.it/1707/1/Safa_Dhaher_Doctoral_Thesis.pdf.

Dhaher, S. 2017. "The Impact of the Current Situation on the Human Rights of the Vulnerable Palestinian Groups in East Jerusalem." *The Heinrich Böll Stiftung (hbs) Palestine and Jordan.* Accessed from https://ps.boell.org/sites/default/files/uploads/2017/03/full_study.final_.pdf.

Friedrichs, J., Galster, G., and S. Musterd. 2003. "Neighbourhood Effects on Social Opportunities: The European and American Research and Policy Context." *Housing Studies,* 18(6): 797–806.

Gordon, N. 2008. "From Colonization to Separation: Exploring the Structure of Israel's Occupation." *Third World Quarterly,* 29(1): 25–44.

Grassroots Palestine. 2010. "Anti-Apartheid Wall." *Palestinian Grassroots Anti-Apartheid Wall Campaign.* Accessed on 12 June 2012 from www.stopthewall.org/news/boycot.

Hever, S. 2007. "The Separation Wall in East Jerusalem: Economic Consequences." *Alternative Information Centre.* Accessed on 10 June 2012 from www.ochaopt.org/documents/opt_econ_aic_separation_wall_eastjerus_ apr_2007.pdf.

Jamal, Amaney A. 2007. *Barriers to Democracy: The Other Side of Social Capital in Palestine and the Arab World.* Princeton: Princeton University Press.

Khatib, Khaled A. 1993. "The Conservation of Jerusalem." *PASSIA: Palestinian Academic Society for the Study of International Affairs.* Accessed from http://www.passia.org/publications/49

Kimhi, I. 2006. "The Security Fence Around Jerusalem: Implications for the City and its Residents." *Jerusalem Institute Israel*. Accessed from http://en.jerusaleminstitute. org.il/?cmd=publication.7&act=read&id=47#.WabL3CgjHIU

Lin, N. 1999. "Building a Network Theory of Social Capital." *Connections*, 22(1): 28–51.

Müller, A. 2004. *A Wall on the Green Line?* Alternative Information Centre, Jerusalem.

Paq, A. 2015. "A Jerusalem Village Under Siege." *Al Jazeera English*, 6 November. Accessed on 11 September 2016 from www.aljazeera.com/indepth/inpictures/2015/11/jerusalem-village-siege-151104071248197.html.

Robinson, G. E. (2008). "Palestinian Tribes, Clans, and Notable Families." *Strategic Insights*, 7(4).

Shlaim, A. 2005. "The Rise and Fall of the Oslo Peace Process." *International Relations of the Middle East*, edited by F. Louis, 241–261. New York: Oxford University Press.

Thawaba, A. S. 2011. "Jerusalem Walls: Transforming and Segregating Urban Fabric." *African and Asian Studies*, 10(2 & 3): 121–142.

Trigilia, C. 2001. "Social Capital and Local Development." *European Journal of Social Theory*, 4(4): 427–442.

Trigilia, C. 2008. *Economic Sociology: State, Market, and Society in Modern Capitalism*. Oxford: John Wiley & Sons.

United Nations, General Assembly Resolution. 181/1947. *Future Government of Palestine A/RES/181*. Accessed from undocs.org/A/RES/181.

UN-OCHA. 2006. "Preliminary Analysis of the Humanitarian Implications of the Fence in the West Bank Based on the Planned Route in April 2006." *Update*, No. 5. United Nations, Office for the Coordination of Humanitarian Affairs (OCHA) in the Occupied Palestinian Territory, East Jerusalem.

UN-OCHA. 2009. *The Planning Crisis in East Jerusalem: Understanding the Phenomenon of 'Illegal' Construction*. United Nations, Office for the Coordination of Humanitarian Affairs (OCHA) in the Occupied Palestinian Territory, East Jerusalem.

World Bank. 2010. *Checkpoints and Barriers: Searching for Livelihoods in the West Bank and Gaza Gender Dimensions of Economic Collapse*. New Haven: Yale University Press.

World Health Organisation (WHO). 2013. *WHO Report of 2013: Crossing Barriers to Access Health in the Occupied Palestinian Territory*. Accessed on 22 February 2017 from www.emro.who.int/images/stories/palestine/documents/WHO__RTH_crossing_barriers_to_access_health.pdf?ua=1.

Yousef, O. 2011. "Jerusalem: Palestinian Space, Behaviours and Attitudes." *Palestine-Israel Journal of Politics, Economics, and Culture*, 17(1 & 2): 43–53.

# 13 Social Regeneration and Environmental Sustainability in Biosphere Reserves[1]

*Silvia Sacchetti and Colin Campbell*

## Introduction

The idea of social regeneration, as framed in this volume, highlights a dynamic or transformative element. Chapter 1 explains that regeneration is a development approach, which is directed towards embedding inclusive and cooperative relations, leading to shared understanding, decisions, and the mutual prosperity of people. In particular, the focus is on types of economic organising that reciprocate communities by reinvesting the surplus produced thanks to natural and community resources (Borzaga and Sacchetti in this volume). The present chapter complements this analysis by considering social regeneration within UNESCO designated biosphere reserves (BRs) and by combining social regeneration with natural justice. By natural justice, we mean solutions that do not hamper the delicate equilibrium of the ecosystems and biodiversity that exist in BRs. In this sense, the UNESCO programme on BRs provides an excellent context to analyse the interaction between the social and the environmental dimensions of development.

BRs have been designated by UNESCO since the 1970s and are located across the globe. Across continents, the challenge of sustainability meets a variety of cultures, histories, natural settings, and forms of economic organisations. Although the need for compatibility between human activities and BRs has been invoked at several policy levels, solutions on how to achieve this outcome have not been considered in the same detail. The chapter then identifies a number of 'spaces' or dimensions (without claiming to be exhaustive) that differentiate BRs and the variety of organisational solutions that can be consistent with social regeneration and natural 'justice'.

To this end, the chapter explores the practice-based approach applied on a number of BRs. Part of the issue is methodological, since BRs may have common aims but greatly differ in terms of their contextual elements. To explore context, the chapter offers illustrations from BRs in Vietnam, Italy, Australia, and Zimbabwe. The analysis derives from a project undertaken by Assist Social Capital (ASC), a community interest company (CIC) based in Scotland that works to bridge the gap between academic evidence of social capital and its practical application.

Firstly, the chapter explains the nature of BRs as defined by UNESCO (Section 2). We then present description of case studies mostly coming from a recently published special issue of the *Journal of Entrepreneurial and Organizational Diversity* on biosphere and community development, addressing cases of UNESCO designated BRs across the world: Cat Ba in Vietnam, Noosa in Australia, Appennino Tosco Emiliano in Italy, and the Middle Zambezi Biosphere Reserve in Zimbabwe (Section 3). Following illustrations, we present the overall framework of analysis and identify the multifaceted 'spatial' dimensions (physical, relational, policy, organisational) which may enable BR communities to take ownership of their own needs, aims, and solutions.

## Biosphere Reserves Across the World—Illustrations

Increasingly, there is a need to reconcile the natural environment with economic as well as social development. Within this context and with a particular focus on preservation and conservation, UNESCO launched the Man and Biosphere (MAB) programme in 1971 (Coetzer et al., 2014; Ishwaran et al., 2008). Out of this framework emerged the BR concept for context-specific conservation in 1974 (Ishwaran et al., 2008), and, two years later, the World Network of Biosphere Reserves (WNBR) was born (Ishwaran, 2009).

The three main functions of a BR are (UNESCO, 1996; Ishwaran et al., 2008; Coetzer et al., 2014):

(i) *Conservation*—preservation of ecosystems, landscape, species, and genetic resources
(ii) *Logistic support*—support projects, research and monitoring, environmental education
(iii) *Development*—foster sustainable economic and human development

To translate the three roles into practice, UNESCO-MAB structured the zoning of the BRs into three: the core, buffer, and transition zones (UNESCO, 1996; Ishwaran, 2009) (see Figure 13.1).

1. The MAB programme aims at turning BRs into '*training grounds*' that develop sustainable development principles translated into local contexts (Ishwaran, 2009: 3). This site-specific application of an international principle is reflected in the recent emphasis on BRs as Learning Laboratories (LLabs) for Sustainable Development to address gaps in implementation of the MAB programme, such as ensuring that the space under consideration includes all three zones of a BR; the core, buffer, and transition areas and that conservation and development are accepted as interdependent and applicable to all three zones (Ishwaran et al., 2008).

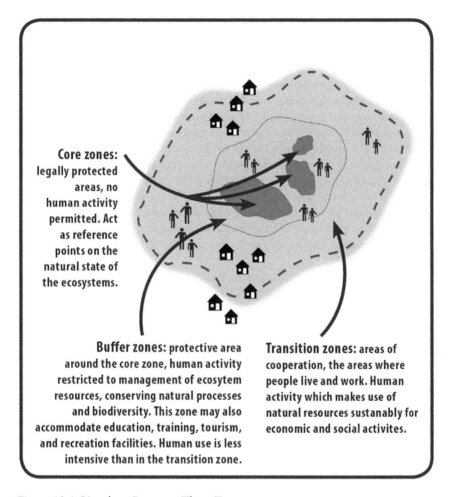

Core zones: legally protected areas, no human activity permitted. Act as reference points on the natural state of the ecosystems.

Buffer zones: protective area around the core zone, human activity restricted to management of ecosytem resources, conserving natural processes and biodiversity. This zone may also accommodate education, training, tourism, and recreation facilities. Human use is less intensive than in the transition zone.

Transition zones: areas of cooperation, the areas where people live and work. Human activity which makes use of natural resources sustanably for economic and social activites.

*Figure 13.1* Biosphere Reserves: Three Zones

The WNBR requires BRs to submit periodic reviews every ten years to ensure that they are compliant with the Seville Strategy and the Statutory Framework (UNESCO, 1996), which formalises the requirements of UNESCO's designation for BRs. The report produced for the review process is then scrutinised by the Advisory Committee for BRs for recommendation to International Coordinating Council (ICC). The objective of the ten-year review is to ensure BRs are functioning as sites for testing and demonstrating approaches to sustainable development, to report on progress being made, and identify any changes required (UNESCO, Periodic Review Process). The review process was introduced as part of the Seville Strategy (UNESCO, 1996), which places a strong emphasis on the importance of BRs for sustainable development and conservation. The Statutory Framework of the WNBR requires BRs to "strive to be sites of excellence to explore and demonstrate approaches to conservation and sustainable development at a regional scale". If the ICC finds that a BR does not satisfy the criteria, it can notify the Director-General of UNESCO that this area will be longer be referred to as "a biosphere reserve". If a State recognises that a BR under its authority does not to satisfy these criteria, it can notify the MAB Secretariat that is will be removed from the WNBR.

The periodic review process is therefore designed to provide evidence that the requirements of the UNESCO designation continue to be met. In this way, it is possible for the ICC to substantiate and endorse the contributions of BRs being managed locally, while ensuring the value and coherence of the network globally. The periodic review also acts as useful methodology to deepen shared understanding of the role of BRs with their stakeholders. As noted by Reed and Egunyu, *"Beyond meeting statutory requirements, the periodic review process can also be considered an opportunity for learning within and beyond the national and international networks"* (July 2013), thus emphasising opportunities to increase shared understanding locally and globally.

Despite continuous challenges in the current 669 BRs in 120 countries worldwide (UNESCO, WNBR, 2016), emanating mainly from the implementation of the BR Framework in diverse local settings, the adapted approach for BRs as LLabs provides an opportunity to learn from their own experiences as well as each other's practices which, in turn, can enable and inform BR management and other stakeholders to develop improved and more balanced strategies and policies (Ishwaran et al., 2008).

After some 40 years in existence, the MAB programme continues to be highly relevant to current global challenges. On the 25th of September 2015, at the seventieth anniversary of the United Nations in New York, member states agreed on new global Sustainable Development Goals (SDGs). There are 17 SDGs and 169 targets for 2030. In March 2016, the 4th World Congress of Biosphere Reserves in Lima, Peru, set out a new vision for MAB for the decade 2016–2025, which mainstreams UNESCO BRs as models for national/regional demonstration of sustainable development within national and global agendas for the 2030 SDGs.

## The Cat Ba Biosphere Reserve in Vietnam

Cat Ba Archipelago Biosphere Reserve (CBBR) is one of eight BRs in Vietnam. It has been part of the UNESCO Man and Biosphere Reserves Programme since 2004. The CBBR archipelago lies 150 kilometres southeast of Hanoi and is made up of 366 islands and islets covering an area of 26,241 ha, 65% (17,000 ha) terrestrial and around 35% (9,200 ha) marine. CBBR is home to some 2,320 different types of fauna and flora. In the region, 60 of CBBR's species are endangered. There are around 6,000 inhabitants on the island. Main income streams are; tourism, fisheries, agriculture, forestry, and service delivery. Unemployment in the Haiphong province is around 4%. The BR connects to Ha Long Bay World Heritage Site (UNESCO World Heritage Centre), one of the seven new natural wonders of the world, and 40 km to the west is Haiphong City, with a population of around two million. CBBR hosts several globally important habitats such as coral reefs, mangroves, sea grass beds, and tropical limestone forests that are under threat due to pressure from surrounding and visiting populations (UNESCO MAB, 2007). The BR is also home to the Cat Ba langur (*Trachypithecus poliocephalus*), a critically endangered primate found only in CBBR.

Since 2007, CBBR has been using engagement initiatives focusing on; local community professions (i.e. farming, fisheries, forestry, tourism), young people, school students, and teachers, as well as all seven village Community Learning Centres on Cat Ba Island. In particular, the model implemented by Assist Social Capital, called the *Social Enterprise and Biosphere Reserve Development Framework*, aimed to "support BRs and their communities to become economically resilient while at the same time maintaining the natural environment in a manner that is appropriate to local strengths, resources and cultural characteristics" (Assist Social Capital, 2013). Facing a risk of overexploitation of the natural asset by tourism, the development model focused on activities designated to promote social capital and place awareness, with the aim to match community needs and the biosphere main functions. The model adopted the OECD's definition of social capital from 'The Wellbeing of Nations' (Healy and, 2001), which defines social capital as "*networks, together with shared norms, values and understanding which facilitate cooperation within and among groups*". Social capital was deemed as key to maximising a community's potential, as it is assumed to enable stakeholders to become actors for sustainable development. Further, ASC's project focused on specific organisational solutions, namely social enterprises. These were identified as a sustainable, not-for-private-profit business model achieved through an asset lock, which strives to be financially independent of grants and have primary objectives to achieve social and/or environmental benefit. This case and the development approach adopted to promote social capital and social enterprise at CBBR have been illustrated in detail in a recent article (Campbell and Sacchetti, 2017), where it is emphasised that further research needs to be done to determine whether this model creates a lasting and sustainable environment. In the meantime, CBBR's approach was identified as a national example of good practice in combining conservation and development for sustainable development at the UN Conference on Sustainable Development, Rio+20 in June 2012.

### The Noosa Biosphere Reserve in Australia

The case of the Noosa region in Queensland has been analysed in Barclay (2017), on which we build this section. Barclay notices that the Noosa region in Queensland, Australia, is recognised for its rich biodiversity and features one of Australia's most-visited national parks. The Noosa Biosphere Reserve, designated by UNESCO in 2007, hosts over 44% of Australia's bird species, 1,365 species of plants, 711 species of native fauna, and 60 distinct ecosystems. Noosa is a popular holiday destination with an active tourism industry and a diversity of local businesses and social enterprises with aspirations to operate ethically and sustainably.

In this work, Barclay explains that the strategy to develop Noosa Biosphere Reserve came about through community partnership with local government. The result was a diverse community governance structure which set up the board of Noosa Biosphere Limited in order to manage the activities of the BR. The Board was comprised of representatives from community-based organisations working in culture, economic development, environment, social engagement, education, and research, together with representation from the local tourism industry and regional political representatives.

To promote a balanced relationship between human interaction and the environment, the BR undertook community engagement, supported innovative projects, as well as research and learning. As part of this process, Noosa Biosphere Limited ran a partnership programme that invited applications from social enterprises, environment and community groups, universities, educational institutions, and businesses that wished to be recognised for their efforts to promote BR principles.

Community participation in Noosa BR was recognised and valued, with the BR being seen as a learning laboratory for collaboration and interdisciplinary thinking. This led to innovative projects and actions that worked for a healthy society, economy, environment, and place. Gaps and opportunities were targeted where innovative projects might act as a catalyst to inspire others. The community engagement and learning aspects were maximised and documented for the benefit of local, national, and international communities.

Consistently with Sacchetti et al. (2009), Barclay identified creativity and culture as being instrumental in the development of social capital and community engagement in the Noosa BR. Creative collaborations and cultural engagement with a multi-stakeholder approach enabled many of the most valuable projects via the social, cultural, environmental, and economic sector boards. A key aim of these projects was to encourage awareness and engagement around BR principles, forming the foundation for social and cultural capital in the Noosa BR community.

According to Barclay, during the first five years of operation, from 2008–2013, Noosa Biosphere Limited produced a broad range of initiatives that had a significant impact within the local community and attracted national and international interest. While they vary in scope and cover a diversity of themes and market sectors, these initiatives have all been critical in underpinning the UNESCO BR framework as interconnected learning laboratories for community-based interdisciplinary collaborations.

## The Appennino Tosco-Emiliano UNESCO Biosphere Reserve in Italy

This case of Appennino Tosco-Emiliano in Italy has been developed in Teneggi and Zandonai (2017), on which we build this section. As Taneggi and Zandonai explain, the Appennino Tosco-Emiliano Biosphere Reserve is located in the Tuscany and Emilia Romagna regions of north-central Italy. It covers the Tuscan-Emilian Apennine ridge from Passo della Cisa to Passo delle Forbici, which marks the geographical and climatic boundary between continental and Mediterranean Europe. The area contains nearly 70% of all species present in Italy, including 122 species of birds, amphibians, reptiles, mammals, and fish, as well as a wide variety of flora comprising at least 260 aquatic and terrestrial plant species.

The main economic activities are tourism, agriculture, craftsmanship, and the processing of high-quality foods, such as Parmigiano Reggiano cheese, Prosciutto di Parma, olive oil, honey, and spelt. Leisure activities and tourism also represent important economic assets for the 100,000 local inhabitants. Some 68,500 tourists and second-home owners represent seasonal boosts to the population. The Appennino Tosco-Emiliano UNESCO BR includes many villages, such as Succiso, Cerreto, Corniglio, Sologno, and Apella, that are highly enterprising and cooperative. In their case studies, the authors emphasise that the cooperatives that have been set up have revitalised public places by turning private businesses on the verge of closure into productive businesses. In some instances, local communities have championed short supply chains through networks of local production companies offering products characteristic of the local culture. In others, small social market economy districts encourage business and non-profit organisations. Cultural initiatives re-forge relationships and revitalise intangible resources and strengths, introducing a new enterprising spirit and a fresh sense of opportunity.

Teneggi and Zandonai also highlight that the Appennino Tosco-Emiliano BR most important output is trust, which is created and circulated on a daily basis by the experiences outlined above. They are *"factories of social cohesion"* (ibid) that keep up the quality of life in the territory. Initiatives that are started by local inhabitants are complemented by people returning to the area or additionally by those from outside the community. The really crucial factor in ensuring these activities are productive for the community and the economy lies in a social contract to take ownership and responsibility and to make the community a home. Rather than simply living in the area, people who make it their home build deep and lasting relationships with the other inhabitants and the place. The same holds true for businesses and companies in the area that incorporate it into their production and/or supply chains. This social contract generates a profound sense of relationship that establishes collective destinies. Similar to life in rural and mountain communities in times gone by, people and their families are bound together by similar activities, not merely for the pursuit of profit but through a feeling of shared future.

As a result, the authors demonstrate, enterprising communities salvage neglected physical spaces, making them into sites for living, interacting, and working once again. Trust, ownership, relationships, and local stakeholders are the assets responsible for the protection and competitiveness of the Appennino Tosco-Emiliano BR, which is acting as a model for similar rural areas in Italy. The Italian Ministry of Economic Development has selected the area as a model site for further experimentation. This process will see strategic programmes established, focusing in particular on health, transport, and school, as well as economic development.

## The Middle Zambezi Biosphere Reserve in Zimbabwe

As set out by Mbereko et al. (2017), the number of protected areas globally, where humans are excluded by law, has grown significantly since the first national park in 1872, particularly in developing countries where biodiversity is at its greatest. Research supports the theory that if fauna and flora are not protected, they degrade at a fast pace (Cf. also Naughton-Treves et al., 2005).

Mbereko et al. (2017) explain that in the late 1980s, a paradigm shift took place from protection and exclusion to involvement and inclusion of humans in national parks management and the sustainable use of natural resources (Stoll-Kleemann et al., 2010). As a result, international conservation initiatives now advocate the use of resource management approaches that centre more on human livelihoods, and BRs are a means to achieve this, under the UNESCO's MAB programme to promote sustainable development based on local community efforts and sound science (Pool-Stanvliet and Clusener-Godt, 2013).

The Middle Zambezi BR became a member of the UNESCO BR network on June 5th 2010. The only BR in Zimbabwe, the Middle Zambezi extends from Lake Kariba and the Matusadona National Park through various National Park and Safari Areas adjacent to the Zambezi River, including Mana Pools National Park and Sapi and Chewore Safari Areas that are already designated as a UNESCO World Heritage Site. Zimbabwe's Middle Zambezi BR covers some 40,000 sq. km in the Zambezi valley. It includes riverine and terrestrial ecosystems unique to the subcontinent, including one of its largest man-made reservoirs, Lake Kariba. The area also contains towns and villages, including Kariba, which depends largely on fishing in Lake Kariba for protein and income.

Research in the Middle Zambezi BR sought to analyse the livelihoods and the conservation issues of natural resources used by farmers bordering the BR, where there is a high inter-dependence between the natural environment and local communities. Evidence suggests that when communities realise economic benefits from wildlife, conservation efforts are aided (Getz et al., 1999; Jones and Weaver, 2009; Ostrom, 1990). Mbereko et al. (2017) highlight that in addition to economic benefit, social capital is fundamental to enabling collective conservation action and equality of shared benefits in communities (Ostrom, 1990; Sacchetti and Campbell, 2014).

A programme in the BR known as CAMPFIRE (Communal Areas Management Programme for Indigenous Resources) was initiated, with the aim of creating economic and ownership incentives in the community. However, due to structural weaknesses and national economic crises, as well as over-exploitation of natural resources, either legally or illegally, CAMPFIRE has not benefitted the poor rural communities of the BR. Community members believe the CAMPFIRE programme had collapsed, citing, for example, the fact that they are not consulted when hunting licences are granted in the area, which they perceive to have negatively impacted their livelihoods. The outcome is therefore conflict between the local inhabitants and the authorities. There have been reports of livestock being left to roam into protected areas and of community members engaging in illegal gold panning in the major rivers using chemicals that kill animals that rely on the river systems downstream.

In an attempt to identify the causes of such failures, Mbereko et al. believe that a focus on support for business with a short-term profit motive (in the case of the Middle Zambezi game hunting) together with a lack of policy to enable local communities to benefit from the natural resources in the BR, results in failure to implement adaptive management strategies that can mitigate threats. Thus, the community uses subtle and illegal methods to benefit from natural resources as they fight to earn sustainable livelihoods. The paper suggests that the CAMPFIRE model needs to be revised to ensure community benefit, increased accountability, and ownership if the aims of the BR are to be assured.

## Biosphere Reserves and Social Regeneration: A Policy Approach

The illustrations reviewed point to a specific challenge that a worldwide programme aimed at BR sustainability faces: how to appreciate diversity of contexts and identify plural and flexible solutions which enable long-term sustainability (Ostrom, 1990). The issue left to be addressed is what elements should be taken into account in order to appreciate the contextual features of each BR and, on those features, design itineraries for social regeneration and natural justice.

In previous work, we had suggested a model of 'community ownership', which identifies the features enabling the promotion of participation and development within social organisations, as well as more broadly within and across communities (Sacchetti and Campbell, 2014). In this work, the 'community ownership' model is compared with one of 'community failure' (Table 13.1), where development goals are defined by restricted groups and do not match the needs of specific publics and communities more broadly (Cf. Sacchetti and Sugden, 2010; Cf. Dewey, 1927 on "publics"). Community ownership identifies a model of development where socio-economic actions

*Table 13.1* Community Failures vs. Community Ownership

|  | *Community failures* | *Community ownership* |
|---|---|---|
| Values and Behaviours | Individuals as passive isolated recipients/direction, competition, and consumerism | Shared pro-social values, trust, reciprocity, cooperation, networking, and deliberation |
| Context | Exclusive and constraining spaces | Inclusive and creative spaces |
| Needs/ Outcomes | Community deficits | Satisfaction of community needs across publics |
| Impacts | Conflict, disillusion and mistrust, inequality | Social regeneration, environmental sustainability leading to community resilience |

Source: adapted from Sacchetti and Campbell (2014)

are based on pro-social values defined by cooperation, reciprocity, trust, and networking, which enable individuals to exert their voice and creativity in deliberative spaces (Cf. Sacchetti et al., 2009; on participatory deliberation see also Lewanski in this volume).

The expected outcomes of promoting a community ownership model is embedding cooperative behaviours, creative deliberative processes, and responsibility, leading to innovative activities and the satisfaction of community needs. Differently, community failure is a model biased towards self-oriented behaviours, consumerism, and the organisation of socio-economic activities by means of exclusive and constraining spaces, where only specific interests are reflected. As a result, the community failure model prevents participation of publics and their capability to bring their experience and knowledge in the deliberative process. It is therefore more likely to disregard community needs, to foster inequality, disillusion, mistrust, and conflict (Sacchetti and Sugden, 2010; Sacchetti and Campbell, 2014: 34–35; Borzaga and Sacchetti, 2015).

Enabling communities in BRs, therefore, consistently point towards a development model embedded in community ownership, leading to a discovery and an appreciation of diversity of conditions and needs across contexts. This approach requires expanding the analysis beyond the particularities of the morphology and natural elements of a territory. Diversity of situational contexts is appreciated by integrating different but complementary levels of analysis, which are relevant for moving towards community resilience. Figure 13.2 summarises the approach. Note that the features of a multi-dimensional, enabling space are all interconnected, pointing to the fact that physical spatiality influences and is in turn influenced by all the other dimensions. The same is true for each and every dimension depicted in Figure 13.2. The dimensions of Figure 13.2 are described in more detail below.

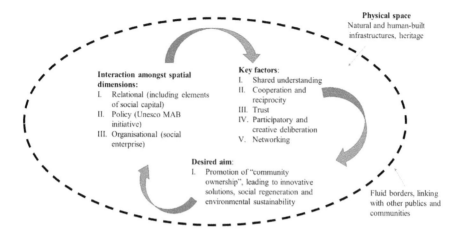

*Figure 13.2* Overview of the Development Approach

## Physical Space

These are the elements of the situational context defined by the physical spatiality of a locality, and the socio-demographic and health features of the population. One of the first questions policy makers ask when approaching common resources is where to put boundaries on the map. In the case of BRs, the issue is to identify the three boundaries of the BR defined by the core, buffer, and transition zones. Within the zones, physical space is made of natural resources and built spaces, including natural and cultural heritage sites and built infrastructures, all of which can provide services to communities and ensure long-term prosperity under sustainability use (Millennium Ecosystem Assessment, 2005).

## Relational Space

These are the elements of a situational context defined by the quality of relations amongst people, organisations, and groups located within the physical space, as well as beyond it. Relational spaces include elements of positive 'social capital', or by those relations, cultures, and related behavioural norms that enable cooperation amongst multiple and diverse actors. Woolcock (2001, 13) suggests that "social capital refers to the norms and networks that facilitate collective action". Such norms have been associated with cooperation, trust, and reciprocity of behaviours. In this sense, a social capital approach contributes to understanding how the relational space may enhance the potential for social regeneration and natural justice by creating a sense of ownership for the members of the community. It is argued that this enables them to become agents for sustainable development themselves (Roseland, 2000). Therefore, social capital has been identified as a crucial aspect to sustainability (see, for example, Barnes-Mauthe et al., 2014).

## Organisational Space

Another question to be addressed in response to the effort to deliver on BRs as models of social and environmental sustainability is what type of organisation shows features consistent with the development of BRs. These are informal as well as organisational solutions and models of enterprise which build on pro-social values and social capital to create participatory governance solutions. Consistently with the participatory nature of solutions, the assets generated by the organisation, such as the provision of innovative social services, relations, jobs, financial resources, cultural resources, and knowledge, are shared with the community (Sacchetti, 2016). At a system level, this identifies a re-investment model aimed at reinforcing the role of economic activities in acting for natural justice and diffused community prosperity. Sacchetti and Tortia (2016) offer an overview of social responsibility across different organisational models.[2] Here we consider, amongst alternatives, the Social Enterprise (SE).

SE is a fairly recent term, and many types exist internationally and continue to evolve. However, the core principle that SEs should work for the common good runs throughout and bridges variants on its definition. Broadly, SEs are businesses which have an explicit social and/or environmental aim and include in their statutory requirements a commitment to reinvest surpluses to achieve this (Borzaga and Tortia, 2010 amongst others). In particular, because they tend to address unresolved community needs, SEs often originate from community publics and are collectively managed by them. More broadly, SEs are characterised by a variety of distinguishing factors, such as the ability to provide innovative services, use specific governance models, and foster social capital (Sacchetti, 2016). SEs are present in almost all economic sectors including manufacturing, tourism, recreational and professional services, agriculture, educational, health, and social services. SEs are distinct from non-profit organisations (NPOs) in that they strive to be independent of grants and donations. They aim to be economically self-sustainable whilst delivering and reinvesting their surpluses into the business to bring about social and environmental benefits for the wider community, whilst also providing space for the development of cooperative relations and increasing community ownership. Reinvestment in the community is a clear feature of SEs, albeit the debate on whether SEs should be able to distribute at least part of the surplus is still open (Galera and Borzaga, 2009). Italy, for example, has recently approved a law to allow more flexibility towards the distribution of produced surplus, mostly to reward and attract financial resources. The aim, as a recent EU/OECD report emphasises, is not to use financial resources to increase scale and profits for investors, but—given the nature of SEs—to scale up their social impacts. This, of course, does not necessarily overlap with growth in their size and can occur via other strategies, such as building collaborative partnerships and knowledge sharing (EU/OECD, 2016).

The organisational space also includes supporting financial elements, such as social impact investment. The rise and interest in social impact investment are strictly tied to the emergence and growing importance of SEs as a reply to the social and environmental challenges of communities (Galera and Borzaga, 2009). Social investment is the provision of finance to address social needs with the expectation of a social, as well as financial, return. Unlike grants and donations, social investments are loans, used to create measurable social impact with the aim of the investment being paid back (OECD, 2015). Social investors attribute different values to the mix of social and financial returns they expect: for example, it includes the offer of capital at rates of return that are lower than the market rate. In fact, it is argued that—besides the aims of the investment—a lower rate of return is a necessary condition to discriminate between standard for-profit loans and social impact investments (ibid.). Such a model is aimed at increasing scaling and financial resilience in SEs.

More broadly, at community level, organisational strategies can be more coherently focused on scaling social impact rather than organisational size by means of participatory and inclusive forms of networking and knowledge sharing (EU/OECD, 2016; Sacchetti and Sugden, 2003). Scaling social impact, in particular, supports linking social capital and brings the attention to the need of taking into account the interaction between multiple coexisting actors and their interests (Borzaga and Sacchetti, 2015).

## Policy Space

A policy space reflects the ability of a community, through public administrations, to transform its norms and values into policy aims, formal rules, and legal frameworks for governing the allocation and distribution of different resources. Likewise, it reflects the capacity of institutions to implement and monitor the implementation of such rules. A policy space is inclusive when the interests of multiple publics and community long-term development goals are promoted through the values of cooperation and deliberation. Differently, an exclusive policy space is defined by lack of deliberation and perspective on broad community interests, typically with a top-down approach (Sacchetti, 2014).

## Key Elements

The key elements of these multiple spaces can be identified in:

a. shared understanding,
b. participatory and creative deliberation,
c. trust,
d. cooperation and reciprocity,
e. networks.

Each of these elements in analysed below.

*Shared Understanding*—describes common standards, expectations, and beliefs which are based on shared values and norms. Shared understanding has been argued to be based on proximity of specific values, based on communication, mutual respect, and deliberation: what Sacchetti and Sugden (2009) call 'mental proximity'. Proximity of values, therefore, is not necessarily defined by co-existence within the same physical space or spatial proximity within the same community (Sacchetti and Sugden, 2009). Shared values and understanding based on inclusive principles contrast with spaces where relations are characterised by power unbalance. This would occur, for example, when the strategic direction of activities within the locality, or more specifically, within the BR, are dominated by concentrated interests (Cowling et al., 2009).

*Participatory and creative deliberation*—relational space forms a discursive platform, a place of transformation, where communication and deliberation engender critical reflection over interacting beliefs, choices, and outcomes. Participatory and creative deliberation is a feature of inclusive relational spaces. It is, in other words, the space of curiosity, enquiry, and discovery, where individuals actively use their creative intelligence to make sense of interactions, understand their needs and shape their aims and existence (Cf. Dewey, 1934; Halsall, 2012; Latour and Weibel, 2005). Creative responses elaborated in this way express what citizens and publics have "reason to value" (Sen, 1999). These solutions represent an innovative benchmark for the ideation and realisation of new courses of economic initiatives, social activities, and policies (Sacchetti, 2015).

*Cooperation, reciprocity, and trust*—cooperation refers to the community members' willingness to support one another (cooperation) and the collectivity and to offer support with the confidence that it will be returned in the future (reciprocity). Both cooperation and reciprocity need trust, or the expectation that other members of the community will not act to the detriment of others. Cooperation occurs when actors are in a relation of mutual dependence, and encompass the interests of multiple interconnected actors (Sacchetti and Sugden, 2003). Reciprocity differs from exchange in important ways. In fact, whilst exchange asks for an equivalence between the goods exchanged between actor A and actor B, reciprocity follows a principle of equity and does not necessarily occur between two actors (say A, the giver, and B, the receiver), but it could involve a third actor, C, who could receive from B as an act of reciprocity of B towards A (Polanyi, 1944).

*Networks*—Trust, cooperation, and reciprocity facilitate the development of a "dense knit" of production interconnections (Camagni and Capello, 2002). In social capital literature, networks describe how people and/or groups are linked through different types of ties: bonding (close, strong ties within the community), bridging (horizontal ties across communities), and linking ties (vertical ties between communities with differing power and authority) (Szreter and Woolcock, 2004, 655).

## Interactions Amongst Spatial Dimensions and Shared Definition of Rules

Institutional economists and political scientists have long studied how norms of cooperation and trust amongst individuals, groups, and organisations are a pre-condition for the management of natural commons and the resilience of the communities living within them. Specifically, Ostrom (1990) argued in favour of self-defined rules by which the community of users and beneficiaries understands the common advantages of cooperating and sharing their knowledge to define and enforce common rules for the use of common natural resources. These are natural resources with clearly identifiable borders which, if left to opportunistic and short-term actions, run the risk of being destroyed. The implication of natural resource abuse is that the livelihood of communities that rely on the common is also compromised. The requirement is, therefore, to find rules of accessing and using the resources that support sustainability of both natural resources and human livelihood, encompassing policy and organisational dimensions. The question, for Ostrom, was what rules would be the most appropriate.

From her work, we learn that there is not one best way that fits all situational contexts and that top-down policy approaches do not always produce the best results. Specifically, top-down approaches would represent a workable solution when: 1) local communities do not have any prior experience of self-management and participation; 2) conflict is high; and 3) individuals are rational opportunists and do not acknowledge reciprocal interdependence in their decision-making (Sacchetti, 2015). Likewise, market solutions will not work if short-term profit maximisation does not also produce shared long-term benefits (Ostrom, 1990; Sacchetti, 2015; Sacconi and Degli Antoni, 2008). For example, the activities of organisations that do not share principles of social and natural justice and do not have representation of those interests in their governing bodies may be argued to have no incentives towards BR sustainability.

Besides top-down solutions and the private market solution, the theory of commons identifies a third way to solve collective challenges, which relies on collective community management. In our case, self-management in BRs can be argued to require:

a.  binding agreements and awareness of environmental issues,
b.  collectively defined rules,
c.  rules on how to access natural resources,
d.  compliance with the rules (mediated through reciprocity).

The requirements of community management are argued to be underpinned by trust, cooperation, and reciprocity of behaviours and that overall, collective action can be best activated through the mobilisation of multiple actors, through social capital, and deliberative practices.

Because each BR offers a specific situational context, the unilateral definition of rules from a super-national authority on how to access and use natural resources may have limited effects. It is not a desirable process either, because it limits the knowledge and experience utilised to standardised models, reducing the validity of the cognitive framework used to address local needs. This is because, where communitarian traditions are strong, disconnecting rules from the locality, from public participation, and understanding is likely to generate "community failure" (Sacchetti and Campbell, 2014). Community management and participatory solutions, moreover, support the building of deliberative skills and social capital and are more promptly respected and enforced by communities.

The overall community resilience, however, can benefit from being positioned in a broader framework. In the case of BRs, the UNESCO MAB framework had the benefit of allowing the recognition of BRs. In the first place, the designation of a site as a BR can raise awareness amongst the local people, citizens, and government authorities on environmental and development issues. Designation becomes a tool to protect communities from being taken over by community failure approaches and, more positively, to activate debate and therefore multiple lines of connection which can enable the development of appropriate rules, whose impacts are evaluated every ten years. Because of the three-zone scale of a BR defined in the MAB programme (Figure 13.1), rule definition and implementation require governance at system level so that multiple actors across the three different zones can coordinate and align their activities. The objective here is to align behaviours and economic activity with the values of local livelihood while protecting natural resources.

What the UNESCO MAB approach did was to provide a framework and rationale, whilst avoiding the imposition of a standard legal framework on BRs: each BR has its own system of governance to ensure it meets its functions and objectives. This is because it is believed that the management system of a BR needs to be open, evolving, and adaptive in order for the local community to better respond to external political, economic, and social pressures, which would affect the ecological and cultural values of the area. The global remit of the MAB programme means that the flexibility of the governance model is critical to the success of the programme given the vast range of local contexts. In Vietnam, for example, BRs are 100% core funded by Local Government, while in other countries, no public funding is available.

## Implications and Concluding Remarks

The UNESCO Man and Biosphere approach provides a framework and rationale for creating itineraries of awareness and endogenous development across communities. This paper has focused on the diversity of contexts, as advocated by Ostrom. Our spaces framework reflects the value of considering multiple types of interacting spaces, i.e. evolving sets of material and immaterial conditions that can hamper or enable communities, their social and natural justice.

A pre-condition to community ownership (Table 13.1) is, in this sense, social capital, or the supporting values and links that determine the ability of community members to engender multi-stakeholder, deliberative and cooperative processes in search of shared development aims. Promotion of social capital and deliberation seems therefore a first step towards the creation of place-awareness (e.g., being aware of living within a BR and a specific community), leading to the endogenous determination of sustainable development strategies for both people and the environment. In terms of *relational space*, our development approach requires forms of social capital and deliberative skills amongst community constituencies that are based on cooperation, shared decision-making, and mutual respect for people and nature. Cases support the idea that taking responsibility or 'ownership' of innovation by all participants and partners should be encouraged to enhance the understanding of sustainability principles within a BR, whilst at the same time to actively encouraging sustainability practices. This brings the community together and acts as a catalyst for the community to learn more about the BR and explore ways to benefit from the natural resources through sustainability principles.

Within the physical space of a BR, *organisational spaces*, such as those defined by social enterprises, have been presented as possible ways to organise economic activities consistently with social and natural justice. They do so when reinvesting their surplus, as a way to reciprocate communities with the surplus produced by using BR resources. In this respect, cases illustrate that reinvestment strategies enable fragile communities to become more resilient and even thrive. The Italian case demonstrates that community-owned cooperatives have revitalised public spaces, turning businesses that were previously on the verge of closing into important spaces for the community. Short supply chains and networks of local producers offer added value through distinctive products and appeal. Reinvestment therefore sustains beneficial social capital maintaining quality of life.

Complementarily, in the *policy space*, resource integration processes must acknowledge the complexity of coordinating the three-zone scale of a BR, as defined in the MAB programme at a more formal level. In this sense, rule definition and implementation requires governance at system level, so that multiple actors across the three different zones can coordinate consistently with deliberative processes within and across communities. Designation under the broader UNESCO MAB framework becomes a tool to activate debate and connections and enable the development of appropriate rules and regulations to align behaviours and economic activity with the values of local livelihood. The global remit of the MAB programme and the ten-year review process means community participation and flexibility of the governance models adopted and is critical to the success of the programme given the vast range of local contexts. The

Space Framework is an open analytical tool for capturing the complexity of interactions across different contexts.

BRs are the physical enabling space for social regeneration and overall community resilience. However, effective and resilient communities only emerge when the relational, organisational, and policy spaces align with the physical space. The SE model can be considered an organisational tool that facilitates social regeneration through cooperation and reinvestment in the community. The success of this organisational space is dependent upon the strength or size of the relational space. All elements must be in synergy in order to reach a sustainable and fully competent community.

The actual working of the proposed approach calls for investigation on:

a. The physical space elements of a BR
b. The policy space and management of the BR
c. The state of social capital within the BR
d. Tools for social capital mobilisation and community engagement to build a shared understanding on BRs
e. How mobilisation of social capital underpins livelihood and sustainability of BRs
f. Specific organisational solutions and enterprise models that are consistent with the development of community participation and BR sustainability.

## Notes

1. The authors wish to thank Tabitha Ewing, OASIIS Project Coordinator, and Licia Claveria, Operations Manager, Assist Social Capital (UK) for the editorial input and Claudia Fernandez for sharing her initial thoughts. We would also like to thank Cat Ba Biosphere Reserve for the opportunity to use the Social Capital Case Study and in particular, Le Thanh Tuyen, Office of Cat Ba Biosphere Reserve (Vietnam), for his continued cooperation.
2. The authors, in particular, address social responsibility in traditional corporations, cooperative firms, social enterprises, and charities.

## References

Assist Social Capital et al. 2013. *Social Enterprise and Biosphere Reserves Framework*. Accessed from http://social-capital.net/wp-content/uploads/2014/11/SEBR-Framework-Summary.pdf.
Barclay, L. 2017. "Biosphere Reserves as Creative Interconnected Learning Laboratories for Community-Based Interdisciplinary Collaborations." Unpublished manuscript.
Barnes-Mauthe, M., Gray, S. A., Arita, S., Lynham, J., and P. Leung. 2015. "What determines social capital in a social–ecological system? Insights from a network perspective." *Environmental management*, 55(2): 392–410.
Borzaga, C., and S. Sacchetti. 2015. "Why Social Enterprises Are Asking to Be Multi-stakeholder and Deliberative: An Explanation Around the Costs of Exclusion." *Euricse Working Paper*, 75/15.

Borzaga, C., and E. C. Tortia. 2010. "The Economics of Social Enterprises." In *The Economics of Social Responsibility: The World of Social Enterprises*, edited by Leonardo Becchetti and Carlo Borzaga, 15–33. London: Routledge.

Camagni, R., and R. Capello. 2002. "Milieux Innovateurs and Collective Learning: From Concepts to Measurement." In *The Emergence of the Knowledge Economy: A Regional Perspective*, edited by Z. Acs, H. de Groot, P. Nijkamp, 15–45. Berlin: Springer Verlag.

Campbell, C., and S. Sacchetti. 2017. "Biosphere Reserves: An 'Enabling Space' for Communities." *Journal of Entrepreneurial and Organizational Diversity*, 5(2).

Coetzer, K. L., Witkowski, E. T. F., and B.F.N. Erasmus. (2014). "Reviewing Biosphere Reserves globally: effective conservation action or bureaucratic label?" *Biological Reviews*, 89: 82–104. doi: http://dx.doi.org/10.1111/brv.12044.

Cowling, K., Sacchetti, S., Sugden, R., and J. Wilson. 2009. "The United Nations and Democratic Globalisation: A Reconnaissance of the Issues." In *Global Social Economy: Development, Work and Policy*, edited by J. B. Davis. London: Routledge.

Dewey, J. 1927. *The Public and Its Problems*. Denver, CO: Holt.

Dewey, J. 1934. *Art as Experience*. London: Penguin.

European Union/OECD. 2016. *Policy Brief on Scaling the Impact of Social Enterprises*. Accessed on January 2017 from www.oecd.org/employment/leed/Policy-brief-Scaling-up-social-enterprises-EN.pdf.

Galera, G., and C. Borzaga. 2009. "Social Enterprise: An International Overview of Its Conceptual Evolution and Legal Implementation." *Social Enterprise Journal*, 5(3): 210–228.

Getz, W. M., Fortmann, L., Cumming, D., Du Toit, J., Hilty, J., Martin, R., and M. I. Westphal. 1999. "Sustaining natural and human capital: villagers and scientists." *Science*, 283(5409), 1855–1856.

Granovetter, M. 1983. "The Strength of Weak Ties: A Network Theory Revisited." *Sociological Theory*, 1: 201–233.

Halsall, F. 2012. "An Aesthetics of Proof: A Conversation Between Bruno Latour and Francis Halsall on Art and Inquiry." *Environment and Planning D: Society and Space*, 30(6): 963–970.

Healy, T., and S. Cote. 2001. *The well-being of nations: the role of human and social capital*. Education and skills, OECD, Paris, Accessed on December 2016 from http://www.oecd-ilibrary.org/education/the-well-being-of-nations_9789264189515-en

Ishwaran, N. 2009. Editorial. "Man and Nature Living in Harmony." *The UNESCO Courier*, No. 6: 3.

Ishwaran, N., and A. Persic. 2008. "Concept and Practice: The Case of UNESCO Biosphere Reserves." *International Journal of Environment and Sustainable Development*, 7(2): 118–131.

Jones, B., and C. Weaver. 2009. "CBNRM in Namibia: growth, trends, lessons and constraints." *Evolution and innovation in wildlife conservation: parks and game ranches to transfrontier conservation areas*, 223–242. London: Earthscan.

Latour, B., and P. Weibel. 2005. *Making Things Public: The Atmospheres of Democracy*. Cambridge, MA: MIT Press.

Le Thanh, T. 2016. "Biosphere Reserves as Models for Sustainable Development: Community Engagement Models in the Cat Ba Biosphere Reserve, Haiphong City, Viet Nam." *Euricse Policy Report*, in preparation.

Mbereko, A. 2017. "Linking Social and Ecological Sustainability: An Analysis of Livelihoods and the Changing Natural Resources in the Middle Zambezi Biosphere Reserve, Zimbabwe." *Journal of Entrepreneurial and Organizational Diversity*, 5(2).

Millennium Ecosystem Assessment. 2005. *Ecosystems and Human Well-being: Synthesis*. Washington, DC: Island Press.

Naughton-Treves, L., Holland, M. B., & Brandon, K. (2005). "The role of protected areas in conserving biodiversity and sustaining local livelihoods." *Annual Review of Environment and Resources*, 30: 219–252.

OECD. 2015. *Social Impact Investment: Building the Evidence Base*. Paris: OECD Publishing. http://dx.doi.org/10.1787/9789264233430-en

Ostrom, E. 1990. *Governing the Commons*. Oxford: Oxford University Press.

Polanyi, Karl. 1994. *The great transformation: Economic and political origins of our time*. New York: Rinehart.

Pool-Stanvliet, R., and M. Clusener-Godt (eds). 2013. *AfriMAb Biosphere Reserves in sub-Saharan Africa: showcasing sustainable development*. (R.) Pretoria: UNESCO.

Reed, M. G., and F. Egunyu. 2013. "Management Effectiveness in UNESCO Biosphere Reserves: Learning From Canadian Periodic Reviews." *Environmental Science & Policy*, 25(January 2013): 107–117.

Roseland, M. 2000. "Sustainable community development: integrating environmental, economic, and social objectives." *Progress in Planning*, 54(2): 73–132.

Sacchetti, F., Sacchetti, S., and R. Sugden. 2009. "Creativity in Socio-Economic Development: Space for the Interests of Publics." *International Review of Applied Economics*, 23(6): 653–672.

Sacchetti, S. 2014. *The Creation of Public Spaces in a Small Italian Town*. Stirling Management School, University of Stirling. Accessed on 8 February 2017 from www.researchgate.net/publication/259849327.

Sacchetti, S. 2015. "Inclusive and Exclusive Social Preferences: A Deweyan Framework to Explain Governance Heterogeneity." *Journal of Business Ethics*, 126(3): 473–485.

Sacchetti, S. 2016. "Governance for a 'Socialised Economy'. A Case Study in Preventive Health and Work Integration." *Euricse Working Papers*, 89/16.

Sacchetti, S., and C. Campbell. 2014. "Creating Space for Communities: Social Enterprise and the Bright Side of Social Capital." *Journal of Entrepreneurial and Organizational Diversity*, 3(2): 32–48.

Sacchetti, S., and R. Sugden. 2003. "The Governance of Networks and Economic Power: The Nature and Impact of Subcontracting Relationships." *Journal of Economic Surveys*, 17: 669–692.

Sacchetti, S. and R. Sugden. 2009. "The Organisation of Production and its Publics: Mental Proximity, Market and Hierarchies." *Review of Social Economy*, 67(3): 289–311.

Sacchetti, S., and R. Sugden. 2010. "Creativity and the Public Interest in Economic Development: A Knowledge Governance Perspective." Translated also in Spanish: "Creatividad e interés public en el desarrollo económico: perspective de la gobernanza del conocimiento." *Ekonomiaz*, 74(2): 36–49.

Sacchetti, S., and E. Tortia. 2016. "The Notion of Social Responsibility Across Different Types of Nonprofit and For-Profit Organizations." In *Handbook on Corporate Social Responsibility*, edited by G. Degli Antoni and L. Sacconi. Cheltenham, Elgar. Forthcoming.

Sacconi, L., and G. Degli Antoni. 2008. "A Theoretical Analysis of the Relationship Between Social Capital and Corporate Social Responsibility: Concepts and Definitions." *Department of Economics Working Papers*, 13/08, University of Trento.

Sen, A. 1999. *Rationality and Freedom*. Cambridge, MA: Harvard University Press.

Stoll-Kleemann, S., De la Vega-Leinert, A., and L. Schultz. (2010). "The role of community participation in the effectiveness of UNESCO Biosphere Reserve management: evidence and reflections from two parallel global surveys." *Environmental Conservation*, 37(3), 227–238.

Szreter, S., and M. Woolcock. 2004. "Health by Association? Social Capital, Social Theory, and the Political Economy of Public Health." *International Journal of Epidemiology*, 33: 650–667.

Teneggi, G., and F. Zandonai. 2017. "The 'Community Enterprises' of the Appennino Tosco Emiliano UNESCO Biosphere Reserve (Italy): Biodiversity Guardians and Sustainable Development Innovators." *Journal of Entrepreneurial and Organizational Diversity*, 5(2).

UNESCO. *Biosphere Reserves 1996: The Seville Strategy and the Statutory Framework of the World Network*. UNESCO, Paris. Accessed from http://unesdoc.unesco.org/images/0010/001038/103849Eb.pdf.

UNESCO. *World Heritage Centre*. Accessed on January 2017 from http://whc.unesco.org/en/list/672.

UNESCO. *World Network of Biosphere Reserves (WNBR)*. Accessed on December 2016 from www.unesco.org/new/en/natural-sciences/environment/ecological-sciences/biosphere-reserves/world-network-wnbr/.

UNESCO MAB. 2007. *Biosphere Reserve Information*. Accessed on January 2017 from www.unesco.org/mabdb/br/brdir/directory/biores.asp?code=VIE+03&mode=all.

Woolcock, M. 2001. "The Place of Social Capital in Understanding Social and Economic Outcomes." *Canadian Journal of Policy Research*, 2(1): 11–17.

# 14 Community Festivals and Their Spaces

## Relational Practice and the Production of a Relational Good?

*Mike Lucas*

## Introduction

This chapter focuses on how, as part of their mutually cooperative practices of organising an annual festival event, a local community group co-produce the space used to celebrate the festival as a form of relational good. This is based in part on the idea that relational goods may be produced by organisations other than the State—in this case, by a group of volunteers organisers of an occasional festival. In examining how such goods are produced in this context, we find that questions arise about the nature and importance of relationality to the organisation of a community festival. Of particular importance is how the productive flow of relationality can be sustained over a longer period than the duration of the festival itself, as the group develops and enhances their festival contribution through discursive as much as social and physical practices. The limited financial resources of the festival, drawn initially from EU grant funding distributed among a number of participating communities and now largely as a self-funding non-profit organisation, highlights the underlying value of this festival space as a form of capital asset to the organising group, invested with collaborative community meaning, and vital to the long-term survival of the festival.

Recent studies of what are termed relational goods suggest a blurred relationship between their production and their consumption. Involvement in the organisation and delivery of such events as the community festival discussed here, contributes to the production of a relational good, but also provides a time-space of engagement, with the "affective, non-instrumental side of personal relationships" which may be viewed as a form of relational consumption. This blurring of the boundary raises further questions about the nature of community relationality, and in particular whether it can be viewed as a tangible outcome, which aligns with its characterisation as a 'good', or as a process. Or, might it indeed be better viewed as a 'practice', integrating both processes and outcomes, as practice theorists have suggested (see Schatzki, 2001)?

A community festival is a particular form of event which offers intensive relational engagement, but unlike shorter events, such as a village or school fete (usually a one-day, themed event), it is offered over an extended period, and unlike a commercially organised festival, it covers a range of activities linked to the interests of community members rather than the specialist interests of the attending audience, e.g., music, arts, books, or films. It is posited, then, that the volunteer organisers of a community festival benefit more from the production/consumption of a relational good than those who simply attend as (consuming) visitors. This chapter explores, using ethnographic data from the author's own research (Lucas, 2014a and b), the nature of relational practices and the goods which are produced and consumed through volunteer involvement in the organisation and delivery of a community festival. The particular focus here is on the space or site which is utilised as part of the community's work to produce its festival celebration. This focus on space offers intriguing insights into the concept of a relational good and the relationship between its production and its consumption. The view of space offered is based on Lefebvre's (1991) theorisation of the social production of space. This is inherently relational in that Lefebvre (1991) considers space as both the outcome and process of three interrelated areas of social practice—design (conceived space), imaginative adaptation (perceived space), and everyday living (lived space)—none of which can be undertaken without some form of relational engagement. Based in part on these ideas of space as socially produced, and in part on Ricoeur's (1971) use of the text paradigm to understand broader social practices of meaning-making, it is argued here that a community festival space is a relational text. In other words, it is a form of relational good linked to the development of shared meanings amongst the members of the volunteer organising group.

## Community Festivals and Their Relational Goods

Becchetti et al. (2008) posited the view that non-instrumental interpersonal relationships produce relational goods which in turn contribute to personal happiness and well-being. "Relational goods include companionship, emotional support, social approval, solidarity, a sense of belonging and of experiencing one's history, the desire to be loved or recognised by others etc. These goods are, on a smaller scale, produced by family relationships or friendships and, on a larger scale, in many kinds of social events" (Becchetti et al., 345). Gui's (1987) interpretation of the concept as a means of understanding the structure of a communitarian economy develops the notion that relational goods are "public because, unlike conventional goods, they cannot be enjoyed by an isolated individual, but only jointly with some others" (Becchetti et al., 346).

Gui and Sugden (2005) stress that relational goods can have important universal public benefits. A traditional reading of their nature is that they are a special kind of public good provided, like other public goods, by state institutions which encourage people to trust others. Relational goods may however be provided by other social arrangements not directly reliant on the state, such as non-profit or temporary organisations who plan and coordinate social events. The acts of coordination involved in the organisation of a community event generates interaction from which all organising participants benefit. The absence of such arrangements can by contrast lead to what Gui and Sugden (2005) term 'relational poverty', "ensuing from individuals allocating too much time to the production of private goods" (p. 347). From this perspective, it may be inferred that a community festival is an example of a mutually shared, or relational, good, which delivers some of the benefits outlined by Becchetti et al. (2008) for at least some of the participants, as well as providing an economic outlet for the artists, performers, makers, and sellers who provide their goods and services.

More recently, however, Pena-Lopez et al. (2017) have questioned the nature of relational goods by positioning them as a nexus of consumption and production. The consumption of 'goods' at the individual level provided by relationships such as belonging, recognition, and personal development are viewed by some (Zamagni, 2004; Iglesias-Vasquez et al., 2013) as the fulfilment of a need for expressive identity. Others, notably Donati (1986), Gui (1987), and Uhlaner (1989), view these as by-products of "non-randomised concrete social relationships . . . in such a way that the agents are at the same time producing and consuming" (Pena-Lopez et al., 2017). This leads us to question whether relational 'goods', as they are characterised, are actually goods at all, or in fact whether this production-consumption nexus should force us to consider them a process. We cannot seemingly subdivide relational goods, however we define them, into sub-units or components which can be quantified in the manner of a traditional economic good, and their nature appears to rule out separate production, exchange, and consumption processes in a division of labour arrangement. Whoever contributes to the production of relationality may almost simultaneously benefit from its consumption.

This raises a number of questions about how the concept of relational goods described by proponents of the theory is relevant to a specific case of a community festival. Community festivals are intensely relational in their nature combining the community volunteers' time and energy to organise a social gathering, with activities of ritual symbolic significance (Douglas, 1996) in which they themselves participate. But what are the relational 'goods' produced and consumed in such a context and how do they relate to the work of the volunteers? Relational goods combine consumption and production at the communal level. They cannot be enjoyed, indeed, cannot be produced/consumed without mutual engagement and relationship building with others who are similarly engaged. So in addition to companionship, a sense of belonging, shared jokes, and general good feeling, we could also, drawing on Lefebvre's (1991) theory of space, include the spaces in which communal events are organised.

To examine this further, it is useful to explore recent interest among scholars of self-organisation among community groups, voluntary organisations, and cooperatives (Steyaert and van Looy, 2015) in the concept of relational practice. These are practices of organisation and self-management which are rooted in collaboration. They may be linked to the affective aspects of relationships which are already developed amongst members of a community, particularly inter-personal trust, but they are more instrumental than relational goods in the sense that they are goal oriented. Bouwen (2015) defines a relational practice as "any communicative or task-oriented interaction among organisational actors, exchanging goods or services, while positioning each other in a mutually inclusive relationship as members of a living community" (p. 22). It is this definition which prompts a further conceptualisation of the relationality encountered in the organisation of a community festival event. In broad terms, Bouwen (2015) characterises a relational practice as any interactive project or exchange between two or more actors which has both a consequence for the relationship between the actors and a perceivable outcome. The fundamental elements of a relational practice are: "the level of reciprocity, the scope for mutual testing and confronting, the openness and directness of expression leading to coownership, the opportunity to mutually reward, and a learning potential for lived interdependence. Relational practices are the negotiated interaction patterns and forms that constitute the building blocks of organising processes" (Bouwen, 2015, 22). Drawing on this view, then, the practices by which community volunteers produce/consume the relational goods to which Becchetti et al. (2008) refer, and which extends to the Lefebvrian concept of space, may also be considered relational. Collaborative, communal organising as a relational practice is intimately connected with the production/consumption of relational goods, such as a community festival space.

Lefebvre's (1991) theorisation of the social production of space incorporates both the outcome and process of three inter-connected practices: the conception of space, its conscious perception, and everyday living. The three conceptualisations of these practices are often characterised as a classic division of labour, with: architects, planners, and designers involved in spatial conception; artists, philosophers and geographers in its conscious perception and the articulation of different social meanings associated with it; and an amorphous group of users involved in 'living' the space, or adapting it for their own everyday practices. This, however, was far from Lefebvre's original aim of a three-way social dialectic which encompassed a variety of social arrangements and relationships. In a social arrangement such as a group of volunteers, with less formal role delineations and with a cooperative organising ethic, all members are thus involved in all three aspects of spatial production as an integral part of their collaborative practices.

## Festival Spaces as Relational Texts

A third strand to this theorisation of a site of collaboration as a relational good is the notion that space can be symbolically organised and read as a form of text. This is examined in Yanow's (1998) study of museums as organisational spaces, where she builds on Ricoeur's (1971) earlier work, in which he views human artefacts and activities as texts whose meanings can be analysed using tools developed by literary theorists and critics. A key facet of this is the relationship between a text's author(s) and its reader(s), as to how meaning is constructed, conveyed, mediated, claimed, and assigned. In the built environment, Yanow (1998) considers the architects and designers of museums to be authors of spatial texts. She examines how the intended meanings of the original authors interact and conflict with those experiencing them—staff, managers, and executives who operate and thus re-interpret the designed space in negotiating their everyday lives.

Schmitt (2012, 17), in his examination of the textual production of "biophysical landscapes", argues that spaces in nature, or the 'outdoors', are assigned meanings by human actors loaded with symbolic significance; space then becomes "a readable object with connotative meaning and association". He asserts that such spaces as "wilderness, mountains, shoreline and other places—become coded with meanings through intertextual relationships" (2012, 19). This draws on the work of twentieth-century literary theorists Bakhtin (1981) and Kristeva (1980), who developed the concept of intertextuality to explain how the meaning of any text was subject to negotiation and change amongst the key actors in its production (normally characterised as the text's authors) and consumption (its readers). In the context of community festival organisation, where production and consumption are intertwined in relational practice, and where the site or space of festival celebration can be construed as the text, we begin to sense something of its intertextual as well as its relational nature.

In his recent examination of the nature of relational practices, Bouwen (2015) examines three main features that characterise the essence of what relational practices do in organisational contexts: they focus essentially (1) on interaction and processes of interaction beyond a mainly individual focus, (2) they draw attention to the quality of these interactions, and (3) they facilitate the creation of conversational spaces" (p. 26). Perhaps most notably for the purpose of this chapter, Bouwen emphasises the discursive nature of a range of relational practices such as collaboration, leadership, conflict, negotiation, and trust. This intersects directly with the notion of space as co-constructed and, intertextual; as both the process and outcome of a relational practice of spatial text construction.

So while community festival organisation is made up of sets of relational practices, the spatial outputs—those artefacts which form the material basis of these practices, a marked festival site—may be viewed as a relational text. In other words, the space which is produced by the volunteer group offers a text which tells both festival attendees and the group members themselves that this is a product of collaboration. It also offers a story of the differing meanings of the festival (and indeed of their community) brought to their collaborative work by the volunteers and how new meanings have been negotiated and authored into the spatial text as a result of their collaboration. This new text may be viewed as a form of relational capital.

It embodies an evolving store of shared meanings which generate and hold value for community members and newcomers and are recognisable by outsiders as part of the (intertextual) fabric of the community. This emphasis on the negotiation and production of shared meaning amongst a group of community festival volunteers indicates a need to recognise, within the analysis, the power relations which underlie the production of any good, relational or otherwise, which is potentially, as Ricoeur (1971) would assert, a social text. In order to address this, the next section of the chapter outlines four broad discourses explored as potentially dominant in the literatures on community festivals and their implications for production of a spatial text

## Discourses of a Community Festival

A community festival is a distinctive form of celebratory event by and for a local community which involves a range of activities reflecting the interests of its members. It expresses aspects of how the community sees itself to visitors and potential visitors through various media. It also tends to be held over more than a single day, offering visitors opportunities to engage with a selection of these activities, and participants such as artists and cultural entrepreneurs to offer their work or goods as part of a programme. It is distinct from a fete, which tends to be a form of fundraising event with local makers and businesses donating their time, goods, or services. It is also distinct from a specialist cultural festival such as film, theatre, or music festivals which tend to be organised by a community of interest rather than a geographically co-located or at least closely clustered community. Nevertheless, the study of community festivals is still largely bound up in the study of the broader field of festival events. Latterly researchers such as Quinn (2003) and Crespi-Vallbona and Richards (2007) have focused on festivals as "contested fields of meaning, in which different groups or stakeholders try to utilise the symbolic capital of the event for their own ends" (Crespi-Vallbona and Richards, 2007). This hints at an understanding of the competing discourses evident in a festival, reflecting struggles for power and dominance between different participant groupings.

Many studies of community festivals by sociologists and anthropologists for most of the last century have tended to focus on the discourse of controlling power groups. A number of studies, for example, have explored the ritualistic aspects of community festivals, underpinned by discourses of spiritual or religious significance. As Falassi (1987, 2) observed, the festival has deep rooted historical meaning as a "a sacred or profane time of celebration marked by special observances", and the annual community event may be considered in many senses part of a ritualistic pattern within the life of a community. In Turner's (1969) classic examination of processes of ritual, he explicitly links the process of liminality, a key component of rituals, involving a suspension of everyday routines in favour of transformational practices amongst ritual participants, to the emergence of communitas, an organic sense of working together. This explicit connection between festivals and liminality, which is principally a temporal phenomenon, is an intriguing one as Turner's (1969) thesis also incorporated the notion of liminal space, a special site identified by the community within which these transforming practitioners could be housed and their practices conducted. This leads us to consider a form of discourse important in our analysis is that of ritual and its associated view of space as liminal.

Some studies have explored the discourse of festivity which views the informal, non-work aspects of community life as a form of resistance to the dominant powers which dictate the terms of ritual celebrations. The concept of festivity is linked to Bakhtin's (1984) examination of the European historical tradition of the carnival—a suspension of everyday working life to engage in "ritual activities for the purpose of popular folk merriment" (p. 219). He elaborated several examples from historical records of behaviours and activities he described as "carnivalesque". Costa (2001), in assessing modernist sociological approaches, developed the concept of festive sociability to describe the distinctive behaviours evident amongst participants during festival times. These incorporate "humour, play, communal eating, sociable work, satiric criticisms, parades etc." (p. 542), the combination of which differs from the pattern of routine, everyday social interactions experienced in modern lives and communities. The spatial implications are not directly evident here, but the recognition of festivity in the relational practice of a community organising group is an important facet of text production in the context of a specific festival space.

A third form of discourse identified by some commentators is that of tradition. Ekman (1999) for example noted the "revival of cultural celebrations in regional Sweden", placing this within a long-standing historical tradition of festivals in the region of Filipstad in central Sweden. She was, however, quick to recognise that some traditions are more recently created than others by "innovative thinking and development in local communities (with a) . . . combination of enthusiasts who have the courage to embark on new ventures and those who are aware of cultural heritage and local culture" (p. 292). The conflicts and differences of opinion between these groups illustrate the contested nature of the concept of tradition and how this impacts on a community festival. Differing interpretations of local history, particularly those which combine social history and folklore, can exert a powerful influence on the practices of community festival organisers. Although no explicit reference is made here to the spatial implications of this, one important link lies in how spatial production is emplaced. In other words, how does a spatial text relate to strands of tradition recognised by inhabitants and visitors to a particular place?

This builds on the tradition of social geographers with an interest in the role of tourism, such as De Bres and Davis (2001), who establish community identity at the centre of festival practice. They put forward a model of community identification comprising the construction of group identity and place identity amongst community members, arguing that both could be strengthened by involvement in community festival activities. Other geographical studies, however (Jackson, 1988; Marston, 1989; Lewis and Pile, 1996), have examined how differing community stakeholder groups with more divergent interests use festival settings to assert their own particular notions of identity.

More recent analyses have offered a more managerial or organisational emphasis, reflecting discourses of market economics. Getz et al. (2010) defined festivals in the more modern context as "themed public celebrations" which acquire a recognisable organisational culture which represents an active celebration of "community values, ideologies, identity and continuity" (p. 30). These contributions offer a fourth discourse, that of place identity, which is useful for our analysis.

In the following section, I will show how these four discourses of community festival—ritual, festivity, tradition, and place identity—are evident in the production of a festival site by a single group of community volunteers engaged in the organisation of their festival contribution. This draws on empirical data from my own research as part of the group. The resolution of these divergent discourses demands the establishment of relational practices amongst community members, which simultaneously produce and consume a collaborative, discursive text, which they know as the community festival space.

## The Relational Practices of a Community Festival Organising Group

Since 2008, I have been peripherally involved in the organisation and delivery of an annual cultural festival which takes place in 15 different villages and sites over a large area of forest in a central region of Sweden. It is one of many such cultural events whose growth in popularity across Europe and rural US during recent years and has also been specifically documented in rural Sweden (Ekman, 1999; Aldskogius, 1993). Its broad goals, understood by the volunteers, participants, and visitors alike, are to highlight the folk-culture heritage of the region, which continues to attract artists, musicians, performers, photographers, and crafts experts with regional, national, and, in some cases, international standing and to promote the development of tourism to the area. From 2009–13, I also spent some time documenting how the organisation of the festival related to the social, cultural, and economic relations embedded in the practices of the host communities. This has developed into an ongoing preoccupation with temporal, spatial, and aesthetic aspects of the organisation of the festival. My interest has been focused largely on the work of a single village community group during several annual iterations of festival planning and delivery.

The volunteer group whose work is explored here is made up of a mix of local friends, family and a small number of holiday homeowners based in and around the village in question. Most volunteer some of their spare time, in some cases, in leave time from their normal work, in order to participate in the organisation of the village's contribution. During the period in which I documented their work, the group comprised between ten to 16 members, varying each year. All the volunteers had differing geographical and emotional ties to the village and differing roles in the festival's planning and delivery. Some members are permanent year-round residents, some are holiday homeowners, and some are related family members. Integral to their practice as organisational members are a number of behaviours, interactions, and material artefacts which, I would argue, exemplify the form of relational practice conceptualised by Steyaert and van Looy (2015) and elaborated by Bouwen (2015).

Following Schatzki (2005), a number of routine patterns can be identified in the practices of the festival organising group of the village. These are linked to the different temporal phases of the festival's planning and delivery, and can be used to analyse the different tasks and activities which make up their relational work:

- Village representation on and liaison with the Festival Organising Committee—this is undertaken by one member at a time, and necessity dictates this must be a permanent, year-round resident, as there are at least six committee meetings per year between January and July, with a post-festival meeting to agree final financial matters.
- Roster planning and assembly—While this can be shared, again, it requires some liaison with the Festival Organising Committee and draws on regional social and business connections. Hence, it is undertaken by six or seven of the permanent residents.
- Site clearance and preparation—This happens over a period in the early summer months of May and June. It involves ground clearance and removal of obstacles which have either grown since last year or are part of the site which has been adopted for use since the previous year. This tends to involve whoever is around, usually a mixture of permanent and holiday residents who can contribute to the physical work.
- Site layout and organisation—On the weekend prior to the festival, the site is laid out with marquee plots designated and exhibition spaces allocated. This also includes the erection of the second-hand sale marquee and food servery bar with seating and overhead awning. The precise layout can take three or four days to agree on and at various times involves almost all of the volunteer group.
- Running the stalls—During the days of the festival itself, the second-hand sale and food servery is staffed on a rota basis by all the Swedish-speaking members of the group.
- Taking down and clearing away—This is generally done on the Sunday after the festival has ended by broadly the same group who cleared and prepared the site in early summer. Many of the older members and members of their family do not tend to take part in this.

The logic of Schatzki's (2001) argument indicates that the village group draws upon prior experience and sources of practical intelligibility to develop these practices. This implies that each of the volunteers bring differing understandings of the objectives of the festival, rooted in their different experiences and in the discourses which they have adopted or developed as a result. For example, it is important to understand the economic and historical context in which the group members live and work. The village was part of the development of the industrial supply chain of a large steel company during the mid-twentieth century, whose economic status has declined considerably since the 1970s. Consequently, it has slowly depopulated to its current low level of permanent, year-round residents. There are three small businesses based in the village, but none provide a stable source of employment beyond their respective owners. There is little economic activity in the village or in its neighbouring settlements; hence, there is a strong focus on the use of place identity in their desire to encourage tourism to the locality. Some older members of the group also have greater investment in discourses of tradition, linked to their practical skills or knowledge of forest history and folklore. No specific individual however claims a dominant leadership of the community and the nature of the group's practice indicates a philosophy of inclusivity and mutual responsibility. The festival, for our volunteer group, represents an opportunity for relational engagement which perhaps acts as a performative for this philosophy.

Despite this apparent backdrop of long-term economic uncertainty, there is a strong sense that the volunteer group engages in their practice imbued with festivity and is aware of the need to support this in the way in which the village site is organised and run. The village festival site is also constructed to maximise festive social interaction between villagers, stallholders, and visitors, accompanied by food and drink prepared by the villagers. Visitors are welcomed into an al fresco food area flanked on two sides by market-type stalls and sitting adjacent to a marquee housing a charity second-hand (loppis) sale. While eating snacks such as älgburgare (moose burgers), and vildsvin korv (wild boar hot dogs), home-baked bread and cakes, and drinking coffee, soft drinks, or the occasional beer, visitors can sit chatting while enjoying views of the lake, or browse around the community fishing club building, in which artists and craftspeople display their wares. Many visitors take a break from their tour of the festival for something to drink or eat at the village, and feedback from several 2011 visitors indicated that this was a particularly valued aspect of it as a festival site. During the festival weekend itself, volunteers wear printed T-shirts symbolising the self-mocking humour of the group and its relationship to their physical surroundings.

However, the humour and friendly banter cannot disguise the fact that members of the group have simply replaced the paid labour of their normal jobs for the unpaid labour of their voluntary festival roles. Several of the group take time out of their working lives and give up part of their formal leave from work period in order to participate in the organisation of the festival. This implies that the festival's value to the community goes much deeper than providing a break from the everyday. Several aspects of the group's practice, particularly the links between the planning group and the volunteer group indicate that the organisation and delivery of the festival is an important ritual in the social and cultural life of the community. The village inhabitants have emotional ties to each other and to the physical maintenance of the village infrastructure which bears out in considerable ongoing work. This is imbued with an ongoing sense of community sociability, which the festival amplifies.

Two major influences on the nature and patterns of social interaction are the socio-demographic profile of the community and the climate. The annual, cyclical nature of social life in such a rurally isolated region, is acutely affected by the extreme seasonal weather variations. The patterns and volume of social interaction during the lengthy, extremely cold winters experienced by the regions' communities differ significantly from that of the short, intense, light-soaked summers. In part, this is because the village population and its festival volunteer group comprise a significant proportion of holiday home owners, whose visits are mainly focused on the summer period between May and September. In part it is also because a high proportion of the permanent, year-round residents are aging and consequently less mobile during the winter months. For both these groups, the festival is part of the fundamental 'ritual' of their community practice. For the holiday residents, it supports their integration into this small, intimate community, reflecting their evolving emotional attachment. For the older residents, most of whom are retired, it is a focus for their social interaction with younger residents and in-comers, and the involvement of a number of retirees in the planning activities symbolises the continued desire for such community rituals. This is very significant in the development of the festival as a whole. As one of the participating artists at a neighbouring village noted, the older, retired residents involved in the festival bring "idealism and enthusiasm" which provides significant impetus to the planning and running of the festival. Without the knowledge, labour, and emotional commitment of this group, it is unlikely the festival would have continued to run for so long.

All official promotional material for the festival as rooted in the region of forest in which it is enacted. This emphasises the artistic connections and a heritage linked to the social history of the forest. Village inhabitants, however, view the festival from the position of their own home village, and it is their emotional ties to their neighbours which underpins much of the work undertaken by the group. Their efforts partly reflect their commitment to the 'corporate' ideals and organisation of the festival and partly their emotional attachment to their village. The link between festival practice and the development of participant identities is a complex one which tells us much about the group members' conceptions of the festival. There is a strong sense of the construction of place identity in the festival promotional materials, and in the theming of the festival each year. The evocation of the forest region as a place of natural beauty, ecological significance, and historical tradition are all familiar themes from previous studies of rural community festivals. The natural and ecological elements of the surrounding forest are also evident in a very high proportion of the art—mostly painting and some sculpture—exhibited at various festival sites, while there is a predominance among the exhibition sites themselves of historic, semi-restored agricultural buildings.

This relationship between the social and natural history of the region is exemplified in the cleverly curated displays of exhibitors' and sellers' artefacts and products amongst the worn and rusting agricultural tools. Many of the craft producers focus on the production of wooden artefacts, including 'traditional' items such as containers for the popular Swedish snack staple, the 'wheel' of cracker bread (knäckerbröd), bark-weave satchels, and slippers similar to those used by past forest inhabitants. Also in evidence are several producers of hunting knives and novelty items made of elk materials (horn and pelts), of decorative metal ornaments and tools produced by traditional black-smithing methods, and of hand-woven rugs, garments, and soft toys. These reflect some of the major historic traditions and preoccupations of the forest inhabitants, timber-craft, hunting, metal-work, and home-weaving. In addition, many of the musical and poetry performances of the festival highlight the history and folk-culture of the region, as does the food menu on each site, with its emphasis on the staples and specialities of the forest workers of the past.

While there are no historic buildings which offer a ready exhibition space in the village, the volunteer group is committed to promoting a sense of place amongst its exhibitors and stallholders, which the core planning group in particular is responsible for assembling. The village festival space plays host to a small number of craft and artistic exhibitors each year who set up their own free-standing stalls. These have included makers of knives, jewellery, hand-made wooden furniture, wood and elk-horn novelty artefacts, and decorative metal items, a bark-weaver, and a traditional baker, several forest landscape or wildlife painters. There have also been performances of acoustic music, a mixture of traditional regional folk music and more contemporary artists with a modern folk repertoire, delivered under a canvas awning or in the open air with the nearby lakeshore as a backdrop.

## Producing a Community Festival Space

Many of the practices I have documented over the past few years offer a picture of relational practices which are rich and complex. They illustrate the multi-faceted nature of the community festival. The dynamic nature of community member relationships is exemplified in the adaptation of community practices with each annual cycle. The connection with non-human actors is also hinted at in the ways that space is used and place is evoked. The economic synergies of relational practice are also in evidence in the distribution of financial benefits between the community and the entrepreneurial artists, makers, and performers and in their mutually beneficial co-location. While many of the artefacts and performances produced by individual makers evoke a communal sense of place, it is the space itself, co-constructed as a complex relational good, a bio-physical text reflecting the interplay of these four key discourses, which is perhaps the most interesting facet of the community's festival. The space presented in the two photographs below (see Figs 14.1 and 14.2) may be interpreted not only as a (socially constructed) backdrop for the activities of the community festival but as both an outcome and part of an iterative process of spatial production which is integral to the relational practices of the community festival.

Figures 14.1 and 14.2 below present the site of a village festival celebration from the angle of a small access track. Figure 14.1 was taken at the opening of the festival in 2010, while Figure 14.2 was taken on the first day of the 2013 festival. The initial intention of the photograph in Figure 14.1 was to capture a *representation* of the space and how the community volunteer group organised it to effect the delivery of their festival contribution. Their choice of location, adjacent to the low wooden building—referred to by community members as the 'fishing cottage', as it was occasionally rented as an overnight sleeping base by visiting anglers—is in some ways obvious (open, and relatively accessible for stall holders' vehicles, and easy for layout planning and construction). Though all the land around village, including this site, is technically owned by a large forestry company it is managed within broader local and national government regulatory frameworks

*Figure 14.1* Festival Site from Access Track 2010

*Figure 14.2* Festival Site from Access Track 2013

which maintain 'rights to roam', and local government planning authority. Hence, the site is viewed by the villagers as 'common' land which can be improved within light regulatory constraints.

With each annual iteration of the festival's organisation, it seemed that an increasing proportion of planning time and activity was spent on the preparation and upgrading of this site. We can see from Figure 14.1, the wet conditions which caused difficulties for the stall holders in setting up their stalls (the distance between them seems odd) and in driving into and out of the space. In Figure 14.2, three years later, we observe that the village group have gravelled the access track, widened it by clearing some of the lying boulders alongside, and provided a hard standing area (middle right, behind the pink flowers) for some of the heavier vehicles. We also begin to see from the photographs the ways in which the non-human elements of the physical landscape (ground surface, geological features, vegetation, weather conditions) are coopted as active agents in the production of a recognisable space of liminality, a space in which the ritual of the annual festival can be performed. These non-human elements contribute to the relational practices of community festival, as well as being components of the spatial outcome we refer to as a relational good.

By observing the photographs of the changing face of the site and the activities involved in its 'construction' more closely, we begin to see some of the relational value of the space. This is the form of the space as a representation of festivity. This is a space which is set aside or protected from visitors' vehicles. It is a short distance from a road, inviting/requiring the visitor to abandon their vehicle and walk down the short track to the festival site. Figure 14.1 invites the viewer to shelter from the weather under the large awning—which incidentally houses a refreshment bar—but still to enjoy the benefits of the fresh air, away from stale cars and houses. The festival is a celebration of the forest area in which it happens. Several of the villages, hamlets, and homesteads spread around the vast 10,000 sq. km tract of forest want their visitors to enjoy the forest's mellow natural beauty, mingle with their non-human as well as human neighbours and produce their own festival space.

The choice of site by the organising group does not simply provide a space for planning and construction, it provides a space for emplacement, for they and their visitors to be close to the lake, potentially the most powerful inhabitant of the village. Their relationship with the lake is complex, encompassing the embodied, affective, and even the political aspects of the space it produces. It is their source of leisure and pleasure, a representation of the vital resources of energy (through the hydro-electric station, 7 km upstream), basic necessities and food stocks (water, fish and the annual moose hunt), and some sources of employment (from the historical practices of timber rafting and water-milling, to the more recent salmon farming). This illustrates an aspect of Lefebvre's (1991) analysis which relates to human: non-human interaction. Control of non-human elements by capitalist organisations creates what he terms abstracted spaces through domination. On the other hand, individuals and informal social groups engaged in spatial production seek to appropriate or coopt non-human elements in a process of identification. It is this place identification with the lake itself which can be seen in the production of a space in such close proximity with it.

## Conclusion

In this chapter, I have examined the view that the organisation of a festival event by a local community volunteer group contributes to the well-being and social wealth of the host community by producing relational goods and extended this by incorporating recent developments in our understanding of organising practices (Steyaert and van Looy, 2015). The recognition by Pena-Lopez et al. (2016) of the blurred boundary between consumption and production in relational goods indicates an interesting processual element to how they may be conceptualised. The case of the community festival presented here indicates that they are also embedded in the broader relational practices of collaboration.

The sites or spaces which are produced as part of the community group's practices offer insights into the ways in which this complex relationship operates. Drawing on Lefebvre's (1991) theory of socially produced space, we see how the practice, process, and outcome of a space are the key dimensions of its production. We also see how relationality is integral to them in the case example offered, not only through the human interactions involved but also through the human/non-human relationships formed. In the context of this community festival, with its twin emphases on collaborative organising and participation, relationality is heightened or intensified to produce a vivid space of social interaction.

The nature of the relational good in this case, is as a collaborative spatial text, the production of which comprises four recognisable types of discourse—ritual, festivity, tradition, and place identity—each drawn upon by the individual volunteers in their practices of meaning-making. The value of this spatial text as a relational good can be seen in the ways in which it is maintained, nurtured, and developed over successive annual iterations of the festival. It is a community capital good which through the group's ongoing collaborative work bestows benefits to the community and visitors alike.

It is hoped that this chapter, with its complex theorisation of an individual case of community festival organisation, can offer insights into the way similar spaces and social arrangements may be theorised in the future.

## References

Aldskogius, H. 1993. "Festivals and Meets: The Place of Music in 'Summer Sweden'." *Geografiska Annaler*, Series B, Human Geography, 75(2): 55–72.

Bakhtin, M. 1981. *The Dialogic Imagination: Four Essays*, edited by C. Emerson and translated by M. Holquist. Austin: University of Texas Press.

Bakhtin, M. 1984. *Rabelais and His World*. Indianapolis: Indiana University Press.

Becchetti, L., Pelloni, A., and F. Rossetti. 2008. "Relational Goods, Sociability and Happiness." *Kyklos*, 61(3): 343–363.

Bouwen, R. 2010. "Chapter 2 Relational Practices for Generative Communal Organizing: Travelling Between Geel and Ecuador." In *Relational Practices, Participative Organizing*, edited by C. Steyaert and B. van Looy, 21–39. Bingley: Emerald Group Publishing

Costa, X. 2001. "Festivity: Traditional and Modern Forms of Sociability." *Social Compass*, 48(4): 541–548.

Crespi-Vallbona, M., and G. Richards. 2007. "The Meaning of Cultural Festivals—Stakeholder Perspectives in Catalunya." *International Journal of Cultural Policy*, 13(1): 103–122.

De Bres, K., and J. Davis. 2001. "Celebrating Group and Place Identity: A Case Study of a New Regional Festival." *Tourism Geographies*, 3(3): 326–337.

Donati, P. 1986. *Introduzione alla sociologia relazionale*. Milan: Franco Angeli.

Douglas, M. 1996. *Natural Symbols: Explorations in Cosmology*. Abingdon, Oxon: Routledge.

Ekman, A.-K. 1999. "The Revival of Cultural Celebrations in Rural Sweden: Aspects of Tradition and Transition." *Sociologia Ruralis*, 39(3): 280–293.

Falassi, A. 1987. *Time Out of Time: Essays on the Festival*, edited by A. Falassi. Albuquerque, NM: University of New Mexico Press.

Getz, D., Andersson, T., and J. Carlsen. 2010. "Festival Management Studies: Developing a Framework and Priorities for Comparative and Cross-cultural Research." *International Journal of Event and Festival Management*, 1(1): 29–59.

Gui, B. 1987. "Elements pour une Définition d'Economie Communautaire." *Notes et Documents de l'Institut International Jacques Maritain*, 19/20.

Gui, B., and R. Sugden. 2005. "Why Interpersonal Relations Matter for Economics." In *Economics and Social Interaction*, edited by B. Gui and R. Sugden. Cambridge: Cambridge University Press.

Iglesias-Vasquez, E., Pena-Lopez, J. A., and J. M. Sanchez Santos. 2013. "Bienestar subjetivo, renta y bienes relacionales. Los determinantes de la felicidad en España." *Revista Internacional de Sociologia*, 71(3): 567–592.

Jackson, P. 1988. "Street Life: The Politics of Carnival." *Environment and Planning D: Society and Space*, 6: 213–227.

Kristeva, J. 1980. *Desire in Language: A Semiotic Approach to Literature and Art.* New York: Columbia University Press.

Lefebvre, H. 1991. *The Production of Space*, Translated by Donald Nicholson-Smith. Malden, MA: Blackwell.

Lewis, C., and S. Pile. 1996. "Woman, Body, Space: Rio Carnival and the Politics of Performance." *Gender, Place and Culture*, 3: 23–41.

Lucas, M. 2014a. "'Nomadic' Organization and the Experience of Journeying: Through Liminal Spaces and Organizing Places." *Culture and Organization*, 20(3): 196–214.

Lucas, M. 2014b. "The Organizing Practices of a Community Festival." *Journal of Organizational Ethnography*, 3(2): 275–290.

Marston, S. 1989. "Public Rituals and Community Power: St. Patrick's Day Parades in Lowell, Massachusetts 1841–1874." *Political Geography Quarterly*, 8: 255–269.

Pena-Lopez, J. A., Sachez-Santos, J. M., and M. Membiela-Pollan. 2017 "Individual Social Capital and Subjective Wellbeing: The Relational Goods." *Journal of Happiness Studies*, 18(3): 881–901.

Quinn, B. 2003. "Symbols, Practices and Myth-making: Cultural Perspectives on the Wexford Festival Opera." *Tourism Geographies*, 5(3): 329–349.

Ricoeur, P. 1971. "The Model of the Text: Meaningful Action Considered as Text." *Social Research*, 38: 529–562.

Schatzki, T. R. 2001. "Introduction: Practice Theory." In *The Practice Turn in Contemporary Theory*, edited by T. R. Schatzki, K. Knorr Cetina, and E. von Savigny. London, UK: Routledge.

Schatzki, T. R. 2005. "Peripheral Vision: The Sites of Organizations." *Organization Studies*, 26(3): 465–484.

Schmitt, C. R. 2012. "'If a Text Falls in the Woods . . .': Intertextuality, Environmental Perception, and the Non-authored Text." *Cultural Analysis*, 11: 17–44.

Steyaert, C., and B. van Looy. 2010. "Chapter 1 Participative Organizing as Relational Practice." In *Relational Practices, Participative Organizing*, edited by C. Steyaert and B. van Looy, 1–17. Bingley: Emerald Group Publishing

Turner, V. W. 1969. *The Ritual Process: Structure and Anti-Structure.* Chicago: Aldine.

Uhlaner, C. 1989. "Relational Goods and Participation: Incorporating Sociability Into a Theory of Rational Action." *Public Choice*, 62: 253–285.

Yanow, D. 1998. "Space Stories: Studying Museum Buildings as Organizational Spaces While Reflecting on Interpretive Methods and Their Narration." *Journal of Management Inquiry*, 7(3): 215–239.

Zamagni, S. 2004. "Towards an Economics of Human Relations: On the Role of Psychology in Economics." *Group Analysis*, 37(1): 17–32.

# Author Index

# Subject Index

For Product Safety Concerns and Information please contact our EU
representative GPSR@taylorandfrancis.com
Taylor & Francis Verlag GmbH, Kaufingerstraße 24, 80331 München, Germany